Logic: Form and Function

LOGIC : FORM AND FUNCTION

The Mechanization of
Deductive Reasoning

J. A. ROBINSON

NORTH·HOLLAND

© J.A.Robinson

First Published in U.S.A. in 1979 by

ELSEVIER NORTH HOLLAND INC.

52 Vanderbilt Avenue

New York, N.Y. 10017

ISBN 0–444–19467–3

Library of Congress Catalog No. 79-52483

Printed in Great Britain

Contents

Acknowledgements

Professor Kenneth Bowen, Dr Robert Kowalski, Mr Kevin Greene and the Rev. Hugh King-Smith (Brother Robert of the Society of St Francis) all read the manuscript of this book and made useful suggestions for which I am most grateful. To Professor F. L. Morris I owe a very special debt of thanks. I had the privileged advantage, throughout the making of this book, of his sage advice and his creative criticism and, in reading and correcting the proofs, of his meticulous perception: few authors are as fortunate, and this one hereby expresses his deep appreciation.

1. Logic : Form and Content

Logic deals with what follows from what. It is the systematic study of the fundamental principles that underlie correct, "necessary" pieces of reasoning (or *true sequents*, as they are called later in the book), as these occur in *proofs*, *arguments*, *inferences*, and *deductions*. The correctness of a piece of reasoning, it is found, does not depend on what the reasoning is about (we can see that the conclusion *all epiphorins are turpy* follows from the premisses *all epiphorins are febrids* and *all febrids are turpy*, without understanding all the words) so much as on how the reasoning is done; on the pattern of relationships between the various constituent ideas rather than on the actual ideas themselves.

To get at the relevant aspects of such reasoning, logic must abstract its *form* from its *content*. We must disregard the epiphorins and the febrids and the turpiness and see the general truth that *all A are C* follows from *all A are B* and *all B are C* quite independently of the particular nature of the *A*, *B* and *C* that happen to occupy those places in the reasoning pattern.

If the content is irrelevant to the correctness of the inference of a conclusion from given premisses, it cannot matter whether the conclusion is true or false, nor whether the premisses are. For example, from the (false) premiss that *all prime numbers are odd* and the (true) premiss that *two is a prime number* the (false) conclusion that *two is odd* follows quite correctly. The form of the inference is: to infer *P is B* from *all A are B* and *P is A*; and this inference form is *valid*.

What does it mean to say that an inference – a piece of reasoning in which a sentence is inferred as conclusion from one or more sentences as premisses – is correct? What is being claimed when it is stated that the conclusion follows from the premisses?

It is not, as we have just seen, that the inference is correct because its conclusion is true: correct inferences can have false conclusions. Moreover, incorrect inferences can have true conclusions, as for example when we infer that *five is prime* from *five is odd* and *some primes are odd*: both premisses are true; the conclusion is true; the inference is nevertheless incorrect. It is incorrect by virtue of its form: to infer *P is B* from *P is A* and *some A are B* is an *invalid* form of inference.

So we have an answer to the question: what makes an inference correct? The answer is: an inference is correct if its form is valid; incorrect if its form is invalid.

This naturally raises a further question: what does it mean to say that a form of inference is valid or invalid? Are not these just alternative words meaning correct or incorrect? It must be confessed that they are. The point is that we must ask (essentially) the same question about inference forms, rather than about inferences themselves. Correctness, or validity, is a property of inference forms rather than of individual inferences. Our answer above begs the question: it says that an inference is correct if its form is correct, and that it is incorrect if its form is incorrect!

However, we now have the question properly posed. Its answer is: an inference form is correct if there is no inference of that form whose premisses are true and whose conclusion is false.

Some people use the word *counterexample* as a convenient short means of expressing this: an inference form is correct if there is no counterexample to it. A counterexample to an inference form is just an inference, having that form, whose premisses are true but whose conclusion is false. Thus when we said that the inference form "to infer *P is B* from *P is A* and *some A are B*" is not correct, we meant that counterexamples to it exist. For instance, here is a counterexample to it: *nine is odd*, and *some primes are odd*, therefore *nine is prime*. Both premisses are true but the conclusion is false; and the form is that of the principle in question, which therefore has a counterexample, and so is not correct.

Notice that the concept of a counterexample introduces the concepts *true* and *false*. These are *semantic* ideas, having to do not only with the *meanings* of sentences and their constituent words and phrases, but also with the *facts*. On the other hand the form of a sentence and of its constituent sub-units is a *syntactic* idea, removed from any consideration of what the facts are or what the "irrelevant" words mean.

Although we are stressing the idea of abstracting away the "irrelevant" meanings, we must not give the impression that all meaning whatsoever is lost when we strip away content and leave behind only form. The "logical words" survive: **all, some, is (are), not, and, or, if ... then**, and so on. We represent and display logical forms as skeletons or schemata made up of various combinations of these logical words, linked together in the *patterns* found in working discourse, but with the "content words" removed and replaced by schematic letters or other symbols. The resulting "formulas" are simply notational devices for revealing, representing, portraying, exhibiting (whatever the term should be) the logical form of the sentences we started with. The transaction involved is better described as separating out the logical meaning from the nonlogical, and depicting the former with the help of special notations.

The exploitation of special notations in studying logical form has reached very high levels of perfection over the past century. The logician Quine says at the beginning of his well-known textbook *Methods of Logic*: "Logic is an old subject, and since 1879 it has been a great one." What happened in 1879? In that year, the German mathematician Gottlob Frege published a short booklet in which he set up a systematic notation for representing logical form. His system was essentially an abstract artificial language, designed with great care and deep insight, in which one could formulate propositions and proofs, with proper emphasis on their form.

Frege called his artificial language the *Begriffsschrift* – a German word he himself coined, to mean something like *the thought notation*, or *the concept language*. In more recent times it has come to be called the *predicate calculus*.

The great central core of modern logic – its mainstream – is the collection of ideas and facts which make up the system of the predicate calculus and its fundamental properties. The predicate calculus system is at one and the same time a notation intended for *use* in formulating and checking pieces of reasoning, and a repository or focus of all of the principal ideas and discoveries – some of them as deep and beautiful as any in the whole of mathematics – that constitute logic as a scientific theory. The chief purpose – or at any rate the chief satisfaction – of logic is the understanding it brings of the reasoning process as such – of the structure of "pure thought", as Frege put it in the title of his booklet: "BEGRIFFSSCHRIFT, a formalized language of pure thought, modelled upon that of arithmetic."

The "formalized language of arithmetic" upon which Frege modelled his predicate calculus is the one we all learn as children for representing numbers, and operations upon them, in both concrete and abstract ways. We learn the concrete algorithms of "counting", "addition", "multiplication", and so on, which help us to write such truths as

$$3 \times (17 + 4) = 63 \tag{1}$$

and we acquire "algebraic" abstract general principles such as

$$a \times (b + c) = (a \times b) + (a \times c) \tag{2}$$

which allow us to represent the form of particular facts like (1). The great power of the system of symbolic representation, manipulation and computation provided by this familiar "formalized language" is available to all people with a standard elementary education. It is the basis for the more extensive, sophisticated, and less widely-known symbolic system of mathematical notation that is the common expressive medium and analytic instrument of the exact sciences.

Frege's predicate calculus, then, is "modelled upon" the notation that is designed to represent *numerical* form and structure. It is *only* modelled upon it: there is an analogy, and a deep one, but that is all. The predicate calculus is designed to represent *logical* form; to permit the construction and application of logical algorithms and analytical procedures. The way in which this representation is done, and what it is that is thereby represented, must be understood independently of the way that the numerical and algebraic symbolic systems work.

Yet there are certain concepts – those, one wants to say, that most nearly correspond to the "forms of pure thought" that Frege wanted to reveal and explain – that are not entirely unfamiliar to the student of the classic "arithmetical" symbolic formalisms. First among these notions is that of a *function*.

One is accustomed to considering, in numerical reasoning, such functions as are "defined" by or "given" by, e.g.

$$3x^2 + 2x + 4 \tag{3}$$

namely, by an *expression* that determines, when some thing (here, a number) x is given as "argument", another thing (here, again a number) as "value" or result. Thus the "expression" (3) defines a function F, which "yields" 9 when "applied to" the number 1, 20 when applied to 2,

$$F(1) = 9$$
$$F(2) = 20$$

and so on; since $3 \cdot (1)^2 + 2 \cdot (1) + 4 = 9$, and $3 \cdot (2)^2 + 2 \cdot (2) + 4 = 20$.

The function F defined by (3) above is applied to an argument a by the simple process of letting "x" denote a in the expression $3x^2 + 2x + 4$, and then "computing out" the resulting expression. This process is known as *evaluating* the expression $3x^2 + 2x + 4$ *at a*.

We can in this fashion define functions that apply to more than one argument, e.g. the function G defined by

$$3x^2 + 2xy + 4y^2 + 5 \tag{4}$$

which applies to pairs of numbers (a, b) and which we compute in the same way, by evaluating its "defining expression" $3x^2 + 2xy + 4y^2 + 5$ after letting x denote a and y denote b. Thus $G(1, 2)$ is

$$3 \cdot (1)^2 + 2 \cdot (1) \cdot (2) + 4 \cdot (2)^2 + 5 = 28$$

There is no reason why we cannot consider functions that yield things other than numbers when applied to numbers. For example, we can consider the "entities" *truth* and *falsehood* (known as the two *truthvalues*) as being yielded when we evaluate such expressions as

$$3x^2 + 12x + 4 \geqslant 0 \tag{5}$$

If x denotes 1 then (5) is true, i.e. "evaluates to truth"; while if x is -3 then (5) is false, i.e. "evaluates to falsehood". So we can look upon the function defined by (5) as one that yields truthvalues when applied to numbers. Similarly,

$$3x^2 + 2xy + 4y^2 + 5 < 21 \tag{6}$$

defines a function of *two* arguments which likewise yields truthvalues as results. Functions that yield truthvalues (and only truthvalues) as their results are called *relations*, or *predicates*.

The arguments of functions need not be numbers, either. For example, we can consider the expression

$$x \text{ is the sister of } y \tag{7}$$

as defining a function of two arguments, which are human beings, and that yields truth when applied to a pair (a, b) of humans such that a is b's sister, and falsehood when applied to other pairs of human beings. Indeed, the notion of function is entirely general, and neutral, as far as the nature of its arguments and results is concerned. We could, for instance, consider the function defined by

$$\text{the father of } x \tag{8}$$

which, when applied to a human being a, yields the human being who is a's father; and we can "nest" such functions just as we do with numerical ones, e.g.

$$x \text{ is the sister of (the father of } y) \tag{9}$$

Frege saw that the general, neutral concept of a function must be made the principal one in his proposed system for symbolically representing the forms of "pure thought". The way in which a function can be defined, or represented, by giving an expression (as in the above examples) for its result as a computable or constructible combination of its arguments, is known as *abstraction*; and Frege's great insight was to see that the activity of "pure thought" he wanted to represent consisted of *acts of abstraction of functions from expressions*, interwoven with *acts of application of functions to arguments*, formulated as *acts of evaluation of expressions*. The interplay between abstraction, application and evaluation is the whole story of the thought that Frege wanted to analyse, explain, and represent.

The distinction (within the general framework of "thought as abstraction, application and evaluation" outlined above) between "pure" thought and the rest, is straightforward enough. Pure thought is not contrasted with impure thought — at least not by Frege, and not in this book — but with "applied thought", in much the same spirit as in the distinction between pure and applied mathematics, or pure and applied science. Certain functions, and certain kinds of result (i.e. the truthvalues) seem to occur in *all* forms of thought, whatever the particular subject matter. So these, along with the bare structure supplied by abstraction, application and evaluation as formative principles, are taken as the primitive ingredients of the "thought-writing" notation.

These functions and entities are the *logical* ones: *truth, falsehood, negation, conjunction, disjunction, universal* and *existential generalization*, and *exemplification*. We shall discuss these, and the notations for their representation, in the following chapter.

"Non-logical" functions and entities co-exist and interact with these logical ones in a completely integrated way: but for each special choice of subject-matter, and of a body of notions with which to organize that subject-matter conceptually, there is a particular "applied" system, or *calculus*. This "applied calculus" contains just the combination of general logical apparatus with the particular special notations deemed appropriate to the subject-matter of the applied calculus and to its particular special way of analysing that subject-matter.

Every "applied" calculus is an example of a particular way of conceptually organizing one's thoughts about some given "universe", or collection of "individuals", as subject-matter. If we then study how reasoning takes place within the framework of such an applied calculus, we are led to the underlying "pure" calculus, which directly depicts the "forms of pure thought" used to organize the subject-matter, without actually introducing that subject-matter.

The first half of this book attempts to clarify the relationship between "pure" and "applied" forms of thought as embodied in the various pure and applied calculi of the symbolic system collectively known as "the" predicate calculus.

Once this formalism is understood, the reader can then easily entertain, and follow the development of, a proposition that has entranced students of logic for centuries: that deductive reasoning can be *mechanized* – literally, performed by a machine – just as many of the routine tasks of numerical computation can be and have been. It was not Frege's main motivation to help make the mechanization of deductive reasoning a practical possibility. He was very much aware, however, of the attempts of earlier thinkers such as Hobbes and Leibniz to argue that this could and must be done, and he well knew that his own work was an indispensable step.

The second half of this book traces the development of the theory of the predicate calculus as it is steered deliberately in the direction of this goal. The discussion culminates in a complete, detailed account of a working computer program for showing "what follows from what". The present author's hope is that the ideas underlying this computer program will be of interest even to those who have no prior experience of computers or of programming – we explain the necessary rudiments of the programming system used (LISP) so as to give the account a self-contained character.

Reasoning *is*, after all, a kind of computation: just as it has always been obvious that computation (as normally understood) is a kind of reasoning. The impressive rôle played by automatic computation in modern science and technology is made possible, ultimately, by the great *notations* of traditional mathematical analysis together with their supporting conceptual frameworks. The mechanization of "pure thought" itself – deductive reasoning as such – is, now that we have been given a notation for it, no longer just the dream of a Leibniz; it is now a reality. In the present author's opinion, mechanizing deductive reasoning is one of the most exciting and potentially fruitful areas of research that there has ever been.

Let us then begin by describing the elements of the predicate calculus system.

2.   Formulas : Syntax and Intuitive Semantics

The predicate calculus has a simple, systematic basic *syntax*, whose principal feature is the characterization of the class of expressions that are its *formulas*. We shall denote this class by *F*.

The formulas are split into two subclasses: the class *T* of *terms*, and the class *S* of *sentences*. The general idea of the calculus is, roughly, that there is a set of things, which are "what the formulas are about". These things are called the *individuals*, and the set containing all of them is called the *universe of individuals*, or the *universe*, for short. The intended meaning of the terms is that they stand for ("denote") individuals. The sentences, on the other hand, are intended to express propositions about the individuals, which are either true or false. In the stylized semantics of the predicate calculus there is a special way of saying that a sentence expresses a *true* proposition; namely, one says that it stands for, or "denotes", *truth*. Similarly, one says of a sentence which expresses a *false* proposition that it stands for, or denotes, *falsehood*. Thus there is a set of two entities, called the *truthvalues*. These truthvalues, namely truth and falsehood, or **t** and **f** for short, are the counterparts, for the sentences, of the individuals. Sentences denote truthvalues; terms denote individuals.

That brief glimpse of the *semantics* of terms and sentences is offered as an aid to understanding the plan behind their *syntax*. We shall later on discuss the semantics much more fully.

So far, then, we have broken down the formulas into two classes, the terms and the sentences:

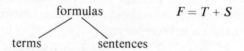

$$F = T + S$$

The class *T* of terms is divided into four classes: these are the *individuals*, the *variables*, the *constructions*, and the *exemplifications*. Let us consider these in order. First, the individuals.

We must emphasize the fact that individuals (i.e. elements of the universe of individuals) are not necessarily "symbolic" entities as usually understood by that notion: they are, rather, the things which the symbolic entities represent. However, the usual notion of "symbol" is quite vague, and it seems to mean nothing more than "what formulas are ultimately made out of". In order to be reasonably clear here about our basic syntax we are taking an abstract attitude towards the formulas, by characterizing them as "constructs" of various kinds, without entering into an unnecessary commitment as to the nature of the basic building-blocks out of which the constructs are put together.

In this spirit we suppose that there are four sets: the universe U; the set V of *variables*; the set C of *constructions* and the set X of *exemplifications*. The universe U is the set of individuals. We assume nothing more about U than that it is a *non-empty* set: it may be finite, or infinite; and in the latter case its cardinal number may be arbitrarily large. (In this book, however, we shall not take advantage of this; we shall in fact be primarily interested in the case where U is finite or at most countably infinite.)

Next, the set V of variables. We assume that V is a countably infinite set, and that indeed there is some given enumeration of it (without repetitions) by reference to which we can unambiguously refer to the jth individual variable, where j is any positive integer.

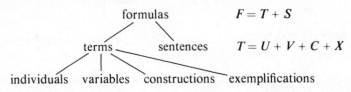

$$F = T + S$$
$$T = U + V + C + X$$

We have so far, then, a countable infinity of variables, and an unknown (but non-zero) number of individuals, among our terms. In writing formulas we shall follow accepted usage and represent variables by letters $x, y, z, \ldots, a, b, c$, etc., affixing numerical subscripts, or further letters, as in x_1, a_2, ab, etc., as is convenient. We do not insist on any standard choice of written representation.

The third kind of term, the constructions, comprise the set C. Each consists of an *operator* and an *operand*. The operator of a construction is a symbol, called a constructor (or, sometimes, a *function symbol*), which is taken from a countably infinite set of such symbols about which we shall say more in a moment. The operand of a construction is *a finite sequence of terms*. This finite sequence may be empty (in which case we say it is *the empty operand*) or it may contain one or more components. These are called the *immediate constituents* of the construction.

With each constructor there is associated a non-negative integer, called the *arity* of the constructor. This number must be the same as the number of components in the operand (i.e. as the length of that operand, considered as a finite sequence).

The set C_k of constructors of arity k, $k \geqslant 0$, is assumed to be equipped with some given enumeration, without repetitions, with respect to which we can unambiguously refer to the jth individual operator of arity k, for all positive integers j. We thus suppose that the constructors of arity k, $k \geqslant 0$, are given as a countably infinite set C_k; so that we have an infinite set of constructors

$$C_0 + C_1 + \ldots$$
$$= \sum_j C_j$$

(Here, we are representing the *union* of sets by symbols for addition, as is usual in discussions of formal syntax when the sets are *disjoint*, i.e. have no common members.)

Now if we have a set A, we denote the set of finite sequences of length k, $k \geqslant 0$, each component of which is a member of A, by A^k. In particular A^0 denotes the set whose only member is the *empty sequence* $(\ )$

$$A^0 = \{(\ )\}$$

while A^1 denotes the set of *unit sequences* of members of A, i.e., if A is $\{a_1, a_2, \ldots\}$ then

$$A^1 = \{(a_1), (a_2), \ldots, \quad \}$$

After these two, the rest are easy, We have

$$A^2 = \{(a_1, a_1), (a_1, a_2), (a_2, a_1), (a_2, a_2), \ldots \quad \}$$

and so on.

Now the "Cartesian" product $(A \times B)$ of two sets is the set of all sequences of length 2 ("pairs")

$$(a, b)$$

whose first component a is in A and whose second component b is in B. Note that A^2 is then the same set as $(A \times A)$.

We have said that a construction is a pair: the operator and the operand of the construction. We can now be more specific. The operator is always a *constructor* of arity $k \geqslant 0$, and, for that k, the operand is always an element of the set T^k. That is, the operand is a sequence of length k whose components are terms.

We can express this definition compactly by the "syntax equation"

$$C = (C_0 \times T^0) + (C_1 \times T^1) + \ldots + (C_k \times T^k) + \ldots$$

or, writing the "infinite sum" more neatly

$$C = \sum_{k=0}^{\infty} (C_k \times T^k)$$

For the purpose of writing down constructions systematically we can conveniently represent them as parenthesized lists, e.g.

$(f\,a\,b)$
$(g(h\,a)(k)(f\,a\,b)(h(h(h\,a))))$

In any such list, its initial component is its operator, and its remaining components, if any, are its immediate constituents and thus comprise its operand. Thus in the above we are supposing that a and b are variables, that f is an individual operator of arity 2, k is an individual operator of arity 0, h is an individual operator of arity 1, and g is an individual operator of arity 4.

Since the immediate constituents of a construction may (some or all of them) be themselves constructions, we can expect in general to meet with terms that have a *nested* structure. This nesting can be arbitrarily deep, but it is always *finite*. (It is, intuitively, the maximum number of nested pairs of parentheses in the written representation of the term.) The nesting depth, or *depth*, of a term may be more formally defined by the recursive rule:

(a) · the depth of a variable, or of an individual, is 0;
(b) the depth of a construction is 1 greater than the maximum of the depths of its immediate constituents;

provided that we interpret the second clause to mean, in the case of a construction with a 0-ary operator (and hence no immediate constituents), that the depth of the term is then 1. Thus the depth of a and b is 0; that of $(f\,a\,b)$ is 1; that of $(h\,a)$ and (k) is also 1; while that of $(g(h\,a)(k)(f\,a\,b)(h(h(h\,a))))$ is 4.

We think of constructions as examples of *applicative* expressions, so called because of the way in which they come to denote the entities they do denote. The general idea is that an applicative expression τ with operator ω and operand δ stands for, or denotes, the entity that results from *applying* a certain function Ω to a certain finite sequence Δ of entities. The function Ω is the one that the symbol ω denotes, while the finite sequence Δ is the one whose components are the entities denoted, in order, by the expressions that are the components of δ.

This general idea is entirely familiar to anyone who has worked with the numerical and algebraic formulas of traditional mathematical notations. The applicative *term*

$$x + y$$

for example, denotes the result of applying the function *addition* to the numbers denoted by "x" and "y". We think of the operator "$+$" as denoting addition, and "x", "y" as denoting numbers α and β; and we think of the expression "$x + y$" as denoting a number γ, namely that yielded by the fundamental process of *application* in the particular case when it is addition which is applied, and the finite sequence (α, β) to which it is applied.

In order to appreciate the definition of the final class of terms – the class X of *exemplifications*, we should first have been introduced to the *sentences*. The reason is that exemplifications are built syntactically from sentences of the kind that, below, will be called *generalizations*. These comprise a class G, which is one of four classes – the truthvalues, the class P of predications, the class B of Boolean combinations, and the generalizations – into which the class S of sentences is divided:

$$S = \{\mathbf{t}, \mathbf{f}\} + P + B + G$$

Each exemplification is a pair consisting of a special logical symbol, "$*$" and a general sentence. So we shall have the syntax equation

$$X = (\{*\} \times G)$$

We shall usually write an exemplification as: $*A$, where A is in G. The intended meaning of an exemplification $*A$ is all tied up with that of the generalization A from which it is constructed, and we shall reserve further discussion until we have been once around the ideas pertaining to the syntax, and intended semantics, of sentences. Suffice it to say, for the time being, that (since it is a term) an exemplification $*A$ is intended to denote an individual, and that *which* individual it denotes is determined by what A says and whether A is true or false. As we shall see, the individual "exemplifies", or illustrates, what it is that the sentence A is saying.

For the purposes of analysing formulas into constituents, an exemplification $*A$ is declared to be "unanalysable" – the only constituent of an exemplification is itself. Of course, its part, A, will have constituents; but these are *not* constituents of the exemplification – not even the part A itself is a constituent of the exemplification.

Before we go on to discuss the basic syntax of sentences, let us elaborate further this notion of the *constituents* of a formula. We are going to define for sentences, as we have already done for terms, the notion of *immediate* constituent, according to which, for example, the immediate constituents of the term

$$(g(h\ a)(k)(f\ a\ b)(h(h(h\ a))))$$

are the terms

$$(h\ a),\quad (k),\quad (f\ a\ b),\quad (h(h(h\ a)))$$

The constituents of a formula are then all those formulas we can obtain from it if we take its immediate constituents, if any; *their* immediate constituents, if any; and so on, together with the formula itself. For each formula φ there is thus a set, (*constituents* φ), which is the set of all constituents of φ in this sense. We define this set somewhat more precisely as follows.

For any formula φ, let φ^* be the *set* of immediate constituents of φ. (Thus φ^* is $\{\}$ when φ has no immediate constituents.) Then by (*constituents* φ) we mean the set of formulas given recursively by

$$(constituents\ \varphi) = \{\varphi\} \cup \bigcup_{\xi\ in\ \varphi^*} (constituents\ \xi)$$

So, for example, (*constituents* $(g(h\ a)(k)(f\ a\ b)(h(h(h\ a))))$) is the set

$$\{(g(h\ a)(k)(f\ a\ b)(h(h(h\ a))))$$
$$(f\ a\ b)$$
$$(k)$$
$$(h(h(h\ a)))$$
$$(h(h\ a))$$
$$(h\ a)$$
$$a$$
$$b\}$$

Now we go on to describe the sentences. They fall, as we have said, into four kinds: truthvalues, predications, Boolean combinations, and generalizations. The second and third kinds of sentences are applicative expressions, and have a very closely related syntactic and semantic explanation to that already given for constructions. The fourth kind of sentence, the generalization, involves a new idea.

Boolean combinations and predications, like constructions, have an operator and an operand. The operator is a symbol, the operand a finite (possibly empty) sequence of formulas; and we write an applicative sentence α as a list

$$(\omega \; \varphi_1 \ldots \varphi_n)$$

whose first component is the operator ω and whose remaining components are those of the operand and are the immediate constituents of α. It is further required, as in the case of constructions, that the arity of the operator symbol ω shall be the number n, which is the length of the operand.

So far the analogy with constructions is exact. However, we have *two* kinds of applicative sentence: predications and Boolean combinations. These are very commonly also referred to as *atomic* sentences and *molecular* sentences. The chemical metaphor (which is in fairly standard use among logicians) is apt enough: one can decompose (as we shall see) a molecular sentence, i.e a Boolean combination, into immediate constituents that are themselves sentences, whereas the immediate constituents of an atomic sentence, i.e. a predication, are not sentences, but terms.

Specifically, we have two kinds of operators: for each $k \geqslant 0$, a countable set P_k of predicate symbols of arity k (sometimes also called *relation symbols* of arity k), and a set B_k of *propositional connectives* of arity k. Analogously with the k-ary constructors, we assume an enumeration of P_k with respect to which we can unambiguously speak of the jth predicate symbol (or jth relation symbol) of arity k, where j is any positive integer. We then define the predications to be the pairs consisting of a predicate symbol of arity k, as operator, and an operand, which is a finite sequence of length k whose components are terms. The terms, which are the components of the operand, are the immediate constituents of the predication. The depth of a predication is greater by 1 than the maximum depth of any of its immediate constituents. We thus have the syntax equation

$$P = (P_0 \times T^0) + (P_1 \times T^1) + \ldots = \sum_{k=0}^{\infty} (P_k \times T^k)$$

The intended meaning of a predication is that it shall denote a truthvalue, and that this truthvalue is determined applicatively, in complete analogy to the way in which an applicative term, or construction, comes to denote the individual that it denotes.

This means that we intend to regard the predicate symbol that is the operator of an atomic sentence as denoting a function applicable to a finite sequence of individuals, but one which yields, when applied to such a sequence, a truthvalue, rather than an individual.

One meets with this idea too, in traditional mathematical notations. For example, the sentence

$$x < y$$

denotes the truthvalue, truth or falsehood, of the proposition that the number denoted by "x" is less than that denoted by "y". We can thus here be construed as taking the predicate symbol "$<$" to denote that function of ordered pairs of numbers that yields truth, or falsehood, when applied to such a pair, according as the first number is less than, or is greater than or equal to, the second.

When the arity of the predicate symbol that is the operator of a predication is 1, as e.g. in the sentence (*prime x*), one has the case of a "property" or "attribute" of individuals being denoted by that operator. A property is regarded as a function that, when applied to (the finite sequence whose only component is) a thing, yields either truth or falsehood, according as the thing has, or has not, got that property.

What does an operator symbol with arity 0 mean? This is a limiting, or degenerate, case of the applicative idea. We can give it an acceptable interpretation, namely, that the function it denotes is to be applied *to the empty sequence* (which is not the same as "not applying" the function!) and that the result of this application is a truthvalue (if the operator is a predicate symbol) or an individual (if it is a construction symbol).

Now Boolean combinations, or molecular sentences, also express propositions about individuals, but they do it by combining, in various ways, the *propositions* expressed by their immediate constituents. The set of *propositional connectives* is

{**not, and, or, if, iff**}

and it is stipulated that the arity of **not** is 1, the arity of **if** is 2, as is the arity of **iff**, and that the operators **and, or** both have *every* arity, from 0 onwards. In keeping with our other applicative formula definitions, we can put $B_1 = \{\textbf{and, or, not}\}$, $B_2 = \{\textbf{and, or, if, iff}\}$, $B_k = \{\textbf{and, or}\}$ if $k \neq 1, 2$, and write

$$B = \sum_{k=0}^{\infty} (B_k \times S^k)$$

Syntactically this means that if S is a sentence so is (**not** S), and if S and T are sentences so are (**if** S T) and (**iff** S T). Here we are maintaining the convention of writing an applicative formula as a list whose initial component is the operator of the formula and whose remaining components comprise the operand of the formula and are its immediate constituents. The statement that the connectives **and,**

or both have *every* arity means syntactically that for every integer $k \geqslant 0$, a list of length $k + 1$ whose initial component is **and** and whose remaining components (if any) are sentences, is a molecular sentence. Similarly for lists whose initial component is **or**. The remaining components comprise the operand, and are the immediate constituents of the molecular sentence.

Sentences of the form (**not** S) are often called *negations*. The negation of S, for any sentence S, is the sentence (**not** S). The operator "**not**" is often represented by the special character "$\neg$", and in either case is known as *the negation symbol*. It is very common to write (**not** S), i.e. ($\neg S$), as $\neg S$; the symbolic analogy being with numerical negation ("minus two" being written as -2 and more properly called "negative two", as we are reminded by our children home from their New Mathematics lessons).

The intended meaning of a negation is that it shall denote the truthvalue that is the "opposite" of that denoted by its immediate constituent: if S denotes **t** then $\neg S$ denotes **f**, while if S denotes **f** then $\neg S$ denotes **t**. Thus the applicative story of the semantics of negations is that the operator **not** denotes the function that, when applied to **t**, yields **f**, and when applied to **f**, yields **t**.

Sentences of the form (**and** ...) are often called *conjunctions*, and their immediate constituents, if any, are said to be their *conjuncts*. The *conjunction symbol* "**and**" is often represented by the special character "$\wedge$". When there are two or more conjuncts $S_1 S_2 \ldots S_n$ it is frequent practice to write the conjunction ($\wedge S_1 S_2 \ldots S_n$) in the "infix" representation

$$(S_1 \wedge S_2 \wedge \ldots \wedge S_n), \text{ or } (S_1 \text{ and } S_2 \text{ and } \ldots \text{ and } S_n)$$

with or without the surrounding pair of parentheses; i.e.

$$S_1 \wedge S_2 \wedge \ldots \wedge S_n, \text{ or } S_1 \text{ and } S_2 \text{ and } \ldots \text{ and } S_n$$

can also be written, if no confusion will arise.

The intended meaning of a conjunction is that it shall denote a truthvalue, and moreover that this shall be **t**, except when it has an immediate constituent that denotes **f**. In particular, the empty conjunction ($\wedge$), having no immediate constituents at all, has none that denotes **f**. Hence ($\wedge$) denotes **t**.

The corresponding applicative story is that the conjunction symbol denotes that function which, when applied to a finite (possibly empty) sequence of truthvalues, yields **t** as result, except when the sequence has **f** as one or more of its components, in which case it yields **f**.

Sentences of the form (or ...) have essentially the same semantic properties as conjunctions, but with the rôles of t and f interchanged. Such sentences are called *disjunctions*, and their immediate constituents, if any, are their *disjuncts*. The *disjunction symbol* "or" is often represented by the special character "∨", and the infix convention is also often used, to write

$$(S_1 \text{ or } S_2 \text{ or } \ldots \text{ or } S_n)$$

instead of (or $S_1 S_2 \ldots S_n$), etc.

A disjunction is intended to denote the truthvalue f, except when it has one or more disjuncts that denote t, in which event it denotes t. Thus in particular the empty disjunction (∨) denotes f.

A "unit" disjunction, (∨ S), and a unit conjunction, (∧ S), according to these explanations, both denote whatever truthvalue the sentence S denotes.

Regarded applicatively, the truthvalue denoted by a disjunction is arrived at by applying the function (denoted by the disjunction symbol) that yields f at every finite sequence of truthvalues except when the sequence has t as one or more of its components, to the particular finite sequence of truthvalues that its disjuncts denote.

Sentences of the form (if S T) are often called *conditionals*; less often, *implications*. The *implication symbol* "if" is also written as the special character "⊃", and sometimes as the special character "→"; when these special characters are used, the infix convention is often preferred, to write the conditional as $(S ⊃ T)$ or $(S → T)$, with omission of the parentheses if desired and if no confusion would arise. However, when the symbol if is used, the infix version becomes

$$(\text{if } S \text{ then } T)$$

with the connective becoming if ... then, and acting, as it were, as both a prefix and an infix operator.

All these notational variations are of purely "window-dressing" interest. The conditional, however it may be represented in written form, has the two immediate constituents S and T. The first of these is called the *antecedent* of the conditional; the second is called the *consequent* of the conditional.

The intended meaning of a conditional is that it shall denote a truthvalue, and that this truthvalue shall be t except in the case that the antecedent denotes t and the consequent denotes f, in which case the conditional shall denote f.

The conditional symbol is thus regarded, from the applicative viewpoint, as denoting the operation that, when applied to a pair of truthvalues, yields t except when the pair is (t, f), in which case it yields f.

Sentences of the form (**iff** *S T*) are often called *biconditionals*; less often, *equivalences*. The *biconditional symbol* "**iff**" can be written as the special character "↔", or as the special character "≡", and biconditionals can be written according to the infix convention, i.e. $S \leftrightarrow T$, $S \equiv T$, S **iff** T. For extra variety the form (*S* **if and only if** *T*) is sometimes used. (The symbol "**iff**" is *pronounced* "if and only if"!) Biconditionals denote t if both their immediate constituents denote the same truthvalue, and denote f in the contrary case.

The notions of constituent and depth carry over to molecular sentences: namely, the constituents of a molecular sentence are itself and the constituents of its immediate constituents (if any); and the depth of a molecular sentence is 1 plus the maximum depth of any of its immediate constituents.

All the formulas so far defined have been, apart from the individuals, the truthvalues, and the variables, applicative, and their intended semantic properties have been informally described in what is intended to be a uniform fashion, based on the *applicative principle* that makes an applicative formula denote the result of applying what its operator denotes to what its operand denotes. An individual or truthvalue denotes itself. A variable, as we shall see, does not denote anything. Its semantic rôle is part of the story explaining the semantics of generalizations and of exemplifications. Let us then complete our discussion of the sentences.

The remaining class of sentences is the class of *generalizations*, which breaks down into two classes, the *universal* generalizations and the *existential* generalizations. The syntactic form of generalizations is threefold: each such sentence has

(a)   an *operator*, which is one of the two *quantification symbols* **all, some**;

(b)   a *bound variable*, which is a variable;

(c)   a *body*, which is a sentence.

The operators **all, some** are also represented by the special characters ∀, ∃, or sometimes (most aptly, as we shall see) as ∧, ∨, the same signs used as conjunction and disjunction symbols, but scaled up. Universal generalizations have **all** as their operator; existential generalizations have **some** as their operator.

The body of a generalization may or may not have, among its constituents, the bound variable of the generalization (as we shall see, however, it is normal, and expected, that it should).

We write the generalization whose operator is Q, whose bound variable is x, and whose body is S, as a list

$$(Q \, x \, S) \quad \text{or} \quad QxS$$

or sometimes as

$$(Q \, x)S$$

the prefixed $(Q \, x)$ being known as the *quantifier* of the generalization. $(\forall x)$ is a *universal*, and $(\exists x)$ an *existential*, quantifier. Formally, we can write the equation

$$G = (((\{"\forall"\} \times V) \times S) + ((\{"\exists"\} \times V) \times S).$$

We depart from the pattern of "constituent analysis" that was established for applicative formulas, and we define the immediate constituents of general sentences (and hence their constituents) in a quite different, but still natural, way. The idea goes as follows.

For every formula φ, variable x, and individual k, we define the formula called *the (x, k)-instance of* φ, denoting it by the notation

$$\varphi[k/x]$$

The definition is given by the five cases:

(a) if φ is the variable x, then $\varphi[k/x]$ is k;

(b) if φ is a variable other than x, or an individual, or a truthvalue, then $\varphi[k/x]$ is φ;

(c) if φ is the applicative formula $(\omega \, \varphi_1 \ldots \varphi_n)$
then $\varphi[k/x]$ is the applicative formula
$(\omega \, \varphi_1[k/x] \ldots \varphi_n[k/x])$

(d) if φ is the generalization $(Q \, x \, S)$, then $\varphi[k/x]$ is φ;

(e) if φ is the generalization $(Q \, y \, S)$, where y is distinct from x, then $\varphi[k/x]$ is the generalization $(Q \, y \, S[k/x])$.

The intuitive idea behind this definition is that to obtain $\varphi[k/x]$ from φ we go through φ, replacing occurrences of x by occurrences of k, but we *leave unchanged* any occurrences of x that are inside constituents of φ that are generalizations whose bound variable is x.

Now we can say what the immediate constituents are of a generalization $(Q \, x \, S)$, whose bound variable is x and whose body is S. They are the sentences

$$S[k/x]$$

which are the (x, k)-instances of the body S, for all individual constants k in the universe U. These are also called the *instances* of $(Q \, x \, S)$. We repeat: there is one immediate constituent, or instance, of $(Q \, x \, S)$, namely $S[k/x]$, for each individual constant k in the universe. If the universe is finite, then $(Q \, x \, S)$ accordingly has finitely many instances. If the universe is infinite, $(Q \, x \, S)$ has infinitely many instances.

This definition of immediate constituents for generalizations extends the notion of *constituents* to them also. The constituents of a generalization are: itself, together with the constituents of its instances. Let us take an example, in which the universe is the set

$$\{1, 2, 3, 4\}$$

Consider the generalization

$(\forall x)$ if $x < 4$ then $(x = 1$ or $x = 2$ or $x = 3)$.

Its body is the (molecular) sentence

if $x < 4$ then $(x = 1$ or $x = 2$ or $x = 3)$

and its immediate constituents are the sentences

if $1 < 4$ then $(1 = 1$ or $1 = 2$ or $1 = 3)$
if $2 < 4$ then $(2 = 1$ or $2 = 2$ or $2 = 3)$
if $3 < 4$ then $(3 = 1$ or $3 = 2$ or $3 = 3)$
if $4 < 4$ then $(4 = 1$ or $4 = 2$ or $4 = 3)$

If "$<$" and "$=$" denote the usual predicates on numbers, then each of these conditionals is true (denotes **t**). Thus the general sentence has no immediate constituent that denotes **f**.

Now let us recall the semantics of conjunctions and disjunctions. We said that a conjunction denotes **t** except when it has an immediate constituent that denotes **f**, and that then it denotes **f**. And we said the same for a disjunction except that the rôles of **t** and **f** were swapped.

These definitions are exactly the same for generalizations: a universal generalization is treated as a conjunction, in that it is intended to denote **t** except when it has an immediate constituent that denotes **f**, in which case it denotes **f**; and an existential generalization is treated as a disjunction, in that it is intended to denote **f** except when it has an immediate constituent that denotes **t**, in which case it denotes **t**.

This shows that (using our sense of "immediate constituents") the universal generalization $(\wedge \, x \, S)$ is in a perfectly straightforward sense the conjunction of its immediate constituents, just as is a conjunction proper. Similarly the existential generalization $(\vee \, x \, S)$ is the disjunction of its immediate constituents, as is a disjunction proper. The instances $S|k/x|$ of a universal generalization $(\wedge \, x \, S)$, as k ranges over all individuals in the universe, cannot (unless the universe happens to be finite) be all written down as can the *actual* conjuncts of an *actual* conjunction: hence the notation of "generalizing" the form common to all these sentences $S\lfloor k/x \rfloor$. This common form is represented by the sentence S, together with the variable x.

The notion of depth extends to generalizations: the depth of $(Q\,x\,S)$ is 1 plus the depth of S. Note that S is not, in general, an immediate constituent of $(Q\,x\,S)$ – the immediate constituents being the sentences $S\lfloor k/x \rfloor$ – but that the depth of $(Q\,x\,S)$ *is*, in fact, "1 + the maximum depth of any of the immediate constituents of $Q\,x\,S)$". It is easy to see that the depth of S is the same as the depth of $S\lfloor k/x \rfloor$, for any individual k.

There is a circumstance in which its body S *is* an immediate constituent (and, in that case, the only immediate constituent) of $(Q\,x\,S)$. That is when the (x, k)-instances of S all turn out to *be* S. For example, the only immediate constituent of $(\wedge x\,(less\ y\ z))$ is $(less\ y\ z)$, the reason being that the body of the generalization contains no occurrence of its bound variable. This being so, the effect of replacing every occurrence of that variable by an individual is, of course, nil.

The matter is rather more subtle than this example illustrates. Consider the sentence

$(\wedge x\ \textbf{if}\ (less\ y\ z)\ \textbf{then}\ (\vee x\ (less\ x\ z)))$

and suppose the universe is

$\{1, 2\}$

The immediate constituents of this sentence are the $(x, 1)$-instance and the $(x, 2)$-instance of the body

$\textbf{if}\ (less\ y\ z)\ \textbf{then}\ (\vee x\ (less\ x\ z))$

However, as the reader will see if he consults the definition of instantiation, these two instances are both identical to the body itself, despite the occurrence, twice, of the variable x in that body! The essential point is contained in clause (d) of the definition of $\varphi\lfloor k/x \rfloor$:

(d) if φ is the generalization $(Q\,x\,S)$, then $\varphi\lfloor k/x \rfloor$ is φ

We are witnessing here a manifestation of the enormously important distinction between two kinds of occurrence of individual variables within formulas: *free* occurrences and *bound* occurrences.

All occurrences of x within the generalization $(Q\,x\,S)$ are *bound* occurrences of x in $(Q\,x\,S)$. As for the occurrences in $(Q\,x\,S)$ of any individual variable y other than x, one notes that they will be occurrences of *y* in *S*. If such an occurrence of *y* in *S* is a bound, or free, occurrence of *y* in *S* then it is defined to be also a bound, or free, occurrence of *y* in (*Q x S*).

We have defined the notion of constituent of a formula in such a way that an individual variable *x* is a constituent of a sentence *S* if, and only if, there is a *free* occurrence of *x* in *S*. If there are only *bound* occurrences of *x* in *S* then *x* is *not* a constituent of *S*. The constituents of the sentence

   (∧*x* **if** (*less y z*) **then** (∨*x* (*less x z*)))

when the universe is {1, 2}, are

   if (*less y z*) **then** (∨*x* (*less x z*))
   (*less y z*)
   (∨*x* (*less x z*))
   (*less* 1 *z*)
   (*less* 2 *z*)
   y
   z
   1
   2

Since *x* has only bound occurrences in the sentence, we do not encounter it when we take constituents. The free variables of a formula are the variables that are among its constituents. Thus *y* and *z* are the free variables of the sentence above.

It is possible for a variable to have both free and bound occurrences in the same formula. Consider the sentence

   if (∧*x* (*less x z*)) **then** (*greater z x*)

Take constituents (assuming the universe is still {1, 2})

   (∧*x* (*less x z*))
   (*greater z x*)
   z
   x
   (*less* 1 *z*)
   (*less* 2 *z*)
   1
   2

It remains to explain the class of terms – the exemplifications – which we set aside earlier in order to consider them after we had been over the various kinds of sentence, in particular the generalizations.

Suppose the universe is $\{1,2,3,4\}$, and that we consider the generalization

$$\forall x(P\,x)$$

whose instances are the predications

$$(P\,1) \quad (P\,2) \quad (P\,3) \quad (P\,4)$$

As we have explained, the truth or falsehood of $\forall x(P\,x)$ is completely determined by that of its instances. If, for example, the respective truthvalues of these instances are

$$\text{t} \quad \text{t} \quad \text{t} \quad \text{t} \tag{1}$$

then $\forall x(P\,x)$ itself has the truthvalue t; while if the respective truth-values of the instances are

$$\text{t} \quad \text{f} \quad \text{f} \quad \text{t} \tag{2}$$

then $\forall x(P\,x)$ has the truthvalue f. Now in the second case, the individual denoted by the exemplification

$$*\forall x(P\,x)$$

of $\forall x(P\,x)$ is either 2, or 3; namely it is an individual k such that the k-instance of $\forall x(P\,x)$ is false.

In general, the exemplification $*A$, where A is a universal generalization, denotes an individual k that satisfies the condition:

$$A \text{ is true if, and only if, the } k\text{-instance of } A \text{ is true} \tag{3}$$

Thus when the instances have the truthvalues (2), only the individuals 2 and 3 satisfy this condition, and hence $*\forall x(P\,x)$ must denote one or other of them. But now suppose the instances have the truthvalues (1). Then *any* individual satisfies the condition (3). Hence, when A is a universal generalization denoting t, the term $*A$ denotes an individual k such that the k-instance of A also denotes t; but when A is a universal generalization denoting f, the term $*A$ denotes an individual k such that the k-instance of A also denotes f.

In either case, $*A$ denotes an individual k with the property that

A and the k-instance of A have the same truthvalue

The same thing applies when A is an existential generalization. That is: $*\exists x(P\,x)$ denotes an individual k such that the k-instance, $(P\,k)$, of $\exists x(P\,x)$, has the same truthvalue as does $\exists x(P\,x)$. So, in case the truthvalues are as in (2), $*\exists x(P\,x)$ must denote either 1 or 4, since $(P\,1)$ and $(P\,4)$ are the only instances that are true. However, if the truthvalues are f   f   f   f   (4)

then $*\exists x(P\,x)$ can denote any of 1, 2, 3, 4, since the corresponding instance will in all cases be false. Thus the individual k denoted by an exemplification $*A$ really does, intuitively, "exemplify" A in the sense that if we instantiate A with respect to k we get a sentence that "shows why" A has the truthvalue that it has.

The reader will have noticed that, in the preceding sketch, we skirted around the question *which* individual $*A$ denotes, when *more than one* individual satisfies the condition (3).

The simple answer is that the *only* logical requirement placed on $v(*A)$ – the individual denoted by $*A$ – is that it must be a member of the set of individuals "represented" by A. This set of individuals is the one described above: the set $\{j \mid j$ is in U and $v(A) = v(A\lfloor j\rfloor)\}$ where $A\lfloor j\rfloor$ is the j-instance of A.

Table 2.1

set	"selected" member
{1}	1
{2}	2
{3}	3
{4}	4
{1, 2}	2
{1, 3}	1
{1, 4}	4
{2, 3}	2
{2, 4}	4
{3, 4}	3
{1, 2, 3}	2
{1, 2, 4}	4
{1, 3, 4}	3
{2, 3, 4}	2
{1, 2, 3, 4}	3

However, it helps to fix ideas by supposing that the denotations of exemplifications are fixed upon with the aid of a *choice function* for U. A choice function for a set S is a function that yields a member of X, when applied to X, for each non-empty subset X of S. For example, Table 2.1 gives a choice function for the set $\{1, 2, 3, 4\}$.

We can now suppose that in working out what formulas denote we use a choice function, when we have determined the set of individuals that are eligible (according to (3)) to be denoted by the term *A, to "choose" an individual from the set, and that it is *this* individual which *A denotes. So, for instance, with the choice function given in table 2.1, the term *∃x(P x) would be found to denote, in the various contexts (1), (2) and (4) mentioned above, the individuals 3, 4 and 3 respectively.

We could then, if we liked, intuitively read an exemplification *A "applicatively", as denoting an individual obtained by applying "what * denotes" to "what A denotes". This works out very nicely if we suppose that the symbol * denotes the choice function and that, *in this context*, the sentence A denotes the set of individuals defined by (3), the set we say is "represented" by A.

Now, the intention of the design of the semantics of the predicate calculus is indeed to provide means for determining (and in some cases, as e.g. when the universe is finite, for constructively computing) the *value* denoted by each formula; *but only if the formula contains no free variables.* Such formulas are said to be *closed* formulas. Thus, ∃x(P x) is closed; but ∃x(R x y) is not, because it contains the free variable y. Formulas that are not closed are said to be *open*.

We have open sentences, such as ∃x(R x y) or (P x), and open terms, such as x, (plus x y), *∃x(R x y). Open formulas do not denote anything: only closed formulas do. This is entirely in accord with conventional ideas about mathematical formulas: whereas, e.g., "3 + 4" denotes 7, the open formula "x + 4" denotes nothing. Granted, we *can* say something like: "x + 4" denotes 7 if "x" denotes 3, but the "if" part has to be added; and one flippant rejoinder might be: but "x" *doesn't* denote 3, because it doesn't denote anything!

What is going on here is this: open formulas do not denote, *but their closed instances do.* The open term "x + 4" has the closed term "3 + 4" as one of its closed instances; and when we say that "x + 4" denotes 7 if "x" denotes 3 we are just using comfortable language for the more pedantic: "the (x, 3)-instance of 'x + 4' denotes 7".

If τ is a closed term and if A is a closed generalization we can consider the "τ-instance of A". By the τ-instance of A, (denoted by A[τ]) we mean the closed sentence that is obtained from the body B of A by putting τ for each of the free occurrences of x (if any) in B; where x is the bound variable of A.

Thus, if A is ∃x(Px → ¬Qx) and τ is (+ 3 4) then A[τ] is (P(+ 3 4)) → ¬(Q(+ 3 4)). Note that A[τ] *is* closed, since τ is closed and A is closed. If the universe is {1, 2, ...} and A is ∀xPx, then we have A[1] = (P 1), A[2] = (P 2), and so on.

For each closed generalization A we shall be particularly interested in its $*A$-instance

$$A[*A]$$

which we also call its *exemplifying instance*. The exemplifying instance of $\forall x(Px \to \neg Qx)$ is thus

$$(P*\forall x(Px \to \neg Qx)) \to \neg(Q*\forall x(Px \to \neg Qx))$$

The reason why we are interested in the exemplifying instance of each generalization A is that *it always has the same truthvalue as A*, and is therefore, intuitively, "equivalent" to A.

The thing denoted by a closed formula X, its *value*, is represented by the notation

$$v(X)$$

("the value of X"). Thus when X is a closed sentence, $v(X)$ is a *truthvalue*. If X is a closed term, $v(X)$ is an *individual*. In this notation, the characteristic property of the exemplifying instance of a generalization is given by the equation

$$v(A) = v(A[*A])$$

which holds for all closed generalizations A.

This v-notation will be our principal tool for defining and analysing the semantic properties of closed formulas. For example, the semantic properties of negations, that is, closed sentences of the form $\neg A$, are entirely expressed in the "conditional" equations

$$v(\neg A) = \mathbf{t} \text{ iff } v(A) = \mathbf{f}$$
$$v(\neg A) = \mathbf{f} \text{ iff } v(A) = \mathbf{t}$$

which say that the truthvalue denoted by a negation $\neg A$ is completely determined by the truthvalue denoted by its negatum A.

The other Boolean combinations also have their characteristic semantic equations. For conditionals $(\to A\ B)$ there are two equations

$$v(\to A\ B) = \mathbf{f} \text{ iff } v(A) = \mathbf{t} \text{ and } v(B) = \mathbf{f}$$
$$v(\to A\ B) = \mathbf{t} \text{ iff } v(A) = \mathbf{f}, \text{ or } v(B) = \mathbf{t}, \text{ or both}$$

so that the truthvalue denoted by a conditional $(\to A\ B)$ is completely determined by those denoted by its antecedent A and its consequent B.

The semantic equations for biconditionals $(\leftrightarrow A\ B)$ are

$$v(\leftrightarrow A\ B) = \mathbf{t} \text{ iff } v(A) = v(B)$$
$$v(\leftrightarrow A\ B) = \mathbf{f} \text{ iff } v(A) \neq v(B)$$

Those for conjunctions $(\wedge A_1 \ldots A_n)$ are

$$v(\wedge A_1 \ldots A_n) = \mathbf{t} \text{ iff } v(A_j) = \mathbf{t}, \text{ for all } j, 1 \le j \le n$$
$$v(\wedge A_1 \ldots A_n) = \mathbf{f} \text{ iff } v(A_j) = \mathbf{f}, \text{ for at least one } j, 1 \le j \le n$$

which must be understood as specializing, when $n = 0$, to the equation:

$$v(\wedge) = \mathbf{t}.$$

The equations for disjunctions are entirely similar to those for conjunctions, except that the rôles of $\mathbf{t}$ and $\mathbf{f}$ are interchanged

$$v(\vee A_1 \ldots A_n) = \mathbf{f} \text{ iff } v(A_j) = \mathbf{f}, \text{ for all } j, 1 \le j \le n$$
$$v(\vee A_1 \ldots A_n) = \mathbf{t} \text{ iff } v(A_j) = \mathbf{t}, \text{ for at least one } j, 1 \le j \le n$$

with the $n = 0$ case giving the equation

$$v(\vee) = \mathbf{f}$$

The semantic equations for the closed sentences $\mathbf{t}$ and $\mathbf{f}$ are

$$v(\mathbf{t}) = \mathbf{t}$$
$$v(\mathbf{f}) = \mathbf{f}$$

("truthvalues denote themselves").

Closed generalizations have semantic equations very similar to those for conjunctions and disjunctions. *Universal* generalizations A denote truthvalues given by

$$v(A) = \mathbf{t} \text{ iff } v(A[j]) = \mathbf{t} \text{ for all } j \text{ in } U$$
$$v(A) = \mathbf{f} \text{ iff } v(A[j]) = \mathbf{f} \text{ for at least one } j \text{ in } U$$

while existential generalizations denote truthvalues given by the same equations but with the rôles of $\mathbf{t}$ and $\mathbf{f}$ reversed: thus when A is an existential generalization we have

$$v(A) = \mathbf{f} \text{ iff } v(A[j]) = \mathbf{f} \text{ for all } j \text{ in } U,$$
$$v(A) = \mathbf{t} \text{ iff } v(A[j]) = \mathbf{t} \text{ for at least one } j \text{ in } U.$$

Thus the value of a closed generalization is completely determined by those of its instances over the universe U of individuals. If U is an infinite set, then there are of course infinitely many such instances to be considered.

The only sentences we have not written down equations for are the *predications*. At this point all we need say is that for each closed predication A we must assume that there is an equation

$$v(A) = w$$

available, where w is either **t** or **f**. Since predications have no immediate constituent sentences, their truthvalues are not determined in the same way as those of sentences that do.

For example, if the universe is $\{1, 2, 3, 4\}$, and we need to know the meaning of the 1-ary predicate Q, we need to be told the truthvalues of the predications $(Q\ 1)$, $(Q\ 2)$, $(Q\ 3)$ and $(Q\ 4)$. Equations giving those truthvalues, as, e.g.,

$$v(Q\ 1) = \mathbf{t}$$
$$v(Q\ 2) = \mathbf{f}$$
$$v(Q\ 3) = \mathbf{f}$$
$$v(Q\ 4) = \mathbf{t}$$

collectively pin down the meaning of Q as a property that belongs to 1 and 4, but does not belong to 2 and 3.

Predications like $(Q\ 1)$, $(Q\ 2)$, $(Q\ 3)$ and $(Q\ 4)$, whose immediate constituents are *individuals*, are called *basic* sentences. As we shall see, if we have equations for the basic sentences and the basic terms, we can deduce the equations for all other formulas! By basic terms we mean constructions whose immediate constituents are individuals. Thus $(+\ 1\ 2)$ is a basic term; and an equation for it might be

$$v(+\ 1\ 2) = 3$$

as it would have to be if the constructor symbol "$+$" was to have its usual meaning.

In general, the semantic equations for closed terms X have the same general form

$$v(X) = w$$

as the semantic equations for closed sentences; the righthand side, w, is the thing denoted by X, its value. When X is a term, the value of X is an individual (and, in particular, when X is an individual, is X itself).

Now the fundamental equation governing the semantics of all applicative formulas (i.e., constructions, predications, and Boolean combinations) is the one that, intuitively, gives the meaning of "application". For any closed applicative formula $(\alpha\ X_1 \ldots X_n)$, we find its value

$$v(\alpha\ X_1 \ldots X_n)$$

by first computing the values

$$v(X_1) \ldots v(X_n)$$

of its immediate constituents. If these are $w_1, \ldots w_n$, we then find the value of the basic formula

$$v(\alpha\, w_1 \ldots w_n)$$

and take its value, w, to be that of $(\alpha\, X_1 \ldots X_n)$.

This "applicative evaluation law" can be written as an equation that tells what the value is of any construction or predication $(\alpha\, X_1 \ldots X_n)$ whose immediate constituents are not all individuals (i.e. any non-basic construction or non-basic predication):

$$v(\alpha\, X_1 \ldots X_n) = v(\alpha\, w_1 \ldots w_n), \text{ where } v(X_j) = w_j, 1 \le j \le n$$

Indeed this equation holds also for the case when $(\alpha\, X_1 \ldots X_n)$ is a closed Boolean combination. In that case we first compute the truth-values $v(X_1), \ldots, v(X_n)$ of the closed sentences $X_1, \ldots, X_n$ that are its immediate constituents, and then, if these truthvalues are $w_1, \ldots, w_n$, obtain the truthvalue w, which is that of the "basic Boolean combination" $(\alpha\, w_1 \ldots w_n)$. From this point of view we can now regard the equations for Boolean combinations, which we gave earlier, as being ways of specifying outright what the values of all basic Boolean combinations are. They tell us, e.g., that

$$v(\neg\, t) = f$$
$$v(\neg\, f) = t$$
$$v(\to f\, t) = t$$
$$v(\wedge\, t\, f\, t\, t\, f\, t) = f$$

and so on.

The only closed formulas for which we do not write down such general equations are the exemplifications $*A$. The reason is that it is not completely determined by the semantic rules which individual (from among those it is eligible to denote) $*A$ actually does denote. All we can do is to express clearly the constraints put upon $v(*A)$ by *logical* considerations.

The condition governing what individual is denoted by a closed exemplification $*A$ is

$$v(*A) \in \{j \mid j \text{ is in } U \text{ and } v(A) = v(A\lfloor j\rfloor)\}$$

On the right-hand side, we are depicting the set

$$\{j \mid j \text{ is in } U \text{ and } v(A) = v(A\lfloor j\rfloor)\}$$

of all individuals j for which $A\lfloor j\rfloor$ and A have the same truthvalue; and all we are saying is that $v(*A)$ is some particular one of these individuals. This set is the one we say is *represented by* A; for convenience we denote it by: $[A]$.

Let us take an example in which U is the set $\{1, 2, 3, 4\}$. We shall use the choice function for U, as given by table 2.1, to determine $v(*A)$ by the rule that $v(*A)$ is the value of the choice function for the set $[A]$. The equations in table 2.2 are provided for all basic formulas containing the 1-ary predicate Q, the 2-ary predicate R, the 0-ary constructor n, the 1-ary constructor g and the 2-ary constructor h.

Table 2.2

$v(Q\ 1) = t$	$v(Q\ 2) = f$	$v(Q\ 3) = f$	$v(Q\ 4) = t$
$v(R\ 1\ 1) = f$	$v(R\ 1\ 2) = t$	$v(R\ 1\ 3) = t$	$v(R\ 1\ 4) = f$
$v(R\ 2\ 1) = t$	$v(R\ 2\ 2) = t$	$v(R\ 2\ 3) = t$	$v(R\ 2\ 4) = f$
$v(R\ 3\ 1) = f$	$v(R\ 3\ 2) = f$	$v(R\ 3\ 3) = t$	$v(R\ 3\ 4) = f$
$v(R\ 4\ 1) = f$	$v(R\ 4\ 2) = t$	$v(R\ 4\ 3) = f$	$v(R\ 4\ 4) = t$
$v(n) = 3$			
$v(g\ 1) = 2$	$v(g\ 2) = 3$	$v(g\ 3) = 4$	$v(g\ 4) = 1$
$v(h\ 1\ 1) = 2$	$v(h\ 1\ 2) = 1$	$v(h\ 1\ 3) = 3$	$v(h\ 1\ 4) = 4$
$v(h\ 2\ 1) = 4$	$v(h\ 2\ 2) = 2$	$v(h\ 2\ 3) = 3$	$v(h\ 2\ 4) = 1$
$v(h\ 3\ 1) = 3$	$v(h\ 3\ 2) = 4$	$v(h\ 3\ 3) = 2$	$v(h\ 3\ 4) = 2$
$v(h\ 4\ 1) = 1$	$v(h\ 4\ 2) = 3$	$v(h\ 4\ 3) = 1$	$v(h\ 4\ 4) = 3$

Given U, a choice function for U, and having "basic equations" for the set

$$\{Q, R, n, g, h\}$$

of non-logical symbols, we have thus available to us enough information to compute the value of *any* closed formula in which no non-logical symbols occur other than those in the set $\{Q, R, n, g, h\}$ covered by the basic equations in Table 2.2. Thus:

$$v(*\ \exists x\ Qx) = 4$$
$$v(*\ \forall x\ \exists y\ Rxy) = 3$$
$$v(h(g(g(n)))\ (g(n))) = 4$$
$$v(R\ *\ \exists x\ Qx\ *\ \forall x\ \exists y\ Rxy) = f$$
$$v(h\ *\ \exists x\ Qx\ *\ \forall x\ \exists y\ Rxy) = 1$$

We call a set like $\{Q, R, n, g, h\}$ a *lexicon*; namely any set whose members are taken from the collection

$$\left(\sum_{k=0}^{\infty} P_k \ \cup \ \sum_{k=0}^{\infty} C_k \right)$$

of all constructor- and predicate-symbols. Once we fix the lexicon L

and the universe U we have fixed the set of all closed formulas "on L and U" – those involving only the symbols in L that can be constructed on the assumption that the universe is U. Thus in our example above we are considering the closed formulas on the lexicon $\{Q, R, n, g, h\}$ and the universe $\{1, 2, 3, 4\}$.

The set of all closed formulas on the lexicon L and the universe U is called the *applied calculus on L and U* and denoted by

> *applied* (L, U)

We can keep L fixed, and let U vary, thereby considering all the various applied calculi *applied* (L, U) in which the lexicon is L and U is *any* non-empty set. Certain closed formulas occur in *all* these applied calculi, namely, those in whose syntactic construction no individuals are used; these closed formulas contain only variables, members of L, and the logical symbols $t, f, \neg, \vee, \wedge, \rightarrow, \leftrightarrow, \forall, \exists$, and $*$. They are the "pure" closed formulas on L, and the set of them is called *the pure calculus on L* and is denoted by

> *pure* (L)

From this discussion it is clear that we always have

> *pure* $(L) \subseteq$ *applied* (L, U)

no matter what set may be chosen as U. The various applied calculi on L and U (i.e. for fixed L and various U) all *include* the pure calculus on L.

One can give a precise characterization of (open and closed) pure formulas, by means of the following recursive specification:

(a)   a variable or a truthvalue is a pure formula

(b)   the formula $(\omega \, \varphi_1 \ldots \varphi_n)$ is a pure formula iff $\varphi_1, \ldots, \varphi_n$ are pure formulas

The form $(\omega \, \varphi_1 \ldots \varphi_n)$ is intended to cover all *applicative* formulas with operator ω and immediate constituents $\varphi_1, \ldots, \varphi_n$, and also to cover generalizations, in which case $n = 2$, ω is $\forall$ or $\exists$, φ_1 is an individual variable, and φ_2 is a sentence; and exemplifications, in which case $n = 1$, ω is $*$, and φ_1 is a generalization. The operator ω and the formulas $\varphi_1 \ldots \varphi_n$ are the *immediate parts* of the formula $(\omega \, \varphi_1 \ldots \varphi_n)$. This notion almost coincides with the notion of the *immediate constituents* of $(\omega \, \varphi_1 \ldots \varphi_n)$ when $(\omega \, \varphi_1 \ldots \varphi_n)$ is an applicative formula. However, these notions very much diverge for generalizations. The immediate *parts* of $(\forall \, x \, S)$ are $\forall$, x, and S, but the immediate *constituents* of $(\forall \, x \, S)$ are the various sentences $S|k/x|$ for k in U.

The *parts* of a formula are: itself, and the parts of its immediate parts. Thus the taking of parts of a formula is, literally, the operation of syntactically dismantling it into its ultimate building blocks and the various intermediate "sub-assemblies" involved in its syntactic construction from those ultimate building blocks. It is an entirely syntactic operation. By contrast, the taking of *constituents* of a formula is a logical analysis of it into those formulas on whose denotations its own denotation depends.

A formula has only finitely many parts. However, a formula may have infinitely many constituents; only when the universe is finite do all formulas have finitely many constituents. When the universe is infinite then, as we have seen, each general sentence has (one immediate constituent for each individual in that universe and hence) infinitely many immediate constituents.

The rôle of the universe U in all of this is therefore, as it were, that of a *parameter* of the entire construction that is the basic syntax. As we vary the set U, so the set of formulas varies. Note, however, that the set of *pure* formulas does *not* vary with the various choices of U. Since, by definition, their syntactic construction does not involve U – none of their parts are individual constants – they are unaffected by changing U to a different set. For this reason the pure formulas enjoy a special "absolute" status in the predicate calculus.

They can also (given sensible choices for the objects acting as basic symbols) be *written*, whereas, for at least some possible choices of U, it is problematic whether even a term that happens to be an individual can always be written: the concept of "writing" is too narrow to extend to such (possible) individuals as the Niagara Falls, the sun, or the population of Brazil.

Another, more important, property of pure formulas is that they collectively form a *countably* infinite set. This is immediately obvious from the fact that there are only countably infinitely many variables and operator symbols, and the fact that we can "flatten" any pure formula into the finite sequence of its basic symbols and brackets as we encounter them in reading the formula from left to right. For example, the formula

$$(\wedge x(\leftrightarrow(P\ x\ y)(\rightarrow(A\ x)(B\ y))))$$

flattens to the sequence of symbols:

$$(\ ,\wedge,x,(\ ,\leftrightarrow,(\ ,P,x,y,)\ ,(\ ,\rightarrow,(\ ,A,x,)\ ,(\ ,B,y,)\ ,)\ ,)\ ,)$$

Thus the pure formulas are no more numerous than the set of all finite sequences of basic symbols and brackets. But in general, if we have a countably infinite set S enumerated, e.g.

$$\{s_1, s_2, \ldots, \quad\} = S$$

we can associate a unique integer with any finite sequence

$$(s_{i_1}, s_{i_2}, \ldots, s_{i_n})$$

of elements of S; namely the integer

$$2^{i_1} \cdot 3^{i_2} \cdot \ldots \cdot p_n^{i_n}$$

which is the product of the first n prime numbers each raised to the power of the index of the corresponding component, relative to the given enumeration. Hence the set of finite sequences of elements of S is countably infinite if S is countably infinite.

So the set of pure formulas is countably infinite. It follows that the set of *all* formulas, pure and impure, is *at least* countably infinite. In fact, if the universe U is not a finite set, then the set of all formulas will have the cardinal number of U, (denoted by $\bar{\bar{U}}$ in the usual notation). For example, if U is the set of the "continuum" of all *real* numbers then the number of formulas is the cardinal number of the continuum, which is strictly greater than the cardinal number $\aleph_0$ of countably infinite sets.

The cardinal number of the set of all formulas is at least $\bar{\bar{U}}$ because U itself is a subset of the set of all formulas. It is (when U is infinite) at most $\bar{\bar{U}}$ because we can then find a one-to-one correspondence between U and the set of all formulas in an analogue of the preceding argument for the countability of the set of pure formulas.

As we shall see, the "parametric" nature of the set U is a central idea of the predicate calculus. We shall be interested in studying properties of pure formulas that remain invariant under *all* choices of U – these properties are essentially the logical properties of pure formulas T. There is also interest in identifying properties of pure formulas that depend on properties of U. The main property of U that is thus studied is its size. For example, it turns out that certain pure formulas cannot be true unless U is infinite.

In many discussions we can illustrate points by supposing U to be a small, finite set and by taking the constituents of sentences. In particular we can refute claims that a certain property holds for a formula for *all* choices of U, by finding a finite U for which the property fails (if there is one). There are many ways to exploit the parametric character of U, and some of the central results of the theory of the predicate calculus are arrived at by this route.

For example, if U is chosen to be the set of all terms in *pure* (L), we have the interesting equation:

$$pure\,(L) = applied\,(L, U)$$

The set of all terms in *pure (L)* is called *the logical universe for L* and is denoted by *logical (L)*. So we have, for all choices of lexicon *L*:

$$pure\,(L) = applied\,(L, logical\,(L)).$$

3. Boolean Analysis of Sentences

In the previous chapter we stated the intended semantics for closed sentences: each one of them is meant to denote one of the two truth-values, t, f. We explained the way in which the truthvalue $v(X)$, denoted by a closed sentence X, depends on those denoted by the closed sentences that are the immediate constitutents of X.

It is traditional, and useful, to separate the study of the predicate calculus into two stages, corresponding roughly to the two kinds of entity – truthvalues and individuals – that closed formulas can denote. In this chapter we shall deal with the first stage, which considers sentences merely as truthvalue-denoters, in isolation from the details involving the denotations of terms and individuals.

From this point of view the only mode of syntactic composition that we consider is the *Boolean composition*, by means of ¬, ∨, ∧, → and ↔, of closed sentences into more complex closed sentences. We ignore the interior structure of closed predications and generalizations, treating them as indivisible wholes that denote either t or f. This "purely Boolean" attitude towards closed sentences leads us to the following definition:

> the *Boolean constituents* of a closed sentence X are: X itself, together with (if X is a Boolean composition) the Boolean constituents of the immediate constituents of X

Thus, if X is a predication or a generalization, there is only one Boolean constituent of X, namely X itself. The only Boolean constituent of t is t; of f, f; of (∧), (∧); and of (∨), (∨).

But, for example, the Boolean constituents of the closed sentence

$$(\wedge(A \to B)(\neg A)(\forall x(Px \to Qx) \to \exists y Py)) \tag{1}$$

are, in addition to itself, the closed sentences:

$(A \to B)$	$(\forall x(Px \to Qx) \to \exists y Py)$ (2)
$\neg A$	$\forall x(Px \to Qx)$
A	$\exists y Py$
B	

but not, e.g., $(Px \to Qx)$, or (Py), for these are both open, and also parts of the interior of generalizations. In the Boolean analysis of the sentence (1) we are interested only in the way that the truthvalues denoted by its "independent" Boolean constituents

$$A, \quad B, \quad \forall x(Px \to Qx), \quad \exists yPy \tag{3}$$

determine the truthvalue denoted by (1).

We call the Boolean constituents (3) independent because they are their own sole Boolean constituents. A and B are predications (i.e., the *symbols* "A", "B" are 0-ary predicates, while the *sentences* "A", "B" should more strictly be written $(A), (B)$); while $\forall x(Px \to Qx)$ and $\exists yPy$ are generalizations. The truthvalues they denote, therefore, do not depend on those denoted by any other of the sentences in (2); hence we say they are independent.

Now, by a *Boolean valuation* of a closed sentence X we mean a set K of $m \geq 1$ *valuation equations* $v(X_j) = w_j$, $1 \leq j \leq m$

$$K = \{v(X_1) = w_1, \ldots, v(X_m) = w_m\}$$

in which $w_1, \ldots, w_m$ are truthvalues and $X_1, \ldots, X_m$ are all of the distinct Boolean constituents of X, and which satisfies the conditions set forth in table 3.1. We have given each condition a label, in the left margin, for later reference.

Note that such a set K of equations will also satisfy the condition:

$\lfloor cons \rfloor$ it does not contain two equations of the form
$v(Y) = \mathbf{f}, v(Y) = \mathbf{t}$

and the condition:

$\lfloor comp\ \mathscr{S} \rfloor$ for each Boolean constituent Y of each sentence in
$\mathscr{S}$, it contains either the equation $v(Y) = \mathbf{t}$ or
the equation $v(Y) = \mathbf{f}$; and if it contains the
equation $v(Z) = w$ then Z is a Boolean constituent of a sentence in $\mathscr{S}$ and w is a truthvalue

when $\mathscr{S}$ is the set $\{X\}$.

We could just as well have defined a Boolean valuation of a closed sentence X to be any set of equations satisfying all of the conditions

$$\lfloor \mathbf{t}, \mathbf{f} \rfloor, \lfloor \neg\ \mathbf{t} \rfloor, \lfloor \neg\ \mathbf{f} \rfloor, \lfloor \to \mathbf{t} \rfloor, \lfloor \to \mathbf{f} \rfloor, \lfloor \leftrightarrow \mathbf{t} \rfloor, \lfloor \leftrightarrow \mathbf{f} \rfloor, \lfloor \wedge \mathbf{t} \rfloor, \lfloor \wedge \mathbf{f} \rfloor,$$
$$\lfloor \vee \mathbf{t} \rfloor, \lfloor \vee \mathbf{f} \rfloor, \lfloor cons \rfloor, \lfloor comp\ \mathscr{S} \rfloor \tag{4}$$

with the set $\mathscr{S}$ taken to be $\{X\}$.

More generally, we say that a set of equations satisfying all the

Table 3.1

[t, f]	it does not contain the equation $v(\mathbf{t}) = \mathbf{f}$, or the equation $v(\mathbf{f}) = \mathbf{t}$; or the equation $v(\wedge) = \mathbf{f}$, or the equation $v(\vee) = \mathbf{t}$
[¬ t]	if it contains the equation $v(\neg\, Y) = \mathbf{t}$ then it also contains the equation $v(Y) = \mathbf{f}$
[¬ f]	if it contains the equation $v(\neg\, Y) = \mathbf{f}$ then it also contains the equation $v(Y) = \mathbf{t}$
[→ t]	if it contains the equation $v(Y \rightarrow Z) = \mathbf{t}$, then *either* it also contains the equation $v(Y) = \mathbf{f}$ *or* it also contains the equation $v(Z) = \mathbf{t}$ *or both*
[→ f]	if it contains the equation $v(Y \rightarrow Z) = \mathbf{f}$, then it also contains the equations $v(Y) = \mathbf{t}$ and $v(Z) = \mathbf{f}$
[↔ t]	if it contains the equation $v(Y \leftrightarrow Z) = \mathbf{t}$ then *either* it contains both of the equations $v(Y) = \mathbf{t}$, $v(Z) = \mathbf{t}$ *or* it contains both of the equations $v(Y) = \mathbf{f}$, $v(Z) = \mathbf{f}$
[↔ f]	if it contains the equation $v(Y \leftrightarrow Z) = \mathbf{f}$ then *either* it contains both of the equations $v(Y) = \mathbf{t}$, $v(Z) = \mathbf{f}$ *or* it contains both of the equations $v(Y) = \mathbf{f}$, $v(Z) = \mathbf{t}$
[∧ t]	if it contains the equation $v(\wedge\, Y_1 \ldots Y_p) = \mathbf{t}$ then it also contains *all* the equations $v(Y_1) = \mathbf{t}, \ldots, v(Y_p) = \mathbf{t}$
[∧ f]	if it contains the equation $v(\wedge\, Y_1 \ldots Y_p) = \mathbf{f}$, then it also contains *at least one* of the equations $v(Y_1) = \mathbf{f}, \ldots, v(Y_p) = \mathbf{f}$
[∨ t]	if it contains the equation $v(\vee\, Y_1 \ldots Y_p) = \mathbf{t}$, then it also contains *at least one* of the equations $v(Y_1) = \mathbf{t}, \ldots, v(Y_p) = \mathbf{t}$
[∨ f]	if it contains the equation $v(\vee\, Y_1 \ldots Y_p) = \mathbf{f}$, then it also contains *all* the equations $v(Y_1) = \mathbf{f}, \ldots, v(Y_p) = \mathbf{f}$

conditions (4), for some *set* $\mathscr{S}$ of closed sentences, is a *Boolean valuation*, and moreover a Boolean valuation *of* $\mathscr{S}$. For example, the following set of equations is a Boolean valuation of the sentence (1):

$$v(\wedge(A \to B)(\neg A)(\forall x(Px \to Qx) \to \exists yPy)) \quad = \quad \mathbf{f} \qquad (5.1)$$

$$v(A \to B) \qquad\qquad\qquad\qquad\qquad\qquad = \quad \mathbf{t} \qquad (5.2)$$

$$v(\neg A) \qquad\qquad\qquad\qquad\qquad\qquad\quad = \quad \mathbf{t} \qquad (5.3)$$

$$* \quad v(A) \qquad\qquad\qquad\qquad\qquad\qquad\quad = \quad \mathbf{f} \qquad (5.4)$$

$$* \quad v(B) \qquad\qquad\qquad\qquad\qquad\qquad\quad = \quad \mathbf{t} \qquad (5.5)$$

$$v(\forall x(Px \to Qx) \to \exists yPy) \qquad\qquad\quad = \quad \mathbf{f} \qquad (5.6)$$

$$* \quad v(\forall x(Px \to Qx)) \qquad\qquad\qquad\quad = \quad \mathbf{t} \qquad (5.7)$$

$$* \quad v(\exists yPy) \qquad\qquad\qquad\qquad\qquad\quad = \quad \mathbf{f} \qquad (5.8)$$

The "independent" equations, marked *, are those for the independent Boolean constituents of (1). None of the conditions in the definition of a Boolean valuation prescribes what the truthvalues on the right-hand sides of these equations (5.4, 5.5, 5.7 and 5.8) should be. The right-hand sides of the remaining "dependent" equations (which correspond to the dependent Boolean constituents of (1)) are completely determined by the conditions of the definition and the presence, in the set, of equations for the immediate constituents of the dependent Boolean constituents.

Thus, the right-hand side of equation 5.6 is determined by the presence of equations 5.7 and 5.8 and by the condition $|\to \mathbf{t}|$, which forbids the right-hand side of 5.6 to be $\mathbf{t}$; hence it must be $\mathbf{f}$.

Similarly, equations 5.4 and 5.5 together with $|\to \mathbf{f}|$ forbid the right-hand side of 5.2 to be $\mathbf{f}$; hence determine it to be $\mathbf{t}$.

Equation 5.4 and condition $|\neg \mathbf{f}|$ require equation 5.3 to have the right-hand side $\mathbf{t}$ since they forbid it to be $\mathbf{f}$.

Finally, the right-hand side of equation 5.1 must be $\mathbf{f}$ since equations 5.2, 5.3 and 5.6, together with condition $|\wedge \mathbf{t}|$, forbid it to be $\mathbf{t}$.

This illustrates the general fact that the right-hand sides of the *dependent* equations are completely determined by those of the *independent* equations, in any Boolean valuation. This is the case whether the valuation contains finitely many, or infinitely many, equations. For note that the number of distinct Boolean constituents of a sentence X, which we can denote by $\beta(X)$, is always a positive integer $\geqslant 1$. In the special case that X is $\mathbf{t}$, $\mathbf{f}$, $(\wedge)$, $(\vee)$, or a predication or a generalization, $\beta(X) = 1$. Note that if Y is an immediate constituent of X, then $\beta(Y) < \beta(X)$. Let us then say that the weight of an equation $v(X) = w$ in a Boolean valuation is the number $\beta(X)$.

It is clear that the right-hand side of an equation of weight $h > 1$ is completely determined by finitely many equations of weight $< h$ together with some condition in the list (4). Hence, if we first determine the right-hand sides of all equations of weight 1 (those whose sentences are $\mathbf{t}$, $\mathbf{f}$, $(\vee)$, $(\wedge)$ are dependent, and are determined by $|\mathbf{t} \, \mathbf{f}|$;

all other equations of weight 1 are independent) we thereby determine those of weight 2; hence those of weight 3; and so on, for all finite weights h.

When $\mathscr{S}$ is a finite set of closed sentences, there can only be finitely many (say, n) distinct, independent Boolean constituents of sentences in $\mathscr{S}$. There are 2^n different ways to write a set of n equations $v(X_1) = w_1, \ldots, v(X_n) = w_n$, corresponding to the distinct ways of choosing the truthvalues $w_1, \ldots, w_n$. Each of these ways of writing the independent equations in a Boolean valuation of $\mathscr{S}$ completely determines what the remaining, dependent equations in that Boolean valuation must be; hence we conclude that

> if there are n distinct independent Boolean constituents of
> the sentences in a set $\mathscr{S}$ of closed sentences, then there are
> 2^n different Boolean valuations of $\mathscr{S}$

It is a purely mechanical task, given a sentence X, to construct and display all of the Boolean valuations of $\{X\}$. There are many ways to organise the work and set up the display. One such way, traditionally called the *truth-table method*, calls for the drawing up of a rectangular table of rows and columns, with the columns headed by the various distinct Boolean constituents of X in a left-to-right arrangement that places sentences with smaller β values earlier than sentences with larger ones, hence putting all those with $\beta = 1$ at the beginning. Among the Boolean constituents with $\beta = 1$, the independent ones precede the dependent ones, if any. Thus if X has n independent Boolean constituents, the leftmost n columns are headed by them, in some arbitrary order. If X has m distinct Boolean constituents in all, the truth table for X will have m columns, one for each; and the rightmost column will be headed by X itself. There will be 2^n rows in the table, one for each distinct Boolean valuation of X.

The entries w_{ij} in row i and column j are either **t** or **f**, representing the fact that each row is a display of the equations $v(X_1) = w_{i1}, \ldots, v(X_j) = w_{ij}, \ldots v(X_m) = w_{im}$ in the ith Boolean valuation of X. The sentence X_j is that displayed at the head of column j.

The order in which the rows are displayed is immaterial, but traditionally a systematic ordering is used, which is illustrated by the pattern below, in which $n = 3$; we show the $2^3 = 8$ rows with the pattern embodied in the first 3 columns of each row, which readers familiar with the binary number notation will recognise as counting from 0 to 7, if **t** is identified with 0 and **f** as 1, in a three-digit counter:

t t t		0 0 0
t t f		0 0 1
t f t	which may be	0 1 0
t f f	thought of as:	0 1 1
f t t		1 0 0
f t f		1 0 1
f f t		1 1 0
f f f		1 1 1

The remaining columns in each row of the table, headed by the dependent Boolean constituents, can then be filled out, the sentence at the head of each column receiving, in that row, the truthvalue not forbidden by the appropriate condition in the definition of Boolean valuations, given the truthvalues already assigned in that row to its immediate Boolean constituents. To illustrate the truth-table method, let us apply it to the sentence $(A \to (\neg B \to (C \vee A)))$. Its seven Boolean constituents are, in an ordering appropriate for heading the columns of a truth table:

$$A, B, C, \neg B, (C \vee A), (\neg B \to (C \vee A)), (A \to (\neg B \to (C \vee A)))$$

The first three Boolean constituents are 0-ary predications and are the independent Boolean constituents. The required table thus has $2^3 = 8$ rows and 7 columns, and is as shown below after the first 3 columns have been filled:

A	B	C	$\neg B$	$(C \vee A)$	$(\neg B \to (C \vee A))$	$(A \to (\neg B \to (C \vee A)))$
t	t	t				
t	t	f				
t	f	t				
t	f	f				
f	t	t				
f	t	f				
f	f	t				
f	f	f				

The remaining values in each row can now be filled in, working from left to right. This mode of working keeps invariant, throughout the computation, the fact that the earliest (leftmost) column not yet filled in each row is headed by a sentence all of whose immediate constituents are already evaluated in that row (since they head columns to the left of that column, and therefore have their columns filled). The result of completing each row in the present case is the table:

A	B	C	¬B	(C ∨ A)	(¬B →(C ∨ A))	(A →(¬B →(C ∨ A)))
t	t	t	f	t	t	t
t	t	f	f	t	t	t
t	f	t	t	t	t	t
t	f	f	t	t	t	t
f	t	t	f	t	t	t
f	t	f	f	f	t	t
f	f	t	t	t	t	t
f	f	f	t	f	f	t

The column headed by ¬B clearly must be filled, in each row, with a truthvalue distinct from that in the same row in the column headed by B.

The column headed by (C ∨ A) must be filled, in each row, with an f, unless one or other of the columns headed by C and by A contains, in that row, a t; in which case the (C ∨ A) column gets a t.

The column headed by (¬B →(C ∨ A)) can now be filled, in each row, with reference to the entries, in that row, in the columns headed by ¬B and by (C ∨ A). The new entry will be a t unless there is a t under ¬B and an f under (C ∨ A), as in the last row; in which case the new entry will be an f.

The column headed by (A →(¬B →(C ∨ A))) can then be filled similarly, by referring to the columns headed by A and by (¬B → (C ∨ A)).

In general each successive column of the dependent section of the table, headed by a sentence X, can be filled by referring to these already-filled columns to its left, which are headed by the immediate Boolean constituents of X. The working is the precise analogue of the numerical evaluation of an algebraic expression such as

$$(x + y) \times (y - z)$$

for various numerical values of its variables. Such work could indeed be arranged in a "number value table", with columns headed by, e.g.

$$x, y, z, (x + y), (y - z), (x + y) \times (y - z)$$

and rows corresponding to the various independent assignments of numbers to x, y, and z. The row whose first three entries are

3, 8, 2

for instance, would be completed to the row

    3, 8, 2, 11, 6, 66.

The analogy breaks down only in that there are infinitely many rows in such a valuation table for number values. The finititude of the set of truthvalues makes the construction of a truth table a finite task.

A Boolean valuation of a closed sentence X is an analysis of one of the two possible denotations (t, or f) of X, together with an "explanation" of how X might well come to denote that value. If the equation $v(X) = t$ is in a Boolean valuation of X, we say that X *denotes* t, or *is true, under that Boolean valuation.* If on the other hand the equation $v(X) = f$ is in a Boolean valuation of X, we say that X *denotes* f, or *is false, under that Boolean valuation.*

Such a table, or its equivalent (the reader will doubtless be able to think of more efficient ways to survey the Boolean valuations of a closed sentence) thus constitutes a complete analysis of the Boolean, or truthvalue, semantics of the given sentence. Sometimes, as in this example, the sentence is true under each of its Boolean valuations. When this is the case, the sentence is said to be a *tautology*. The method of truth tables is a completely general decision procedure for determining whether or not a sentence is a tautology.

In the other extreme case, namely when a sentence is *false* under each of its Boolean valuations, the sentence is said to be a *contradiction*. For example, the sentence $(A \wedge \neg A)$ is a contradiction. The truth-table method is thus also a decision procedure for determining whether or not a sentence is a contradiction.

Tautologies and contradictions naturally occur in pairs: if S is a tautology then $\neg S$ is a contradiction, and conversely. (There is really only one notion: denoting the same fixed truthvalue in all Boolean valuations. We make two cases of it by also stating *which* truthvalue.)

If a conjunction is a tautology, then each of its conjuncts is, and conversely.

If a disjunction is a contradiction, then each of its disjuncts is, and conversely.

In particular, the empty conjunction $(\wedge)$ is a tautology, as, of course, is the truthvalue t.

Similarly, the empty disjunction $(\vee)$ is a contradiction, as is the truthvalue f.

Suppose that the sentences $A_1, ..., A_n$ and B are such that the sentence $(\wedge A_1 ... A_n) \rightarrow B$ is a tautology. Then we say that $A_1, ..., A_n$ *tautologically imply* B. The relationship is thought of as holding between the set of sentences $\{A_1, ..., A_n\}$ and the sentence B. We can extend this idea to the case when infinitely many sentences together tautologically imply a given sentence. The idea is as follows.

If $\mathscr{S}$ is a (finite or infinite) set of closed sentences, and K is a Boolean valuation of $\mathscr{S}$, we say that K *satisfies* $\mathscr{S}$ if each sentence in $\mathscr{S}$ is true under K. When $\mathscr{S}$ is satisfied by at least one of its Boolean valuations, we say that $\mathscr{S}$ is *Boolean satisfiable*; but if $\mathscr{S}$ is satisfied by none of its Boolean valuations, we say that $\mathscr{S}$ is *Boolean unsatisfiable*.

When $\mathscr{S}$ is finite, we can obviously adapt the idea of the truth-table method to obtain a complete survey of all the (finitely many) Boolean valuations of $\mathscr{S}$; we simply take the Boolean constituents of all the sentences in $\mathscr{S}$ and arrange them in order of non-decreasing β value across the top of the table. Thus when $\mathscr{S}$ is finite we can decide mechanically whether $\mathscr{S}$ is Boolean satisfiable or Boolean unsatisfiable. We use the truth-table method.

When $\mathscr{S}$ is infinite, this method obviously will not work. The concepts of Boolean satisfiability and Boolean unsatisfiability are the same for finite as for infinite sets $\mathscr{S}$, but *deciding whether they apply* to a given set $\mathscr{S}$ is a quite different problem as we go from finite to infinite $\mathscr{S}$.

We can now return to the notion of tautological implication of a sentence by a set of sentences. Let B be a sentence, as before, but now let $\mathscr{A}$ be any set (possibly infinite) of sentences. The required definition of the relationship $\mathscr{A}$ *tautologically implies B* is that *the set*

$$\mathscr{A} \cup \{\neg B\}$$

is Boolean unsatisfiable.

This definition subsumes the earlier one, which covered only the case when $\mathscr{A}$ is a finite set of sentences. For when $\mathscr{A}$ is finite, say, the set $\{A_1, ..., A_n\}$, then

$$\{A_1, ..., A_n\} \cup \{\neg B\}$$

is Boolean unsatisfiable if, and only if, the sentence

$$(\wedge A_1 ... A_n) \to B$$

is a tautology.

Whereas, however, the truth-table method affords a mechanical procedure for deciding whether $\mathscr{A}$ tautologically implies B *when $\mathscr{A}$ is finite*, it no longer suffices for this purpose when $\mathscr{A}$ is an *infinite* set of sentences.

The definition of tautological implication given above is intended to capture, within the semantics of the Boolean part of the predicate calculus, the essential, intuitive idea behind the usual notion of *implication*. In that intuitive idea, to say that $\mathscr{A}$ "logically implies" B is to say that there is no way (i.e. it is impossible) that all the sentences in $\mathscr{A}$ can "come out true" and yet "at the same time" B can still "come out false". Our definition virtually transcribes this intuitive conception: we are saying exactly that "$\mathscr{A}$ tautologically implies B" means that there is no Boolean valuation (of the set $\mathscr{A} \cup \{\neg B\}$) under which all the sentences in $\mathscr{A}$ are true and yet the sentence B is false.

For example, the set of sentences

$$\{(A \to B), (B \to (C \vee D)), \neg C, A\} \tag{6}$$

tautologically implies the sentence D. This fact can be checked by carrying out a process that closely corresponds to the intuitive idea mentioned above, as reflected in the formal definition that embodies it. We have to show the non-existence, or "impossibility", of a Boolean valuation under which D is false but which satisfies the given set (6).

Of course, one way to do this is the already-discussed truth-table method. One might characterize that method as the "bottom-up" method: it starts by laying out all the different possibilities for the "bottom" Boolean constituents, and then proceeds, upwards, to *deduce* the truthvalues for the remaining "higher" constituents.

The following method works in the other direction – "top-down". We start by saying: suppose K were such a Boolean valuation of the set

$$\{(A \to B), (B \to (C \vee D)), \neg C, A, D\}$$

The equations in K that we "know" must be there can then be listed:

1 $v(A \to B) = \mathbf{t}$
2 $v(B \to (C \vee D)) = \mathbf{t}$
3 $v(\neg C) = \mathbf{t}$
4 $v(A) = \mathbf{t}$
5 $v(D) = \mathbf{f}$

and contemplated. If they are not already "obviously" impossible, we can reason about them, in an attempt to make the impossibility of such a K obvious. For example, equation 3 requires that the equation $v(C) = \mathbf{f}$ (by $[\neg \mathbf{t}]$) should also be in K. Hence we expand the list of equations we know must be in K by adding this on:

6 $v(C) = \mathbf{f}$

Equation 1 requires (with $[\to \mathbf{t}]$) only that it should *not* be the case that K contains both $v(A) = \mathbf{t}$ and $v(B) = \mathbf{f}$. We can express this by saying: equation 1 requires that K contain *either* $v(A) = \mathbf{f}$ *or* $v(B) = \mathbf{t}$, *or both*. This means that there are two equations:

7.1 $v(A) = \mathbf{f}$
7.2 $v(B) = \mathbf{t}$

at least one of which must be added to the first 6 already adduced. There are now, then, two sets of 7 equations: they are

    $\{1, 2, 3, 4, 5, 6, 7.1\}$
and
    $\{1, 2, 3, 4, 5, 6, 7.2\}$

We have found that K must include at least one of these two sets.

But consider the first of these sets: it contains equations 4 and 7.1, namely

    $v(A) = \mathbf{t}$
    $v(A) = \mathbf{f}$

and so it is *obviously* impossible because of [*cons*]. This leaves only the second set of equations as a set which K *must* include. Let us continue to contemplate it.

Equation 2 requires, for similar reasons to those adduced for equation 1, that at least one of the further equations

8.1 $v(B) = \mathbf{f}$
8.2 $v(C \vee D) = \mathbf{t}$

be in K. We thus have two sets of equations:

    $\{1, 2, 3, 4, 5, 6, 7.2, 8.1\}$
    $\{1, 2, 3, 4, 5, 6, 7.2, 8.2\}$

at least one of which must be included in K. The first of these contains 7.2 and 8.1, namely

    $v(B) = \mathbf{t}$
    $v(B) = \mathbf{f}$

and so it is *obviously* impossible that a Boolean valuation K should include it. We are thus left with only the one possibility: K *must* include the second set.

Well: the second set contains equation 8.2. This means that K must, by [$\vee$ t], also contain at least one of the equations

9.1 $v(C) = \mathbf{t}$
9.2 $v(D) = \mathbf{t}$

We therefore again split our reasoning into two cases: we now know that K must include at least one of the two sets of equations:

$$\{1, 2, 3, 4, 5, 6, 7.2, 8.2, 9.1\}$$
$$\{1, 2, 3, 4, 5, 6, 7.2, 8.2, 9.2\}$$

However: it is *obviously* impossible that K should include the first set by virtue of

6     $v(C) = \mathbf{f}$
9.1 $v(C) = \mathbf{t}$

while it is also *obviously* impossible that K should include the second set, by virtue of

5     $v(D) = \mathbf{f}$
9.2 $v(D) = \mathbf{t}$

We must conclude, therefore, that it is impossible that the original set of equations:

$$\{1, 2, 3, 4, 5\}$$

be included in a Boolean valuation K. We cannot say this set is *obviously* impossible: one cannot, so to speak, see its impossibility at a glance. So: we conclude that D is tautologically implied by the set $\{(A \rightarrow B), (B \rightarrow (C \vee D)), \neg C, A\}$.

Now the reasoning process illustrated above can be laid out systematically and economically in the form of a *tree* figure. The original equations form its "trunk":

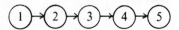

The step corresponding to pursuing the requirement imposed by equation 3 produces the figure

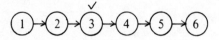

in which we have added the new equation 6 and checked off the equation 3 as "duly noted".

The next step involved pursuing the requirement imposed by equation 1, and produces the tree figure:

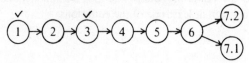

in which equation 1 is checked off as "duly noted", and the new equations 7.1 and 7.2 now are the "tips" of two distinct "branches" of the tree. The branches correspond to the *two* sets of equations that we arrived at, at this stage. However, we then found the first set to be inconsistent because of its containing 7.1 and 4. So the figure becomes:

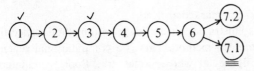

with the impossible branch marked as "dead".

We next duly noted equation 2. This produced the result represented in the figure:

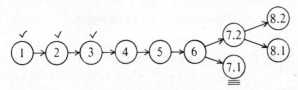

namely: equation 2 is now checked off as duly noted, and the branch with tip 7.2 is now sprouted into two branches with tips 8.1 and 8.2.

We then observed the obvious inconsistency of the branch with tip 8.1; this produces the figure in which *that* branch is marked as dead:

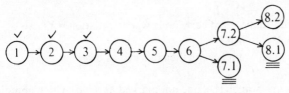

We then duly noted equation 8.2, producing the figure:

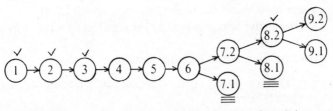

But then in contemplating both "live" branches we found them to be obviously inconsistent. The 9.1 branch by virtue of 9.1 and 6; the 9.2 branch by virtue of 9.2 and 5. This yields the final figure:

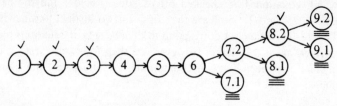

in which all branches are marked as dead.

This example has illustrated a beautiful general method, called the Boolean *semantic tableau* method. This is a computational scheme that produces tree figures at whose nodes are "Boolean valuation equations", i.e. equations of the form

$$v(X) = w$$

in which X is a closed sentence and w is a truthvalue.

The steps of the computation each have two stages:

A

(a) *Mark* as *dead* any "obviously inconsistent" branch of the tree, i.e., any branch containing a node whose equation has one of the forms
$$v(\mathbf{t}) = \mathbf{f}, v(\mathbf{f}) = \mathbf{t}$$
or one of the forms:
$$v(\vee) = \mathbf{t}, v(\wedge) = \mathbf{f}$$
or two nodes whose respective equations are of the form:
$$v(X) = \mathbf{t}, v(X) = \mathbf{f}.$$

(b) *Mark* as "duly noted" any node whose equation $v(X) = w$ has an X with $\beta(X) = 1$.

(c) H A L T if all branches are then marked as dead.

B

(a) *Find* a *live* branch (i.e. one not marked as *dead*) which contains a node whose equation is not marked as "duly noted".

(b) *Select* some such node N on some such branch L.

(c) *Extend* all live branches passing through N, and mark N as "duly noted".

(d) H A L T if there are no such live branches.

We must explain precisely what "*extending* all live branches passing through node N" means.

A branch is a sequence of nodes starting at the *origin*, or *root* node (e.g. the node ① in our example) and continuing with all the nodes encountered, in the order of their being encountered, en route to some *tip* node. Such a branch is uniquely determined by its tip: indeed we can traverse the branch backwards by starting at the tip and travelling "down" the tree in the direction opposite to that in which the arrows point.

Thus if a node is not a tip, there may be more than one branch of the tree that passes through it, i.e., on which that node occurs. In stage B, then, having selected node N to be duly noted, we must identify all the branches that pass through N and that are not marked *dead*. (There will be at least one such branch in view of the fact that this was how the node N got selected!) Each such branch is then to be extended by the appropriate operation described below, which will depend on the form of the equation $v(X) = w$.at N. These operations fall into two kinds: *stretching* and *splitting*.

A stretching operation appends a sequence of one or more new nodes $t_1, \ldots t_n$ to the tip t of the branch, creating a *single* new branch, i.e., from the branch:

$$\boxed{1} \rightarrow \boxed{2} \rightarrow \ldots \rightarrow \boxed{t}$$

creating the branch:

$$\boxed{1} \rightarrow \boxed{2} \rightarrow \ldots \rightarrow \boxed{t} \rightarrow \boxed{t_1} \rightarrow \ldots \rightarrow \boxed{t_n}$$

We denote this stretching operation by: $|t_1 \ldots t_n|$.

A splitting operation creates *two or more* new branches by appending, to the tip t, $k \geqslant 2$ sequences of new nodes $t_{11}, \ldots, t_{1n_1}; \ldots t_{k1}, \ldots t_{kn_k}$ in k different continuations, i.e. from the branch

$$\boxed{1} \rightarrow \boxed{2} \rightarrow \ldots \rightarrow \boxed{t}$$

creating the k new branches:

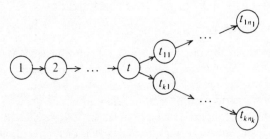

We denote this splitting operation by: $|t_{11} \ldots t_{1n_1}| \ldots | t_{k1} \ldots t_{kn_k}|$

Thus in our earlier example, when we selected the node whose equation was

$$v(\neg C) = t$$

we performed the stretching operation: $[v(C) = f]$, and when we selected the node whose equation was $v(C \vee D) = t$ we performed the splitting operation: $[v(C) = t \mid v(D) = t]$. A complete list of the operations is shown in table 3.2, keyed to the two "parameters" X and w in the equation at the selected node, $v(X) = w$.

Table 3.2

Case	X	w	operation
$[\neg t]$	$\neg Y$	t	$[v(Y) = f]$ (stretch)
$[\neg f]$	$\neg Y$	f	$[v(Y) = t]$ (stretch)
$[\rightarrow t]$	$Y \rightarrow Z$	t	$[v(Y) = f \mid v(Z) = t]$ (split)
$[\rightarrow f]$	$Y \rightarrow Z$	f	$[v(Y) = t, v(Z) = f]$ (stretch)
$[\leftrightarrow t]$	$Y \leftrightarrow Z$	t	$\begin{bmatrix} v(Y) = t & v(Y) = f \\ v(Z) = t & v(Z) = f \end{bmatrix}$(split)
$[\leftrightarrow f]$	$Y \leftrightarrow Z$	f	$\begin{bmatrix} v(Y) = t & v(Y) = f \\ v(Z) = f & v(Z) = t \end{bmatrix}$(split)
$[\wedge t]$	$(\wedge\, Y_1 \ldots Y_n)$	t	$[v(Y_1) = t, \ldots, v(Y_n) = t]$ (stretch)
$[\wedge f]$	$(\wedge\, Y_1 \ldots Y_n)$	f	$[v(Y_1) = f \mid \ldots \mid v(Y_n) = f]$ (split)
$[\vee t]$	$(\vee\, Y_1 \ldots Y_n)$	t	$[v(Y_1) = t \mid \ldots \mid v(Y_n) = t]$ (split)
$[\vee f]$	$(\vee\, Y_1 \ldots Y_n)$	f	$[v(Y_1) = f, \ldots, v(Y_n) = f]$ (stretch)

This semantic tableau method accepts as input a finite collection of valuation equations

$$v(X_1) = w_1, \ldots, v(X_n) = w_n$$

where $X_1, \ldots, X_n$ are sentences and $w_1, \ldots, w_n$ are truthvalues. We *initialize the tableau* by applying the stretch operation:

$$[v(X_1) = w_1 \ldots v(X_n) = w_n]$$

to the "empty tree", i.e. by creating a single branch whose equations are the given ones. We then *develop the tableau* by repeatedly performing steps, as explained, as long as they can be performed.

The following properties of this method will now be shown:

(a)   if the set of input equations is impossible, i.e., if it is included in no Boolean valuation, the method will HALT after finitely many steps, in stage A, i.e., with a *dead* tree figure

(b)   if the input conditions are not impossible, the method will HALT after finitely many steps, in stage B, i.e., with one or

more *live* branches that are *fully developed*, i.e., whose nodes
are all checked off as "duly noted".

First let us show that the method will indeed eventually halt after
finitely many steps.

To do this, we will identify a quantity that *strictly decreases* at
each step of the computation, and which cannot continue to decrease
indefinitely. This quantity is called the "remaining work index" of a
semantic tableau. The remaining work index (RWI) of a semantic
tableau is a finite sequence of integers defined in the following
way.

Consider all nodes $v(X) = w$ in the tableau, which

are not checked off as duly noted;

are on a live branch;

satisfy the condition $\beta(X) = j$.

Let the number of all such nodes in the tableau be n_j. Let d be the
largest number such that $n_d > 0$, or if $n_j = 0$ for all j, let $d = 0$. Then
the sequence $(n_d, ..., n_1)$ of length d (if $d > 0$) or the sequence ( ),
(if $d = 0$) is defined to be the RWI of the tableau.

We will consider the set of all finite sequences of non-negative
integers that are either empty or whose first component is not 0. For
example, ( ) is in the set. (3, 0, 2) is in the set, as is (3, 4, 0, 0). But
(0, 2, 0, 3) is not. RWI's are such sequences. Let us call them *indices*.
The *length* of such an index is the number of components it has. So
the length of ( ) is 0, that of (3, 0, 2, 8) is 4 and so on.

Now there is an ordering $\prec$ of these indices which is defined, for
any two distinct indices α and β, as follows:

(a)   if the length of α is less than that of β, then $\alpha \prec \beta$

(b)   if the length of α is the *same* as that of β, then: if α and β agree
     in their leftmost $j - 1$ components, and if the jth component
     of α is less than the jth component of β, then $\alpha \prec \beta$.

Thus $(2, 0) \prec (1, 1, 8)$; but $(7, 1, 89) \prec (7, 2, 0)$ since the second component of $(7, 1, 89)$ is less than that of $(7, 2, 0)$, and they do not differ
in earlier components.

In this ordering of the indices, the "empty index" ( ) precedes all
the others. The crucial property of indices is that, with respect to this
ordering,

every descending sequence of indices is finite.

That is to say, if $\alpha_1, \alpha_2, ...,$ is a sequence of indices such that $\alpha_{j+1} \prec$
α_j, for $j \geqslant 1$, then there is a *last* member α_n, for some integer $n \geqslant 1$.

This is not self-evident. The ideas involved here – Cantor's system
of ordinal numbers and its applications – deserve their own expo-

sition, and we shall give a brief one in the appendix. It meanwhile suffices to note that indices generalize the usual notation for natural numbers, yielding "numerals" for the ordinal numbers far beyond the natural numbers. The property of the natural numbers that every descending sequence of them is finite also holds for the ordinal numbers in general. The appendix need not be read now in order to follow the rest of the reasoning.

Returning, then, to the process of developing the semantic tableau. We need only notice that each step of the procedure changes the tableau in such a way that the R W I of the tableau *after* the step *strictly precedes* the R W I of the tableau *before* the step.

For, consider the node N with equation $v(X) = w$, selected for the step. Suppose that $\beta(X) = j$. Then for every immediate Boolean constituent Y of X, we shall obviously have $\beta(Y) < \beta(X)$. Consider the R W I of the new tableau in relation to that of the old tableau. In the new tableau, the node $v(X) = w$ will be checked off, so that the component n_j of the R W I will have been decreased; but the only components of the R W I that can have *increased* will be those *to the right of* n_j – those corresponding to the new nodes added to the tableau by stretching or splitting. The new R W I will thus be strictly earlier in the $\prec$ ordering than the old R W I.

The conclusion is that there can be only finitely many steps taken in developing the tableau. The process must eventually halt.

What will be shown next is that, if the tableau upon termination has any live branches in it, we can take any one of them as the basis for constructing a Boolean valuation that includes the set of input equations that initiated the process in the first place.

Consider any such live branch. Since the process terminated, we know that all nodes on the branch must have been marked as duly noted (for otherwise at least one more step of the procedure would have been possible). If we let K be the set of equations occurring on the branch, this means that:

> K satisfies all of the conditions
> ⌊t, f⌋, ⌊¬ t⌋, ⌊¬ f⌋, ⌊→ t⌋, ⌊→ f⌋, ⌊↔ t⌋, ⌊↔ f⌋, ⌊∧ t⌋, ⌊∧ f⌋, ⌊∨ t⌋,
> ⌊∨ f⌋ ⌊*cons*⌋

What we do *not* know, and indeed it need not in general be the case, is that K *also* satisfies the condition ⌊*comp* $\mathscr{S}$⌋, when $\mathscr{S}$ is the set:

$$\mathscr{S} = \{X_1, ..., X_n\}$$

of closed sentences involved in the set

$$E = \{v(X_1) = w_1, ..., v(X_n) = w_n\}$$

of equations that were the input to the procedure. However, we can always *extend K*, by adding further equations, in such a way that the condition $|comp \, \mathscr{S}|$ is satisfied, without disturbing the fact that all of the other conditions $|t, f|, \ldots, |cons|$ are satisfied. The resulting, extended, K is a *Boolean valuation* that includes E. This is an important result; the Boolean semantic tableau procedure would not work without it.

We form a set J of equations $v(X) = w$, containing one equation for each independent constituent X of $\mathscr{S}$, as follows:

> if K contains an equation $v(X) = w$ for X, let J contain that equation for X also;
> if K contains no equation $v(X) = w$ for X, let J contain the equation $v(X) = t$.

Now let M be the Boolean valuation of $\mathscr{S}$ that is completely determined by J. We claim that $K \subseteq M$, (and hence $E \subseteq M$, since $E \subseteq K$). For − suppose it were not so. That would mean that K contained equations *not* contained in M.

Let $v(X) = w$ be such an equation: and let us choose it so that the quantity $\beta(X)$ is a minimum when taken over all such equations. We must have $\beta(X) > 1$, since $J \subseteq M$.

The fact that $\beta(X)$ is a minimum means that all the equations

$$v(Y_1) = u_1, \ldots, v(Y_r) = u_r$$

in K that involve immediate Boolean constituents $Y_1, \ldots, Y_r$ of X, are also in M. (We are not saying here that $Y_1, \ldots, Y_r$ are *all* the immediate Boolean constituents of X.)

But inspection of the process by which the set K was created shows that the equation $v(X) = w$ is completely determined by the equations $v(Y_1) = u_1, \ldots, v(Y_r) = u_r$ − indeed, by those of them that were added to the tableau at the step when the node bearing the equation $v(X) = w$ was duly noted. This means, however, that M, too, must contain $v(X) = w$, since M contains all of $v(Y_1) = u_1, \ldots, v(Y_r) = u_r$. Our conclusion is that K *cannot* contain equations that are not contained in M. So: $K \subseteq M$, as claimed.

We have so far shown that, given the finite set E of input equations

> the procedure halts;
> if the procedure halts with a live tableau, then $E \subseteq M$ for some Boolean valuation M of $\mathscr{S}$.

We shall show next that

if $E \subseteq M$ for some Boolean valuation M of $\mathscr{S}$, then the
procedure halts with a live tableau

Consider the procedure after initialization. The equations in E have
been installed and are the sole occupants of the sole branch in the
tableau. This *initial* tableau cannot be dead: for otherwise we could
not have $E \subseteq M$. Thus we have that, before executing the first step
of the cycle,

there is at least one branch in the tableau, all of whose
equations are contained in M (7)

We claim that, if (7) is true before stage A of a given step, it will
remain true *after* the step is completed.

Suppose L is such a branch. Then L may be extended, or not, in
stage B. If not, (7) will still hold as required; if so, there will in the
new tableau be one or more branches $L_1, ..., L_p$ that are extensions
of L. Inspection of the various stretching and splitting steps with
which L might be extended shows that *at least one* of the new
branches $L_1, ..., L_p$ will have all its equations in M. If $p = 1$ (i.e.
the operation is a stretch) this is immediately obvious; if $p > 1$ (i.e.
the operation is a split), M's being a Boolean valuation requires that
the equations in at least one of the arms of the split should also be
in M.

Thus the procedure cannot halt with a dead tableau; and since it
does halt, it must do so with a live one.

So we have shown that

the procedure halts; and moreover
the procedure halts with a *live* tableau if, and only if,
$E \subseteq M$ for some Boolean valuation M of $\mathscr{S}$

which latter proposition is therefore equivalent to this one:

the procedure halts with a *dead* tableau if, and only if,
the input set E of equations is impossible

By E *is impossible* we mean: there is *no* Boolean valuation M of $\mathscr{S}$
such that $E \subseteq M$.

We conclude therefore that the semantic tableau procedure is a
complete, mechanical procedure for testing whether a finite subset of
the equations of an alleged Boolean valuation really is so, or is an
impossibility. It can be used to test whether a finite set $\mathscr{A}$ of sentences
is Boolean unsatisfiable by running it with the set of input equations
$v(X) = \mathbf{t}$, for all X in $\mathscr{A}$. It can be used to test whether $\mathscr{A}$ tautologically

implies a sentence B by running it with the previous set of equations together with the extra equation $v(B) = \mathbf{f}$.

Of course, the truth-table procedure is already an instrument with equivalent capability! To test whether $\{A_1, ..., A_n\}$ is a Boolean unsatisfiable set of sentences one need only draw up a truth table for the sentence $(\wedge A_1 ... A_n)$, and observe whether its rightmost column contains only $\mathbf{f}$'s or has at least one $\mathbf{t}$. And to test whether $\{A_1, ..., A_n\}$ tautologically implies the sentence B, we need only draw up a truth table for the sentence $(\wedge A_1 ... A_n) \rightarrow B$, and observe whether its rightmost column contains only $\mathbf{t}$'s, or has at least one $\mathbf{f}$.

There are two reasons why the semantic tableau method is of independent interest, one psychological, and the other technical. The psychological interest of semantic tableaux lies in the way that consulting them serves to *organize the mind's ability to discern the obvious*. If a set $\{A_1, ..., A_n\}$ of sentences is at all large, or complicated, or both, it will in general not be evident "in one glance" whether the set is Boolean satisfiable or not. The property is a "global" one, involving a complex network of inter-relationships between the Boolean constituents of $A_1, ..., A_n$ that in general is too intricate to observe all at once. The method of semantic tableaux is a technique for *managing* and *taming* this complexity. The steps of development, by which a tableau is extended, are each designed to dissolve an equation $v(X) = w$ into a set of one or more *simpler* equations or into several, alternative, sets of simpler equations. The psychology of the transformation is that it requires only a *surface* perception of the syntactic structure of X as a Boolean composition: only its "outermost" structure

$$X = (\kappa\, X_1 ... X_n)$$

is at issue, and not any structural detail that is "inside" the immediate parts $X_1, ..., X_n$ of X. We need to see X as having the operator κ, and we need to see $X_1, ..., X_n$ only as wholes – the analysis of *their* internal structure, if any, being relegated to future steps of development of the tableau.

The relationship between the equation

$$v(\kappa\, X_1 ... X_n) = w$$

and the simpler equations

$$v(X_i) = w_i$$

into which it is dissolved by a development step is likewise a matter of *surface structure*, in which the X_i are throughout regarded as indivisible wholes whose internal structure is irrelevant to the transaction. Ideally, the internal structure of the X_i would actually be *hidden* from the agent developing the tableau, so as not to confuse his perceptions with structural detail which plays no part in the step.

Each development step must be accompanied, psychologically speaking, by the *conviction* that the new tableau "obviously" represents the same problem as the old. Specifically, the conviction must be that a Boolean valuation of the set $\{A_1, ..., A_n\}$ of sentences will include the equations on some branch of the *new* tableau if, but only if, it will include the equations on some branch of the *old* tableau.

The "local" character of the transformation is designed to make possible this conviction; indeed, the conviction is rooted in the essence of what it means to understand the meaning of the connective κ.

The observation, on a branch, of any of the "lethal" constraints $v(t) = f$, $v(f) = t$, $v(\wedge) = f$, $v(\vee) = t$ is a matter of direct perception that (after the first step of development) can always be confined to the *newly added* node or nodes. The observation of the "lethal" pairs $v(X) = t$, $v(X) = f$ on a branch is, again a *surface* matter in which X is regarded as an indivisible whole, however complex its structure might in fact be.

The psychological complexity of the process of comparing two constraint equations to see if they have the form $v(X) = t$, $v(X) = f$ depends very much on whether the inner structure (if any) of X is hidden or not. It is possible (and for example in computer realizations of logical algorithms it is most natural) to represent formulas in such a way that one can compare the representations of two sentences to test whether they are the *same* or *distinct* sentences, without having to probe *any* of their syntactic structure. For instance one might represent each formula by a unique non-negative integer, corresponding to some enumeration

$$\varphi_1, \varphi_2, ...,$$

of all formulas without repetition. Then a "lethal" pair of equations, such as $v(382146) = t$, $v(382146) = f$, could be recognized as such without any knowledge of the syntactic structure of the formula φ_{382146}. Of course, one still would have to be prepared to test pairs of *numerals* for being the same or distinct, and since in many respects a formula is just a string of symbols, it may be thought that comparing two numerals digit by digit is no different from comparing two formulas, symbol by symbol.

The acts of recognition that a tableau is fully developed, or that it is dead, are psychologically simple and direct. One need only be able to perceive the presence or absence of a checking-off mark against an equation $v(X) = w$ and to maintain some indication of the status of each node as to whether it has, or has not, at least one live branch passing through it. One interesting way to do this is to introduce a special mark to attach to a node, having the intuitive meaning "no live branches pass through this node". Let us call a node, through which no live branches pass, a *dead node*. Thus a dead node is one through which only dead branches pass.

Clearly, the tip of a dead branch is a dead node, and can be so marked at the same time that it is marked as the tip of a dead branch.

But, in general, if all the immediate successor nodes of a given node are dead, then that node too is dead, and so we should mark as dead any node all of whose immediate successors are already marked as dead. This can be done, recursively, in stage A, propagating the marks up the tree as far as they must go. Note that, if the tree as a whole is dead, then a mark will be propagated all the way up the tree to its root.

Such a system of marking dead nodes obviates the need to *search*, in stage B, for live branches. The live branches are immediately discernible by the fact that they consist entirely of nodes not marked as dead. It aids the imagination to picture the process of tableau development as taking place on a large display screen, with different light intensities, colours, and on-and-off blinkings, etc., for drawing attention to features of the tableau. If we picture the live (i.e. not marked as dead) nodes as being brilliantly lit, and the dead nodes as dimly lit, possibly a darker colour such as blue or green as compared with, say, the yellow or orange colour of the live nodes, then the phenomenology of tableau properties becomes more vividly imaginable. The live branches of a tableau can be made brightly and clearly discriminable from the dead branches. Or – perhaps the simplest scheme of all! – one could arrange to have dead nodes just *disappear*.

Those nodes on live branches which are still awaiting selection, and which are therefore eligible in stage B for selection as development node for the step, can be pictured as, say, blinking on and off in the manner of the displays at airports which draw attention to the flights whose departure is imminent.

Finally, the decision as to *which* eligible node has been selected as the development node for the step can be indicated by some suitably prominent feature – say, by its remaining blinking while the non-selected eligible nodes stop blinking.

As a matter of topical interest, displays of this kind, behaving more or less exactly as described, are now quite practical possibilities with modern computer-controlled "graphics display" equipment. If a human being is to be a part of the process of developing a semantic tableau, such "engineering" of his perceptions of, and his intellectual interactions with, the symbolic complexities of the logical analysis, can be of enormous utility. One need only complete the scenario by supposing that (as is entirely feasible) the human selects the development node merely by pointing at it, with a "light pen". Thereupon the computer immediately takes over, extending the live branches passing through the selected node by carrying out the corresponding stretch or split; executing stage A, including the propagation of the dead-node marks, and once again returning the control to the human for selection of another development node.

We have elaborated this phenomenological reflection on the nature of the semantic tableau procedure to bring out its properties as a device for managing the mental states of the human analyst. It is important to see that it is the *active development process of construct-ing the tableau* that has the desired effect on the mind, of producing conviction: it would not be any use merely to present the human with a finished tableau in whose construction he had not participated. A finished tableau can itself be a very large symbolic construction, and its compelling force is not so much *to be what it is*, as *to have come into being as it did*. It is not essential that the human actually *partici-pate* in the process by making the selection in stage B. There is no reason why the computer should not do that too. The human can then be a "mere" spectator – but he *must* be at least that. In order for a "proof" to do its job, one must read it, or "go through" it; not just "take delivery of it" and file it away.

The psychological interest of the semantic tableau method is, then, one of the reasons for its appeal. By comparison, the truth-table method is simply a "brute force" search through the set of all Boolean valuations of $\{A_1, ..., A_n\}$. Its outcome is objectively equivalent to the outcome of the semantic tableau method, yet its impact on the *under-standing* of $\{A_1, ..., A_n\}$ is subjectively different. The difference is something like the difference between being *told* (by a source one knows is infallible) that a proposition is true, and *seeing for oneself* that the same proposition is true.

There is a technical, as well as the preceding psychological, reason for interest in the semantic tableau method. This rests in the fact that it can be very easily adapted to accept *infinite* sets of equations $v(A) = w$ as input. Specifically, if we are given an enumeration

$$v(A_1) = w_1, v(A_2) = w_2, \ldots$$

of a countably *infinite* set of such equations, we can develop a semantic tableau for them just as if we were handling a *finite* set of equations, and indeed the modified semantic tableau procedure can be run on *either* a finite, *or* an infinite, enumeration of equations as input.

In either case, the basic property remains: the tableau development will eventually halt in stage A after finitely many steps with a dead tableau if, but only if, there is no Boolean valuation of the set $\{A_1, A_2, \ldots, \}$ that includes all of the input equations.

The main difference, in running an *infinite* set of input equations through the procedure, is that the development of the tableau will *not* halt if there *is* a Boolean valuation of the set of sentences $\{A_1, A_2, \ldots, \}$ that includes the input equations. The criterion for halting in stage B – that there are no more live nodes eligible for selection as development nodes – becomes, in the revised semantic tableau procedure, a criterion for *extending the tableau in a new way*.

The revised semantic tableau procedure accepts as input an enumeration of a (possibly infinite) set of equations of the form

$$v(A_1) = w_1, v(A_2) = w_2, \ldots$$

in which the A_i are sentences and the w_i are truthvalues. The *initialization* of the tableau consists of creating the single node consisting of the first input equation

$$v(A_1) = w_1$$

and *marking* this equation as "entered in the tableau". The tableau is then *developed*, exactly as before. However, the instruction in stage B that said

HALT if there are no such live branches

is now deleted, and is replaced by the following instruction:

If no such live branch exists, *stretch* each live branch by performing the operation $[v(A_i) = w_i]$, where $v(A_i) = w_i$ is the first *unmarked* input equation; and *mark* that equation, in the input list, as "entered in the tableau".

Thus the revised procedure can still halt in stage A. However, instead of *halting* in stage B when the tableau (as it eventually must, by the RWI argument, if it does not halt in stage A) becomes fully developed, the revised procedure uses this circumstance as a signal to reach for the next input equation and tack it onto the end of each of its live branches. Since a *finite* input list will eventually be exhausted by this repeated entering of input equations into the tableau, we add to the above instruction the extra sentence:

If there are no input equations left unmarked, HALT.

Considered, therefore, as a procedure for working on *finite* sets of input equations, the revised semantic tableau procedure is in all essential respects the same; the only difference being that the input equations are introduced into the tableau one at a time instead of all at once. It is as a procedure for working on *infinite* sets of input equations that the revised semantic tableau procedure (henceforth we shall drop the word "revised" and still *mean* the revised procedure) takes on a new and, as we shall see, rather startling significance.

The key to the significance of semantic tableaux for infinite inputs is this: that if the input equations are impossible, the development of the tableau will halt in stage A after finitely many steps. The tableau will, of course, be dead.

Think what this means. After only *finitely* many steps of development, the procedure will have entered into the tableau only finitely many of the input equations! It is as though the procedure can forego all need to examine the infinitely many remaining input equations, and pronounce their collective impossibility on the strength of only a *finite* subset of them. How can this be?

The answer is straightforward: the finitely many equations taken into the tableau must already constitute a *finite* impossible set of equations: for had we run the procedure with just *those* equations as input set, the result would of course have been the same.

What this really shows is not some miraculous property of the semantic tableau procedure itself, but a fact about countably infinite sets of equations $v(X) = w$. This fact is: if such a set is impossible, then some *finite* subset of it is impossible.

The name given to this phenomenon is *compactness*. It is one of the cornerstones of modern logical theory. In the next chapter we shall take a detailed look at compactness and see why the semantic tableau procedure is guaranteed to halt with a dead tableau, as claimed, when applied to even an infinite input set that is impossible.

Exercise. Try to contrive a countably infinite set of conditions $v(X) = w$ that (a) is impossible, and (b) has no finite subset that is impossible. By coming to *see* why you can't succeed, you may well anticipate the explanation given in chapter 4.

4. Infinite Finitary Trees and Boolean Compactness

The semantic tableaux constructed by the procedure described in the previous chapter are examples of what in general are known as *finitary trees*. Finitary trees in turn are a particular kind of *trees*, which are configurations of things called *nodes* and which seem to turn up everywhere in mathematics, especially where *computation* of some sort is involved.

From the abstract viewpoint a tree is a system of nodes, which we can think of simply as elements of some given set N, for which there is defined a notion of *level* and a notion of *successor*. Each node x in N is assigned a positive integer, *the level of x*, and a subset of N, *the successor set of x*, whose members are called *successors of x*. These notions are required to satisfy the following conditions:

(a)   there is exactly one node of level 1, called the *root node* of the tree;

(b)   the level of each successor of x is 1 greater than the level of x, for all nodes x in the tree;

(c)   each node x other than the root node is a successor of exactly one node, called *the predecessor of x*.

Some remarks are in order concerning this definition.

There may be nodes in the tree whose successor set is empty. Such nodes therefore have no successors; they are called *tips* of the tree.

Each node x uniquely determines a sequence of nodes, called *the branch leading to x*, namely, the sequence

$$x_1, \ldots, x_n$$

in which x_1 is the root node, x_n is x, and in which (if $n > 1$) x_j is the predecessor of x_{j+1}, for all j, $1 \leqslant j < n$.

More generally we define the *branches* of a tree to be the sequences of nodes

$$x_1, x_2, \ldots x_j, x_{j+1}, \ldots$$

in which x_1 is the root node and in which, for all $j \geqslant 1$, either x_j is the last node in the sequence (in which case the branch is that leading to x_j) or else is the predecessor of x_{j+1}, This general notion of a branch admits the possibility that a branch may not *have* a last member. Such branches are called *infinite* branches, whereas branches that have a last member are called *finite* branches.

The *length* of a finite branch is the level of its last member, i.e., it is the number of nodes in the sequence. Infinite branches, having no last member, cannot be assigned a length in this sense. We shall simply say that their length is infinite.

For example, consider the tree whose nodes are the various finite strings of characters ("words") taken from the alphabet $\{a, b\}$, which begin with the letter b. Let the *level* of a word be its length, so that b is of level 1, *baa* of level 3, etc. And let the successor set of a word W be the set $\{Wa, Wb\}$; that is, the successors of a word are obtained by adding one more letter to its righthand end. So the successors of b are *ba* and *bb*, and so on. Call this tree the *word-tree*.

In the word-tree, the branch leading to *babaa*, for example, is

   b, ba, bab, $baba$, $babaa$

But there are infinite branches: for example, the branch that starts off

   b, ba, baa, ...

and is continued by tacking on another a to the most recently generated word, forever.

In the word-tree all successor sets are of size 2. So we can say that there is a finite upper bound (namely, 2) on the size of successor sets in this tree. Some trees lack this feature. For example, consider the "wide" tree whose nodes are the positive integers. In this tree, the level of a node is 1 if it is the integer 1, and otherwise the level is 2. The successors of 1 are all the other integers, and no integer except 1 has any successors. This tree then looks like:

In the "wide" tree the size of successor sets has no finite upper bound, for the very good reason that one of its successor sets (indeed, its only non-empty one) is an *infinite* set.

It is, however, possible for a tree to have only finite-sized successor sets, and yet for there to be no finite upper bound on the size of its successor sets. Consider, for example, the "powers-of-two" tree whose nodes are the positive integers, in which the level of a node x is the exponent n of the smallest power of 2 that exceeds x. The level of 1 is thus 1, that of 2 and 3 is 2, that of 4, 5, 6 and 7 is 3, and so on.

The successor set of 2^n is the set of integers k in the interval $2^{n+1} \leqslant k < 2^{n+2}$; the successor set of an integer is empty if that integer is not a power of 2. This tree looks like:

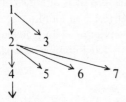

and has just one infinite branch

$$1, 2, 4, 8, \ldots, 2^n, \ldots$$

consisting of the successive powers of 2 (starting with $2^0 = 1$). The successor sets of this tree:

$\{2, 3\}$
$\{4, 5, 6, 7\}$
$\{8, 9, 10, 11, 12, 13, 14, 15\}$

etc., are all finite sets. However, there is no finite upper bound to the size of these sets. So the powers-of-two tree illustrates how a tree can have all of its successor sets be *finite* sets *without* necessarily having these sets all be of size less than some fixed integer. It is the trees *whose successor sets are all finite* that are called *finitary* trees.

Now a tree may have a finite, or an infinite, set of nodes. The tree

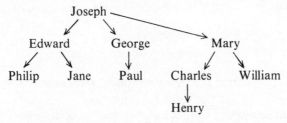

for example, has ten. We say that it is a *finite tree*. In general, a finite tree is one having only finitely many nodes and an infinite tree is one having infinitely many nodes.

So a finite tree is something very different from a finitary tree. Every finite tree is of course finitary – there being only finitely many nodes in it altogether, it can scarcely be expected to muster an infinite set of nodes as one of its successor sets. The point is that *not every finitary tree is finite*. There are infinite finitary trees. They fall into two kinds: those whose successor sets are (as in the word-tree) bounded in size by some fixed number, and those (like the powers-of-two tree) for which this is not the case.

Now the "wide" tree is an example of an infinite tree all of whose branches are finite. Indeed, all its branches are of length 2. You do not have to have infinite branches in order to be an infinite tree. We can also find examples of trees whose branches are all finite in length, but which are not bounded in length by any fixed number. Consider, for example, the "festooned-pairs" tree:

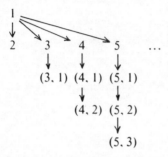

which we get from the "wide" tree by adding, as further nodes, the *pairs* (n, k) of integers such that $n \geqslant 3$ and $1 \leqslant k \leqslant (n - 2)$, and by letting the successor of each integer $n \geqslant 3$ be the pair $(n, 1)$ and the successor of each pair (n, k) be the *pair* $(n, k + 1)$ unless $k = n - 2$ (in which case (n, k) is a tip).

The "festooned-pairs" tree has a branch of length n, for every $n \geqslant 2$. The branch

$$1, 2$$

is of length 2, while for $n > 2$ the branch

$$1, n, (n, 1), \ldots, (n, n - 2)$$

is of length n. Note that the "festooned-pairs" tree is not finitary, in view of the infinite successor set of 1.

Is there an infinite *finitary* tree that, like the "festooned-pairs" tree, has branches of all finite lengths but no infinite branch? Can one somehow rearrange the structure of the "festooned-pairs" tree to avoid its infinite successor set without introducing an infinite branch; or is perhaps some new construction needed, involving an ingenious trick? To appreciate to the full the truth of the matter, which we are about to reveal, the reader who enjoys puzzles might at this point set aside the book and try to come up with an example of a tree with the three properties: it is infinite; it is finitary; it has no infinite branch.

Well: the truth of the matter is that there are no such trees. As we have seen in the examples, there *are* trees that have *any two* of these three properties. What we are saying then is that *any tree that has some two of these three properties must necessarily lack the third.* This is a very interesting and important fact. It is known as *König's Lemma.* We may state it as the proposition

> every infinite finitary tree has an infinite branch

and prove it by the following argument.

In any tree, let us say that the *descendants* of a node are: the node itself, and the descendants of its successors. And let us say that a node is *immortal* if it has infinitely many descendants, but *mortal* if it has only finitely many descendants.

Obviously a finite tree has only mortal nodes, but in any infinite tree there is always at least one immortal node, namely the root node (whose descendants are *all* the nodes in the tree). (This may be the *only* immortal node; for example, the "festooned-pairs" tree has no immortal nodes except its root node.)

If the infinite tree is also finitary, however, the root node is *not* the only immortal node: at least one of its successors must be immortal. Why? Consider: the root node x has only finitely many successors, say, $x_1, \ldots, x_n$. Every descendant of x, except for x itself, must be a descendant of x_1, or of $x_2, \ldots,$ or of x_n. But if each of $x_1, \ldots, x_n$ were mortal, they would have only finitely many descendants between the lot of them! So, at least one of $x_1, \ldots, x_n$ must be immortal.

More generally, this argument shows that

> in any infinite finitary tree each immortal node has at least one immortal successor

The point can be made in a different way, as a property of any infinite set D. Namely, if we partition D into finitely many sets $D_1, \ldots, D_n$, so that:

$$D = D_1 \cup \ldots \cup D_n$$

then at least one of the sets $D_1, \ldots, D_n$ must be infinite.

In the case of the immortal node x we are just taking D to be the set of all its descendants other than itself, and $D_1, \ldots, D_n$ to be the sets of descendants of its successors $x_1, \ldots, x_n$.

But if every immortal node has an immortal successor, and if the root-node is immortal, the tree must have at least one infinite branch consisting entirely of immortal nodes:

$$x_0, x_1, x_2, \ldots, x_j, x_{j+1}, \ldots,$$

in which x_0 is the root node, and, in general, x_{j+1} is one of the immortal successors of x_j, for all $j \geqslant 0$.

One can see how the fact that the infinite tree is *finitary* plays the essential rôle in this argument. It is this fact that causes immortality to be passed on to (at least one member of) the next generation. An immortal node with an infinite successor set can easily fail to have any immortal successor (as witness the "wide", and even the "festooned-pairs", tree).

We return, then, to our discussion of semantic tableaux, armed with König's Lemma. We can expect to be able to apply it to semantic tableaux since, considered as trees, they are finitary, even when they are infinite. In view of the trickiness of the discussion of infinite semantic tableaux, and the weight of the theory that rests on the compactness theorem, we must now take the trouble to give a more precise characterization of what a semantic tableau actually is.

In the previous chapter's informal presentation we loosely said that a semantic tableau was a tree with an equation $v(X) = w$ "at" each of its nodes. This notion is often called a *labelled* tree. That is, in addition to the tree itself we also have a collection of things, distinct from the nodes, which can be attached to nodes as their *labels*. If the node x has the thing y attached to it in this way, we say that y is *the label on node x*.

It is important to notice that two *distinct* nodes can have the *same* label. This can easily happen in semantic tableaux, in which the labels are the various equations $v(X) = w$, with X a sentence and w one of the two truthvalues.

In a labelled tree we think of a node and its label as inseparable, and when we refer to a node we often really mean the label on that node. Thus a branch of a semantic tableau is a sequence of *labelled* nodes, not just of the bare nodes: our attention is on the equations and not particularly on the little whatnots to which they are attached.

In our general notion of a tree there is no order given in which the successor set of a node is thought of as being arranged. However, in representing the tree as a diagram in the usual way, we perforce exhibit the successors of each node in a left-to-right order; and in any case it is often useful in applications to have *ordered* successor sets instead of just plain, unordered, successor sets.

A tree with ordered successor sets is called an *ordered* tree. Each node (other than a tip) has a first successor, ..., jth successor, etc.; if its successor set is infinite then it has a jth successor for all $j \geqslant 1$; otherwise it has a *last* successor.

Semantic tableaux are ordered trees. When we create new labelled nodes as the successors of a current tip we therefore must be construed as imposing an order on these successors; it is, in fact, the order given in the table of "splits" and "stretches" in the previous chapter.

The nodes of ordered trees can be conveniently taken to be finite sequences of positive integers, according to the scheme:
(a) the root node is the empty sequence ( );
(b) the jth successor of the node $(a_1, \ldots, a_k)$ is the finite sequence
     $(a_1, \ldots, a_k, j)$
Thus the node (3) is the 3rd successor of the root node, (3, 4) is the fourth successor of *that* node, and so on:

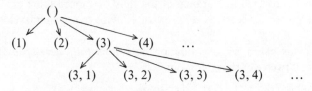

In this notation, a *branch* is a sequence

$$( ), (b_1), (b_1, b_2), (b_1, b_2, b_3)$$

of finite sequences of positive integers, beginning with ( ), with the property that if we omit the last component of any finite sequence, we get the immediately preceding finite sequence. To save writing we may write this as the single sequence (which may be *infinite*):

$$(b_1, b_2, b_3, \ldots \ )$$

on the understanding that we are merely representing, in a telescoped way, the sequence of nodes given above.

Thus both nodes and branches of ordered trees can be represented as sequences of positive integers. (Observe that a node is identified with the branch leading to that node; but there is no such thing as "the" node corresponding to an *infinite* branch.)

Now let us consider the semantic tableau generated by an infinite set of equations:

$$E = \{v(A_1) = w_1, v(A_2) = w_2, \ldots, \quad \} \tag{1}$$

for which the procedure *never halts*. We claim that the failure to halt means that the equations in (1) are included in at least one Boolean valuation of the set of sentences

$$\mathscr{S} = \{A_1, A_2, \ldots, \quad \} \tag{2}$$

We establish this claim by the following argument.

A. We note that the semantic tableau generated by the procedure is an *infinite* tree. This is clear because it contains, for each equation $v(A_j) = w_j$ in (1), at least one node labelled with $v(A_j) = w_j$.

B. We note that the semantic tableau is a *finitary* tree.

C. Hence we conclude by König's Lemma that the semantic tableau *has at least one infinite branch b*.

Let us next consider the set K of valuation equations labelling the nodes of b.

D. It is clear that among the equations in K are all those in the input sequence (1). The construction of the tableau called for each equation in (1), in turn, to be entered into the tableau as the (label on the) new tip of each live branch of the fully developed finite tableau encountered in stage B as a result of running out of undeveloped nodes. So: $E \subseteq K$.

E. Let us call a set of valuation equations *fully developed* if it satisfies all twelve of the conditions

$$[\mathbf{t}, \mathbf{f}], [\neg \mathbf{t}], [\neg \mathbf{f}], [\to \mathbf{t}], [\to \mathbf{f}], [\leftrightarrow \mathbf{t}], [\leftrightarrow \mathbf{f}], [\wedge \mathbf{t}], [\wedge \mathbf{f}],$$
$$[\vee \mathbf{t}], [\vee \mathbf{f}], [cons]$$

It is clear that K is fully developed. Every equation in K corresponds to a node of the branch that, at some step of the construction of the tableau, was duly noted; thus at that time further equations were added to the branch b as called for in the appropriate condition above. Furthermore, since b is not dead, K also satisfies $[\mathbf{t}, \mathbf{f}]$ and $[cons]$.

F. Note that if K also satisfied $[comp \; \mathscr{S}]$ it would itself be a Boolean valuation of $\mathscr{S}$ that included E, and we would be done. But in general this will not be the case, and we must find a Boolean valuation M of $\mathscr{S}$ such that $K \subseteq M$. Since $E \subseteq K$ we will then have $E \subseteq M$ and we *will* be done.

The construction of M is essentially the same for the infinite case we now have as it was for the finite case. We first define the set J of valuation equations $v(X) = w$, where X is an *independent* constituent of $\mathscr{S}$, by the rule: if K contains an equation for X, let it be the one for X which goes into J; otherwise let $v(X) = \mathbf{t}$ be put into J.

We next define M to be *that unique Boolean valuation of $\mathscr{S}$ that includes J*.

> For the sceptic, we need to show that there is such a unique M. We need only indicate, for each Boolean constituent X of $\mathscr{S}$, which of the two valuation equations, $v(X) = \mathbf{t}$, $v(X) = \mathbf{f}$, M is to contain. We do this by induction on $\beta(X)$. If $\beta(X) = 1$ and X is independent, we put into M whichever equation for X is in J; if X is dependent, i.e., is $\mathbf{t}, \mathbf{f}, (\wedge)$ or $(\vee)$, we put into M

the corresponding correct equation: $v(\mathbf{t}) = \mathbf{t}$, $v(\mathbf{f}) = \mathbf{f}$, $v(\wedge) = \mathbf{t}$, $v(\vee) = \mathbf{f}$.

Now suppose we have determined which equation M contains for Y, for all Y such that $\beta(Y) < X$. This means in particular that we have determined which equations M shall contain for each immediate constituent of X.

There are five cases to consider, corresponding to the five possible forms of X:

$$\neg Y, (\rightarrow Y_1 \ Y_2), (\leftrightarrow Y_1 \ Y_2), (\wedge Y_1 \ldots Y_n), (\vee Y_1 \ldots Y_n)$$

E.g. if X is $\neg Y$, and we have already determined that $v(Y) = \mathbf{t}$ is to be in M, we now must determine that $v(X) = \mathbf{f}$ is to be in M; but if we have already determined that $v(Y) = \mathbf{f}$ is to be in M, then we must now determine that $v(X) = \mathbf{t}$ is to be in M.

The remaining cases are handled entirely similarly, but are tedious to write out in full. The essential idea is that the equation we determine must satisfy the appropriate one of the conditions

(3) $[\neg \mathbf{t}] \ [\neg \mathbf{f}] \ [\rightarrow \mathbf{t}] \ [\rightarrow \mathbf{f}] \ [\leftrightarrow \mathbf{t}] \ [\leftrightarrow \mathbf{f}] \ [\wedge \mathbf{t}] \ [\wedge \mathbf{f}] \ [\vee \mathbf{t}] \ [\vee \mathbf{f}]$

and that therefore, since we already have determined the equations that are to be in M for the immediate constituents of X we have one and only one choice for the equation that is to be in M for X.

M is "generated" by J, by these forced choices being propagated from the sentences with smaller β's to the sentences with larger β's.

G. Now that we have our Boolean valuation M, it remains to show that $K \subseteq M$. Well, let K_j be the set of all equations $v(X) = w$ in K for which $\beta(X) = j$. Let us show that $K_j \subseteq M$ for all $j \geqslant 1$.

Obviously, $K_1 \subseteq M$, since if $v(X) = m$ is in K_1 it is either in J or else is one of the equations $v(\mathbf{t}) = \mathbf{t}$, $v(\mathbf{f}) = \mathbf{f}$, $v(\wedge) = \mathbf{t}$, $v(\vee) = \mathbf{f}$, and so was put into M at the start of the construction. Assume then that $K_1 \subseteq M, \ldots, K_{j-1} \subseteq M$; and let us prove that $K_j \subseteq M$, for $j > 1$.

Well: if $v(X) = w$ is in K it must be (since K is fully developed) that the equations for the immediate constituents of X are such that the appropriate condition in the list (3) is satisfied. But these constituents are all in $K_1 \cup \ldots \cup K_{j-1}$, and are therefore in M. Hence the equation $v(X) = w$ must also be in M. Hence $K_j \subseteq M$. This shows that for all $j \geqslant 1$, $K_j \subseteq M$, and hence that $K \subseteq M$.

This argument establishes the fundamental property of a fully developed set K of valuation equations for Boolean constituents of a set $\mathscr{S}$ of closed sentences: that it is essentially a *consistent description* of a Boolean valuation M of $\mathscr{S}$.

The Boolean valuations M described by a fully developed set K of equations are not, in general, uniquely determined by K. The reader will have noted that in the construction of M, we decided to put $v(X) = \mathbf{t}$ into J if K contained no equation for X, when $\beta(X) = 1$. The choice of $v(X) = \mathbf{t}$ rather than $v(X) = \mathbf{f}$, for such X, is quite arbitrary and does not affect the argument at all. It would have been adequate to say: choose from $v(X) = \mathbf{t}$, $v(X) = \mathbf{f}$ at random, for such X. Of course, the Boolean valuation M will be different, for each collection of such "irrelevant" choices.

The main thrust of the argument is to show that there *are* Boolean valuations of $\mathscr{S}$ that include the fully developed set K. To be fully developed is, intuitively, to have had one's consistency completely checked out.

Our conclusion, then, concerning the semantic tableau procedure, is that when applied to an infinite set E of valuation equations it will halt with a dead tableau if, and only if, there is no Boolean valuation that includes E, i.e. if, and only if, E is impossible.

The *compactness theorem for Boolean semantics* follows at once:

> An *enumerably infinite* set of closed sentences is Boolean unsatisfiable if and only if *some finite* subset is Boolean unsatisfiable.

Let $\mathscr{S}$ be such an infinite set of closed sentences. We just need to apply the semantic tableau procedure to the set of equations: $\{v(X) = \mathbf{t} \mid X \text{ in } \mathscr{S}\}$.

The compactness theorem for Boolean semantics sounds even more interesting, to some people, if we negate both sides of the "if and only if" and state it in the equivalent, positive, version

> An *enumerably infinite* set of closed sentences is Boolean satisfiable if and only if *every finite* subset of it is Boolean satisfiable.

5. Semantic Analysis of Sentences and Terms

Boolean valuations are concerned only with the semantics of truth-values and Boolean combinations. They ignore entirely the semantics of predications and generalizations, apart from assigning truthvalues to them as indivisible wholes.

A Boolean valuation might well, therefore, violate the intended semantic properties of generalizations. For example, it might contain both of the equations

$$v(\exists x Q x) = \mathbf{f}$$
$$v(Q a) = \mathbf{t}$$

(here, the symbol "Q" is taken from P_1 and the individual "a" from U).

But one of the fundamental properties of an existential generalization is that if it is false then all its instances are false. Since Qa is an instance of $\exists x Q x$, the two equations together violate this property.

For the complete semantical analysis of the predicate calculus system we need to introduce the idea of a *total valuation* of an applied calculus

$$applied\,(L, U)$$

with lexicon L and universe U. In chapter 2 we defined *applied* (L, U) to be the set of all closed sentences and closed terms in whose syntactic construction only symbols from L and individuals from U occur, in addition to the logical symbols $\mathbf{t}, \mathbf{f}, \neg, \rightarrow, \leftrightarrow, \vee, \wedge, \forall, \exists$, and $*$.

A total valuation of the calculus $K = applied\,(L, U)$ is a collection of equations $v(X) = w$, one for each closed formula X in K, such that if X is a sentence, w is a truthvalue, while if X is a term, w is an individual in U; this collection of equations must satisfy the conditions set forth in table 5.1 as well as the conditions in table 5.2.

In writing condition B1 of table 5.2 we are assuming that $\tau_1, \ldots, \tau_n$ are closed terms in K, and that α is a symbol in L that is *either* in P_n or in C_n; thus $w_1, \ldots, w_n$ are individuals and w is either a truthvalue or an individual, according as α is in P_n or C_n.

Condition B1 says that the total valuation must reflect the seman-

Table 5.1

	it contains	iff it contains
A1	$v(\mathbf{t}) = \mathbf{t}$	—
A2	$v(\mathbf{f}) = \mathbf{f}$	—
A3	$v(\neg\, Y) = \mathbf{t}$	$v(Y) = \mathbf{f}$
A4	$v(\neg\, Y) = \mathbf{f}$	$v(Y) = \mathbf{t}$
A5	$v(\rightarrow Y Z) = \mathbf{t}$	either $v(Y) = \mathbf{f}$ or $v(Z) = \mathbf{t}$ or both
A6	$v(\rightarrow Y Z) = \mathbf{f}$	$v(Y) = \mathbf{t}$ and $v(Z) = \mathbf{f}$
A7	$v(\leftrightarrow Y Z) = \mathbf{t}$	both of $v(Y) = \mathbf{t}, v(Z) = \mathbf{t}$
		or else both of $v(Y) = \mathbf{f}, v(Z) = \mathbf{f}$
A8	$v(\leftrightarrow Y Z) = \mathbf{f}$	both of $v(Y) = \mathbf{t}, v(Z) = \mathbf{f}$
		or else both of $v(Y) = \mathbf{f}, v(Z) = \mathbf{t}$
A9	$v(\wedge\, Y_1 \ldots Y_n) = \mathbf{t}$	$v(Y_j) = \mathbf{t}$, for all j, $1 \leqslant j \leqslant n$
A10	$v(\wedge\, Y_1 \ldots Y_n) = \mathbf{f}$	$v(Y_j) = \mathbf{f}$, for at least one j, $1 \leqslant j \leqslant n$
A11	$v(\vee\, Y_1 \ldots Y_n) = \mathbf{t}$	$v(Y_j) = \mathbf{t}$, for at least one j, $1 \leqslant j \leqslant n$
A12	$v(\vee\, Y_1 \ldots Y_n) = \mathbf{f}$	$v(Y_j) = \mathbf{f}$, for all j, $1 \leqslant j \leqslant n$
A13	$v(\forall\, x\, A) = \mathbf{t}$	$v(A[\tau/x]) = \mathbf{t}$, for all individuals τ in U
A14	$v(\forall\, x\, A) = \mathbf{f}$	$v(A[*\forall x A/x]) = \mathbf{f}$
A15	$v(\exists\, x\, A) = \mathbf{t}$	$v(A[*\exists x A/x]) = \mathbf{t}$
A16	$v(\exists\, x\, A) = \mathbf{f}$	$v(A[\tau/x]) = \mathbf{f}$, for all individuals τ in U

Table 5.2

B1	if it contains the equations
	$\quad v(\tau_1) = w_1, \ldots, v(\tau_n) = w_n$ and $v(\alpha\, w_1 \ldots w_n) = w$
	then it must also contain the equation: $v(\alpha\, \tau_1 \ldots \tau_n) = w$
B2	if it contains the equations
	$\quad v(*A) = j$ and $v(A) = w$
	then it must also contain: $v(A[j]) = w$
B3	it must contain the equation $v(j) = j$
	for every individual j in U.

tics of the *applicative* notation in which predications and constructions are expressed. A total valuation E for K is a complete description of the denotational behaviour of the closed formulas in K: it provides us with a "denotational map", in the form of the set of equations, which tells us, for each closed formula X in K, the (truthvalue or individual) w which X denotes. The denotational map tells us this by containing the equation $v(X) = w$.

For example, suppose $L = \{g, h, n, Q\}$, with:

g in C_1, h in C_2, n in C_0, Q in P_1

and suppose $U = \{1, 2, 3\}$. Then condition B1 says, e.g., that if a denotational map for *applied* (L, U) has in it the equations:

$v(h\ 2\ 3) = 2, v(g\ 1) = 2, v(n) = 3$

then it *must* contain also the equation:

$v(h(g\ 1)\ n) = 2$

and that if it contains, in addition, the equation:

$v(Q\ 2) = \mathbf{t}$

then it *must* contain the equation:

$v(Q(h(g\ 1)n)) = \mathbf{t}$

as well.

Condition B2 of table 5.2 says that the denotation map of a total valuation must respect the intended meaning of *exemplifications* $*A$ by seeing to it that $*A$ denotes an individual in the set of individuals "represented" by A in the total valuation, this being the set of individuals j for which the instance $A\lfloor j\rfloor$ denotes the same truthvalue as does A.

Table 5.1 covers all the ground that was covered previously when we considered Boolean valuations. Conditions A1 to A12 say collectively that if we drop from the denotation map of a total valuation all equations $v(X) = w$ in which X is a term, we must be left with a Boolean valuation *of the set of all sentences in K*.

However, it will be *more* than just a Boolean valuation of the sentences in K, for it also satisfies conditions A13 to A16, which say that it must respect the semantics of *generalizations*. Conditions A13 and A16 reflect the "universality" of a true universal generalization or of a false existential generalization. Conditions A14 and A15 reflect the "exemplifiability" of a false universal generalization or of a true existential generalization.

One cannot defend this definition of a total valuation of an applied calculus K, except on grounds of its appropriateness to the *intended* semantics; for it is nothing more than a formalization of those intentions.

Now in the system of the predicate calculus that we are setting up in this book it is the intention to regard applied calculi and the various total valuations of them as a formal way of dealing with the semantics of *pure* calculi. It will be recalled that a pure calculus is determined completely by its lexicon *L* of constructor and predicate symbols, and that it consists of all the closed formulas (sentences and terms) in which only symbols in *L* occur, besides the logical symbols **t**, **f**, ¬, →, ↔, ∧, ∨, ∀, ∃, ∗. In particular there are no individuals involved in the formulas of a pure calculus. The pure calculus with lexicon *L* is denoted, it will be recalled, by *pure* (*L*).

One can regard the various applied calculi with lexicon *L* as "extensions" of *pure* (*L*); since we obviously have

$$pure\,(L) \subseteq applied\,(L, U)$$

for all sets *U*, what we are doing, intuitively, as we pass from *pure* (*L*) to *applied* (*L*, *U*) is simply adding some more closed terms, namely the individuals in *U*, to *pure* (*L*) and then "forming the closure" of the resulting set under the various operations of syntactic construction. If we consider a total valuation of *applied* (*L*, *U*), then each formula in *pure* (*L*) denotes a value under it, as specified by the denotation map.

The preceding remarks have prepared us for the fundamental definition of the semantics of the predicate calculus. This definition says what is meant by a *model* of a pure calculus:

A *model* of the calculus *pure* (*L*) is a total valuation of some calculus *applied* (*L*, *U*).

That is, we give a model for *pure* (*L*) by choosing a set *U* as universe of individuals and then supplying a total valuation of the calculus *applied* (*L*, *U*).

For example, let *L* be the lexicon⁻{*Q*, *n*, *g*, *h*} considered in our earlier example. Then among the terms of *pure* (*L*) would be, for example:

$$n, (g\ n), (h\ n\ n), (h(g\ n)n), \ast \exists x Q x, (g \ast \forall x \neg Q x)$$

and among the sentences of *pure* (*L*) would be:

$$\exists x Q x, \forall x \neg Q x, (\exists x Q x \leftrightarrow Q \ast \exists x Q x), Q(h(g\ n)n).$$

As we consider various different models of *pure* (*L*), its formulas will denote various different entities. For example, let *U* be the set {1, 2, 3}. Then let the denotation map be any set of equations, one for each formula in *applied* (*L*, {1, 2, 3}) that satisfies the conditions of tables 5.1 and 5.2 and contains the equations shown in table 5.3.

Table 5.3

$v(n) = 3$		
$v(g\ 1) = 2$	$v(g\ 2) = 3$	$v(g\ 3) = 1$
$v(h\ 1\ 1) = 2$	$v(h\ 1\ 2) = 3$	$v(h\ 1\ 3) = 1$
$v(h\ 2\ 1) = 3$	$v(h\ 2\ 2) = 1$	$v(h\ 2\ 3) = 2$
$v(h\ 3\ 1) = 1$	$v(h\ 3\ 2) = 2$	$v(h\ 3\ 3) = 3$
$v(Q\ 1) = \mathbf{t}$	$v(Q\ 2) = \mathbf{f}$	$v(Q\ 3) = \mathbf{t}$

The equations in table 5.3 cover all of the "basic" formulas in *applied* $(L, \{1, 2, 3\})$, i.e. all formulas that consist of a symbol from L followed by the appropriate number of members of $\{1, 2, 3\}$.

But once we have decided on the equations for all basic formulas, these, and the conditions in tables 5.1 and 5.2, allow us to write proper equations for *all* formulas in *applied* $(L, \{1, 2, 3\})$. For example, we can easily see that the denotation map *must* contain

$$v(g\ n) = 1, \quad v(h(g\ n)n) = 1, \quad v(\forall x \neg Qx) = \mathbf{f},$$
$$v(h\ n\ n) = 3, \quad v(\exists xQx) = \mathbf{t}$$

but that there is freedom to choose between the equations

$$v(*\exists xQx) = 1, \quad v(*\exists xQx) = 3 \tag{1}$$

We *cannot* choose

$$v(*\exists xQx) = 2$$

because the equation

$$v(Q\ 2) = \mathbf{f}$$

is already in table 5.3, and the condition B2 says that if we already have

$$v(*\exists xQx) = 2 \text{ and } v(\exists xQx) = \mathbf{t}$$

then we must also have

$$v(Q\ 2) = \mathbf{t}$$

which we would not be able to do. So (1) is the range of our choice: it does not matter which equation we do choose.

However, if we choose, say,

$$v(*\exists xQx) = 3$$

then our choice for the equation for $(g*\exists xQx)$ is forced to be

$$v(g(*\exists xQx)) = 1$$

while if we had chosen

$$v(*\exists xQx) = 1$$

our choice for $(g*\exists xQx)$ would have had to be

$$v(g(*\exists xQx)) = 2$$

The point is that table 5.3 does not fully determine *all* other equations; the inherent "indeterminacy" in the semantics of the exemplification terms leaves a certain amount of leeway in the choice of their valuation equations. But *only* a certain amount! It is crucial that the individual denoted by an exemplification $*A$ in a total valuation be a member of the set *represented by A in that valuation*. That is, if the equation for A in the valuation is

$$v(A) = w$$

then A represents the set $\lfloor A \rfloor$ of all individuals j for which the valuation contains the equation

$$v(A\lfloor j \rfloor) = w$$

Consequently, the equation for $*A$, while not necessarily *completely determined* (that would happen *only* if $\lfloor A \rfloor$ was a singleton set) is *constrained*; there are certain choices for it that are *excluded* by the semantical rules codified in tables 5.1 and 5.2.

One *might* decide to select the equations for exemplifications $*A$ by picking from the set $\lfloor A \rfloor$ whatever individual in $\lfloor A \rfloor$ was the value of some *choice function* for U when applied to $\lfloor A \rfloor$. There is nothing in the semantic rules that says one *must* do so, and a purely arbitrary choice from $\lfloor A \rfloor$ may be made (in giving a total valuation) each time the issue arises. Thus: if the *same* set of individuals comes up on separate occasions during the writing of the total valuation, a *different* choice might indeed be made on each occasion. For example, the sentence $\exists yQy$ must be given the same truth value, **t**, as was $\exists xQx$, according to the semantic rules. They are both "saying the same thing". But we are free, in giving a total valuation, to choose (given table 5.3) the equations:

$$v(*\exists xQx) = 1, \quad v(*\exists yQy) = 3 \tag{2}$$

Since $\exists xQx$ and $\exists yQy$ are "logically equivalent" they both denote the same truthvalue, no matter what the total valuation is. We must have either

$$v(\exists xQx) = \mathbf{t} \text{ and } v(\exists yQy) = \mathbf{t}$$

or

$$v(\exists xQx) = \mathbf{f} \text{ and } v(\exists yQy) = \mathbf{f}$$

in every total valuation. But even though $\exists xQx$ and $\exists yQy$ are logically equivalent, the terms $*\exists xQx$ and $*\exists yQy$ are not – as (2) clearly shows.

The principle that "logically equivalent closed formulas may be substituted for each other in all contexts" does not carry over to the contexts of exemplifications. We do *not* have:

> if A is logically equivalent to B
> then $*A$ is logically equivalent to $*B$ (3)

Nor should we *expect* to have (3). Exemplifications are terms whose interiors are "lost" once the terms are formed.

Now, no matter how we choose our equation for $*\exists xQx$ in our example, we shall find that we have *no* choice but

$$v(\exists xQx \leftrightarrow Q*\exists xQx) = \mathbf{t}$$

for the sentence

$$\exists xQx \leftrightarrow Q*\exists xQx$$

and, for that matter, *no* choice but

$$v(\exists yQy \leftrightarrow Q*\exists xQx) = \mathbf{t}$$

for the sentence

$$\exists yQy \leftrightarrow Q*\exists xQx$$

Now if we changed table 5.3 to contain some different equations for the basic formulas of *applied* $(\{Q, g, h, n\}, \{1, 2, 3\})$ we would in general of course get different "forced" equations for the formulas $(g\,n)$, $(h\,n\,n)$, etc. considered above. For example, if we put

$$v(Q\,1) = \mathbf{f}, \quad v(Q\,2) = \mathbf{f}, \quad v(Q\,3) = \mathbf{f}$$

we would get different equations for $\exists xQx$ and $\forall x\neg Qx$:

$$v(\exists xQx) = \mathbf{f} \text{ and } v(\forall x\neg Qx) = \mathbf{t}$$

However, we would *still* get the same equation for $(\exists xQx \leftrightarrow Q*\exists xQx)$:

$$v(\exists xQx \leftrightarrow Q*\exists xQx) = \mathbf{t}$$

as we did before. Indeed, no matter *what* equations are written in table 5.3 for the basic formulas in *applied* (L, U), we would still get this equation. As a matter of fact, *no matter what model* of *pure* $(\{Q, g, h, n\})$ we consider, the sentence

$(\exists x Q x \leftrightarrow Q * \exists x Q x)$

will *always* have the equation

$v(\exists x Q x \leftrightarrow Q * \exists x Q x) = \mathsf{t}$

in the denotation map of the model! This property – being true in *all* models – is the defining property of a "logically true" sentence.

Clearly, all *tautologies* are logically true in this sense, and all *contradictions* are "logically false" in the sense that they are false in all models. But $(\exists x Q x \leftrightarrow Q * \exists x Q x)$ is not a tautology. Its logical truth depends on something semantically deeper than the Boolean structure it exhibits.

A set $\mathscr{S}$ of the sentences in *pure* (L) is *satisfied* by a given model of *pure* (L) if every sentence in $\mathscr{S}$ is true in that model. (Similarly we say that $\mathscr{S}$ is *falsified* by the model if *every* sentence in $\mathscr{S}$ is false in that model; note that "falsified" does *not* just mean "not satisfied".)

A set $\mathscr{S}$ of the sentences in *pure* (L) is *satisfiable* if there is a model of *pure* (L) that satisfies $\mathscr{S}$.

These notions were partly anticipated by the notions "Boolean satisfiable" and so on; but we should now note carefully that while we (of course) have:

if $\mathscr{S}$ is satisfiable then $\mathscr{S}$ is Boolean satisfiable

we do *not* in general have:

if $\mathscr{S}$ is Boolean satisfiable then $\mathscr{S}$ is satisfiable.

For example, $\{\neg(\exists x Q x \leftrightarrow Q * \exists x Q x)\}$ is Boolean satisfiable!

In chapter 2 we introduced the notion of the *logical universe*:

logical (L)

for a lexicon L, and noted that when we take the applied calculus

applied (L, *logical* (L))

whose lexicon is L and whose universe is *logical* (L), we simply get *pure* (L) again:

pure (L) = *applied* (L, *logical* (L))

Among the various models of *pure* (L), it is those whose universe is *logical* (L) in which our main interest will be centred. These models of *pure* (L) are called its *logical models*. It should be noted that, although a closed term has *two* personalities in a logical model (one as an *individual,* and one as the *construction* or *exemplification* that it syntactically is) the prescriptions of table 5.2 coincide for it. So we *can* in fact take the closed terms as our universe and still give total valuations in accordance with tables 5.1 and 5.2. It turns out that for the purposes of a complete logical analysis of a pure calculus, *it is only its logical models that need to be taken into account.* This is so because of the theorem:

> A set $\mathcal{S}$ of sentences of *pure* (L) is satisfiable if, and only if, it is satisfied by some *logical* model of *pure* (L).

We shall see why this theorem is true a little later on, when we have been over some of the ground opened up by the notion of a logical model. Let us consider some of the special characteristics of logical models.

The *individuals* in a logical model of *pure* (L) are simply the various closed terms in *pure* (L). Condition B3 of table 5.2 tells us that in the denotation map of a model we must have, for each *individual w*, the equation $v(w) = w$. This means that, in a logical model,

> every closed term τ denotes itself

Thus, in every logical model of the calculus *pure* $(\{Q, g, h, n\})$ of our earlier example, we shall have the equations

$$v(n) = n$$
$$v(h(g\ n)n) = (h(g\ n)n)$$
$$v(*\exists xQx) = *\exists xQx$$

and so on.

Since every closed term denotes *itself* in a logical model, we know that, in particular, *exemplifications denote themselves.* Thus in *logical* models there is none of the indeterminacy, arising from the condition B2, that we face in other models. In a logical model we always have the equation

$$v(*A) = *A$$

to tell us which individual, in the set of individuals represented by A, is denoted by the exemplification $*A$.

In logical models, the set of individuals ($\equiv$ closed terms) represented by a generalization A always contains the individual ($\equiv$ closed term) $*A$. We are guaranteed that this is so by conditions A14 and A15 in table 5.1.

Let us call a model whose denotation map "admits a choice

function" a *uniform* model. More precisely, a uniform model is one for which *there exists* a choice function, *ch*, for its universe of individuals, satisfying the condition that the equation

$$v(*A) = ch \{j \mid j \text{ an individual and the equation}$$
$$v(A[j]) = w \text{ is in } D\} \tag{4}$$

is in its denotation map D, where w is the truthvalue on the right-hand side of the equation $v(A) = w$ in D, which the model has for A.

Given a denotation map D satisfying tables 5.1 and 5.2, it is a matter of fact whether the corresponding model admits a choice function *ch* or not.

For a *non-uniform* model, there *is*, by definition of "non-uniform", no choice function *ch* for its universe of individuals which satisfies condition (4). As long as condition B2 holds:

$$\text{if } v(*A) = j \text{ and } v(A) = w \text{ are both in } D$$
$$\text{then } v(A[j]) = w \text{ is in } D \tag{5}$$

the model provides denotations for all sentences and terms, including exemplifications, exactly in accord with our intuitions as to what these denotations should be.

Now, logical models are always *non-uniform*. To see this, consider the exemplifications $*\exists xQx$ and $*\exists yQy$. These are *distinct* closed terms. In any *uniform* model, they will always denote the *same* individual because each of the generalizations $\exists xQx$ and $\exists yQy$ will always represent the same set as the other. (Indeed, each of $\exists xQx$ and $\exists yQy$ will always represent the same set as the other in any model, uniform or non-uniform: they are, as we shall say later on, *logically equivalent* to each other.) Hence, in a uniform model, the individual denoted by $*\exists xQx$ will necessarily be the same as that denoted by $*\exists yQy$.

In any *logical* model, however, each of $*\exists xQx$ and $*\exists yQy$ denotes *itself*. Hence they denote *distinct* individuals, despite the fact that $\exists xQx$ and $\exists yQy$ both represent the same *set* of individuals. Thus, no logical model can be uniform.

Non-uniformity of a model is by no means an unnatural, unwanted, or impractical feature of it. One can easily conceive of schemes for computing denotations of formulas in a model, wherein the denotation of an exemplification $*A$ is found by some kind of a *search* process in which the various instances $A[j]$ are evaluated and their truthvalues compared with that of A. It is then very natural, and sensible, to suppose that $v(*A)$ should be taken to be the *first j found* that satisfies $v(A[j]) = v(A)$. In this conception we may suppose that the truthvalue $v(A)$ is known already, in order that the search can take place as described. We may, for instance, have recorded $v(A)$ in the corpus of "values already computed" but omitted to record the various values $v(A[j])$.

Because of B3, the part of a logical model's denotation map that contains the equations for *terms* is trivial, and we need not be explicitly concerned with it in considering the denotation maps of logical models. Indeed, in order to construct a logical model it suffices to construct a set D of equations *for the sentences only*, so as to satisfy the conditions of table 5.1.

A logical model for *pure* (L) is completely determined by any set D of equations $v(X) = w$, one for each sentence X in *pure* (L), which satisfies table 5.1. Let us call such a set D of equations a *logical denotation map* for *pure* (L). To specify a logical model for a calculus *pure* (L), then, we need only specify a logical denotation map for it. In specifying a logical denotation map, the only guide we need is table 5.1.

Now, we are ready to appreciate why it is that if a set of sentences of *pure* (L) is satisfiable at all, it is satisfied by some *logical* model of *pure* (L).

Suppose that N is some arbitrary model of *pure* (L). This means that N is a total valuation of some calculus *applied* (L, U). Let M be that subset of the set N of equations, which consists of all equations $v(X) = w$ in N for which X is a sentence of *pure* (L):

$$M = \{v(X) = w \mid X \text{ is a sentence in } pure\ (L)\}$$

Since N satisfies table 5.1, so must M! That is to say, M is a logical model of *pure* (L). This reasoning shows that we have the following *logical model theorem*:

every model includes a logical model

The logical model M in question is of course uniquely determined by the given model N; so we may justifiably call it "the" logical model included in N, and denote it by $\mathscr{L}(N)$. It is now immediately obvious that if $\mathscr{S}$ is a set of sentences of *pure* (L) that is satisfied by a model N, then $\mathscr{S}$ is satisfied by the logical model $\mathscr{L}(N)$ included in N. For $\mathscr{S}$ is satisfied by N if, and only if, N contains the equation $v(X) = \mathbf{t}$ for each X in $\mathscr{S}$; but then M will contain all these equations too.

So we see that as far as *pure* (L) is concerned, all its models are "classified" into classes, each of which is associated with some particular *logical* model M of *pure* (L); indeed each class of models of *pure* (L) has the form

$$\{N \mid \mathscr{L}(N) = M\}$$

for some logical model M of *pure* (L). One might say that M (which is itself in the class) *represents* the class; and that all its members are in a sense *equivalent* to each other, and *not* equivalent to any model in any other such class.

Since the universe of a logical model is a countably infinite set, we have the nice theorem:

> If a (finite or infinite) set $\mathscr{S}$ of sentences in *pure* (L) is satisfiable, then it is satisfied by a model whose universe is countably infinite.

which is known as the Skolem-Löwenheim theorem.

Given the calculus *pure* (L), it is interesting to try to get some intuitive feel for what the various logical models of *pure* (L) are. There is a "space" of logical models of *pure* (L) – one might say it is the *logical space* of *pure* (L) – that is, the "points" in the space are the distinct logical models of *pure* (L). What is this space like?

One way to imagine it is as an infinite tree whose branches correspond to the various logical denotation maps of *pure* (L). For this purpose we need to assume a particular enumeration

$$X_1, X_2, \ldots \tag{6}$$

of the countably infinite set of sentences in *pure* (L). Each logical denotation map for *pure* (L) can then be thought of as a corresponding enumeration

$$w_1, w_2, \ldots \tag{7}$$

of the truthvalues assigned to the sentences in (6) by the logical denotation map. The two enumerations (6) and (7) are just a way of representing the set of equations

$$\{v(X_1) = w_1, v(X_2) = w_2, \ldots, \quad \} \tag{8}$$

which *is* the logical denotation map. From this point of view, the logical denotation maps of *pure* (L) are certain of the sequences (7) of truthvalues – namely, those for which the corresponding set (8) of equations satisfies table 5.1.

How can we tell which sequences (7) do, and which do not, give us a logical denotation map (8)? The obvious reply is: given such a sequence, *check it against table 5.1*. If it satisfies table 5.1 (in the sense that the corresponding set (8) of equations does), then it gives a logical denotation map (namely, the set (8)); if it violates table 5.1 in any respect, then it does not, i.e., the set (8) is *not* a logical denotation map.

Now, in order to certify that (8) *does* satisfy table 5.1, we would have to have examined all of the infinitely many equations and confirmed that in each case the appropriate condition in table 5.1 was met. For example, if (8) contained an equation

$$v(\forall xA) = \mathbf{t} \tag{9}$$

then it would have been necessary to check condition A13 and to verify that *every* equation

$$v(A[\tau]) = \mathbf{t} \tag{10}$$

was also in (8), for each closed term τ in *pure* (L).

But in order to certify that (8) *does not* satisfy table 5.1, we need only have examined *finitely many* (say, the first n, for some $n \geqslant 1$) of the equations. For example, if we find among the first n equations not only (9) but also

$$v(A[\tau]) = \mathbf{f} \tag{11}$$

for some closed term τ, we would know with certainty that condition A13 of table 5.1 could not be satisfied.

With this point in mind let us study table 5.1 more closely. The following fact presents itself:

> if the set (8) does not satisfy table 5.1, then this will become immediately obvious after only *finitely* many, (say, the first n, for some $n \geqslant 1$) of the equations have been examined.

For: if (8) does not satisfy table 5.1, it must fail to satisfy one of the conditions A1 to A16. Consider each possibility in turn. If (8) fails to satisfy A1 or A2, then (since $\mathbf{t}$ is X_i and $\mathbf{f}$ is X_j for some i, j) we shall eventually encounter in (8) either the equation $v(\mathbf{t}) = \mathbf{f}$ or the equation $v(\mathbf{f}) = \mathbf{t}$, at which point we shall be able to state with certainty that (5) violates table 5.1.

Next, consider the conditions A3 to A12, and A14 and A15. Suppose (8) fails to satisfy one of *these* conditions. Then, in every case, there will come a time in the successive examination of the sequence of subsets of (8):

$$\{v(X_1) = w_1\}$$
$$\{v(X_1) = w_1, v(X_2) = w_2\}$$
$$\{v(X_1) = w_1, v(X_2) = w_2, v(X_3) = w_3\}$$
$$\cdots$$

$$\{v(X_1) = w_1, v(X_2) = w_2, \ldots \qquad\qquad v(X_n) = w_n\}$$
...

when we will have before us a set of equations in which "all of the evidence is in"; namely we shall have an equation for each of the sentences mentioned in the violated condition, and we shall then be able to compare these equations with the ones that table 5.2 says we should have.

For example, (8) might violate A11 (and A12!) by containing the equations

$$v(\vee X_i X_j X_k) = \mathbf{t}, v(X_i) = \mathbf{f}, v(X_j) = \mathbf{f}, v(X_k) = \mathbf{f}$$

where the sentence $(\vee X_i X_j X_k)$ is X_m; hence we would know this with certainty by the time we had reached the set:

$$\{v(X_1) = w_1, \ldots, v(X_n) = w_n\}$$

where n is the maximum of i, j, k and m; for this set would contain those four offending equations.

Again, (8) might fail to satisfy A15: it might, that is, contain the pair of equations

$$v(\exists xA) = \mathbf{t}, \quad v(A[*\exists xA/x]) = \mathbf{f}$$

or the pair

$$v(\exists xA) = \mathbf{f}, \quad v(A[*\exists xA/x]) = \mathbf{t}$$

We would know this with certainty once we had reached the point in the enumeration at which the later of the two sentences

$$\exists xA, \quad A[*\exists xA/x]$$

appears.

In all of the above cases we would know, at the appropriate point in the enumeration, not only that these little bundles of equations were errors, if they were, but also that they were *not*, if they were not. For example, if (8) contained the equations

$$v(\vee X_i X_j X_k) = \mathbf{f}, \quad v(X_i) = \mathbf{f}, \quad v(X_j) = \mathbf{f}, v(X_k) = \mathbf{f} \tag{12}$$

we could *certify* the equation

$$v(\vee X_i X_j X_k) = \mathbf{f} \tag{13}$$

as being "downwards consistent" with table 5.1. This simply means that, if (8) *does* fail to satisfy table 5.1, it will *not* be because of equation (13) having the wrong right-hand side, *given the equations* *for the immediate constituents of its sentence X_m.* Of course (13) might not be "upwards consistent" with table 5.1: the sentence $(\vee X_i X_j X_k)$ might have to have the value **t** because of its being an immediate constituent of a sentence (e.g., the sentence $(\neg(\vee X_i X_j X_k))$) whose equation in (8) would itself not be downwards consistent otherwise: e.g. (8) might contain the equation

$$v(\neg(\vee X_i X_j X_k)) = \mathbf{f}$$

The only equations that can never be certified "downwards consistent" in this sense are those of conditions A13 and A16, in their left column.

In order to certify, e.g. the equation

$$v(\forall xA) = \mathbf{t}$$

as downwards consistent, we would have to have observed that (8) contained *all* of the equations $v(A\,|\,\tau|) = \mathbf{t}$.

But we *can* certify $v(\forall xA) = \mathbf{t}$ as *downwards inconsistent, if* indeed it is: for then we will eventually come upon an equation

$$v(A\,|\,\tau|) = \mathbf{f}$$

Thus, without any exceptions, *every* equation, in any set thereof of the form (8), can eventually be detected, after only finitely many steps of the enumeration, as being downwards inconsistent with table 5.1, *if indeed it is so.* But, if (8) does not satisfy table 5.1, it *must* in fact contain *at least one* equation that is downwards inconsistent. Expressed the other way round, we have just said: if no equation in (8) is downwards inconsistent, then (8) satisfies table 5.1.

In the light of this discussion, let us return to the logical space of *pure (L),* and undertake the following thought-experiment: we shall construct the infinite binary tree whose nodes are

$$( ), (\mathbf{t}), (\mathbf{f}), (\mathbf{t}, \mathbf{t})\ (\mathbf{t}, \mathbf{f}), (\mathbf{f}, \mathbf{t}), (\mathbf{f}, \mathbf{f}), (\mathbf{t}, \mathbf{t}, \mathbf{t}), \text{etc.} \qquad (14)$$

i.e., the tree

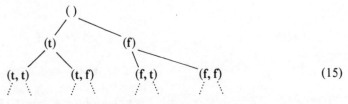

$$(15)$$

and we shall *label* each node of length j with the equation $v(X_j) = \mathbf{t}$ if the node's rightmost component is **t**, and the equation $v(X_j) = \mathbf{f}$ if the node's rightmost component is f:

$$
\begin{array}{c}
( ) \\
\end{array}
$$

$$v(X_1) = t \quad (t) \qquad (f) \quad v(X_1) = f$$

$$v(X_2) = t \quad (t, t) \qquad (t, f) \quad v(X_2) = f \qquad (16)$$

Next, we traverse the nodes of the tree (16) in the order given by (14), and, for each node $(w_1, \dots w_n)$, we examine the set

$$\{v(X_1) = w_1, \dots, v(X_n) = w_n\} \qquad (17)$$

of equations that label the nodes of the tree between the rootnode ( ) and the node $(w_1, \dots, w_n)$. If we find that this set (17) contains an equation that is downwards inconsistent with table 5.1, we mark the node $(w_1, \dots w_n)$ *dead* by drawing a line beneath it, and we *discard* all nodes of the tree (16) that are proper descendants of it (i.e. all nodes of the form $(w_1, \dots, w_n, t, \dots)$ or $(w_1, \dots w_n, f, \dots)$).

The tree produced by this process is a complete survey of the logical space of *pure* (L). Its infinite branches are enumerations of the various logical models of *pure* (L): every logical model corresponding to one particular infinite branch, and every infinite branch corresponding to one particular logical model. Let us call it a "logical tree" for *pure* (L). Provided the truncations are done at the earliest moment at which "the evidence is all in", the logical tree for *pure* (L) is uniquely determined by the enumeration (6) of the sentences in *pure* (L) that is being considered.

For example, if the enumeration (6) of the sentences in *pure* (Q, g, h, n) begins:

$$(\exists x Q x), t, (Q*\exists x Q x), (Q(g\, n)), \dots \qquad (18)$$

then the logical tree for *pure* $(\{Q, g, h, n\})$ starts off (omitting the details of the nodes, for readability):

$$(19)$$

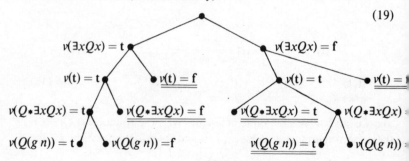

Node (t, f) is dead because condition A1 is violated; similarly for node (f, f).

Node (t, t, f) is dead because condition A15 says that node (t) is downwards inconsistent with node (t, t, f).

Node (f, t, t) is dead because condition A16 says that node (f) is downwards inconsistent with node (f, t, t).

Node (f, t, f, t) is dead because condition A16 says that node (f) is downwards inconsistent with node (f, t, f, t).

And so on.

One can quite readily program a computer to develop the logical tree for *pure* (L) if it is provided with the enumeration (6) for the sentences of *pure* (L) that uniquely determines it. The checking of each node, to see if any of the equations on the branch leading to it are certifiably downwards inconsistent, is a purely mechanical task. It can be materially aided by sensible programming techniques – for instance, we could mark a node as downwards *consistent* as soon as it becomes certifiably so; ever thereafter, *that* node need not be checked to see if it is downwards *in*consistent.

Of course, the computer, like the human, can only ever grow a finite initial portion of the logical tree for *pure* (L): but in principle (if not in practice!) either of them can carry the construction arbitrarily far. Our intuitive imaginations, however, are able to "complete" the construction and contemplate the entire infinite logical tree for *pure* (L). Let us reflect on what an extraordinarily powerful device it is.

Suppose we are given a sentence X in *pure* (L) and asked whether it is logically true. This is the same thing as being asked whether the equation $v(X) = f$ occurs in any logical model of *pure* (L)! In order to answer it, we take the logical tree for *pure* (L) and mark as dead all of the nodes labelled $v(X) = t$ that are not already marked as dead, (and discarding all nodes of the logical tree that are proper descendants of them). This simple operation leaves us with what might be called "the logical tree for the set of equations $\{v(X) = f\}$". It is a complete survey of *all* the logical models of *pure* (L), if any, that contain the equation $v(X) = f$.

The beautiful thing is that if there are no such logical models of *pure* (L), then *the logical tree for the set* $\{v(X) = f\}$ *is finite!* We know this is so because of König's Lemma, discussed in chapter 4, which says *if* the logical tree for the set $\{v(X) = f\}$ were infinite, it would, being finitary (indeed, binary), have an *infinite* branch; and since we saw to it that all branches containing the equation $v(X) = t$ stopped growing immediately (i.e., ended with the node labelled by

$v(X) = \mathbf{t}$ as tip), any such infinite branch must contain the equation $v(X) = \mathbf{f}$. Hence, in the absence of any such logical models of *pure* (L), the logical tree for $\{v(X) = \mathbf{f}\}$ is finite.

By revising our scheme a little, we can apply this "complete logical survey" idea to *infinite* sets of equations. Suppose we are given an enumeration

$$v(Y_1) = u_1, v(Y_2) = u_2, \ldots \tag{20}$$

of equations in which Y_1, Y_2, ... are sentences of *pure* (L) and u_1, u_2, ... are truthvalues. We would like to know whether the set of equations in (20) is "logically possible" or "logically impossible", by which we mean: is there, or is there not, a logical model of *pure* (L) that includes all of the equations in (20)?

The set enumerated in (20) can be finite, or infinite; it does not affect what we are about to do. We may assume that the order in which the equations are enumerated in (20) agrees with the order (6) in which all the sentences of *pure* (L) are enumerated; that is, we have, that if Y_r is X_{j_r} and Y_s is X_{j_s} then $r < s$ if, and only if $j_r < j_s$. Thus (20) is also writable as

$$v(X_{j_1}) = u_1, v(X_{j_2}) = u_2, \ldots \tag{21}$$

But now let us repeat the process by which we "constructed" the logical tree for *pure* (L) from the enumeration (6) of its sentences; only this time we shall, in examining each node $(w_1, \ldots w_n)$, not only look to see whether the set of equations $\{v(X_1) = w_1, \ldots, v(X_n) = w_n\}$ violates table 5.1, as we looked to see before, but also look to see if this set of equations is inconsistent with the enumeration (20). This we do by noting whether the equation $v(X_{j_r}) = u_r$ is in the set $\{v(X_1) = w_1, \ldots, v(X_n) = w_n\}$, as soon as n is j_r: i.e., whether $w_n = u_r$.

This process grows a tree, which we might call the logical tree of *pure* (L) for the set (20). It is a complete survey of all the logical models of *pure* (L), if any, that include (20). If there are no such models, *this tree will be finite.* König's Lemma again!

Thus if (20) is impossible, we can know this with certainty after only finitely many steps of the construction. For if the logical tree for (20) is finite and is, say, of depth $n \geqslant 1$, then the construction process will terminate, with a dead tree, after at most 2^{n+1} steps.

But think what this says about (20): it says that, if (20) is infinite, but impossible, then the first r of the equations in (20) are already collectively impossible: where r is the largest number for which $j_r \leqslant n$. In short:

If the infinite set of equations (20) is logically impossible, then some finite subset of (20) is logically impossible.

This immediately gives the *logical compactness theorem*:

If an infinite set $\mathscr{S}$ of sentences of *pure* (*L*) is unsatisfiable, then some finite subset of $\mathscr{S}$ is unsatisfiable.

For unsatisfiability of $\mathscr{S}$ is simply the logical impossibility of the set of equations $\{v(X) = \mathbf{t} \mid X \text{ in } \mathscr{S}\}$.

The compactness theorem borrows its name from *topology*, the branch of mathematics that studies the properties of *spaces* that have a certain kind of structure, analogous to that of the geometrical spaces such as the Euclidean plane, or three-dimensional Euclidean space, or the one-dimensional continuum of points comprising the real numbers line. The common features of all such spaces derive from the notion of *continuity*, which shows up in each, and has the same abstract characterization no matter what the particular details of the space may be.

A *topological space* consists of a set X of "points" together with a collection T of subsets of X, called the *topology* of the space. The sets in T are known as the *open* sets of the topological space, and they satisfy the fundamental conditions:

the *intersection* of any two open sets is an open set;
the *union* of any collection of open sets is an open set;
the *empty set*, and *the set X itself*, are open sets.

This definition is deceptively simple. It serves as the basis for a beautiful, deep mathematical theory, whose definitions and theorems search out the essence of our ideas about space and continuity. However: back to logic!

The logical models of a calculus *pure* (*L*) can be considered as the points of a topological space in which the open sets have a less intuitive characterization than the *closed* ones. Since the closed sets of a topological space are simply the *complements* of its open sets, we can just as easily give the topology of a topological space by saying what are its closed sets as by saying what are its open sets.

The closed sets of logical models of *pure* (*L*) are those that satisfy some set $\mathscr{S}$ of sentences of *pure* (*L*). That is, for each set $\mathscr{S}$ of sentences, the set $\{M \mid M \text{ satisfies } \mathscr{S}\}$ is a closed set; and these are all the closed sets. Let us write $\mathscr{S}{\uparrow}$ for the set $\{M \mid M \text{ satisfies } \mathscr{S}\}$, and $\mathscr{S}{\downarrow}$ for its *complement*, viz. the set $\{M \mid M \text{ does not satisfy } \mathscr{S}\}$. Thus the open sets are the sets $\mathscr{S}{\downarrow}$, for various sets $\mathscr{S}$ of sentences in *pure* (*L*).

One must verify that the open sets, so defined, are a topology. Well: the empty set is $\{t\}\downarrow$ and the set of all models is $\{f\}\downarrow$, so both of these sets are open. If $\{\mathscr{S}_i\downarrow\}$ is an arbitrary collection of open sets, its union $\underset{i}{\cup}\{\mathscr{S}_i\downarrow\}$ is the set $(\underset{i}{\cup}\mathscr{S}_i)\downarrow$, and so is also open.

(Think: if M is in $\underset{i}{\cup}\{\mathscr{S}_i\downarrow\}$ it fails to satisfy some $\mathscr{S}_i$ and hence fails to satisfy $(\underset{i}{\cup}\mathscr{S}_i)$, so M is in $(\underset{i}{\cup}\mathscr{S}_i)\downarrow$. But if M is in $(\underset{i}{\cup}\mathscr{S}_i)\downarrow$ some sentence A in $(\underset{i}{\cup}\mathscr{S}_i)$ is false in M; but since A is in some $\mathscr{S}_i$, M fails to satisfy $\mathscr{S}_i$ and so is in $\mathscr{S}_i\downarrow$. Hence M is in $\underset{i}{\cup}\{\mathscr{S}_i\downarrow\}$.)

Finally, if $\mathscr{S}_1\downarrow$ and $\mathscr{S}_2\downarrow$ are open sets, so is the intersection $(\mathscr{S}_1\downarrow)\cap(\mathscr{S}_2\downarrow)$. This is because $(\mathscr{S}_1\downarrow)\cap(\mathscr{S}_2\downarrow)$ is the same set of models as

(22) $\{A_1 \vee A_2 \,|\, A_1 \text{ in } \mathscr{S}_1 \text{ and } A_2 \text{ in } \mathscr{S}_2\}\downarrow$

which is an open set. (For: if M is in both of $\mathscr{S}_1\downarrow$ and $\mathscr{S}_2\downarrow$, there must be a sentence A_1 in $\mathscr{S}_1$ that M makes false, and a sentence A_2 in $\mathscr{S}_2$ that M makes false; so M makes the disjunction $A_1 \vee A_2$ false and hence is in (22). On the other hand, if M is in the set (22) it makes some sentence $A_1 \vee A_2$ false, where A_1 is in $\mathscr{S}_1$ and A_2 is in $\mathscr{S}_2$. So M is in both $\mathscr{S}_1\downarrow$ and $\mathscr{S}_2\downarrow$.)

The set of logical models of *pure* (L) being thus furnished with a not unnatural (if we consider what its *closed* sets are) topology, we can ask what are its topological properties: what *kind* of a topological space is it? Well: what kinds of topological space *are* there?

One important kind of topological space is the kind called *compact*. To be compact, a topological space (X, T) must satisfy the property:

For any family K of open sets such that X is the union of K: there is a *finite* subfamily $F \subseteq K$ such that X is the union of F.

Such a family K of open sets is called an *open cover*; and the proposition above is often expressed briefly as

every open cover has a finite subcover

What are the open covers in the logical model space? They are the various families $\{\mathscr{S}_i\downarrow\}$ of open sets of models for which the union $\underset{i}{\cup}\{\mathscr{S}_i\downarrow\}$ is the entire set of models. If we translate this into logical language, we get: an open cover $\{\mathscr{S}_i\downarrow\}$ corresponds to a collection $K = \{\mathscr{S}_i\}$ of sets of sentences whose union $\underset{i}{\cup}\mathscr{S}_i$ is unsatisfiable. (For $\underset{i}{\cup}\{\mathscr{S}_i\downarrow\} = (\underset{i}{\cup}\mathscr{S}_i)\downarrow = X$).

But if the set of sentences $(\underset{i}{\cup}\mathscr{S}_i)$ is unsatisfiable, the *logical com-*

pactness theorem tells us that some *finite* subset of $(\underset{i}{\cup} \mathscr{S}_i)$ is unsatisfiable, say, the set $\{A_1, ..., A_n\}$. Each of these sentences A_j is a member of some set $\mathscr{S}_{i_j}$ in the family $\{\mathscr{S}_i\}$. So there is a *finite* collection, viz.

$$F = \{\mathscr{S}_{i_1}, ..., \mathscr{S}_{i_n}\}$$

of the sets in $\{\mathscr{S}_i\}$ whose union is unsatisfiable.

Thus we have found that the space of logical models is *compact* in the topological sense of the word, and in showing that this is so we have called upon the logical compactness theorem. Thus

> the logical compactness theorem implies the proposition
> that the topological space of logical models is compact

Now let us take it the other way round. Suppose we *assume* that the topological space (X, T) of logical models is compact. Does it follow that the logical compactness theorem is true?

Yes. Consider: if $\mathscr{S}$ is an unsatisfiable set of sentences $\{A_1, A_2, ...\}$, we can regard $\mathscr{S}$ as the union of the sets $\mathscr{S}_i = \{A_i\}$ and its unsatisfiability as the fact that the family $\{\mathscr{S}_i\downarrow\}$ of open sets is an open cover:

$$X = \{A_1\}\downarrow \cup \{A_2\}\downarrow \cup ...$$

But the assumed compactness of the topological space of logical models then tells us that this open cover has a *finite* subcover, say, $\{\{A_{i_1}\}\downarrow, ..., \{A_{i_n}\}\downarrow\}$:

$$X = \{A_{i_1}\}\downarrow \cup ... \cup \{A_{i_n}\}\downarrow = \{A_{i_1}, ..., A_{i_n}\}\downarrow$$

and therefore that some finite subset of $\mathscr{S}$, viz. $\{A_{i_1}, ..., A_{i_n}\}$, is unsatisfiable. So we have:

> the proposition that the topological space of logical models is
> compact implies the logical compactness theorem.

The upshot of the discussion is simply this: that the logical compactness theorem is equivalent to the proposition that the topological space of logical models is a compact space.

6. Logical Consequence: Sequents and Proofs

The intuitive idea of "logical consequence" is that a collection of assertions $\mathcal{A}$ has an assertion B as a logical consequence if B "must be true whenever all the assertions in $\mathcal{A}$ are true". The implicit assumption, that assertions are sometimes true and sometimes not, is somewhat mysterious in ordinary contexts, where the assertions presumably say something specific and hence *are* true, or not. The solution to the mystery lies in the distinction between a sentence, pure and simple, and a sentence-together-with-a-model. Sentences by themselves are just that: syntactic constructs that simply sit there, exhibiting their logical form but not actually expressing any proposition. Sentences together with a model are *interpreted* by that model, and express propositions that are either true or false. In some models, they are true sentences; in other models, false sentences. This is what is behind the notion that assertions, i.e. sentences, are sometimes true, sometimes false.

Accordingly the technical definition that we are about to give gets at the essence of the intuitive idea of logical consequence by explicitly using the relationship of sentences in a pure calculus to the logical models of that calculus:

> A sentence B in *pure* (L) is a *logical consequence* of a set $\mathcal{A}$
> of sentences in *pure* (L) if there is no logical model of *pure* (L)
> that satisfies $\mathcal{A}$ and yet falsifies B.

This definition says that B is a logical consequence of $\mathcal{A}$ if whenever (i.e. in some model M) the sentences in $\mathcal{A}$ are all true then the sentence B must be true (i.e. in M); and thus it virtually transcribes the intuitive idea.

It turns out to be convenient and indeed enlightening to work with a slightly more general and symmetric technical notion of logical consequence than this one, however: In the more general relationship we replace the single sentence B by a *set $\mathcal{B}$* of sentences, and say:

> A set $\mathcal{B}$ of sentences in *pure* (L) is a *logical consequence* of a set

$\mathscr{A}$ of sentences in *pure* (*L*) if there is no logical model of *pure* (*L*) that satisfies $\mathscr{A}$ and falsifies $\mathscr{B}$.

Recall that a model falsifies a *set* of sentences if it makes *every* sentence in the set false (so *falsifying* a set of sentences is not the same as merely *failing to satisfy* it).

We write

$$\mathscr{A} \Rightarrow \mathscr{B}$$

as an abbreviation of $\mathscr{B}$ *is a logical consequence of* $\mathscr{A}$, and when one or both of $\mathscr{A}$, $\mathscr{B}$ is finite we often drop the curly brackets from around a set of sentences and write, e.g.

$$A_1, A_2, A_3 \Rightarrow B \quad \text{for: } \{A_1, A_2, A_3\} \Rightarrow \{B\}$$

and

$$A_1, A_2, A_3 \Rightarrow B_1, B_2 \quad \text{for: } \{A_1, A_2, A_3\} \Rightarrow \{B_1, B_2\}.$$

It is immediately obvious that the more general definition subsumes the first definition we gave, as a special case.

The definition of $\mathscr{A} \Rightarrow \mathscr{B}$ explicitly permits $\mathscr{A}$ and $\mathscr{B}$ to be *any* sets of sentences in *pure* (*L*). In particular, either or both of them can be *infinite*; and either or both of them can be *empty*.

Instead of saying: $\mathscr{B}$ *is a logical consequence of* $\mathscr{A}$, we can use any of the other synonymous expressions

    $\mathscr{A}$ *entails* $\mathscr{B}$
    $\mathscr{B}$ *follows from* $\mathscr{A}$
    $\mathscr{A}$ *logically implies* $\mathscr{B}$

which are in general use. The relationship, not the form of words used to express it, is what counts.

The propositions $\mathscr{A} \Rightarrow \mathscr{B}$ are called *sequents*, and when $\mathscr{A}$ and $\mathscr{B}$ are both finite, *finite sequents*. Sequents are *not* formulas; not even finite sequents are. They are, rather, meaningful (and hence either true, or false) assertions *about* formulas. Some people like to make this point by saying that whereas the formulas are expressions in the *object language*, namely, in *pure* (*L*), the sequents are expressions in the *metalanguage*, namely, the part of the natural English language that one uses to talk about *pure* (*L*). This is a little ponderous, and we shall not use this terminology here. The main point, however, must be stressed: sequents *say* something quite specific, and what they say either is so, or is not so; therefore they are true or they are false. We may not always be able to tell which; but each sequent is certainly one or the other.

The point *can* be missed. In particular, when $\mathscr{A}$ and $\mathscr{B}$ are both finite – say, $\mathscr{A}$ is $\{A_1, ..., A_m\}$ and $\mathscr{B}$ is $\{B_1, ..., B_n\}$ – there is a tendency for people to confuse the sequent

$$A_1, ..., A_m \Rightarrow B_1, ..., B_n \qquad (1)$$

with the formula

$$(A_1 \wedge ... \wedge A_m) \rightarrow (B_1 \vee ... \vee B_n) \qquad (2)$$

In fact the sequent (1) is, in effect, a proposition *about* the formula (2): it says that (2) is logically true.

For a formula (sentence) to be true, or false, there must be given a *model, in* which the sentence is true, or *in* which it is false. Whereas a sentence of *pure* (*L*) can be, in this sense, "sometimes true, sometimes false", it is nonsense to say that a sequent can be "sometimes true, sometimes false".

Nevertheless we *can* study sequents in a rather formal way. In saying things about them, as we shall, we are then, no doubt, speaking in the metametalanguage.

In the sequent $\mathscr{A} \Rightarrow \mathscr{B}$, $\mathscr{A}$ is called its *antecedent*, and $\mathscr{B}$ its *succedent*.

In studying sequents, we will really be getting down to the proper business of logic, conceived of as the science of "what follows from what". One might almost say: the task of logic is to separate the true sequents from the false ones, and to find ways of *establishing* the truth of true sequents and the falsehood of false sequents. The latter task obliges logic to come up with methods of "revealing", or "making obvious", the truth of true sequents and the falsehood of false sequents: this being a matter of taking into account the way the human mind works, and in particular what its "information-processing" capacities are. The mind apparently has quite definite limitations on the *complexity* of what it can handle, just as the muscles and bones have their limitations on what they can lift.

Let us consider some features of sequents that are immediately perceivable and which make it completely obvious that they are true. We confine our attention, for the time being, to finite sequents. It is clear that if, in the finite sequent $\mathscr{A} \Rightarrow \mathscr{B}$, the set $\mathscr{A}$ contains the sentence **f**, or the set $\mathscr{B}$ contains the sentence **t**, then there is no model that will satisfy $\mathscr{A}$ and falsify $\mathscr{B}$: such a model would have to contain the equation $v(\mathbf{f}) = \mathbf{t}$, or the equation $v(\mathbf{t}) = \mathbf{f}$, or both, and there are no such models.

It seems reasonable therefore to classify all such sequents as "axioms": meaning that *they are self-evidently true*:

if f is in $\mathscr{A}$ then $\mathscr{A} \Rightarrow \mathscr{B}$ is an *axiom*

if t is in $\mathscr{B}$ then $\mathscr{A} \Rightarrow \mathscr{B}$ is an *axiom*

So, for example, we have in particular that the following sequents are axioms:

$$f \Rightarrow, \quad \Rightarrow t, \quad f \Rightarrow t$$

(In general, when $\mathscr{A}$ is the empty set we write the sequent $\mathscr{A} \Rightarrow \mathscr{B}$ as $\Rightarrow \mathscr{B}$. Similarly, if $\mathscr{B}$ is empty, we write $\mathscr{A} \Rightarrow \mathscr{B}$ as $\mathscr{A} \Rightarrow$. If *both* $\mathscr{A}$ and $\mathscr{B}$ are empty, then $\mathscr{A} \Rightarrow \mathscr{B}$ becomes simply $\Rightarrow$. Note that, in effect, $\mathscr{A} \Rightarrow$ says "$\mathscr{A}$ is unsatisfiable", and $\Rightarrow \mathscr{B}$ says "$\mathscr{B}$ is unfalsifiable". The *empty sequent* $\Rightarrow$, as it is called, is quite obviously *false*. It says: there is no logical model that satisfies every sentence in $\{ \}$ and falsifies every sentence in $\{ \}$. But *every* logical model does that. The empty sequent, in short, couldn't be more mistaken!

Suppose, next, that in a finite sequent $\mathscr{A} \Rightarrow \mathscr{B}$ there is some sentence X *that is in both $\mathscr{A}$ and $\mathscr{B}$*. This circumstance is certainly immediately observable, or at least (if $\mathscr{A}$ and $\mathscr{B}$ are very big) detectable by a patient comparison of the two sets. Any such sequent is obviously true: there obviously can be no logical model that satisfies $\mathscr{A}$ and falsifies $\mathscr{B}$ if X is in both $\mathscr{A}$ and $\mathscr{B}$, for the model would have to contain both of the equations $v(X) = t$ and $v(X) = f$. So we can say:

if there is a sentence X that is in both $\mathscr{A}$ and $\mathscr{B}$ then $\mathscr{A} \Rightarrow \mathscr{B}$ is an axiom

It is useful to have a system of mnemonically efficient labels for the various classes of axioms. We shall say that an axiom $\mathscr{A} \Rightarrow \mathscr{B}$ is an $f \Rightarrow$-axiom if it is an axiom because f is in $\mathscr{A}$; a $\Rightarrow t$-axiom if it is an axiom because t is in $\mathscr{B}$; and an $X \Rightarrow X$-axiom if it is an axiom because the sentence X is in both $\mathscr{A}$ and $\mathscr{B}$. We can, if we like, think of $f \Rightarrow$, $\Rightarrow t$ and $X \Rightarrow X$ as the classes of axioms in question. Thus, the axiom $f \Rightarrow t$ is in both of the classes $f \Rightarrow$ and $\Rightarrow t$. Note that we have a class $X \Rightarrow X$ for each sentence X.

Consider next a finite sequent $\mathscr{A} \Rightarrow \mathscr{B}$ with the property that $\mathscr{B}$ contains the sentence:

$$(\wedge \, Y_1 \dots Y_n)$$

and $\mathscr{A}$ contains all of the sentences:

$$Y_1, \dots, Y_n$$

It is clear (referring to table 5.1) that $\mathscr{A} \Rightarrow \mathscr{B}$ is true: no logical model could satisfy $\mathscr{A}$ and also falsify $\mathscr{B}$, for it would have to contain the equations:

$$v(Y_1) = \mathbf{t}, \ldots, v(Y_n) = \mathbf{t}, v(\wedge\, Y_1 \ldots Y_n) = \mathbf{f}$$

The property in question is an immediately observable property of $\mathscr{A} \Rightarrow \mathscr{B}$. We invent an appropriate label for such sequents and have another class of axioms:

if $\mathscr{A}$ contains sentences $Y_1, \ldots, Y_n$ and $\mathscr{B}$ contains $(\wedge\, Y_1 \ldots Y_n)$, then the sequent $\mathscr{A} \Rightarrow \mathscr{B}$ is an axiom in the class:
$$Y_1, \ldots, Y_n \Rightarrow (\wedge\, Y_1 \ldots Y_n)$$

On the other hand a sequent $\mathscr{A} \Rightarrow \mathscr{B}$ in which it is $\mathscr{A}$ that contains the sentence $(\wedge\, Y_1 \ldots Y_n)$, while $\mathscr{B}$ contains one of the sentences $Y_1, \ldots, Y_n$, say Y_j, is also obviously true: no model can satisfy $\mathscr{A}$ and falsify $\mathscr{B}$ because it would have to contain the equations:

$$v(\wedge\, Y_1 \ldots Y_n) = \mathbf{t}, v(Y_j) = \mathbf{f}$$

which (as table 5.1 insists) no model can. So

if $\mathscr{A}$ contains the sentence $(\wedge\, Y_1 \ldots Y_n)$ and $\mathscr{B}$ contains Y_j, for some j, $1 \leqslant j \leqslant n$, then $\mathscr{A} \Rightarrow \mathscr{B}$ is an axiom in the class
$$(\wedge\, Y_1 \ldots Y_n) \Rightarrow Y_j$$

The pattern that is guiding us, in classifying and labelling finite sequents as various kinds of axioms, should by now be emerging. We are consulting table 5.1 and finding that each of its rows suggests another family of axiom classes. The two we have just described arise from rows A9 and A10, which deal with conjunctions. The classes $\mathbf{f}\Rightarrow$ and $\Rightarrow\mathbf{t}$ arise from rows A2 and A1 respectively.

The general scheme for the labelling is that we label a sequent $\mathscr{A} \Rightarrow \mathscr{B}$ with the *sequent*

$$Y_1, \ldots, Y_m, X \Rightarrow X_1, \ldots, X_n \tag{3}$$

or

$$X_1, \ldots, X_n \Rightarrow X, Y, \ldots, Y_m \tag{4}$$

where X is a sentence and $X_1, \ldots, X_n$, $Y_1 \ldots Y_m$ are immediate constituents of X (not necessarily *all* of the immediate constituents of X) according as table 5.1 forbids a model to contain the equations

$$v(X_1) = \mathbf{f}, \ldots, v(X_n) = \mathbf{f}, v(X) = \mathbf{t}, v(Y_1) = \mathbf{t}, \ldots, v(Y_m) = \mathbf{t} \tag{5}$$

or forbids it to contain the equations

$$v(X_1) = \mathbf{t}, \ldots, v(X_n) = \mathbf{t}, v(X) = \mathbf{f}, v(Y_1) = \mathbf{f}, \ldots, v(Y_m) = \mathbf{f} \tag{6}$$

and where (in case (3)) $X, Y_1, \ldots, Y_m$ are in $\mathscr{A}$ and $X_1, \ldots, X_n$ are in $\mathscr{B}$ or (in case (4)) $X_1, \ldots, X_n$ are in $\mathscr{A}$ and $X, Y_1, \ldots, Y_m$ are in $\mathscr{B}$.

We thus have two such families of axioms and labels for each logical symbol: one for sequents in which a sentence X occurs in $\mathscr{A}$ and has that logical symbol as its main symbol, and the other for sequents in which such a sentence occurs in $\mathscr{B}$.

In this way we can make up table 6.1, laying out the various classes of axioms. Thus any finite sequent $\mathscr{A} \Rightarrow \mathscr{B}$ is an axiom in the class labelled by the sequent $\mathscr{L} \Rightarrow \mathscr{R}$, if $\mathscr{L} \subseteq \mathscr{A}$ and $\mathscr{R} \subseteq \mathscr{B}$. In particular, $\mathscr{L} \Rightarrow \mathscr{R}$ is in the class labelled by $\mathscr{L} \Rightarrow \mathscr{R}$!

Table 6.1

		$X \Rightarrow X$	fill axiom
$f\Rightarrow$	$f \Rightarrow$	$\Rightarrow t$	$\Rightarrow t$
$\neg\Rightarrow$	$\neg Y, Y \Rightarrow$	$\Rightarrow Y, \neg Y$	$\Rightarrow\neg$
$\rightarrow\Rightarrow$	$(\rightarrow Y Z), Y \Rightarrow Z$	$Z \Rightarrow (\rightarrow Y Z)$	
		$\Rightarrow (\rightarrow Y Z), Y$	$\Rightarrow\rightarrow$
$\leftrightarrow\Rightarrow$	$(\leftrightarrow Y Z), Y \Rightarrow Z$	$Y, Z \Rightarrow (\leftrightarrow Y Z)$	$\Rightarrow\leftrightarrow$
	$(\leftrightarrow Y Z), Z \Rightarrow Y$	$\Rightarrow (\leftrightarrow Y Z), Y, Z$	
$\wedge\Rightarrow$	$(\wedge Y_1 \ldots Y_n) \Rightarrow Y_j$	$Y_1, \ldots, Y_n \Rightarrow (\wedge Y_1 \ldots Y_n)$	$\Rightarrow\wedge$
	$(1 \leqslant j \leqslant n)$		
$\vee\Rightarrow$	$(\vee Y_1 \ldots Y_n) \Rightarrow Y_1, \ldots, Y_n$	$Y_j \Rightarrow (\vee Y_1 \ldots Y_n)$	$\Rightarrow\vee$
		$(1 \leqslant j \leqslant n)$	
$\forall\Rightarrow$	$(\forall x A) \Rightarrow A[\tau/x]$	$A[*\forall x A/x] \Rightarrow (\forall x A)$	$\Rightarrow\forall$
	τ any term of *pure* (L)		
$\exists\Rightarrow$	$(\exists x A) \Rightarrow A[*\exists x A/x]$	$A[\tau/x] \Rightarrow (\exists x A)$	$\Rightarrow\exists$
		τ any term of *pure* (L)	

It is quite natural to "read" a sequent $\mathscr{A} \Rightarrow \mathscr{B}$ as saying "if all the sentences in $\mathscr{A}$ are true then at least one of the sentences in $\mathscr{B}$ is true". In reading $\mathscr{A} \Rightarrow \mathscr{B}$ like this we must be careful to remember that this is a shortened version of "for any logical model M, if all the sentences in $\mathscr{A}$ are true in M, then at least one of the sentences in $\mathscr{B}$ is true in M". Alternatively, as we have pointed out previously, we can read $\mathscr{A} \Rightarrow \mathscr{B}$ as: the conjunction of the sentences in $\mathscr{A}$ *logically implies* the disjunction of the sentences in $\mathscr{B}$.

The sequents displayed in table 6.1 and all sequents that they label are, in any case, *true sequents whose truth is immediately apparent* by virtue of the semantics of some one of the logical symbols (or in the cases $\Rightarrow \forall$ and $\exists \Rightarrow$, the semantics of $\forall$, $*$ together or $\exists$, $*$ together). The one exception to this pattern is the sequent $X \Rightarrow X$, whose truth is immediately apparent independently of the semantics of any logical symbols that X may contain. Indeed, X may not contain any: it may be a predication.

Now we have called these sequents *axioms* because they can be employed as such in certain *deductions*, by which a true sequent can be *deduced* from other true sequents. Deduction is in general a technique for "revealing" or "making obvious" the truth of true sequents when their truth is not *immediately* obvious.

To make deductions we need one or more ways – called *inference principles* or *rules of inference* – by which the truth of some sequent (called the *conclusion* of the inference) can be immediately recognised once the truth of some other sequent or sequents (called the *premisses* of the inference) has been recognised. There is one such principle, which is known as the *cut principle*, (or the *cut rule*) whose efficacy in this regard is readily apparent.

An inference made according to the cut principle always has two premisses, whose forms are very closely related. They are two sequents of the form:

$$\mathcal{A} \Rightarrow \mathcal{B} \cup \{X\} \quad \{X\} \cup \mathcal{A} \Rightarrow \mathcal{B} \tag{7}$$

where $\mathcal{A}$ and $\mathcal{B}$ are finite sets of sentences, neither of which contains the sentence X, and X is a sentence. We usually write $\{X\} \cup \mathcal{A} \Rightarrow \mathcal{B}$ as $X, \mathcal{A} \Rightarrow \mathcal{B}$; and $\mathcal{A} \Rightarrow \mathcal{B} \cup \{X\}$ as $\mathcal{A} \Rightarrow \mathcal{B}, X$. The conclusion of the inference is then the sequent:

$$\mathcal{A} \Rightarrow \mathcal{B} \tag{8}$$

Since neither $\mathcal{A}$ nor $\mathcal{B}$ contains X, it is natural to say that one obtains (8) from (7) by "cutting", or *eliminating*, the sentence X from each premiss; when this is done to either premiss, the resulting sequent is (8).

Now we wish to point out that, *if* both premisses (7) are true, *then* the conclusion (8) is. For suppose that $\mathcal{A} \Rightarrow \mathcal{B}$ is false, i.e., that there is some logical model, say M, that satisfies $\mathcal{A}$ and falsifies $\mathcal{B}$. Well: the sentence X is either true in M or false in M. Hence (in the first case) M satisfies $\{X\} \cup \mathcal{A}$ and falsifies $\mathcal{B}$, which means that $\{x\} \cup \mathcal{A} \Rightarrow \mathcal{B}$ is false. In the other case, M satisfies $\mathcal{A}$ and falsifies $\mathcal{B} \cup \{X\}$, so that $\mathcal{A} \Rightarrow \mathcal{B} \cup \{X\}$ is false.

So we can reason from (8) to (7) and say: if $\mathcal{A} \Rightarrow \mathcal{B}$ is false, then *either* $\mathcal{A} \Rightarrow \mathcal{B}, X$ or $X, \mathcal{A} \Rightarrow \mathcal{B}$, is false. Or we can reason in the other direction, from (7) to (8), and say: if *both* $\mathcal{A} \Rightarrow \mathcal{B}, X$ and $X, \mathcal{A} \Rightarrow \mathcal{B}$ are true, then $\mathcal{A} \Rightarrow \mathcal{B}$ is true.

Now by a *cut deduction* we mean a binary tree whose nodes are labelled by finite sequents in such a way that each node N that is not a tip of the tree is labelled by a sequent $\mathscr{A} \Rightarrow \mathscr{B}$, which is the *conclusion* of an inference, by the cut principle, whose premisses are the sequents labelling the two immediate successors of N:

$$\mathscr{A} \Rightarrow \mathscr{B}, X \qquad X, \mathscr{A} \Rightarrow \mathscr{B}$$
$$\mathscr{A} \Rightarrow \mathscr{B}$$

A cut deduction whose rootnode is labelled with $\mathscr{A} \Rightarrow \mathscr{B}$ is said to be a cut deduction *of $\mathscr{A} \Rightarrow \mathscr{B}$ from* the sequents $\mathscr{A}_1 \Rightarrow \mathscr{B}_1, \ldots, \mathscr{A}_n \Rightarrow \mathscr{B}_n$ that label its tips; and $\mathscr{A} \Rightarrow \mathscr{B}$ is said (generalizing the terminology already introduced for a *single* inference by the cut principle) to be the *conclusion* of the cut deduction, while $\mathscr{A}_1 \Rightarrow \mathscr{B}_1, \ldots, \mathscr{A}_n \Rightarrow \mathscr{B}_n$ are said to be its *premisses*.

When the premisses of a cut deduction whose conclusion is $\mathscr{A} \Rightarrow \mathscr{B}$ *are all axioms* the deduction is said to be a *cut proof* of $\mathscr{A} \Rightarrow \mathscr{B}$. For example, we give below a cut proof of the sequent

$$A, A \rightarrow (B \vee C), \neg B \Rightarrow C$$

For convenience, we label each axiom, and also write the "cut sentence" X as the rightmost sentence in the left premiss and the leftmost sentence in the right premiss of each cut inference:

In this style of display of a cut proof, we write the sentences of each premiss of a cut in exactly the order in which they appear in the conclusion of the cut, and write the cut sentence as the rightmost sentence, or the leftmost sentence, in the left and right premisses respectively. This convention makes it virtually effortless for the mind to verify that each cut inference really is one. Similarly, by writing above each axiom a sequent that is its label we make it virtually effortless for the mind to verify that the sequent is indeed an axiom. Let us call such a cut proof display an *annotated* cut proof.

It is clear that the conclusion of a cut proof is always a *true* sequent: for axioms are true sequents, and the conclusion of a cut inference is true if the premisses of the cut inference are true. This observation is decomposable into two observations:

> axioms are true;
> if the premisses of a cut deduction are all true
> then its conclusion is true

The second observation makes the point about cut deductions that is often expressed by saying they are *sound*; their soundness being an immediate consequence of the soundness of the cut principle itself.

What is not so immediately obvious is that *every true sequent has a cut proof*, that is, for *any* sequent $\mathscr{A} \Rightarrow \mathscr{B}$, if $\mathscr{A} \Rightarrow \mathscr{B}$ is true then there is a cut proof of $\mathscr{A} \Rightarrow \mathscr{B}$. The following argument and construction shows that this is so.

Let us take an arbitrary true finite sequent $\mathscr{A} \Rightarrow \mathscr{B}$ (in *pure (L)*) and construct a cut proof for it by the following procedure. Let $X_1, X_2, \ldots$, be an enumeration of all closed sentences of *pure (L)*. For each $n \geqslant 0$ we shall make a cut deduction of $\mathscr{A} \Rightarrow \mathscr{B}$, which we shall call D_n. The deduction D_0 is simply (the rootnode labelled by) the sequent $\mathscr{A} \Rightarrow \mathscr{B}$ itself.

Now suppose we have constructed, for some $n \geqslant 0$, the deduction D_n. This deduction will have one or more tips, the sequent at each of which will satisfy one of the conditions

(a) it is an axiom

(b) it is not an axiom, but does contain the sentence X_{n+1}

(c) it is not an axiom, and does not contain the sentence X_{n+1}

We then construct the deduction D_{n+1} from D_n by performing the following operation on each tip of kind (c), if any, in D_n. Suppose the sequent at such a tip is $\mathscr{L} \Rightarrow \mathscr{R}$. We then affix two nodes to the tip, labelled respectively by $\mathscr{L} \Rightarrow \mathscr{R}, X_{n+1}$ and $X_{n+1}, \mathscr{L} \Rightarrow \mathscr{R}$, so that $\mathscr{L} \Rightarrow \mathscr{R}$ follows from the newly affixed sequents by a cut:

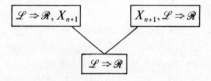

This then yields a deduction D_{n+1} of $\mathscr{A} \Rightarrow \mathscr{B}$ in which each tip sequent contains the sentence X_{n+1} or else is an axiom.

If there are no tips of kinds (b) and (c) in D_n, the construction halts: the deduction D_n is in that case a *proof* of $\mathscr{A} \Rightarrow \mathscr{B}$. Otherwise, the construction continues for at least one more cycle.

Clearly, for all $n \geqslant 1$, the deduction D_n has the property that each of its premisses is *either* an axiom *or* a sequent that contains the sentence X_n (or both).

Now, we claim that *if* $\mathscr{A} \Rightarrow \mathscr{B}$ is a true sequent, *then* the above construction will terminate after only finitely many steps, say $n \geqslant 0$. The deduction D_n will then be a *proof* of $\mathscr{A} \Rightarrow \mathscr{B}$.

For consider the sequence $D_0, D_1, \ldots$ of deductions produced by the construction if the construction does *not* terminate. This sequence can be regarded as the sequence of successive stages in the construction of a single *infinite* tree D that, by König's Lemma, will (since it is finitary, indeed binary) contain at least one infinite branch, whose sequents are, say,

$$\mathscr{A}_0 \Rightarrow \mathscr{B}_0, \mathscr{A}_1 \Rightarrow \mathscr{B}_1, \ldots, \mathscr{A}_j \Rightarrow \mathscr{B}_j \qquad (\text{with } \mathscr{A}_0 \Rightarrow \mathscr{B}_0 = \mathscr{A} \Rightarrow \mathscr{B})$$

in which (by the construction) each sequent $\mathscr{A}_j \Rightarrow \mathscr{B}_j$ is exactly like its immediate predecessor except that it contains the sentence X_j either on the left or on the right:

for all $j \geqslant 1, \mathscr{A}_j \Rightarrow \mathscr{B}_j$ is either $X_j, \mathscr{A}_{j-1} \Rightarrow \mathscr{B}_{j-1}$ or $\mathscr{A}_{j-1} \Rightarrow \mathscr{B}_{j-1}, X_j$.

Since none of $\mathscr{A}_j \Rightarrow \mathscr{B}_j$ is an axiom, no sequent contains the same sentence in both its antecedent $\mathscr{A}_j$ and its succedent $\mathscr{B}_j$.

Now let E_j $(j \geqslant 0)$ be the set of equations

$$\{v(A) = \mathbf{t} \mid A \text{ in } \mathscr{A}_j\} \cup \{v(B) = \mathbf{f} \mid B \text{ in } \mathscr{B}_j\}$$

and define E to be the set of equations.

$$\bigcup_{j=0}^{\infty} E_j = (E_0 \cup E_1 \cup \ldots \quad)$$

We can also define the infinite sequent

$$\left(\bigcup_{j=0}^{\infty} \mathscr{A}_j\right) \Rightarrow \left(\bigcup_{j=0}^{\infty} \mathscr{B}_j\right)$$

call it $\mathscr{A}_\infty \Rightarrow \mathscr{B}_\infty$, and take E to be

$$\{v(A) = \mathbf{t} \mid A \text{ in } \mathscr{A}_\infty\} \cup \{v(B) = \mathbf{f} \mid B \text{ in } \mathscr{B}_\infty\}$$

By our remarks above, E contains *exactly one* equation $v(X_j) = \dot{w}_j$ for each sentence X_j in the enumeration $X_1, X_2, \ldots$ that we used in the construction. Moreover, since none of the sequents $\mathscr{A}_j \Rightarrow \mathscr{B}_j$ is an axiom, the set E cannot violate any of the conditions of table 5.1. In short, the set E of equations is a logical model of *pure* (L). E obviously satisfies $\mathscr{A}_\infty$ and falsifies $\mathscr{B}_\infty$; hence, for each j, satisfies $\mathscr{A}_j$ and falsifies $\mathscr{B}_j$; hence (with $j = 0$), satisfies $\mathscr{A}$ and falsifies $\mathscr{B}$.

This logical model E satisfies the $\mathscr{A}$, and falsifies the $\mathscr{B}$, of the sequent $\mathscr{A} \Rightarrow \mathscr{B}$, alias $\mathscr{A}_0 \Rightarrow \mathscr{B}_0$? But it was given that $\mathscr{A} \Rightarrow \mathscr{B}$ is a *true* sequent, and hence there can be no such logical model! In that case, it must inevitably be that the sequence $D_0, D_1, \ldots$ *does* terminate after finitely many steps, say, n of them. The proof D_n of $\mathscr{A} \Rightarrow \mathscr{B}$ thus generated is, so to speak, produced by the enumeration $X_1, X_2, \ldots$ of the sentences of *pure* (L) that was used to determine the cut sentence X_j for each cut inference at level j in the proof. Different enumerations will produce different proofs of the same true sequent $\mathscr{A} \Rightarrow \mathscr{B}$, but each enumeration, no matter on what principle of ordering it is based, *must* produce a proof of $\mathscr{A} \Rightarrow \mathscr{B}$.

For example, the proof of the sequent

$$A, A \to (B \vee C), \neg B \Rightarrow C$$

which we gave earlier as an illustration, would have been generated by an enumeration that began

$$(B \vee C), B, \ldots$$

It is clear that some enumerations will produce a proof of a true sequent $\mathscr{A} \Rightarrow \mathscr{B}$ at an earlier stage in the construction than others: some enumerations are "more appropriate" than others for a given sequent. Indeed, reflection on the nature of proofs by cut shows that, for each true (hence provable) sequent $\mathscr{A} \Rightarrow \mathscr{B}$ there exists a proof D_n of *minimum* "height" n. (There will in general be several proofs of $\mathscr{A} \Rightarrow \mathscr{B}$ having that height, and some may have fewer nodes than others. For that matter, some proofs of $\mathscr{A} \Rightarrow \mathscr{B}$ of height greater than n may have fewer nodes than some proofs – or even all proofs – of height n.)

The thought immediately suggests itself that, for a given $\mathscr{A} \Rightarrow \mathscr{B}$, the enumeration might well be taken to be one of those that is, or at least appears to be, "appropriate" to $\mathscr{A} \Rightarrow \mathscr{B}$ in this sense. If one's objective is to be done as soon as possible with the construction, it will be the minimum height proofs that ideally one would like to hit upon.

The cut proofs automatically generated by this "Cut-Proof Procedure" for a true sequent $\mathscr{A} \Rightarrow \mathscr{B}$ have the interesting property that *none of their premisses are fill axioms*, except in the trivial case that $\mathscr{A} \Rightarrow \mathscr{B}$ itself is such an axiom.

It is not hard to see why this is so: if $\mathscr{A} \Rightarrow \mathscr{B}$ itself does not contain some sentence X in both its antecedent and succedent then no sequent created by the Cut-Proof Procedure will. Recall that it is only in case (c), when a tip sequent $\mathscr{L} \Rightarrow \mathscr{R}$ does not contain the sentence X_{n+1} at all, that the procedure creates new sequents from $\mathscr{L} \Rightarrow \mathscr{R}$. These are the sequents:

$$\mathscr{L} \Rightarrow \mathscr{R}, X_{n+1} \qquad X_{n+1}, \mathscr{L} \Rightarrow \mathscr{R}$$

from which $\mathscr{L} \Rightarrow \mathscr{R}$ then follows by a cut. Neither of them can contain the same sentence in both antecedent and succedent, since $\mathscr{L} \Rightarrow \mathscr{R}$ does not (it is not an axiom); and since $\mathscr{L} \Rightarrow \mathscr{R}$ does not contain X_{n+1} at all, there is no danger that in the new sequents, X_{n+1} might occur in antecedent and succedent.

So: the Cut-Proof Procedure automatically produces a cut proof for a "non-trivial" true sequent $\mathscr{A} \Rightarrow \mathscr{B}$ from axioms *none of which are fill axioms*. This says, roughly, that every true sequent has a proof exhibiting a certain "normal form".

This result is symmetrically in contrast to a well-known fact about proofs of true sequents, which was discovered by Gerhard Gentzen in the early 1930s. He found that every true sequent has a proof exhibiting a different "normal form", one feature of which is that *every* premiss is a fill axiom, while *no* inference is a cut inference! Since so far we have not encountered any inference patterns for sequents *other* than the pattern of the cut, we are not yet in a position to appreciate Gentzen's "cut-free" normal form for proofs of true sequents.

The fact is that there is a very natural family of inference *rules* for sequents, which corresponds to the family of sequent *axioms* that we have laid out in table 6.1 of this chapter. In table 6.2, we display the various kinds of sequent inference in the notation:

$$\frac{\mathscr{A}_1 \Rightarrow \mathscr{B}, \quad \ldots, \quad \mathscr{A}_n \Rightarrow \mathscr{B}_n}{\mathscr{A} \Rightarrow \mathscr{B}}$$

which says: if (the *premisses*) $\mathscr{A}_1 \Rightarrow \mathscr{B}_1, \ldots, \mathscr{A}_n \Rightarrow \mathscr{B}_n$ are true, then (the *conclusion*) $\mathscr{A} \Rightarrow \mathscr{B}$ is true; so that the cut principle is written, in this notation, as:

$$\frac{\mathscr{A} \Rightarrow \mathscr{B}, X \qquad X, \mathscr{A} \Rightarrow \mathscr{B}}{\mathscr{A} \Rightarrow \mathscr{B}}$$

The inference patterns in the table reflect an attitude to inference-making that is extremely natural. This attitude is that an inference should be associated with a particular logical symbol, and should consist of concluding that a sentence beginning with that symbol should have a certain truthvalue if certain of its immediate constituents have certain truthvalues.

For example, in the inference pattern $\neg\Rightarrow$ we deduce the sequent $\neg X, \mathcal{A} \Rightarrow \mathcal{B}$ from the premiss $\mathcal{A} \Rightarrow \mathcal{B}, X$:

$$\frac{\mathcal{A} \Rightarrow \mathcal{B}, X}{\neg X, \mathcal{A} \Rightarrow \mathcal{B}}$$

with the following rationale: if $\mathcal{A} \Rightarrow \mathcal{B}, X$ is true, i.e., if there is no model that satisfies $\mathcal{A}$ and falsifies $\mathcal{B}$ and X, then there can be no model that satisfies $\neg X$ and $\mathcal{A}$, and falsifies $\mathcal{B}$; i.e., $\neg X, \mathcal{A} \Rightarrow \mathcal{B}$ is true.

In the inference-pattern $\Rightarrow\neg$ we deduce $\mathcal{A} \Rightarrow \mathcal{B}, \neg X$ from $X, \mathcal{A} \Rightarrow \mathcal{B}$

$$\frac{X, \mathcal{A} \Rightarrow \mathcal{B}}{\mathcal{A} \Rightarrow \mathcal{B}, \neg X}$$

with essentially the same rationale: if $X, \mathcal{A} \Rightarrow \mathcal{B}$ is true, i.e. if no model satisfies X and $\mathcal{A}$ while falsifying $\mathcal{B}$, then no model can satisfy $\mathcal{A}$ while falsifying $\mathcal{B}$ and $\neg X$, i.e., $\mathcal{A} \Rightarrow \mathcal{B}, \neg X$ is true.

Note that, in both patterns, the conclusion is identical with the premiss except for the presence of X in the premiss and its absence in the conclusion and the presence of $\neg X$ in the conclusion and *its* absence in the premiss.

The same spirit pervades the other inference patterns. Let us consider the patterns associated with conjunction: $\wedge\Rightarrow$ and $\Rightarrow\wedge$. The pattern $\wedge\Rightarrow$ is:

$$\frac{X_1, \ldots, X_n, \mathcal{A} \Rightarrow \mathcal{B}}{(\wedge X_1 \ldots X_n), \mathcal{A} \Rightarrow \mathcal{B}}$$

and its explanation and justification goes as follows. If the sequent $X_1, \ldots, X_n, \mathcal{A} \Rightarrow \mathcal{B}$ is true, i.e., if there exists no model that satisfies each of $X_1, \ldots, X_n$ and $\mathcal{A}$ while falsifying $\mathcal{B}$, then there can be no model that satisfies $(\wedge X_1 \ldots X_n)$ and $\mathcal{A}$ while falsifying $\mathcal{B}$; i.e., the sequent $(\wedge X_1 \ldots X_n), \mathcal{A} \Rightarrow \mathcal{B}$ is true.

The pattern $\Rightarrow\wedge$ is:

$$\frac{\mathcal{A} \Rightarrow \mathcal{B}, X_1 \quad \ldots \quad \mathcal{A} \Rightarrow \mathcal{B}, X_n}{\mathcal{A} \Rightarrow \mathcal{B}, (\wedge X_1 \ldots X_n)}$$

The supporting reasoning for $\Rightarrow\wedge$ is that if each of the n sequents above the line are true, then for each $\mathcal{A} \Rightarrow \mathcal{B}, X_j, 1 \leqslant j \leqslant n$, it can be assumed that there is no model M_j that satisfies $\mathcal{A}$ but falsifies $\mathcal{B}$ and X_j; but, this being so, we can therefore be assured that there is no model M that satisfies $\mathcal{A}$ but falsifies $\mathcal{B}$ and $(\wedge X_1 \ldots X_n)$ – for if there were, M would in effect have to be an M_j since it would have to falsify some X_j. Hence, the sequent $\mathcal{A} \Rightarrow \mathcal{B}, (\wedge X_1 \ldots X_n)$ is true.

As one might expect, the inference patterns for disjunction are like those for conjunction, except that the rôles of truth and falsehood are interchanged. The patterns are $\vee \Rightarrow$:

$$\frac{X_1, \mathcal{A} \Rightarrow \mathcal{B} \quad \ldots \quad X_n, \mathcal{A} \Rightarrow \mathcal{B}}{(\vee X_1 \ldots X_n), \mathcal{A} \Rightarrow \mathcal{B}}$$

and $\Rightarrow \vee$:

$$\frac{\mathcal{A} \Rightarrow \mathcal{B}, X_1, \ldots, X_n}{\mathcal{A} \Rightarrow \mathcal{B}, (\vee X_1 \ldots X_n)}$$

and the reader will be able to supply their rationales by analogy with those for $\wedge \Rightarrow$ and $\Rightarrow \wedge$.

The patterns for the conditional and the biconditional are based upon essentially similar ideas. For the conditional we have $\rightarrow \Rightarrow$:

$$\frac{\mathcal{A} \Rightarrow \mathcal{B}, X \quad\quad Y, \mathcal{A} \Rightarrow \mathcal{B}}{X \rightarrow Y, \mathcal{A} \Rightarrow \mathcal{B}}$$

and $\Rightarrow \rightarrow$:

$$\frac{X, \mathcal{A} \Rightarrow \mathcal{B}, Y}{\mathcal{A} \Rightarrow \mathcal{B}, X \rightarrow Y}$$

while for the biconditional we have $\leftrightarrow \Rightarrow$:

$$\frac{X, Y, \mathcal{A} \Rightarrow \mathcal{B} \quad\quad \mathcal{A} \Rightarrow \mathcal{B}, X, Y}{X \leftrightarrow Y, \mathcal{A} \Rightarrow \mathcal{B}}$$

and $\Rightarrow \leftrightarrow$:

$$\frac{X, \mathcal{A} \Rightarrow \mathcal{B}, Y \quad\quad Y, \mathcal{A} \Rightarrow \mathcal{B}, X}{\mathcal{A} \Rightarrow \mathcal{B}, X \leftrightarrow Y}$$

and the supporting rationales are easy to supply, following the examples already given.

The four inference patterns involving generalizations, $\forall \Rightarrow$, $\exists \Rightarrow$, $\Rightarrow \forall$ and $\Rightarrow \exists$, follow essentially the same plan in their design as the Boolean combinations. The two cases $\exists \Rightarrow$ and $\Rightarrow \forall$ are simple, and reflect the semantics of exemplifications. We have for $\exists \Rightarrow$:

$$\frac{A[*\exists xA], \mathcal{A} \Rightarrow \mathcal{B}}{\exists xA, \mathcal{A} \Rightarrow \mathcal{B}}$$

and for $\Rightarrow \forall$:

$$\frac{\mathcal{A} \Rightarrow \mathcal{B}, A[*\forall xA]}{\mathcal{A} \Rightarrow \mathcal{B}, \forall xA}$$

which are self-explanatory in the light of the semantic fact that the exemplifying instance of a generalization always denotes the same truthvalue as the generalization.

The other two cases, $\forall \Rightarrow$ and $\Rightarrow \exists$, display a certain departure from the practice followed in all the other inference patterns. They are:

$$\frac{A \lfloor k \rfloor, \forall x A, \mathcal{A} \Rightarrow \mathcal{B}}{\forall x A, \mathcal{A} \Rightarrow \mathcal{B}} \qquad \frac{\mathcal{A} \Rightarrow \mathcal{B}, \exists x A, A \lfloor k \rfloor}{\mathcal{A} \Rightarrow \mathcal{B}, \exists x A}$$

The term k is any closed term, in either of the two patterns.

For the first time, we encounter inference patterns in which the sentence "introduced" into the conclusion *is already present in the premiss*. In none of the other cases is this sentence (the so-called *principal sentence* of the inference) present in premisses of the inference (it is $\neg X$ in $\neg \Rightarrow$ and $\Rightarrow \neg$; $(\wedge X_1 \ldots X_n)$ in $\wedge \Rightarrow$ and $\Rightarrow \wedge$; $(\vee X_1 \ldots X_n)$ in $\vee \Rightarrow$, and $\Rightarrow \vee$; $(X \rightarrow Y)$ in $\rightarrow \Rightarrow$ and $\Rightarrow \rightarrow$; $(X \leftrightarrow Y)$ in $\leftrightarrow \Rightarrow$ and $\Rightarrow \leftrightarrow$; $\exists x A$ in $\exists \Rightarrow$; and $\forall x A$ in $\Rightarrow \forall$).

The force of the inferences here is: we can *drop* the instance $A \lfloor k \rfloor$ from the premiss, without affecting its truth. The presence of $\forall x A$ or $\exists x A$ on the same side of $\Rightarrow$ guarantees that $A \lfloor k \rfloor$ is, in the obvious sense, "redundant". If we know $\forall x A$ is true, then we "already" know that $A \lfloor k \rfloor$ is; while if we know $\exists x A$ is false, we "already" know that $A \lfloor k \rfloor$ is. Or, giving to $\Rightarrow$ its reading "logically implies", we are saying that, e.g., if the sentences $A \lfloor k \rfloor$, $\forall x A$ and those in $\mathcal{A}$ together logically imply $\mathcal{B}$, then $\forall x A$ and $\mathcal{A}$ do so without the aid of $A \lfloor k \rfloor$.

A similar explanation suffices to justify the two inference patterns associated with $\mathbf{t}, \mathbf{f}$:

$$\frac{\mathbf{t}, \mathcal{A} \Rightarrow \mathcal{B}}{\mathcal{A} \Rightarrow \mathcal{B}} \qquad \frac{\mathcal{A} \Rightarrow \mathcal{B}, \mathbf{f}}{\mathcal{A} \Rightarrow \mathcal{B}}$$

namely that the truth of the sequents above the line is not affected if we omit the $\mathbf{t}$ or the $\mathbf{f}$: they do none of the work in the logical entailment of succedent by antecedent.

And so we have our table of inference patterns, table 6.2, whose general layout is intended to recall that of the table of axioms, table 6.1.

By a *deduction* of a sequent $\mathcal{A} \Rightarrow \mathcal{B}$ we mean a finite tree whose nodes are labelled by sequents; the rootnode is labelled by $\mathcal{A} \Rightarrow \mathcal{B}$, and all other nodes, if any, are labelled in such a way that a sequent labelling a node that is not a tip is the conclusion, according to some particular one of the rules in table 6.2, of an inference whose premisses are the sequents labelling the immediate successors of that node.

Table 6.2. The principal sentence in each rule is underlined.

rule	$\dfrac{\mathcal{A} \Rightarrow \mathcal{B}, X \qquad X, \mathcal{A} \Rightarrow \mathcal{B}}{\mathcal{A} \Rightarrow \mathcal{B}}$		cut rule
	antecedent rules	succedent rules	

	antecedent rules	succedent rules	
$t\Rightarrow$	$\dfrac{t, \mathcal{A} \Rightarrow \mathcal{B}}{\mathcal{A} \Rightarrow \mathcal{B}}$	$\dfrac{\mathcal{A} \Rightarrow \mathcal{B}, f}{\mathcal{A} \Rightarrow \mathcal{B}}$	$\Rightarrow f$
$\neg\Rightarrow$	$\dfrac{\mathcal{A} \Rightarrow \mathcal{B}, X}{\neg X, \mathcal{A} \Rightarrow \mathcal{B}}$	$\dfrac{X, \mathcal{A} \Rightarrow \mathcal{B}}{\mathcal{A} \Rightarrow \mathcal{B}, \neg X}$	$\Rightarrow\neg$
$\rightarrow\Rightarrow$	$\dfrac{\mathcal{A} \Rightarrow \mathcal{B}, X \qquad Y, \mathcal{A} \Rightarrow \mathcal{B}}{X \rightarrow Y, \mathcal{A} \Rightarrow \mathcal{B}}$	$\dfrac{X, \mathcal{A} \Rightarrow \mathcal{B}, Y}{\mathcal{A} \Rightarrow \mathcal{B}, X \rightarrow Y}$	$\Rightarrow\rightarrow$
$\leftrightarrow\Rightarrow$	$\dfrac{X, Y, \mathcal{A} \Rightarrow \mathcal{B} \qquad \mathcal{A} \Rightarrow \mathcal{B}, X, Y}{X \leftrightarrow Y, \mathcal{A} \Rightarrow \mathcal{B}}$	$\dfrac{X, \mathcal{A} \Rightarrow \mathcal{B}, Y \qquad Y, \mathcal{A} \Rightarrow \mathcal{B}, X}{\mathcal{A} \Rightarrow \mathcal{B}, X \leftrightarrow Y}$	$\Rightarrow\leftrightarrow$
$\wedge\Rightarrow$	$\dfrac{X_1, \ldots, X_n, \mathcal{A} \Rightarrow \mathcal{B}}{(\wedge X_1 \ldots X_n), \mathcal{A} \Rightarrow \mathcal{B}}$	$\dfrac{\mathcal{A} \Rightarrow \mathcal{B}, X_1 \quad \ldots \quad \mathcal{A} \Rightarrow \mathcal{B}, X_n}{\mathcal{A} \Rightarrow \mathcal{B}, (\wedge X_1 \ldots X_n)}$	$\Rightarrow\wedge$
$\vee\Rightarrow$	$\dfrac{X_1, \mathcal{A} \Rightarrow \mathcal{B} \quad \ldots \quad X_n, \mathcal{A} \Rightarrow \mathcal{B}}{(\vee X_1 \ldots X_n), \mathcal{A} \Rightarrow \mathcal{B}}$	$\dfrac{\mathcal{A} \Rightarrow \mathcal{B}, X_1, \ldots, X_n}{\mathcal{A} \Rightarrow \mathcal{B} (\vee X_1 \ldots X_n)}$	$\Rightarrow\vee$
$\forall\Rightarrow$	$\dfrac{A[k], \forall x A, \mathcal{A} \Rightarrow \mathcal{B}}{\forall x A, \mathcal{A} \Rightarrow \mathcal{B}}$	$\dfrac{\mathcal{A} \Rightarrow \mathcal{B}, A[*\forall x A]}{\mathcal{A} \Rightarrow \mathcal{B}, \forall x A}$	$\Rightarrow\forall$
$\exists\Rightarrow$	$\dfrac{A[*\exists x A], \mathcal{A} \Rightarrow \mathcal{B}}{\exists x A, \mathcal{A} \Rightarrow \mathcal{B}}$	$\dfrac{\mathcal{A} \Rightarrow \mathcal{B}, \exists x A, A[k]}{\mathcal{A} \Rightarrow \mathcal{B}, \exists x A}$	$\Rightarrow\exists$

For example, figure 6.1 shows a deduction of the sequent:

$$\Rightarrow (\exists x(A \rightarrow Qx) \rightarrow (A \rightarrow \exists x Qx))$$

In the sentences of this deduction we abbreviate the term

$$*\exists x(A \rightarrow Qx)$$

by τ. We have labelled the inferences and axioms, for convenience of the reader of the deduction who wishes to check each step and each premiss. If, as in this example, each premiss of a deduction of a sequent is an axiom, we say that the deduction is a *proof*.

In this example, we have an illustration of a proof that is *cut-free*, in that none of the inferences in it are by the cut rule. It also has the "fill-only" property that it restricts its axioms to the fill-axiom type. This is diametrically opposed to the organisation of a cut proof, which eschews fill axioms and restricts its inferences to those sanc-

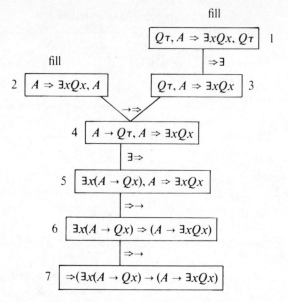

Figure 6.1

tioned by the cut rule. Let us say that a proof is *normal* if it is, like this example, both *cut-free* and *fill-only*.

Normal proofs have very nice psychological properties. Every inference step in a normal proof corresponds to some feature of the sentences in the conclusion of the proof: the sentences in the conclusion of the proof are "built up" from certain of their constituents. For example, in sequent 7 of the example, we have as the only sentence a conditional, both of whose immediate constituents are sentences – indeed, the only sentences – in sequent 6. Sequent 5 in turn is composed of the immediate constituents of one of the sentences in sequent 6, together with the remaining sentence of sequent 6. Sequent 4 is just like sequent 5 except that in place of $\exists x(A \to Qx)$ it has its exemplifying instance $(A \to Q_*\exists x(A \to Qx))$. (Note that, when the universe is the *logical* universe, the immediate constituents of generalizations are the instances that turn up in these sequent proofs). Sequents 2 and 3 are populated by the sentences in sequent 4, except for the sentence $A \to Q\tau$, which has been broken down into its immediate constituents A and $Q\tau$, which in turn are the remaining members of sequents 2 and 3.

In short, normal proofs have the *constituent* property (often called the *subformula* property) that every sentence that is a member of a sequent anywhere in the proof is a constituent of a sentence *in the conclusion of the proof.* A cut proof in general need not have the constituent property (although it may, as in our earlier example).

In view of the fact that every true sequent has a cut proof using no fill axioms it is interesting and pleasing that every true sequent also has a cut-*free* proof using *only* fill axioms. In short:

> every true sequent has a normal proof

To see why this is so, we must contemplate the properties of a certain *normal proof procedure*, which accepts as input a finite sequent $\mathscr{A} \Rightarrow \mathscr{B}$ and constructs a sequence $D_0, D_1, \ldots,$ of cut-free deductions of $\mathscr{A} \Rightarrow \mathscr{B}$ in such a way that

> D_n is a normal proof of $\mathscr{A} \Rightarrow \mathscr{B}$, for some $n \geqslant 0$, if, and only if, $\mathscr{A} \Rightarrow \mathscr{B}$ is true

If $\mathscr{A} \Rightarrow \mathscr{B}$ is false, the normal proof procedure simply continues (in general) to generate the sequence of deductions $D_0, D_1, \ldots$ indefinitely, without ever terminating. However, in certain cases it *does* terminate, even when $\mathscr{A} \Rightarrow \mathscr{B}$ is false; and in such cases the last deduction it constructs contains sufficient evidence for constructing a model that satisfies $\mathscr{A}$ and falsifies $\mathscr{B}$. As we shall see, even when the sequence $D_0, D_1, \ldots,$ continues infinitely, it may still be interpreted as specifying one or more logical models that satisfy $\mathscr{A}$ and falsify $\mathscr{B}$. The deduction D_0 is the (single node labelled by the) sequent $\mathscr{A} \Rightarrow \mathscr{B}$ itself.

The idea of the normal proof procedure is to show $\mathscr{A} \Rightarrow \mathscr{B}$ *true* by the *reductio ad absurdum* strategy, namely: to assume that it is *false*, and to arrive at a contradiction by pursuing the ramifications of that assumption. The contradiction, if forthcoming, is then conclusive evidence that $\mathscr{A} \Rightarrow \mathscr{B}$ must, after all, be true.

In applying this strategy the normal proof procedure is aided by the fact that each inference rule in table 6.2 can be read equally well "bottom-up" as "top-down". When read bottom-up, each rule says that if the sequent below the line is false, then at least one of the sequents above the line must also be false.

It may be noted that if we specify which sentence in a sequent is to serve as the principal sentence of an inference in a cut-free proof that has that sequent as its conclusion, then the *rule* by which that inference must take place is completely determined (by the operator of the principal sentence, and which side of the sequent the sentence is). Indeed not only the *rule*, but also (except in the case of $\forall \Rightarrow$ and $\Rightarrow \exists$) the *premisses* to which that rule must be applied, are completely determined.

For instance, there is only one way to infer by a non-cut rule the sequent that is the conclusion of our example proof:

$$\Rightarrow (\exists x(A \rightarrow Qx) \rightarrow (A \rightarrow \exists xQx)) \tag{9}$$

since it contains only the one sentence, and since that sentence must perforce serve as principal sentence for the inference. It being a conditional, and in the succedent, the rule must be $\Rightarrow \rightarrow$; and so the premiss must be:

$$\exists x(A \rightarrow Qx) \Rightarrow (A \rightarrow \exists xQx) \tag{10}$$

as, indeed, in our example, it is. There are now two choices for the principal sentence in the inference by which (10) may be inferred; in our example we chose the sentence in the succedent, thereby determining that the rule should again be $\Rightarrow \rightarrow$ and the premiss (up to within the order of the sentences):

$$A, \exists x(A \rightarrow Qx) \Rightarrow \exists xQx \tag{11}$$

However, we could have chosen as principal sentence for inferring (10) the sentence in its *antecedent*; *that* choice would fix the rule to be $\exists \Rightarrow$ and the premiss to be:

$$(A \rightarrow Q*\exists x(A \rightarrow Qx)) \Rightarrow (A \rightarrow \exists xQx) \tag{12}$$

and so on.

But instead of thinking of these determinations of the rule and the premisses as *a way of inferring the conclusion to be true if those premisses are*, we can equally well think of them as *a way of inferring that at least one of the premisses is false if the conclusion is.*

That is how, intuitively, the normal proof procedure looks at the rules and at the deduction D_j it has already constructed. The input sequent $\mathcal{A} \Rightarrow \mathcal{B}$ is at the rootnode of each D_j, and each D_j is a cut-free deduction of $\mathcal{A} \Rightarrow \mathcal{B}$. Hence, by the iteration of the reasoning above to support the bottom-up reading of each rule, *at least one of the premisses of D_j must be false, if $\mathcal{A} \Rightarrow \mathcal{B}$ is false.*

Each deduction D_j is transformed into the next one, D_{j+1}, by choosing a tip N_j of D_j, which is labelled by a sequent S_j that is *not* a fill axiom; and further choosing a sentence P_j in S_j to serve as principal sentence in an inference whose conclusion is to be the sequent S_j. (If D_j has no such tips, it must be a normal proof, so the whole procedure halts.) D_{j+1} is then the deduction obtained from D_j by adding one or more nodes as immediate successors of N_j, labelled by just those sequents that are required to be premisses in an inference of S_j with P_j as principal sentence.

For example, if D_1 is the deduction:

$$\boxed{\exists x(A \to Qx) \Rightarrow (A \to \exists xQx)}$$

$$\Rightarrow \to$$

$$\boxed{\Rightarrow(\exists x(A \to Qx) \to (A \to \exists xQx))}$$

then there is only one choice for N_1 and S_1, but two choices for P_1. If $\exists x(A \to Qx)$ is selected as P_1, then D_2 is:

$$\boxed{(A \to Q \ast \exists x(A \to Qx) \Rightarrow (A \to \exists xQx)}$$

$$\exists \Rightarrow$$

$$\boxed{\exists x(A \to Qx) \Rightarrow (A \to \exists xQx)}$$

$$\Rightarrow \to$$

$$\boxed{\Rightarrow(\exists x(A \to Qx) \to (A \to \exists xQx))}$$

but if $(A \to \exists xQx)$ is selected as P_1, then D_2 is:

$$\boxed{\exists x(A \to Qx), A \Rightarrow \exists xQx}$$

$$\Rightarrow \to$$

$$\boxed{\exists x(A \to Qx) \Rightarrow (A \to \exists xQx)}$$

$$\Rightarrow \to$$

$$\boxed{\Rightarrow(\exists x(A \to Qx) \to (A \to \exists xQx))}$$

The normal proof procedure must be provided therefore with a *selection rule*, which decides, given the deduction D_j, which of its tips shall be N_j, hence which of its premisses shall be S_j; and which further decides what sentences in S_j shall be the principal sentence P_j. The rule must decide also, in the particular cases when the selection of S_j and P_j determines that the inference is to be an $\forall \Rightarrow$ or an $\Rightarrow \exists$, *what the term k shall be*.

The overall behaviour of the normal proof procedure is thus a simple cycle, initiated by setting $D_0 = $ (the node labelled by) $\mathcal{A} \Rightarrow \mathcal{B}$. The cycle simply repeats the steps:

(1)   given D_j $(j \geqslant 0)$, *halt* if D_j is a normal proof; otherwise
(2)   use the *selection rule* to detemine N_j
       S_j, P_j (and, if called for, k); *halt* if no selections exist.
(3)   construct D_{j+1} from D_j by adding above N_j the premisses required to infer S_j with principal sentence P_j (using k, if the inference is $\forall \Rightarrow$ or $\Rightarrow \exists$):

(4)   change j to $j + 1$ and return to step 1.

The *halt* in step 2 may occur in some cases. The deduction D_j may be such that none of its premisses, which are not fill axioms, can be inferred by any of the non-cut rules. For example, a sequent *all of whose sentences are predications* cannot be so inferred.

We shall work with selection rules that call for a halt in step 2 *only* when D_j provides sufficient information for specifying a model that satisfies $\mathcal{A}$ and falsifies $\mathcal{B}$, i.e., shows $\mathcal{A} \Rightarrow \mathcal{B}$ to be false.

So: if the normal proof procedure halts in step 1, we have conclusive evidence (viz. the proof D_j) that $\mathcal{A} \Rightarrow \mathcal{B}$ is true; if the halt comes in step 2, we have conclusive evidence (whose cogency will be explained in the sequel) that $\mathcal{A} \Rightarrow \mathcal{B}$ is false; but it is possible that *neither* of these two events will ever occur once the procedure is set in motion. As we shall see, *this* response of the normal proof procedure is also conclusive evidence that $\mathcal{A} \Rightarrow \mathcal{B}$ is false. However, it is hardly *usable* in practice as such evidence, since the telling of it never ends!

From our overall description of the fundamental cycle of the normal proof procedure, it is clear that we can get different procedures by "plugging in" different selection rules. The selection rule fully determines what the procedure does. In particular we can find selection rules that cause the resulting procedure to fall short of the claims made for it in the previous paragraph. What we must do next is to work out selection rules that guarantee the "completeness" of the procedure.

Let us call a sentence P in a sequent S *active* if either P is a *universal generalization in the antecedent* of S, or P is an *existential generalization in the succedent* of S. A sentence in S that is not active and not a predication is passive.

Suppose a selection rule has the property that, if the deduction D_j contains any premisses at all that have one or more passive sentences in them, the rule will choose such a premiss and one of those sentences in it as S_j and P_j respectively. We then say that the selection rule *favours passivity*.

A selection rule favouring passivity in this sense gives the normal proof procedure a certain purposiveness: it is "trying" persistently to produce *deductions in which no premiss contains any passive sentence*. It is quite easy to show that with such a rule we have that, for each deduction D_j in the sequence $D_0, D_1, \ldots$ of deductions, there will be a sequence

$$D_j, D_{j+1}, \ldots, D_{j+k}$$

$(k \geqslant 0)$ starting with D_j, such that each successive deduction (if any) comes from its predecessor via the selection of a passive sentence in some premiss of that predecessor, and such that *either D_{j+k} is a normal proof or D_{j+k} has no premiss containing a passive sentence*.

In the latter case we say the deduction D_{j+k} is *passively developed*. A passively developed deduction is thus one each of whose premisses is *either* a fill axiom *or* a sequent *containing only predications and (possibly) active sentences*.

A selection rule that favours passivity will therefore be required to select an active sentence *only* when there are no premisses left that contain passive ones. One of the possibilities is that there are no premisses that contain *active* sentences either. That is one of the main circumstances under which a *halt* is called for in step 2 – no selections exist, either passive or active. In general, however, the selection rule must be prepared to decide which of several active sentences to select, and must furthermore be prepared to specify a closed term k.

Consider again the deduction shown in figure 6.1. It is D_5 in the sequence sketched below (using the numbering of the nodes used in figure 6.1):

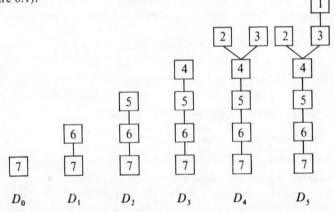

$$D_0 \qquad D_1 \qquad D_2 \qquad D_3 \qquad D_4 \qquad D_5$$

D_4 is a passively developed deduction. Premiss 2 of D_4 is a fill axiom, but premiss 3 is not, and contains the active sentence $\exists x Q x$ in its succedent. This being the only active sentence in D_4, it is selected; and thus $\Rightarrow \exists$ will be used to infer 3. The term k selected is the term $*\exists x(A \to Qx)$, *which was already introduced in going from D_2 to D_3, when $\exists \Rightarrow$ was the selected rule and 5 the selected premiss.

What was it about this particular term k which caused it to be selected by the selection rule in going from D_4 to D_5? What *other* terms might have been selected instead? We are at the heart of the matter, with these two questions.

The normal proof procedure is always brought into action for a specific sequent $\mathscr{A} \Rightarrow \mathscr{B}$ whose sentences are taken from some pure calculus *pure* (L): if the L is not specified, we can take it to be the smallest set of non-logical (i.e. constructor and predicate) symbols for which *pure* (L) contains all sentences that appear in $\mathscr{A}$ and $\mathscr{B}$.

The term k mentioned in the inference rules $\forall \Rightarrow$ and $\Rightarrow \exists$ has hitherto been only rather generally restricted to "any closed term", meaning any closed term in *pure* (L), the pure calculus that is the context of the sequent $\mathscr{A} \Rightarrow \mathscr{B}$ we are considering. Now, indeed, k may *be* any closed term of *pure* (L), as far as the *correctness* of rules $\forall \Rightarrow$ and $\Rightarrow \exists$ is concerned. But in the normal proof procedure we can, it turns out, restrict, with great advantage, the choice of k to a much "smaller" set of the closed terms in *pure* (L) than the set of *all* closed terms. (We use apologetic quotes because in general the "smaller" set is also countably infinite, and so is *not* smaller in the strict sense! We should perhaps say, *simpler*.)

Note that the smallest lexicon L such that the proved sequent of figure 6.1 has all its sentences in *pure* (L) is $\{A, Q\}$, where A is in P_0 and Q is in P_1. There are no *constructors* in this lexicon. Consequently, the *only* closed terms k in *pure* (L) are the exemplifications, such as the very one

$$*\exists x(A \rightarrow Qx)$$

which is used in this deduction.

But of course, *pure* (L) contains infinitely many such exemplifications. In addition to the one above, there are

$$*\exists x Qx, \ *\forall x(\neg Qx \rightarrow Qx), \ \ldots$$

and so on. Why, then, was it that $*\exists x(A \rightarrow Qx)$ was chosen in passing from D_4 to D_5, and not any of these other exemplifications?

The answer is: the term $*\exists x(A \rightarrow Qx)$ was *generated* (in going from D_2 to D_3) *by the normal proof procedure itself*: it was brought into the deduction in the act of applying an *exemplification rule* of inference (i.e. $\exists \Rightarrow$ or $\Rightarrow \forall$; it was $\exists \Rightarrow$ in this case), which act, so to speak, *created* the term out of the principal sentence (i.e., in this case, the sentence $\exists x(A \rightarrow Qx)$) that was selected (as a *passive* sentence) for the application of the inference rule.

In general, in any deduction D_j built by the first j cycles of the normal proof procedure, there will be a set, call it E_j, of exemplifications *that have been introduced into D_j* by applications of $\exists \Rightarrow$ or $\Rightarrow \forall$. In our example, we have

$$E_0 = E_1 = E_2 = \{\ \}; \quad E_3 = E_4 = \{*\exists x(A \rightarrow Qx)\}$$

We can also define, for each D_j, the set U_j of all closed terms in *pure* (L) that are either exemplifications in E_j or else are constructions built up, using constructors in L, from these exemplifications, in all possible ways.

For example, if instead of the lexicon $\{A, Q\}$ for the deduction of figure 6.1 we had used the lexicon $\{A, Q, g, h, n\}$, where g is in C_1, h is in C_2, and n is in C_0, then we would have had

$$U_0 = U_1 = U_2 = \{n, (g\ n), (h\ n\ n), (g(h\ n\ n)), (h\ n(g\ n)), \ldots\ \}$$

since these terms are built up using only constructors from the lexicon and exemplifications in E_0, E_1, E_2 (of which there are none). But we would then have had:

$$U_3 = U_4 = \{n, *\exists x(A \to Qx), (g\ n), (g*\exists x(A \to Qx)), \ldots,\ \}$$

since E_3 now contains $*\exists x(A \to Qx)$.

The set U_j is called *the self-generated universe of D_j*, and is the set from which the selection rule (if D_j is passively developed) must select its k. Moreover, the selected k must not have been used before to instantiate the same selected active sentence, anywhere on the branch leading to the selected premiss. With the selection rule thus limited in how it may select its k for applications of $\forall \Rightarrow$ and $\Rightarrow \exists$, we must *still* say *which* k is actually selected. This point will be discussed in full, very soon. But note: in the deduction of figure 6.1, the normal proof procedure actually had only *one* choice available for the term k, in passing from D_4 to D_5. It is *that* choice, namely of $*\exists x(A \to Qx)$, which was therefore taken.

As the deduction of figure 6.1 shows, the normal proof procedure, which is equipped with a selection rule that favours passivity and which is restricted to the self-generated universe of a deduction for its choices of terms for use with $\forall \Rightarrow$ and $\Rightarrow \exists$, may well march straight to a normal proof of its input sequent in an almost completely determined way – the only room for choice being within the "passive" sequences of cycles when there is leeway as to *which* passive sentences are selected.

The limitation of the selected terms k to the self-generated universe of the deduction also causes *halts* in step 2 where they might not otherwise (with more liberal criteria for k) occur. Consider, for example, the sequent:

$$\forall x(Ax \to Bx), \exists xBx \Rightarrow \exists xAx$$

It is, as it happens, false (it says "if all A's are B's, and there are some B's, then there must be some A's": try that out with A's as unicorns and *B*'s as quadrupeds). Let us see what the normal proof procedure will do with this sequent, when its selection rule not only favours passivity but also is limited to self-generated universes.

The first deduction D_0 is:

$$1 \quad \boxed{\forall x(Ax \to Bx), \exists xBx \Rightarrow \exists xAx}$$

The only passive sentence is $\exists xBx$ in the antecedent, so the second deduction is D_1:

$$2 \quad \boxed{B*\exists xBx, \forall x(Ax \to Bx) \Rightarrow \exists xAx}$$

$$\exists \Rightarrow$$

$$1 \quad \boxed{\forall x(Ax \to Bx), \underline{\exists xBx} \Rightarrow \exists xAx}$$

and the self-generated universe U_1 *is:* $\{*\exists xBx\}$. Now D_1 is passively developed, with two active sentences. Selection of the first of these, $\forall x(Ax \to Bx)$, produces the deduction D_2:

$$3 \quad \boxed{B*\exists xBx, (A*\exists xBx \to B*\exists xBx), \forall x(Ax \to Bx) \Rightarrow \exists xAx}$$

$$\forall \Rightarrow, *\exists xBx$$

$$2 \quad \boxed{B*\exists xBx, \underline{\forall x(Ax \to Bx)} \Rightarrow \exists xAx}$$

$$\exists \Rightarrow$$

$$1 \quad \boxed{\forall x(Ax \to Bx), \underline{\exists xBx} \Rightarrow \exists xAx}$$

with $U_2 = U_1 = \{*\exists xBx\}$. D_2 now has a passive sentence in its only premiss, viz. the conditional in the antecedent. D_3 is therefore:

$$5 \quad \boxed{B*\exists xBx, \forall x(Ax \to Bx) \Rightarrow \exists xAx}$$

$$4 \quad \boxed{B*\exists xBx, \forall x(Ax \to Bx) \Rightarrow \exists xAx, A*\exists xBx}$$

$$\to \Rightarrow$$

$$3 \quad \boxed{B*\exists xBx, (A*\exists xBx \to B*\exists xBx), \forall x(Ax \to Bx) \Rightarrow \exists xAx}$$

$$\forall \Rightarrow, *\exists xBx$$

$$2 \quad \boxed{B*\exists xBx, \underline{\forall x(Ax \to Bx)} \Rightarrow \exists xAx}$$

$$\exists \Rightarrow$$

$$1 \quad \boxed{\forall x(Ax \to Bx), \underline{\exists xBx} \Rightarrow \exists xAx}$$

D_3 is now passively developed. Its active sentences are now:

$\forall x(Ax \to Bx)$ in the antecedent of the first premiss and also in that of the second premiss;

$\exists xAx$ in the succedent of the first premiss and also in that of the second premiss.

If we select $\exists xAx$ in the second premiss, D_4 is:

6 | $B * \exists xBx, \forall x(Ax \to Bx) \Rightarrow A * \exists xBx$

$\Rightarrow \exists, * \exists xBx$

5 | $B * \exists xBx, \forall x(Ax \to Bx) \Rightarrow \underline{\exists xAx}$

4 | $B * \exists xBx, \forall x(Ax \to Bx) \Rightarrow \exists xAx, A * \exists xBx$

$\to \Rightarrow$

3 | $B * \exists xBx, (A * \exists xBx \to B * \exists xBx), \forall x(Ax \to Bx) \Rightarrow \exists xAx$

$\forall \Rightarrow, * \exists xBx$

2 | $B * \exists xBx, \underline{\forall x(Ax \to Bx)} \Rightarrow \exists xAx$

$\exists \Rightarrow$

1 | $\forall x(Ax \to Bx), \underline{\exists xBx} \Rightarrow \exists xAx$

and now if we select $\exists xAx$ in the first premiss, D_5 is:

7 | $B * \exists xBx, \forall x(Ax \to Bx) \Rightarrow A * \exists xBx, \exists xAx$

$\Rightarrow \exists, * \exists xBx$

6 | $B * \exists xBx, \forall x(Ax \to Bx) \Rightarrow A * \exists xBx, \exists xAx$

$\Rightarrow \exists, * \exists xBx$

5 | $B * \exists xBx, \forall x(Ax \to Bx) \Rightarrow \underline{\exists xAx}$

4 | $B * \exists xBx, \forall x(Ax \to Bx) \Rightarrow \underline{\exists xAx}, A * \exists xBx$

$\to \Rightarrow$

3 | $B * \exists xBx, (A * \exists xBx \to B * \exists xBx), \forall x(Ax \to Bx) \Rightarrow \exists xAx$

$\forall \Rightarrow, * \exists xBx$

2 | $B * \exists xBx, \underline{\forall x(Ax \to Bx)} \Rightarrow \exists xAx$

$\exists \Rightarrow$

1 | $\forall x(Ax \to Bx), \underline{\exists xBx} \Rightarrow \exists xAx$

In D_5, there are two *branches*, terminating in the two premisses. The active sentences in those premisses have been selected, somewhere along the branch, and have been instantiated, with respect to all of the terms in U_5, (there being only one, $*\exists xBx$). Since the term selected must not have previously been selected, to instantiate the *same* selected sentence, anywhere along the branch of the deduction that leads to the selected premiss, we see that in D_5 we have run out of selections for the selection rule to make; so we get a halt, in step 2, of the normal proof procedure.

Now D_5 is not a normal proof, nor indeed a proof of any kind. What it is, however, is a piece of evidence that certainly shows the sequent

$$\forall x(Ax \to Bx), \exists xBx \Rightarrow \exists xAx$$

to be false, by providing us with a description of a model of *applied* (L, U_5). The set $U_5 = \{*\exists xBx\}$ is the set of individuals of the model. Next we choose some branch (say, the one leading to sequent 7) in the deduction which does *not* lead to a fill axiom. (There are none that *do*, in this deduction.) We then form the set M_0 of equations $v(X) = w$ such that X is a sentence of a sequent on this branch, and w is **t** if X is in the antecedent, and **f** if X is in the succedent. In the present case, this yields the equations:

$$
\begin{aligned}
v(\forall x(Ax \to Bx)) &= \mathbf{t} \\
v(\exists xBx) &= \mathbf{t} \\
v(\exists xAx) &= \mathbf{f} \\
v(B*\exists xBx) &= \mathbf{t} \\
v(A*\exists xBx \to B*\exists xBx) &= \mathbf{t} \\
v(A*\exists xBx) &= \mathbf{f}
\end{aligned}
$$

This set M_0 of equations can now be expanded to a *total valuation M* of *applied* $(\{A, B\}, \{*\exists xBx\})$ by a construction that provides, for each closed formula X in *applied* $(\{A, B\}, \{*\exists xBx\})$, the equation $v(X) = w$ that is to go into M for that X.

The equations $v(\mathbf{t}) = \mathbf{t}$ and $v(\mathbf{f}) = \mathbf{f}$ go into M.

For all terms X that are individuals in the universe we put the equation $v(X) = X$ into M. In the present example, there is only one such term; so in this case we put into M the equation

$$v(*\exists xBx) = *\exists xBx.$$

Next we must put into M equations for all *basic* formulas. (Recall that these are the predications and constructions whose immediate constituents are individuals.) In the present example there are no basic *constructions*. In the general case we shall, for each basic construction X, simply put the equation $v(X) = X$ into M; this will be because the universes U we deal with will always have the property that whenever the entities $u_1, \ldots, u_n$ are in U, so is the basic construction $(\Omega\, u_1 \ldots u_n)$, for each n-ary constructor Ω in the lexicon.

For each basic *sentence* X we choose our equation for X as follows. If the set M_0 contains an equation for X, we put *that* equation into M. Otherwise, we choose an arbitrary truthvalue w (say, $\mathbf{t}$, to be specific) and put the equation $v(X) = w$ into M. In the present case, there are only two basic sentences in the applied calculus we are considering: $A * \exists x B x$ and $B * \exists x B x$. There is an equation for each in our set M_0; so these equations go into M.

We now have equations in M for all closed formulas X such that:

X is a truthvalue or an individual
X is a basic formula

It is now necessary to add equations to M for each closed formula in the applied calculus in such a way that M is a total valuation of it. We must add these equations level by level, so that when we decide what equation to add to M for a closed formula X we will have already decided on the equations to add to M for all constituents of X, and all parts of X that are closed. In doing this we shall observe the constraints imposed by the definition of total valuations, as laid down in tables 5.1 and 5.2.

Consider, then, a formula X for which we have not yet determined an equation $v(X) = w$ to be added to M; and suppose that we *have* determined equations, and have added them already to M, for all closed formulas that are constituents of X, or parts of X. Well, X is either a term or a sentence. Let us take the first possibility.

If X is a term, it is either a construction or an exemplification. If it is a construction, say, $(\Omega\, X_1 \ldots X_n)$, then since $X_1, \ldots, X_n$ are constituents of X we have equations for them in M, say:

$$v(X_1) = w_1, \ldots, v(X_n) = w_n$$

and we also have the equation for the basic term $(\Omega\, w_1 \ldots w_n)$:

$$v(\Omega\, w_1 \ldots w_n) = (\Omega\, w_1 \ldots w_n)$$

hence condition B1 of table 5.2 obliges us to add to M the equation:

$$v(X) = (\Omega\, w_1 \ldots w_n)$$

If, on the other hand, the term X is an exemplification, say, $*Y$, then we have an equation, say,

$$v(Y) = w$$

in M for the generalization Y, since Y is a part of $*Y$. Furthermore we have in M equations for each instance $Y[k]$ of Y, where k is an individual in the universe, for these instances are constituents of Y. Hence the set of individuals

$$\{k \mid v(Y[k]) = w \text{ is an equation in } M\}$$

(where w is the truthvalue assigned to Y by the equation for Y in M) is well-determined by the current contents of M. We are now at liberty to choose, by any means we like, an individual u from this set and put into M the equation $v(X) = u$, i.e.

$$v(*Y) = u$$

thereby satisfying the constraint laid down in B2 of table 5.2.

This then takes care of X, if X is a term. Suppose X is a sentence. We have three cases: X is a predication; X is a Boolean combination; X is a generalization.

If X is a *predication*, say $(\Omega\, X_1 \ldots X_n)$, we determine the equation for it by essentially the same process as for the case when X is a construction. For M will already contain equations

$$v(X_1) = w_1, \ldots, v(X_n) = w_n, v(\Omega\, w_1 \ldots w_n) = w$$

and so we have no choice (in view of B1) but to add to M the equation $v(X) = w$.

If X is a *Boolean combination*, say $(\Omega\, X_1 \ldots X_n)$, we have essentially the same case once again. M will contain equations

$$v(X_1) = w_1, \ldots, v(X_n) = w_n$$

for the immediate constituents of X, and so the relevant conditions of table 5.1 will completely determine the equation $v(X) = w$ for X that must be added to M.

If X is a *generalization*, then M will already contain equations $v(X[k]) = w_k$ for the various instances $X[k]$ of X with respect to individuals k in the universe. If X is universal, and the w_k are all **t** then we add $v(X) = \mathbf{t}$ to M, otherwise $v(X) = \mathbf{f}$; but if X is existential, and the w_k are all **f**, we add the equation $v(X) = \mathbf{f}$ to M, otherwise $v(X) = \mathbf{t}$.

Thus, level by level, we determine equations to be put into M for *all* closed formulas X of the applied calculus. In particular we determine equations for those closed sentences for which we already *have* equations picked out, in M_0. What we want is that $M_0 \subseteq M$ – i.e. that the total valuation M agrees with M_0 whenever they both have equations for the same sentence, X. We saw to it that this was so when the sentence X was a *basic* sentence – for then, if M_0 contained an equation for X, it was *that* equation which went into M.

What about the agreement between M_0 and M when X is a sentence, *not* a basic one, for which both M_0 and M contain an equation? It turns out that they must always agree. For suppose not: then there would be a simplest sentence X such that M_0 contains an equation $v(X) = w$ and M contains $v(X) = \bar{w}$ where w and $\bar{w}$ are distinct truthvalues. X cannot be *basic*. But then the equations in M_0 and M for the immediate constituents of X must agree; and since M_0 is "downwards consistent" with table 5.1, the equation for X in M_0 must satisfy the constraints of table 5.1 as does that for X in M. So w and $\bar{w}$ must in fact be the same. Hence M_0 and M agree whenever they have equations for the same sentence; $M_0 \subseteq M$.

What is this "M_0 is downwards consistent with table 5.1" claim, which just popped up like a *deus ex machina*? It is the nub of the whole construction. What it means is that whenever M_0 contains an equation of the form mentioned in some row the *left* column of table 5.1, then it *also* contains equations as specified in the corresponding row of the *right* column of table 5.1.

For example, if M_0 contains the equation

$v(\wedge\, Y\, Z) = \mathbf{t}$

then it *also* contains the equations

$v(Y) = \mathbf{t}$ and $v(Z) = \mathbf{t}$

while if M_0 contains the equation

$v(\exists x Q x) = \mathbf{f}$

then it also contains all the equations

$v(Q k) = \mathbf{f}$

for every individual k in the universe: and so on.

The point is that sets of equations M_0 defined by some branch of a deduction generated by the normal proof procedure *must* be downwards consistent with table 5.1 in the described sense, if none of the sequents on the branch are fill axioms. This is the case, as in our example, when the procedure halts in step 2 and we take M_0 from a branch whose tip is not a fill axiom; and it is also the case, in general, when the branch is infinite. The upshot is that since $M_0 \subseteq M$, M satisfies $\mathcal{A}$ and falsifies $\mathcal{B}$, and thus shows $\mathcal{A} \Rightarrow \mathcal{B}$ to be false.

In our example, we have thus found that the sequent

$\forall x(A x \to B x),\ \exists x B x \Rightarrow \exists x A x$

is false, and we have been provided with a model whose universe has one member, namely the closed term $*\exists x B x$, in which the basic sentences $A*\exists x B x$ and $B*\exists x B x$ are false and true respectively. In this model, the sentences $\forall x (A x \rightarrow B x)$ and $\exists x B x$ are both true, but the sentence $\exists x A x$ is false.

It remains to discuss the details of the selection rule for the normal proof procedure, on which rests the claim that the sets M_0 are always downwards consistent with table 5.1.

In the general case we have to be able to provide a set M_0 of equations that is downwards consistent with table 5.1, whenever the normal procedure does not halt in step 1. This may mean, as in our example, that the procedure halts in step 2; in that case M_0 is a *finite* set taken from any branch of the deduction that does not lead to a fill axiom.

When the normal proof procedure does not halt, it generates an infinite tree D, of which $D_1, D_2, \ldots$, are simply finite initial subtrees. The set M_0 of equations is then taken from some infinite branch, say R, of D. R is an infinite sequence

$$\mathscr{A}_0 \Rightarrow \mathscr{B}_0, \mathscr{A}_1 \Rightarrow \mathscr{B}_1, \ldots$$

of sequents $\mathscr{A}_i \Rightarrow \mathscr{B}_i$, in which $\mathscr{A}_0 \Rightarrow \mathscr{B}_0$ is the given sequent $\mathscr{A} \Rightarrow \mathscr{B}$. Indeed, if we form the sets of sentences

$$T = \bigcup_i \mathscr{A}_i \text{ and } F = \bigcup_i \mathscr{B}_i$$

then M_0 is just the set of equations $v(X) = \mathbf{t}$, for X in T, and $v(X) = \mathbf{f}$, for X in F.

We have to take care, in designing the selection rule that creates the infinite tree D, and hence each infinite branch R, that M_0 is downwards consistent with table 5.1. For only then can we argue successfully that there exists a model M, with $M_0 \subseteq M$, in which all sequents $\mathscr{A}_i \Rightarrow \mathscr{B}_i$ are true.

The universe U of the model M is going to be the *union* of all the sets U_j associated with the deductions D_j. These "self-generated universes" for each D_j are pooled to form a single "self-generated universe" for D.

Recall how U_j is defined. It is the set of all closed terms that can be constructed, using constructors from the lexicon of the calculus from which the sentences in $\mathscr{A}$ and $\mathscr{B}$ are taken, from the exemplifications in the set E_j. Recall that E_j is the set of exemplifications introduced into D_j by applications of $\exists \Rightarrow$ or $\Rightarrow \forall$. Now, in general, U_j is infinite. The set U, also infinite, is thus introduced, as it were, layer by layer, as the deductions D_j come along one by one.

Suppose M_0 contains the equation $v(X) = \mathbf{t}$, where X is a universal generalization. Then table 5.1 says M_0 *must also contain the equation* $v(X[k]) = \mathbf{t}$ *for every k in U*. (Similarly, for M_0's containing $v(X) = \mathbf{f}$ with X an existential generalization.)

The equation $v(X) = \mathbf{t}$ will be in M_0 only if X is in $\mathscr{A}_j$, for some j – but then as an *active* sentence of $\mathscr{A}_j \Rightarrow \mathscr{B}_j$, it will be in $\mathscr{A}_m$ for *all* $m \geqslant j$. Active sentences of a sequent always occur in the premisses of that sequent.

The requirement that $v(X[k]) = \mathbf{t}$ be in M_0 for all k in U translates to the requirement that *for each k in U* there must be some sequent on the branch R that is inferred from its successor by $\forall \Rightarrow$ with k as the term.

The same remarks apply, *mutatis mutandis*, when $v(X) = \mathbf{f}$ is in M_0 and X is an existential generalization.

The selection rule must be designed, therefore, in such a way that on every infinite branch of D every active sentence is selected infinitely many times, once for each k in U, as the principal sentence in an inference, using k, of its sequent by $\forall \Rightarrow$ (or $\Rightarrow \exists$, as the case may be). Selection rules that do this are a little intricate to describe. We shall explain the design ideas for one such rule, essentially due to Kleene in §50 of his book *Mathematical Logic*. In Kleene's rule, there are two "states" to be distinguished for the workings of the normal proof procedure. We shall call these the *passive* state and the *active* state.

In the passive state of the procedure, Kleene's selection rule operates as a passivity-preferring selection rule, persistently selecting passive sentences and extending the finite deductions accordingly, until no passive sentences are left.

Thereupon, the normal proof procedure *switches to the active state*. With the proof procedure in the active state, Kleene's selection rule no longer prefers passive sentences, even when, as in general happens, its selections cause some to come into existence. Rather, it prefers active sentences to passive ones: and persistently selects active sentences until each has been selected with respect to every k satisfying a condition that we shall now describe.

At the moment when the procedure switches from the passive state to the active state, there is in general a collection of active sentences, say,

$$S_j = \{X_1, \ldots, X_n\} \tag{13}$$

each in a premiss of the (passively developed) current deduction D_j, which is not a fill axiom. We call these *the active sentences of the state*. During the lifetime of the active state, other active sentences may come into existence as the normal proof procedure continues to cycle and produce more and more of the tree; but these are not counted as active sentences of the state. Only those in (13) are so dignified, the ones that were in existence at the beginning of the state's lifetime.

Furthermore, at the moment when the procedure switches from the passive to the active state, several "layers" of the self-generated universe U of D will already have come into existence. Indeed, the deduction D_j will have generated the universe U_j; but this will be a union

$$U_j = U_1 \cup U_2 \cup \ldots \cup U_j$$

in which each earlier self-generated universe is in general extended to the next one by the creation of a new exemplification $*A$ and hence of all closed terms which contain $*A$. (Of course the next universe may be simply the same as the previous one, if no exemplification is introduced by the inference by which the next deduction extends the previous one.)

Let us actually define these *layers* of U_j. As each new exemplification $*A_1$, $*A_2$, ... is introduced, we immediately have an extended universe that contains all of the previous terms but now has a new, infinite collection of terms

$$\{k_{i1}, k_{i2}, \ldots \} \tag{14}$$

in which $*A_i$ actually occurs. Let us call (14) the *layer* L_i. In general a new exemplification $*A_i$ is not created at each step of the proof procedure, and so we have:

$$U_j = L_1 \cup L_2 \cup \ldots \cup L_{j'}$$

where $j' \leqslant j$. Now, we must suppose that each of these layers L_i is enumerated:

$$L_1 = k_{11}\, k_{12} \ldots$$
$$L_2 = k_{21}\, k_{22} \ldots$$
$$\ldots$$
$$L_{j'} = k_{j'1}\, k_{j'2} \ldots \tag{15}$$

giving a layout of U_j as a j'-rowed infinite table, and indeed, for the entire infinite tree, giving a layout of the whole universe U as a table with infinitely many rows and columns.

Now, Kleene's selection rule is going to select the active sentences in (13) repeatedly until each of them has been selected for every term k in U_j that occurs in any of *the first j columns* of the table (15), in every branch of the resulting deduction. There are at most j^2 of these terms, so eventually this goal will have been accomplished. Thereupon, the lifetime of *this* active state is completed, and the procedure switches back to the passive state. Let K_j be the set of terms k that occurs in any of the first j columns of the table (15).

With Kleene's selection rule governing its behaviour, the normal proof procedure exhibits a rhythmic alternation between active and passive states. During each passive state, the tree is developed to the point where it no longer contains any premisses with passive sentences in them, except possibly for some premisses that may be fill axioms. During the ensuing active state, the deduction D_j as it then stands is extended, by $\forall \Rightarrow$ and $\Rightarrow \exists$ rules alone, to one, say D_m, in which every active sentence of the state has been instantiated with respect to every term k in K_j on every branch in which it occurs.

The plan behind Kleene's selection rule is such that every infinite branch of the infinite tree D, generated by the procedure when it does not halt, has the properties necessary for the corresponding set M_0 of equations to be downwards consistent with table 5.1. The idea behind its behaviour in the active state is simply that, as active state succeeds active state (separated by passive states in each of which, so to speak, the passive consequences of the preceding active state are pursued to completion) the branches of D take in more and more of the terms in U. No term in U can escape; eventually it will be reached, in some active state; and at that time it will be used to instantiate every active sentence of that active state, on every branch in which it occurs.

This long discussion, when the pieces are all pulled together, has established that

> every true sequent has a normal proof

in a rather strong sense; since the normal proof provided by the procedure satisfies an extra condition that not all normal proofs need satisfy.

The extra condition is that, in all applications of the rules $\forall \Rightarrow$ and $\Rightarrow \exists$ in the proof, the term k can be restricted to lie in what might be called a "natural universe" for the sequent, namely, the self-generated universe of some deduction generated for the sequent by the normal proof procedure. We might therefore express the outcome of the discussion as being that

> every true sequent has a natural normal proof

the extra adjective signifying the extra condition that we now know the normal proof can be made to satisfy.

We do not seriously suggest that the normal proof procedure should be used, as stated, for the purposes of *seeking* a proof of a sequent. One can very frequently do much better than it will do, in finding a proof of a given sequent.

Even when the terms k can be restricted, in instantiation steps ($\forall \Rightarrow$ and $\Rightarrow \exists$ steps), to those in the natural universe of the problem, it is still entirely possible to choose k "inappropriately". The inappropriateness affects the *efficiency* of one's search, and the *size* of the proof one finally obtains: for some instantiations may not in fact be necessary in a given proof and could, if one had only known this was so, have been omitted.

For example, suppose we wish to prove the sequent:

$$\forall x(Hx \rightarrow Mx), (H(F\,S)) \Rightarrow (M(F\,S))$$

in which the lexicon H, M, F, S has the character: H, M are in P_1, F is in C_1, and S is in C_0. This sequent might have arisen, for instance, from the argument:

> all humans are mortal, the father of Socrates is a human,
> $\therefore$ the father of Socrates is mortal.

Now the self-generated universe of this sequent is the set

$$\{S, (F\,S), (F(F\,S)), \dots \quad \}$$

and we have a proof very quickly if we select from it the "appropriate" term for the inference by $\forall \Rightarrow$, which is the only one available for inferring it:

The term $(F\,S)$ is, however, not the only one eligible for selection. We could have tried S first, but this would have led nowhere. Only when $(F\,S)$ is used, on every active sentence in every branch of the deduction, will we finally get our proof, and it will be littered with the useless debris of the "inappropriate" selections. For example, choosing S first, and then $(F\,S)$, gives the proof shown opposite:

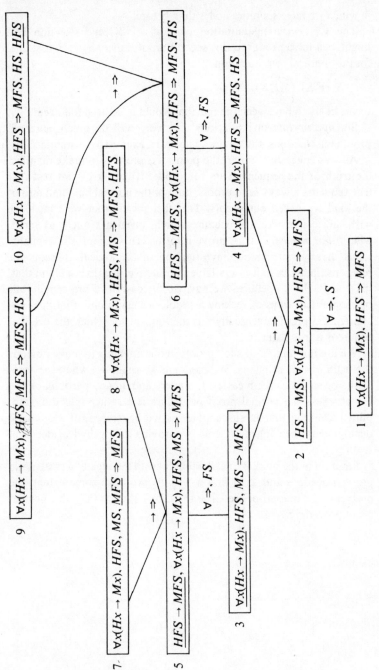

in which we have six more nodes than before.

The *systematic* instantiation plan of the Kleene selection rule might well have produced this second proof rather than the first one, for the "natural" enumeration

$$S, (F\ S), (F(F\ S)), \ldots,$$

seems likely to have been the one that would have been followed.

So: *appropriate* instantiations may very well do much better, in proof constructions, than mere systematic, exhaustive instantiations.

As was suggested earlier, the point of a proof is to make manifest the truth of the sequent at its root node. It is of great interest that true sequents always *have* proofs, both of the normal kind and also of the kind we called cut proofs. This fact means that we can, if we wish, always invoke a procedure which, given a sequent as input, will, *if that sequent is true*, prove it for us. This recourse is available to us at any time in our investigation of the logical consequence relationship; at least, it is available in principle. We do not claim that, in general, the procedures we have so far described are expeditious or economical ways of seeking a proof. We claim only that they will construct a proof "eventually", if the sequent for which the proof is sought is a true sequent.

We are not *limited* to such proofs in our attempts to make obvious the truth of true sequents. We can, and we shall, use whatever arguments or evidence seem easiest to understand, in any particular case. Nevertheless the normal proof procedure is a rather splendid, standard technique that is susceptible, as we have seen, of systematic deployment when ingenuity fails to provide the desired evidence of truth.

Later on in the book we shall again take up the idea of a systematic proof procedure and shall find a way to avoid, to some extent, the problem of "inappropriate" instantiations that afflicts the normal proof procedure.

When each of two closed sentences X and Y is a logical consequence of the other, both of the sequents

$$X \Rightarrow Y \text{ and } Y \Rightarrow X$$

are true, and we say that X and Y are *logically equivalent*. We can then, for short, write the "double sequent", or "equivalence":

$$X \Leftrightarrow Y$$

For example, the equivalences

$$A \wedge (B_1 \vee \ldots \vee B_n) \Leftrightarrow (A \wedge B_1) \vee \ldots \vee (A \wedge B_n)$$
$$(B_1 \vee \ldots \vee B_n) \wedge A \Leftrightarrow (B_1 \wedge A) \vee \ldots \vee (B_n \wedge A)$$

are saying that "conjunction is (left- and right-) distributive through disjunction".

The assertion $X \Leftrightarrow Y$ may of course be read as "each of X and Y is a logical consequence of the other". In order to *prove* $X \Leftrightarrow Y$ it is *sufficient* to prove $X \Rightarrow Y$ and to prove $Y \Rightarrow X$; but it is not *necessary* — later we shall discuss other ways of proving sentences to be logically equivalent to each other. Whereas $X \Rightarrow Y$ is called a *sequent*, $X \Leftrightarrow Y$ is called an *equivalence*. Since we have both

$$A \vee B \Leftrightarrow B \vee A$$

and

$$A \wedge B \Leftrightarrow B \wedge A$$

i.e., that "conjunction and disjunction are commutative", it is easy to infer that if conjunction is *left*-distributive through disjunction then it must also be *right* distributive through disjunction. The equivalence

$$A \wedge (B_1 \vee \ldots \vee B_n) \Leftrightarrow (A \wedge B_1) \vee \ldots \vee (A \wedge B_n)$$

is often called the (left-) *distributive law* of conjunction through disjunction. We also have a (left-) distributive law of *disjunction* through *conjunction*:

$$A \vee (B_1 \wedge \ldots \wedge B_n) \Leftrightarrow (A \vee B_1) \wedge \ldots \wedge (A \vee B_n)$$

and hence also a *right*-distributive law, by commutativity of disjunction.

There are a number of such logical equivalences, or "laws", which hinge on, and display, characteristic properties of the Boolean operators and relationships between them:

$\neg\neg A \Leftrightarrow A,$	the law of double negation
$A \vee B \Leftrightarrow \neg(\neg A \wedge \neg B)$ $A \wedge B \Leftrightarrow \neg(\neg A \vee \neg B)$	De Morgan's Laws
$A \leftrightarrow B \Leftrightarrow (A \rightarrow B) \wedge (B \rightarrow A)$	the law of double implication
$A \rightarrow B \Leftrightarrow (\neg A \vee B)$	the elimination of the conditional
$\neg(A \rightarrow B) \Leftrightarrow (A \wedge \neg B)$	the denial of the conditional
$(A \vee (B \vee C)) \Leftrightarrow ((A \vee B) \vee C)$	the associativity of disjunction
$(A \wedge (B \wedge C)) \Leftrightarrow ((A \wedge B) \wedge C)$	the associativity of conjunction
$A \vee \neg A \Leftrightarrow \mathbf{t}$	the law of the excluded middle
$A \wedge \neg A \Leftrightarrow \mathbf{f}$	the law of noncontradiction
$A \vee A \Leftrightarrow A$	the idempotence of disjunction
$A \wedge A \Leftrightarrow A$	the idempotence of conjunction
$A \wedge \mathbf{t} \Leftrightarrow A$	the fact that $\mathbf{t}$ is the identity for conjunction
$A \vee \mathbf{f} \Leftrightarrow A$	the fact that $\mathbf{f}$ is the identity for disjunction
$\neg\mathbf{f} \Leftrightarrow \mathbf{t}$ $\neg\mathbf{t} \Leftrightarrow \mathbf{f}$	complementarity of $\mathbf{f}$ and $\mathbf{t}$

Some of these laws bear a strong formal resemblance to laws governing the fundamental arithmetic operators. If we let $\neg$ correspond to $-$ (numerical negation), $\vee$ to $+$, $\wedge$ to $\cdot$, $\mathbf{f}$ to 0, and $\mathbf{t}$ to 1, we note that, e.g. the algebraic laws

$$a + b = b + a$$
$$a \cdot b = b \cdot a$$
$$-- a = a$$
$$a + (b + c) = (a + b) + c$$
$$a \cdot (b \cdot c) = (a \cdot b) \cdot c$$
$$a \cdot (b_1 + \ldots + b_n) = (a \cdot b_1) + \ldots + (a \cdot b_n)$$
$$a + 0 = a$$
$$a \cdot 1 = a$$
$$a + (-a) = 0$$

all have their Boolean counterparts, but that some Boolean laws have counterparts in the algebraic domain which are not in general true. For example, the counterparts of De Morgan's laws

$$a + b = -(-a \cdot -b)$$
$$a \cdot b = -(-a + -b)$$

are not algebraic laws; addition and multiplication are not idempotent:

$$a + a = a$$
$$a \cdot a = a$$

nor is addition distributive through multiplication:

$$a + (b_1 \cdot \ldots \cdot b_n) = (a + b_1) \cdot \ldots \cdot (a + b_n),$$

and 0 and 1 are not mutual complements:

$$-0 = 1$$
$$-1 = 0$$

Nevertheless, the cultural and technical habits associated with those algebraic laws that *do* correspond to Boolean equivalences are by no means to be shaken off; we can (as we shall see) "manipulate" logical formulas by appeal to logical equivalences in just the same sort of way that we manipulate algebraic formulas by appeal to algebraic "identities". It is in such manipulations that we find ourselves carrying out the *calculation* that it is one of the main purposes of the predicate *calculus* to make possible and indeed easy.

Certain equivalences and sequents involving the quantifier structure of generalizations are also worthy of note because of their constant recurrence in logical calculations.

Perhaps the most fundamental of these is the logical equivalence of *variants*: two formulas being variants each of the other, if they "differ only in their bound variables". For example, the sentences $\exists x P x$ and $\exists y P y$ are variants, and we have:

$$\exists x P x \Leftrightarrow \exists y P y$$

Although the intuitive notion of this variant relationship is reasonably clear, it can in intricate cases be difficult both to recognise as present between two formulas and also to characterize properly. We shall postpone a proper analysis of the variant relationship until a little later.

The following are fundamental:

$\neg \exists x A \Leftrightarrow \forall x \neg A$ negation of an existential generalization
$\neg \forall x A \Leftrightarrow \exists x \neg A$ negation of a universal generalization

One might loosely sum up these two laws by saying: "it is OK to replace $\neg \exists x$ by $\forall x \neg$ and $\neg \forall x$ by $\exists x \neg$".

We also have the intimate connection between conjunction and universal generalization:

$$\forall x(A_1 \wedge \ldots \wedge A_n) \Leftrightarrow (\forall x A_1 \wedge \ldots \wedge \forall x A_n)$$

and a similar one between disjunction and existential generalization:

$$\exists x(A_1 \vee \ldots \vee A_n) \Leftrightarrow (\exists x A_1 \vee \ldots \vee \exists x A_n)$$

neither of which is surprising in view of the close resemblance in the semantics of each pair.

One also has:

$$\exists x A \Leftrightarrow A \quad \text{vacuous existential generalization}$$

and

$$\forall x A \Leftrightarrow A \quad \text{vacuous universal generalization}$$

for all *closed* sentences A; that is, to put it another way, if A does not contain at least one free occurrence of x, then one gains nothing by prefixing either $\exists x$ or $\forall x$ to A.

Finally, if Q is either $\forall$ or $\exists$, we have the very important laws for *changing scopes*:

$$Qx(\wedge \, A \, B_1 \ldots B_n) \Leftrightarrow (\wedge \, QxA \, B_1 \ldots B_n)$$
$$Qx(\vee \, A \, B_1 \ldots B_n) \Leftrightarrow (\vee \, QxA \, B_1 \ldots B_n)$$

which hold *whenever the sentences $B_1 \ldots B_n$ are closed*, i.e., do not contain free occurrences of x. (There is nothing special about A and QxA being the *first* conjunct or disjunct; by the commutativity of $\vee$ and $\wedge$ the laws above also hold when the A is placed anywhere among the B_j's and the QxA in the same place.)

None of these laws is hard to prove: the reader may like to try his hand at some of them.

The relationship of logical equivalence between sentences boils down simply to this: that *each of the sentences denotes the same truthvalue as the other, in every model*. Logical equivalence enjoys the three basic defining properties of an "equivalence relation". It is *reflexive*, i.e. we have

$$X \Leftrightarrow X$$

for all closed sentences X. It is *symmetric*, i.e. we have

$$\text{if } X \Leftrightarrow Y \text{ then } Y \Leftrightarrow X$$

for all closed sentences X, Y. And it is *transitive*, i.e. we have if $X \Leftrightarrow Y$ and $Y \Leftrightarrow Z$ then $X \Leftrightarrow Z$

for all closed sentences X, Y, Z.

In addition to its reflexivity, symmetry and transitivity, logical equivalence has a very important fourth property – its *substitutivity* – which gives it a fundamental role in the technology of logic. A full characterization of the substitutivity property must await a new idea, which we shall shortly explain; but an intuitive notion of it is that, if $X \Leftrightarrow Y$, then we may freely replace X by Y within some sentence Z to obtain another sentence Z' and know with certainty that $Z \Leftrightarrow Z'$.

For example, we noted in the previous chapter that

$$(A \to B) \Leftrightarrow (\neg A \vee B)$$

By the substitutivity of logical equivalence we therefore know immediately that

$$A \wedge (A \to B) \Leftrightarrow A \wedge (\neg A \vee B) \tag{1}$$

by taking Z to be $(A \wedge (A \to B))$, X to be $(A \to B)$ and Y to be $(\neg A \vee B)$. But since we also know that

$$(\neg A \vee B) \Leftrightarrow (B \vee \neg A)$$

we immediately have:

$$A \wedge (\neg A \vee B) \Leftrightarrow A \wedge (B \vee \neg A) \tag{2}$$

by another appeal to the substitutivity principle. The distributivity of conjunction through disjunction gives the equivalence

$$A \wedge (B \vee \neg A) \Leftrightarrow (A \wedge B) \vee (A \wedge \neg A) \tag{3}$$

while, because of the law of non-contradiction

$$(A \wedge \neg A) \Leftrightarrow \mathbf{f}$$

we have

$$(A \wedge B) \vee (A \wedge \neg A) \Leftrightarrow (A \wedge B) \vee \mathbf{f} \tag{4}$$

by substitutivity again. But then the fact that $\mathbf{f}$ is the identity for disjunction gives

$$(A \wedge B) \vee \mathbf{f} \Leftrightarrow (A \wedge B) \tag{5}$$

So, if we repeatedly use the transitivity of $\Leftrightarrow$, we can start from the equivalences (1) through (5) and get

$$A \wedge (A \to B) \Leftrightarrow (A \wedge B) \tag{6}$$

This little exercise illustrates how one can "manipulate" sentences to produce logically equivalent sentences, after the fashion of the algebraic manipulation of a formula:

$$(x - 3) \cdot (x + 4)$$

to produce an equivalent formula:

$$x^2 + x - 12$$

In algebra it is the relationship of "equality", represented by the "equation symbol" =, which is being exploited for its reflexivity, symmetry, transitivity and substitutivity; and whereas logical equivalence between sentences means that they denote the same *truthvalue* in each model, equality between algebraic formulas means that they denote the same *number* in each "model".

One gives a "model" for an algebraic formula such as $(x - 3) \cdot (x + 4)$ by saying what number is denoted by x. Thus if x denotes 5, $(x - 3) \cdot (x + 4)$ denotes 18; but then so does $x^2 + x - 12$. If x denotes 3, $(x - 3) \cdot (x + 4)$ denotes 0, as also does $x^2 + x - 12$, and so on.

Giving a model is saying what the symbols mean which don't already *have* a meaning: the symbols 3, 4, 12, +, ·, − are the "arithmetical" symbols, analogues in algebraic formulas of the "logical" symbols t, f, ¬, ∧, ∨, →, ↔, ∀, ∃, ∗, in logical formulas. The symbol x in $(x - 3) \cdot (x + 4)$ is the analogue of the constructor and predicate symbols.

Now, so far in this book we have dealt only with *closed* formulas in the predicate calculus. The idea has been firmly held to, that only closed formulas denote anything; open formulas, those with one or more free variables in them, being regarded only as syntactic way-stations encountered en route to the finished formula as it is assembled from its parts.

It is possible to relax this attitude to some extent and in various useful ways. One way is to broaden the notion of a pure calculus by permitting its lexicon to contain one or more variables, and admitting as its sentences and terms all formulas in which the only *free* variables, if any, are those in its lexicon. The semantic definitions must then be modified to accommodate the newcomers appropriately. A total valuation of an applied calculus *applied* (L, U) must now include equations $v(X) = w$ for formulas X that may now possibly contain free occurrences of the variables, if any, that are in L. But this is quite simple to arrange: if X *is* one of the variables in L, then it must be required that w is an *individual*; the equation $v(X) = w$

then intuitively says that the variable X denotes the individual w. If on the other hand X merely *contains* one or more free occurrences of a variable in L, but is not actually identical with one of them, then the conditions of table 5.1 and table 5.2 specify what $v(X) = w$ must be. Intuitively, it is as though the variables, if any, in L were being conscripted for service as *constructors of arity* 0.

Once we allow variables to occur free in formulas, without at all disturbing any of the basic semantic arrangements we have made, we can work happily with formulas containing free variables in essentially the same spirit as that of algebra. Free variables become, intuitively, "indeterminate" individuals, just as the "unknowns" x, y, z, etc., in traditional algebraic formulas are "indeterminate numbers". Algebraists have taken this sensible view for generations.

But we must issue a warning: a formula of a pure calculus *pure* (L) may contain free variables *only* if those variables are official members of its lexicon L. If the free variables of a formula constructed from some lexicon L are *not* all in that lexicon, then the formula is *not* in *pure* (L). The point might be expressed thus: we are *still* interested only in the closed formulas constructible from a given lexicon; but by putting some *variables* into the lexicon we are *extending the notion of closed formula* to include a specially privileged class of open formulas, namely those whose free variables are "officially registered" by being explicitly listed among the symbols comprising the lexicon.

A pure calculus whose lexicon contains variables will be referred to as a *pure calculus with indeterminates*. We shall display its lexicon as, e.g., $L \cup \{x\}$, $L \cup \{x, y\}$; showing the set L of constructors and/or predicates (the "proper" lexicon) separately from the indeterminates. Evidently we have:

$$pure\,(L) \subseteq pure\,(L \cup X)$$

where X is any set of variables introduced as indeterminates. So, any model of *pure* $(L \cup X)$ will include a model of *pure* (L).

All of the ideas we have introduced for pure calculi carry over easily and naturally to pure calculi with indeterminates. This includes the ideas of logical consequence, logical equivalence, sequents, and proofs.

For example, the sequent

$$Ax, Bxy \Rightarrow (Ax \wedge Bxy)$$

is true: there is no model of *pure* $(\{A, B, \ldots\} \cup \{x, y\})$ in which we have the equations

$$v(Ax) = \mathbf{t}, v(Bxy) = \mathbf{t}, v(Ax \wedge Bxy) = \mathbf{f}$$

Again, the equivalence

$$\neg\neg Bxy \Leftrightarrow Bxy$$

is true; no new ideas are involved, once the status of free variables as indeterminates has been accepted.

It is now possible to study the connection between certain sequents and equivalences in a "determinate" calculus *pure* (L), and related sequents and equivalences in various "indeterminate extensions" *pure* ($L \cup X$) of *pure* (L). Suppose, for example, that in *pure* ($L \cup \{x\}$) we have

$$A \Leftrightarrow B$$

(where A and B may now contain free occurrences of the variable x). Then in *pure* (L) we must have

$$\forall xA \Leftrightarrow \forall xB$$

and, for similar reasons, we must have

$$\exists xA \Leftrightarrow \exists xB$$

For: the sequent $A \Leftrightarrow B$ says that there is *no* model (of *pure* ($L \cup \{x\}$)) in which A and B denote different truthvalues. In that event, there can be *no* model (of *pure* (L)) in which $\forall xA$ and $\forall xB$ denote different truthvalues; since if there were one (say, M), we would have, say, that $\forall xA$ is true in M while $\forall xB$ is false in M. That would mean that for some individual k of M, $B[k/x]$ is false in M while $A[k/x]$ is true in M. But now this immediately provides us with a model M' of *pure* ($L \cup \{x\}$), which we get by adding the equation $v(x) = k$, and all the other equations which are thereby entailed, to M. In this model M' we shall have that B is false but A is true, contradicting the fact that $A \Leftrightarrow B$.

Similarly, if $A \Leftrightarrow B$ there can be no model of *pure* (L) in which $\exists xA$ and $\exists xB$ have different truthvalues. For if M were such, and (say) $\exists xA$ were true in M while $\exists xB$ were false in M, we would again have an individual k for which $A[k/x]$ is true in M while $B[k/x]$ is false in M. If M' is defined as before, this would mean that A and B have different truthvalues in M', contradicting $A \Leftrightarrow B$.

In addition to broadening our ideas of logical consequence and logical equivalence to cover the possible presence of indeterminates, we should also at this point in our discussions make a distinction, hitherto unremarked, between "ordinary" formulas, which do not contain the logical symbol "$*$", and "auxiliary" formulas (as we shall call them), which do.

In an *ordinary* formula (whether it be a term or a sentence, and whether it contains indeterminates or not) there is no use made of the facility of "exemplifying" a generalization A by introducing the term $*A$. This facility is, indeed, accorded a special status in our calculi: its use is regarded as an *auxiliary* device *to be invoked in the elaboration of a proof*, rather than as a standard means of expressing oneself in an ordinary way.

The purpose of an exemplification such as

$*\forall x\ (even\ x \rightarrow \exists p\ \exists q\ (prime\ p \wedge prime\ q \wedge (sum\ p\ q\ x)))$

is to name an object k in the universe of discourse "for the sake of argument". For example, if we were interested in trying to prove Goldbach's Conjecture that

every even number is the sum of two prime numbers

we might well first express it as a sentence GC in some pure calculus

$\forall x\ (even\ x \rightarrow \exists p\ \exists q\ (prime\ p \wedge prime\ q \wedge (sum\ p\ q\ x)))$

and then try to prove a sequent of the form

$\mathscr{A} \Rightarrow GC$

in which $\mathscr{A}$ is a collection of suitably formulated (ordinary) sentences expressing the axioms of arithmetic, the definitions of *even*, *prime*, *sum*, and so on. In the course of trying to construct such a proof we would very naturally introduce the name of a certain number $*GC$, which is the one written out above. All we know about the number $*GC$ is that, *if* Goldbach's Conjecture is false, and there are in fact even numbers that are *not* obtainable by adding together a couple of prime numbers, *then* $*GC$ will be one of them.

It is as though the general format of a proof of GC can always be thought of as:

> "*Suppose GC is false.* Then $*GC$ in particular is a number for which GC fails. But ..." (reasonings about $*GC$, leading to a contradiction) ... "This is a contradiction! Hence GC is true."

In proving the "ordinary" sequent $\mathscr{A} \Rightarrow GC$ (assuming it could be done) we would thus encounter "auxiliary" sentences only within the analytical reasoning that is intended to make manifest the truth of $\mathscr{A} \Rightarrow GC$.

It is reasonable, then, to suppose that it is the *ordinary* sentences and terms of a pure calculus that are the medium in which we shall formulate the assertions and concepts of interest to us, while the auxiliary sentences and terms of that pure calculus stand in reserve to be deployed, if desired, in the course of a logical analysis of those ordinary formulas such as is the elaboration of a proof.

The principle of substitutivity of logical equivalence holds, without any qualifications, for all *ordinary* sentences:

> if X, Y, Z and Z' are *ordinary* sentences, and if Z' comes
> from Z by the replacement of an occurrence of X in Z by
> an occurrence of Y, then:
> if $X \Leftrightarrow Y$ then $Z \Leftrightarrow Z'$ (7)

However, as we have previously noted, it is possible, e.g., for two generalizations X and Y, that $X \Leftrightarrow Y$ but $*X$ and $*Y$ denote distinct individuals in some (e.g. logical) models. Hence we could easily find Z and Z', say:

> $Q*X$ and $Q*Y$

which are *not* logically equivalent even though X and Y are.

Thus the principle of substitutivity (7) does not hold if we delete the word *ordinary* from it. If we wish to assert the principle for all sentences, we have to guard against the above kind of counter-example by limiting the kind of occurrence of X that can be replaced by Y:

> if X, Y, Z and Z' are any sentences and if Z' comes from
> Z by the replacement of an occurrence of X in Z, *not*
> *within an exemplification*, by an occurrence of Y, then:
> if $X \Leftrightarrow Y$ then $Z \Leftrightarrow Z'$ (8)

We shall only use (7) in the rest of this book, but will prove (8); which is the same proposition as (7) when X, Y, Z and Z' are ordinary.

Suppose, then, that X, Y, Z, and Z' are sentences, and that Z and Z' are related by one of the ways exhibited in the table opposite.

Then it is immediately clear that:

> if $X \Leftrightarrow Y$ then $Z \Leftrightarrow Z'$ (9)

But Z and Z' can now be related in more general ways than those of the table, without losing the truth of (9). Specifically, if Z' comes from Z by replacing *any* one "replaceable" occurrence of X in Z, i.e., one not within an exemplification, by an occurrence of Y, then (9) is true. The replaceable occurrence of X need not be an immediate part of Z as in the table.

Z is	Z' is
$\neg X$	$\neg Y$
$(\rightarrow X\, W)$	$(\rightarrow Y\, W)$
$(\rightarrow W\, X)$	$(\rightarrow W\, Y)$
$(\leftrightarrow X\, W)$	$(\leftrightarrow Y\, W)$
$(\leftrightarrow W\, X)$	$(\leftrightarrow W\, Y)$
$(\wedge\, X_1 \ldots X_m\, X\, Y_1 \ldots Y_n)$	$(\wedge\, X_1 \ldots X_m\, Y\, Y_1 \ldots Y_n)$
$(\vee\, X_1 \ldots X_m\, X\, Y_1 \ldots Y_n)$	$(\vee\, X_1 \ldots X_m\, Y\, Y_1 \ldots Y_n)$
$\forall x X$	$\forall x Y$
$\exists x X$	$\exists x Y$

Consider the case where Z is:

$$(A \wedge \neg(B \rightarrow \exists b X))$$

and Z' is:

$$(A \wedge \neg(B \rightarrow \exists b Y))$$

Then we show (9) true in this case by repeatedly appealing to the above easy special cases:

> if $X \Leftrightarrow Y$ then $\exists b X \Leftrightarrow \exists b Y$
> if $\exists b X \Leftrightarrow \exists b Y$ then $(B \rightarrow \exists b X) \Leftrightarrow (B \rightarrow \exists b Y)$
> if $(B \rightarrow \exists b X) \Leftrightarrow (B \rightarrow \exists b Y)$ then $\neg(B \rightarrow \exists b X) \Leftrightarrow \neg(B \rightarrow \exists b Y)$
> if $\neg(B \rightarrow \exists b X) \Leftrightarrow \neg(B \rightarrow \exists b Y)$ then $(A \wedge \neg(B \rightarrow \exists b X)) \Leftrightarrow$
> $(A \wedge \neg(B \rightarrow \exists b Y))$

and then telescoping the series of if … then's:

> (if A_1 then A_2; if A_2 then A_3; …; if A_{n-1} then A_n)

into the desired one:

> if A_1 then A_n

namely:

> if $X \Leftrightarrow Y$ then $(A \wedge \neg(B \rightarrow \exists b X)) \Leftrightarrow (A \wedge \neg(B \rightarrow \exists b Y))$

Obviously this method can be used to show that (9) is true, no matter how deeply buried in the sentences Z and Z' the corresponding occurrences of X and Y may be, provided they are "replaceable". Our conclusion must be that (9) is true for all sentences X, Y, Z and Z', where Z and Z' are identical except that Z has a "replaceable" occurrence of X where Z' has one of Y. In short, the principle (8) of the substitutivity of logical equivalence can be used to get new equivalences $Z \Leftrightarrow Z'$ from given ones $X \Leftrightarrow Y$.

There is an important case of logical equivalence between ordinary sentences that we have not yet discussed. This case arises in its simplest form when we have two generalizations that have the same logical operator, i.e. two universal generalizations

$$\forall x A, \forall y B$$

or two existential generalizations

$$\exists x A, \exists y B$$

whose bound variables x, y are distinct, but whose bodies – the sentences A and B – are *identical except that A has free occurrences of x exactly where B has free occurrences of y*. When A and B are related in this way, we have

$$\forall x A \Leftrightarrow \forall y B$$

and

$$\exists x A \Leftrightarrow \exists y B$$

For example: $\exists x \, \exists z (Pxz \wedge Qx) \Leftrightarrow \exists y \, \exists z (Pyz \wedge Qy)$. Two such generalizations are said to be *variants* of each other. Intuitively, they are the *same* formula written in two *inessentially different* ways. For example, if k is some closed term and we have the sentence

$$\exists z (Pkz \wedge Qk)$$

then we can "existentially generalize" it using any variable we like as bound variable:

$$\exists a \, \exists z (Paz \wedge Qa)$$
$$\exists b \, \exists z (Pbz \wedge Qb)$$
$$\exists x \, \exists z (Pxz \wedge Qx)$$
$$\exists y \, \exists z (Pyz \wedge Qy)$$

etc., *except* for z; for if we used z, we would have the sentence

$$\exists z \, \exists z (Pzz \wedge Qz)$$

which says the same as

$$\exists z (Pzz \wedge Qz)$$

and is thus different in its meaning from all of the other generalizations, each of which is a variant of the others. The sentence $\exists z \, \exists z (Pzz \wedge Qz)$ is *not* a variant of, e.g., $\exists y \, \exists z (Pyz \wedge Qy)$; their respective bodies are *not* "identical except that one has free z exactly where the other has free y".

Variants are often said to be identical "up to bound variables", meaning that, intuitively, they are all the same formula except that we have made different choices for which variables we use as bound variables in generalizations.

Actually, two formulas X and Y can be variants, written

$$X \sim Y$$

("X is a variant of Y") in more complicated ways than this example illustrates. In general, $X \sim Y$ if and only if there is a one-to-one correspondence θ between the occurrences of symbols in X and the occurrences of symbols in Y, in which corresponding occurrences are of *identical* symbols except possibly when one of them is a *bound* occurrence of a variable; in that case, the other is *also* a *bound* occurrence of a variable, but not necessarily of the identical variable. However, the correspondence must "preserve scopes" of bound occurrences in the sense that the particular occurrence of $\forall$ or $\exists$ that binds an occurrence ξ of a variable in X must correspond to the particular occurrence of $\forall$ or $\exists$ in Y that binds the corresponding occurrence $\theta(\xi)$ in Y. A very wordy definition, alas!

An example of more complicated variants is the pair:

$$\forall x(Px \wedge (\forall x \, \exists y \, \forall z \;\, Axyz) \wedge Qxy)$$
$$\forall z(Pz \wedge (\forall y \, \exists x \, \forall w \, Ayxw) \wedge Qzy)$$

in which the correspondence θ is simply the set of pairs of occurrences of symbols that are vertically aligned. The diagram:

(called a "scope diagram") shows the abstract pattern of bindings in each of these two formulas. We replace each *bound* occurrence of a variable by a dot, to mark the "place" of that occurrence, and then indicate below, for each occurrence of $\forall$ or $\exists$ in the formula, which of these places it "owns". The idea of *the scope diagram for a formula* is perfectly general and should be clear from this example. We then have:

$X \sim Y$ **iff** X and Y have the same scope diagram

It is not difficult to show that *ordinary variants are logically equiv-*

alent (but not, of course, *all* variants, as witness $Q*X \sim Q*Y$ when $X \sim Y$):

if $X \sim Y$ then $X \Leftrightarrow Y$ for all ordinary sentences X and Y

We may note that the variant relationship is itself an equivalence relation. We have all three of the required properties:

$X \sim X$
if $X \sim Y$ then $Y \sim X$
if $X \sim Y$ and $Y \sim Z$ then $X \sim Z$

The eye soon becomes accustomed to running along formulas X, Y, and, so to speak, seeing only their scope diagrams – ignoring the particular choices of bound variable in generalizations and paying attention only to the pattern of the bindings. Even so, in cases that are too complex for the eye to analyse it is always possible to fall back on the process of actually drawing the scope diagrams of the formulas and comparing them directly to see whether X is a variant of Y.

8. Normal Forms of Sentences and Sequents

A given sentence in a pure calculus is logically equivalent to many other sentences – indeed, to infinitely many others – of that pure calculus. For any sentence X in the pure calculus, there is in fact a *set* of sentences, denoted by $[X]$, such that $[X]$ is the set of all sentences Y in the pure calculus that are logically equivalent to X:

$$[X] = \{Y \mid Y \Leftrightarrow X\}.$$

Intuitively, every sentence in $[X]$ "expresses the same proposition as X expresses". Each sentence in X is in a sense a different way of formulating the common meaning which they all share.

For example, we can express the proposition that *every human has a mother* in the following ways:

$\forall x(\text{Human } x \rightarrow \exists y(\text{Mother } y\, x))$
$\forall a\, \exists b(\neg\text{Human } a \lor \text{Mother } b\, a)$
$\neg\exists u\forall v(\text{Human } u \land \neg\text{Mother } v\, u)$

and infinitely many more, some of them quite silly, such as

$\neg\neg\neg\neg\neg\neg\neg\neg\neg\neg\neg\neg\forall x(\text{Human } x \rightarrow \exists y(\text{Mother } y\, x))$

or

$\forall x((\text{Human } x \lor \text{Human } x \lor \text{Human } x) \rightarrow \exists y(\text{Mother } y\, x))$

It is useful to have some "standard ways of saying things" within each logical equivalence class $[X]$ – that is, to distinguish, within each $[X]$, some particular kinds of sentences that "say what X says" but do so in a fixed-format style. Such sentences are called *normal forms* of X.

One of the most important types of normal form is called the *prenex* normal form. A prenex normal form of an ordinary sentence X is a prenex sentence in $[X]$, i.e. an ordinary sentence having the special syntactic structure:

$$Q_1 x_1 \ldots Q_n x_n M$$

where $Q_1 \ldots Q_n$ are quantifier symbols (each of them is either $\forall$ or $\exists$), $x_1, \ldots, x_n$ are variables, and M is a sentence *in which no quantifiers occur* (a so-called *quantifier-free* sentence). The sequence of quantifiers $Q_1x_1 \ldots Q_nx_n$ is called the *prefix*, and the sentence M the *matrix*, of the prenex sentence $Q_1x_1 \ldots Q_nx_nM$. The special case $n = 0$ is possible: a quantifier-free sentence M is a prenex sentence.

Prenex sentences are nicely organized into two portions; first comes the prefix, telling how the variables are quantified, and then comes the matrix, telling the quantifier-free condition that those variables are to satisfy. For example,

$$\forall x(\text{Human } x \to \exists y \text{ Mother } y\, x)$$

is not a prenex sentence, but

$$\forall x \, \exists y(\text{Human } x \to \text{Mother } y\, x)$$

is.

Every ordinary sentence X has a prenex normal form, i.e. is logically equivalent to, a prenex sentence; i.e. $|X|$ always contains prenex sentences. If X has no quantifiers, X already is prenex, and so the claim is obvious in this case. If X has quantifiers, then it is either prenex, or not. If not, let us manipulate X, using the substitutivity of logical equivalence, by replacing parts of X by logically equivalent parts, until X becomes prenex. More precisely, let us construct a sequence of sentences, each logically equivalent to the next, which starts with X and ends with a prenex sentence.

First, we will eliminate all occurrences of $\leftrightarrow$ by successive replacements of parts of the form $A \leftrightarrow B$ by parts of the form $(A \to B) \wedge (B \to A)$. Next, we will eliminate all occurrences of $\to$ by successive replacements of parts of the form $(A \to B)$ by parts of the form $(\neg A \vee B)$. (At this stage, the only Boolean operators present are at most $\neg, \vee, \wedge$.)

We next proceed to *move all quantifiers to the left of all Boolean operators*, by successive replacements of parts of the form $\neg\exists xA$ by parts of the form $\forall x\neg A$, and parts of the form $\neg\forall xA$ by parts of the form $\exists x\neg A$ ("moving negation signs inside quantifiers"); and of parts of the form

$$(B \ldots QxA \ldots)$$

by parts of the form

$$Qx'(B \ldots A' \ldots)$$

(where Q is either $\forall$ or $\exists$, B is either $\wedge$ or $\vee$, and $Qx'A'$ is a variant of QxA so chosen that the variable x' is not free in the part $(B \ldots QxA \ldots)$), until no such parts remain.

A special replacement step is available for parts of the form:

$$(\wedge \ \forall x_1 A_1 \ldots \forall x_n A_n)$$

or

$$(\vee \ \exists x_1 A_1 \ldots \exists x_n A_n)$$

which can be transformed in two steps; first, to

$$(\wedge \ \forall x A'_1 \ldots \forall x A'_n)$$

or

$$(\vee \ \exists x A'_1 \ldots \exists x A'_n)$$

where $\forall x A'_1, \ldots, \forall x A'_n$ are variants of $\forall x_1 A_1, \ldots, \forall x_n A_n$ so chosen that the new variable x is the same for all (similarly for $\exists x A'_1, \ldots, \exists x A'_n$); and second, to

$$\forall x (\wedge \ A'_1 \ldots A'_n)$$

or

$$\exists x (\vee \ A'_1 \ldots A'_n).$$

This replacement has the advantage of shortening the ultimate prefix of the prenex sentence eventually arrived at.

Since the replaced parts are always logically equivalent to the replacing parts, the sentence we reach after all these replacement operations is logically equivalent to X.

An example of this process follows, in which the starting sentence X is

$$\forall x (Px \leftrightarrow \exists y (Rxy \wedge \forall z \ Rzy)) \tag{1}$$

Eliminating $\leftrightarrow$ gives

$$\forall x ((Px \rightarrow \exists y (Rxy \wedge \forall z \ Rzy)) \wedge (\exists y (Rxy \wedge \forall z \ Rzy) \rightarrow Px))$$

and then eliminating $\rightarrow$ gives

$$\forall x ((\neg Px \vee \underline{\exists y}(Rxy \wedge \forall z \ Rzy)) \wedge (\neg \exists y (Rxy \wedge \forall z \ Rzy) \vee Px))$$

Now we move out to the prefix each quantifier in turn, taking them in order from left to right, the underlined one in each sentence being the one to be moved:

$$\forall x (\underline{\exists y}(\neg Px \vee (Rxy \wedge \forall z \ Rzy)) \wedge (\neg \exists y (Rxy \wedge \forall z \ Rzy) \vee Px))$$
$$\forall x \ \exists y ((\neg Px \vee (Rxy \wedge \underline{\forall z} \ Rzy)) \wedge (\neg \exists y (Rxy \wedge \forall z Rzy) \vee Px))$$
$$\forall x \ \exists y ((\neg Px \vee \underline{\forall z}(Rxy \wedge Rzy)) \wedge (\neg \exists y (Rxy \wedge \forall z \ Rzy) \vee Px))$$
$$\forall x \ \exists y (\underline{\forall z}(\neg Px \vee (Rxy \wedge Rzy)) \wedge (\neg \exists y (Rxy \wedge \forall z Rzy) \vee Px))$$
$$\forall x \ \exists y \ \forall z ((\neg Px \vee (Rxy \wedge Rzy)) \wedge (\neg \underline{\exists y}(Rxy \wedge \forall z \ Rzy) \vee Px))$$
$$\forall x \ \exists y \ \forall z ((\neg Px \vee (Rxy \wedge Rzy)) \wedge \ (\underline{\forall y}\neg(Rxy \wedge \forall z \ Rzy) \vee Px))$$
$$\forall x \ \exists y \ \forall z ((\neg Px \vee (Rxy \wedge Rzy)) \wedge \underline{\forall y}(\neg(Rxy \wedge \forall z \ Rzy) \vee Px))$$

Now note the need to choose a variant before the next replacement:

$\forall x \exists y \ \forall z \ \forall v((\neg Px \vee (Rxy \wedge Rzy)) \wedge (\neg(Rxv \wedge \underline{\forall z} \ Rzv) \vee Px))$
$\forall x \ \exists y \ \forall z \ \forall v((\neg Px \vee (Rxy \wedge Rzy)) \wedge (\neg\underline{\forall z}(Rxv \wedge Rzv) \vee Px))$
$\forall x \ \exists y \ \forall z \ \forall v((\neg Px \vee (Rxy \wedge Rzy)) \wedge (\underline{\exists z} \ \neg(Rxv \wedge Rzv) \vee Px))$
$\forall x \ \exists y \ \forall z \ \forall v((\neg Px \vee (Rxy \wedge Rzy)) \wedge \underline{\exists z}(\neg(Rxv \wedge Rzv) \vee Px))$

Once again, we must choose a variant before the next step:

$$\forall x \ \exists y \ \forall z \ \forall v \ \exists w((\neg Px \vee (Rxy \wedge Rzy)) \wedge (\neg(Rxv \wedge Rwv) \vee Px)) \qquad (2)$$

which, finally, is in prenex form. The prefix is thus

$$\forall x \ \exists y \ \forall z \ \forall v \ \exists w$$

and the quantifier-free matrix is:

$$((\neg Px \vee (Rxy \wedge Rzy)) \wedge (\neg(Rxv \wedge Rwv) \vee Px)).$$

Now (2) is not by any means the only prenex sentence that is logically equivalent to (1). We could have brought the interior quantifiers out to the prefix in a different order from the systematic left-to-right order that we used. All we are really saying when we claim that every ordinary sentence has a prenex normal form is that we can in fact manipulate its quantifiers outside all Boolean operators, and hence into the prefix, with the Boolean operators all in the matrix. (Of course, we could not do this for an auxiliary sentence – some of its quantifiers would be locked inside exemplications.)

The process just illustrated becomes much easier to grasp if we lay out the sentence as a tree. For example, after elimination of → and ↔, the sentence we have just treated looks like figure 8.1.

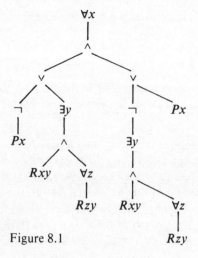

Figure 8.1

When a sentence is displayed in this way, it is easy to see whether or not its quantifiers are in the prefix or not. In this example, one of them is and four are not. Of the four that are not, two are "uppermost"; that is, we reach them first, if we travel down from the root node. Each such quantifier is reached after an *odd*, or an *even*, number of negation symbols has been passed. If the number is even, the quantifier will find its way to the prefix unchanged in "sign" (i.e., if it is ∀, it will wind up as ∀ in the prefix; if it is ∃, it will wind up as ∃). If the number is odd, then by the time the quantifier winds up in the prefix it will have "changed sign", from ∀ to ∃ or from ∃ to ∀.

We can, however, take any uppermost non-prefix quantifier and bring it to the prefix *in a single step.* For example, we can select the right-hand one (at node $(1, 2, 1, 1)$) and move it in one step to the prefix, getting the tree shown in figure 8.2. Note the change of sign from ∃ to ∀.

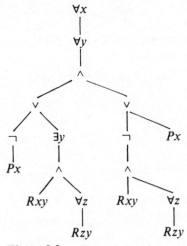

Figure 8.2

If we next select the quantifier at node $(1, 1, 1, 2)$, rather than that at node $(1, 1, 2, 1, 1, 2)$, for removal to the prefix, we must first change the subsentence it heads to a variant, using, say, u instead of y; then we may move the quantifier directly to the prefix, as shown in figure 8.3.

Now we may select either of the two remaining non-prefix quantifiers, since each is uppermost. The one at node $(1, 1, 1, 2, 1, 1, 2)$, if selected, will change sign because of the ¬ at node $(1, 1, 1, 2, 1)$, but we need not first change the sentence at $(1, 1, 1, 2, 1, 1, 2)$ to a new

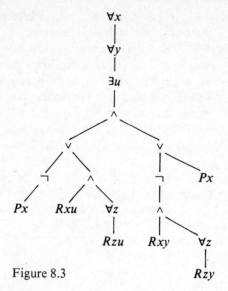

Figure 8.3

variant since *z* is not free in the sentence at (1, 1, 1). Moving this quantifier gives the tree shown in figure 8.4.

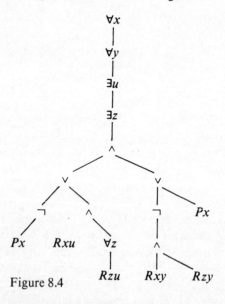

Figure 8.4

Before moving up the final quantifier we change its sentence to a variant, since *z* is free in the sentence at (1, 1, 1, 1). The final sentence, in prenex form, is shown in figure 8.5.

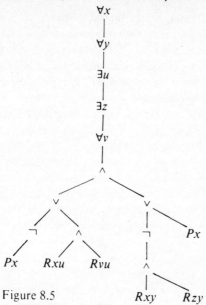

Figure 8.5

Written linearly and with infixed operators, this sentence looks like

$$\forall x\, \forall y\, \exists u\, \exists z\, \forall v((\neg Px \vee (Rxu \wedge Rvu)) \wedge (\neg(Rxy \wedge Rzy) \vee Px))\qquad(3)$$

and if we compare it with the other prenex normal form of (1), namely

$$\forall x\, \exists y\, \forall z\, \forall v\, \exists w((\neg Px \vee (Rxy \wedge Rzy)) \wedge (\neg(Rxv \wedge Rwv) \vee Px))\qquad(2)$$

we notice some interesting differences. These are obscured somewhat by the fact that corresponding bound variables are different. But after we take scope diagrams, the essential structures of each stand out:

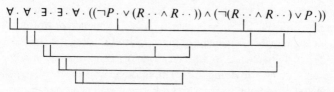

being the scope diagram of (3), while

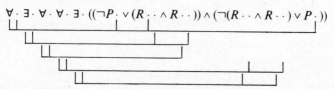

is that of (2). These diagrams bring out the patterns of binding associated with each quantifier and allow us to see where each one came to rest, in each prenex normal form. These final positions in the prefix are determined by the choices made during the "prenexing" process between the non-prefix quantifiers which are uppermost at each stage. By making these choices in all the possible ways, we can arrive at all of the different prefixes possible for a prenex normal form of a given sentence. As we shall see, there may well be a reason for preferring some of the prefixes over others.

Now, the structure of the matrix of a prenex sentence can be made considerably more orderly by replacing it by any one of several *Boolean normal forms*. There are two main Boolean normal forms, the *conjunctive normal form* (c.n.f.) and the *disjunctive normal form* (d.n.f.), the ideas underlying each being symmetric versions of those underlying the other.

These forms are best described with reference to the tree representation of a sentence. In c.n.f., the tree of a sentence contains only branches of the forms $\wedge, \vee, P$ and $\wedge, \vee, \neg P$, where P is a predication. (In d.n.f., the branches can only be $\vee, \wedge, P$ and $\vee, \wedge, \neg P$). Thus the tree

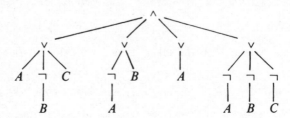

is a c.n.f. sentence. In linear format, this looks like:

$$(A \vee \neg B \vee C) \wedge (\neg A \vee B) \wedge (A) \wedge (\neg A \vee \neg B \vee \neg C)$$

Every quantifier-free sentence is logically equivalent to one in conjunctive normal form, and also to one in disjunctive normal form; and it is a matter of elementary manipulations, using the substitutivity of logical equivalence, to find a c.n.f. of a given sentence, or a d.n.f. of a given sentence. In doing the manipulations we shall need, in general, to appeal repeatedly to several Boolean equivalences, namely:

$$(A \rightarrow B) \Leftrightarrow (\neg A \vee B)$$
$$(A \leftrightarrow B) \Leftrightarrow (\neg A \vee B) \wedge (A \vee \neg B)$$

(elimination of $\rightarrow$ and $\leftrightarrow$),

$$(\neg \neg A) \Leftrightarrow A$$

(elimination of double negation),

$$\neg(\wedge A_1 \ldots A_n) \Leftrightarrow (\vee \neg A_1 \ldots \neg A_n)$$
$$\neg(\vee A_1 \ldots A_n) \Leftrightarrow (\wedge \neg A_1 \ldots \neg A_n)$$

(driving negation across conjunction and disjunction). In addition to these, it will in general be necessary to use (in transforming a sentence to c.n.f.) the *distributivity of disjunction through conjunction*, which says, e.g., that

$$(\vee(\wedge A\ B\ C)(\wedge D\ E)) \Leftrightarrow (\wedge(\vee A\ D)(\vee A\ E)$$
$$(\vee B\ D)(\vee B\ E)$$
$$(\vee C\ D)(\vee C\ E))$$

and which in general says that a disjunction of conjunctions $C_1, \ldots, C_n$ is logically equivalent to the conjunction of all disjunctions $(\vee X_1 \ldots X_n)$ in which X_j is an immediate constituent of C_j, for $1 \leqslant j \leqslant n$. This means that if C_j contains, say k_j different immediate constituents, then there are $k_1 \cdot k_2 \cdot \ldots \cdot k_n$ such disjunctions to be conjoined. (In our simple case above, $n = 2$, $k_1 = 3$, $k_2 = 2$; so we have $6 = 3 \cdot 2$ disjunctions conjoined on the right-hand side.)

(The formation of a d.n.f. will require the use of the similar principle of the *distributivity of conjunction through disjunction*.)

We shall, during the transformation process, also perhaps wish to simplify the sentence as much as possible by appeal to:

$$\left.\begin{array}{l} (\wedge) \Leftrightarrow \mathbf{t} \\ (\vee) \Leftrightarrow \mathbf{f} \end{array}\right\} \quad (4)$$

$$\left.\begin{array}{l} (\wedge A_1 \ldots A_m\, \mathbf{t}\, B_1 \ldots B_n) \Leftrightarrow (\wedge A_1 \ldots A_m\, B_1 \ldots B_n) \\ (\vee A_1 \ldots A_m\, \mathbf{f}\, B_1 \ldots B_n) \Leftrightarrow (\vee A_1 \ldots A_m\, B_1 \ldots B_n) \end{array}\right\}\ m, n \geqslant 0 \quad (5)$$

$$\left.\begin{array}{l} (\wedge A_1 \ldots A_m\, \mathbf{f}\, B_1 \ldots B_n) \Leftrightarrow \mathbf{f} \\ (\vee A_1 \ldots A_m\, \mathbf{t}\, B_1 \ldots B_n) \Leftrightarrow \mathbf{t} \end{array}\right\}\ m, n \geqslant 0 \quad (6)$$

$$\left.\begin{array}{l} \neg \mathbf{t} \Leftrightarrow \mathbf{f} \\ \neg \mathbf{f} \Leftrightarrow \mathbf{t} \end{array}\right\} \quad (7)$$

$$\left.\begin{array}{l} (\wedge A_1 \ldots A_n\, A_j) \Leftrightarrow (\wedge A_1 \ldots A_n) \\ (\vee A_1 \ldots A_n\, A_j) \Leftrightarrow (\vee A_1 \ldots A_n) \end{array}\right\}\ (1 \leqslant j \leqslant n) \quad (8)$$

$$\left.\begin{array}{l} (\wedge A_1 \ldots A_n) \Leftrightarrow (\wedge A_{j_1} \ldots A_{j_n}) \\ (\vee A_1 \ldots A_n) \Leftrightarrow (\wedge A_{j_1} \ldots A_{j_n}) \end{array}\right\}\ \begin{array}{l} (j_1, \ldots, j_n \text{ any permutation} \\ \text{ of } \{1, \ldots, n\}) \end{array} \quad (9)$$

which will enable us to eliminate $\mathbf{t}$ and $\mathbf{f}$, and all duplications of disjuncts within a disjunction and of conjuncts within a conjunction (8). The equivalences (9) will enable us to reveal the essential identity between disjunctions or conjunctions that differ only in the order of their immediate constituents.

Finally we shall need to be able to "flatten" nested conjunctions and disjunctions by appeal to:

$$\left.\begin{array}{l}(\wedge A_1 \ldots A_m (\wedge B_1 \ldots B_n) C_1 \ldots C_r) \Leftrightarrow (\wedge A_1 \ldots A_m B_1 \ldots B_n C_1 \ldots C_r) \\ (\vee A_1 \ldots A_m (\vee B_1 \ldots B_n) C_1 \ldots C_r) \Leftrightarrow (\vee A_1 \ldots A_m B_1 \ldots B_n C_1 \ldots C_r)\end{array}\right\}$$ (10

There are many straightforward ways to organize a systematic process of manipulation that will produce a c.n.f. or a d.n.f. of a given ordinary sentence X that is quantifier-free. For example, to get a c.n.f. of X we would:

First, eliminate $\rightarrow$'s and $\leftrightarrow$'s.

Next, drive $\neg$'s to innermost positions; i.e., persistently replace

$$\neg\neg A \text{ by } A$$
$$\neg f \text{ by } t$$
$$\neg t \text{ by } f$$
$$\neg(\wedge A_1 \ldots A_n) \text{ by } (\vee \neg A_1 \ldots \neg A_n)$$
$$\neg(\vee A_1 \ldots A_n) \text{ by } (\wedge \neg A_1 \ldots \neg A_n)$$

until no such contexts remain.

Next, drive $\vee$'s inside $\wedge$'s; i.e. persistently replace

$$(\vee(\wedge A_{11} \ldots A_{1n_1}) \ldots (\wedge A_{k1} \ldots A_{kn_k}))$$
by
$$(\wedge(\vee A_{11} \ldots A_{k1})$$
$$(\vee A_{11} \ldots A_{k2})$$
$$\ldots$$
$$(\vee A_{1j_1} \ldots A_{kj_k}) \quad 1 \leqslant j_1 \leqslant n_1, \ldots, 1 \leqslant j_k \leqslant n_k$$
$$\ldots$$
$$(\vee A_{1n_1} \ldots A_{kn_k}))$$

until no such contexts remain. Note that in the replacement we have to form all possible disjunctions $(\vee A_{1j_1} \ldots A_{kj_k})$ whose disjuncts are taken one each from the k conjunctions in the replaced sentence.

Next, flatten conjunctions and disjunctions; i.e., persistently replace

$$(\wedge A_1 \ldots A_m (\wedge B_1 \ldots B_n) C_1 \ldots C_r) \text{ by}$$
$$(\wedge A_1 \ldots A_m B_1 \ldots B_n C_1 \ldots C_r)$$

and

$$(\vee A_1 \ldots A_m (\vee B_1 \ldots B_n) C_1 \ldots C_r) \text{ by}$$
$$(\vee A_1 \ldots A_m B_1 \ldots B_n C_1 \ldots C_r)$$

until no such contexts remain.

The sentence is now in c.n.f., but not necessarily in the simplest form. It may still contain redundancies. We can thus add the steps:
First: simplify the disjunctions; i.e. persistently replace

$(\vee A_1 \ldots A_m \, \mathbf{t} \, B_1 \ldots B_n)$ by $\mathbf{t}$

$(\vee A_1 \ldots A_m \, \mathbf{f} \, B_1 \ldots B_n)$ by $(\vee A_1 \ldots A_m \, B_1 \ldots B_n)$

$(\vee A_1 \ldots A_m \, A \, B_1 \ldots B_n \, \neg A \, C_1 \ldots C_r)$ by $\mathbf{t}$

$(\vee A_1 \ldots A_m \, A \, B_1 \ldots B_n \, A \, C_1 \ldots C_r)$ by

   $(\vee A_1 \ldots A_m \, A \, B_1 \ldots B_n \, C_1 \ldots C_r)$

$(\vee)$ by $\mathbf{f}$

until no such disjunctions remain. After this step, no disjunction will contain a disjunct more than once; no disjunction will contain a truth-value; and no disjunction will contain a predication A and also its negation $\neg A$. Nor will there be any empty disjunctions.

Next: simplify the conjunction; i.e.

(a)   replace it by $\mathbf{f}$ if it has $\mathbf{f}$ as a conjunct; or has two conjuncts of the form $(\vee A)(\vee \neg A)$

(b)   replace it by $\mathbf{t}$ if it has no conjuncts, or only $\mathbf{t}$'s as conjuncts; otherwise:

(c)   drop any $\mathbf{t}$'s it may have as conjuncts;

(d)   if any of its conjuncts are subsumed by others, *drop* the ones that are subsumed. (We say $(\vee B_1 \ldots B_n)$ is *subsumed* by $(\vee A_1 \ldots A_m)$ if each A_i is one of the B_j.)

After this step, the sentence will have either become $\mathbf{t}$, or $\mathbf{f}$, or else will be a conjunction of one or more disjunctions, none of which subsumes any of the rest.

To illustrate the process let us find a c.n.f. duly simplified, for the matrix of sentence (2), namely, the sentence (in tree format):

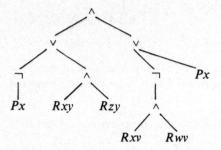

There are no $\rightarrow$'s or $\leftrightarrow$'s to eliminate. A single replacement drives $\neg$'s to innermost positions:

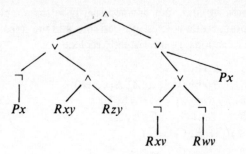

Another single replacement drives ∨'s inside ∧'s:

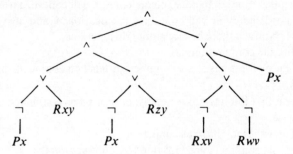

and two more flatten disjunctions and conjunctions; the resulting sentence requires no simplification, and so we have our c.n.f.:

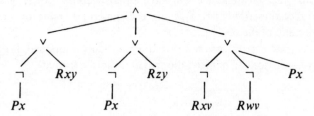

Combining these two normal form results, we see that

> every ordinary sentence is logically equivalent to one in prenex normal form whose matrix is in conjunctive normal form.

(and we see that in the above we can substitute "disjunctive" for "conjunctive").

For instance, the sentence (1) of our running example:

$$\forall x(Px \leftrightarrow \exists y(Rxy \wedge \forall z\ Rzy))$$

has now been found to have the sentence:

$$\forall x\ \exists y\ \forall z\ \forall v\ \exists w (\wedge (\vee\ \neg Px\ Rxy)$$
$$(\vee\ \neg Px\ Rzy)$$
$$(\vee\ \neg Rxv\ \neg Rwv\ Px)) \tag{11}$$

as one of its "prenex conjunctive" normal forms. We also can complete the transformation of the other one of its prenex forms that we have found, (3), to obtain a further prenex conjunctive normal form:

$$\forall x\ \forall y\ \exists u\ \exists z\ \forall v (\wedge (\vee\ \neg Px\ Rxu)$$
$$(\vee\ \neg Px\ Rvu)$$
$$(\vee\ \neg Rxy\ \neg Rzy\ Px)) \tag{12}$$

The regularity and simplicity of the prenex conjunctive normal format makes it easier to analyse the sentence systematically. However, there is one more step of normalization we can take, which simplifies the form of the sentences still further.

Suppose that we are interested in the question whether the ordinary sequent (i.e. one whose sentences are ordinary sentences)

$$A_1, ..., A_m \Rightarrow B_1, ..., B_n$$

is true. Clearly this question is the same as asking whether the sequent

$$A_1, ..., A_m, \neg B_1, ..., \neg B_n \Rightarrow$$

is true, or in other words whether the set of sentences

$$\{A_1, ..., A_m, \neg B_1, ..., \neg B_n\}$$

is *unsatisfiable*. Now, by our preceding discussion we know that we can simplify the question, without changing its meaning, by replacing each of the sentences in the set by one of its prenex normal forms.

Let us then consider the question, in general, whether a given finite ordinary sequent

$$C_1, ..., C_r \Rightarrow \tag{13}$$

i.e. one whose sentences are ordinary sentences in prenex normal form, is true. It turns out that we can always reduce such a question to a very special, and simple, case: namely the case in which *none of the prefixes in $C_1, ..., C_r$ contains any existential quantifiers*, i.e., each C_j has the form

$$\forall x_1 ... \forall x_n A$$

(where the matrix A, of course, contains no quantifier of either kind). If (13) is not already in this simple case, we shall construct a sequent

$$C'_1, \ldots, C'_r \Rightarrow \tag{14}$$

that *is*, and moreover which is true if, and only if, (13) is true.

Let C be a sentence in (13) in whose prefix at least one existential quantifier appears. Thus C will have the form

$$\forall x_1 \ldots \forall x_k \, \exists y \, N(x_1, \ldots, x_k, y) \tag{15}$$

where N is in prenex form and will in general contain free occurrences of $x_1, \ldots, x_n$ and y, as we have indicated above by writing them in parentheses.

Now suppose that g is a k-ary constructor symbol that *does not occur in any of the sentences in (13)*, and let C' be the sentence

$$\forall x_1 \ldots \forall x_k \, N(x_1, \ldots, x_k(g \, x_1 \ldots x_k)) \tag{16}$$

which comes from C by

(a)   deleting the quantifier ($\exists y$) from the prefix
(b)   replacing each free occurrence of y in N by an occurrence of
      the *term* $(g \, x_1 \ldots x_k)$

We claim that the sequent

$$\{C_1, \ldots, C_r\} - \{C\} + \{C'\} \Rightarrow \tag{17}$$

obtained by discarding C from (13) and adding C' in its place, is true if, and only if, (13) is true. Note that, in view of the new constructor symbol g, the lexicon of (17), i.e. that containing just the constructors, predicates and free variables in (17) is $L \cup \{g\}$, where L is the lexicon of (13).

It is clear that, if M is a model of *pure* $(L \cup \{g\})$ satisfying the left-hand side of (17), then M will also satisfy that of (13), for M in particular makes the sentence (16) true and so must make (15) true as well. On the other hand, if M is a model of *pure* (L) satisfying the left-hand side of (13), it will contain no semantic equations for formulas involving the constructor symbol g and so we cannot say either that M does, or does not, make (16) true – it does neither!

But consider, for each k-tuple of individuals $u_1, \ldots, u_k$, in the universe U of the model M, the term

$$*\exists y \, N(u_1, \ldots, u_k, y) \tag{18}$$

which exemplifies the existential generalization obtained from (15) by successively instantiating x_1 with u_1, \ldots, etc., \ldots, and x_k with u_k. We have an equation in M

$$v(*\exists y \, N(u_1, \ldots, u_k, y)) = w \tag{19}$$

for each such term (18); and so we can add a corresponding equation

$$v(g\, u_1 \ldots u_k) = w \tag{20}$$

into M, for each k-tuple $u_1, \ldots, u_k$, and thereby (after also adding the implied equations for the other formulas in *applied* $(L \cup \{g\}, U)$) that are not in *applied* (L, U)), get a model M of *pure* $(L \cup \{g\})$ that agrees with M on *pure* (L) and makes the sentence (16) true.

What this discussion shows is that we can *eliminate* the leading existential quantifier in the sentence (15) by *introducing* the new function symbol g and replacing (15) by (16), without thereby affecting the truth or falsehood of the sequent under scrutiny. The original sequent (13) is true if, and only if, the new sequent (17) is true.

However, there is no reason why we cannot repeat this transformation and eliminate (if any remain) another leading existential quantifier by introducing another new function symbol. Clearly, by carrying out as many of these steps as there were distinct existential quantifiers in the various prefixes of sentences in the sequent (13), we can produce the promised sequent (14) whose sentences all have prefixes which contain *no* existential quantifiers and which is true if and only if (13) is. It is obviously possible to identify, in (14), the sentence C'_j that comes ultimately from the sentence C_j in (13); we say that C'_j is a *Skolem transform* of C_j. For example, a Skolem transform of (11) is:

$$\forall x\, \forall z\, \forall v (\wedge(\vee \neg Px\, Rx(g\, x)) \\ (\vee \neg Px\, Rz(g\, x)) \\ (\vee \neg Rxv\, \neg R(h\, x\, z\, v)v\, Px)) \tag{21}$$

and a Skolem transform of (12) is:

$$\forall x\, \forall y\, \forall v (\wedge(\vee \neg Px\, Rx(g\, x\, y)) \\ (\vee \neg Px\, Rv(g\, x\, y)) \\ (\vee \neg Rxy\, \neg R(h\, x\, y)y\, Px)) \tag{22}$$

The arity of the introduced function symbols (often called the *Skolem function symbols* of the Skolem transform) is always equal to the number of *universal* quantifiers that precede, in the prefix, the eliminated existential quantifier. If this number is zero, as in, e.g.

$$\exists x\, \forall y\, \varphi(x, y)$$

then the Skolem transform will have a zero-ary Skolem function symbol, e.g.

$$\forall y\, \varphi(g, y).$$

The intuitive idea underlying the Skolem transformation is simple. We pass from, e.g. $\forall x\, \exists y\, \varphi(x, y)$ to $\forall x\, \varphi(x(g\,x))$ by reasoning that if indeed there *is* always a y, for each x we might pick, such that $\varphi(x, y)$ is true of that x and y, then the y can be thought of as being determined by our choice of x, and this dependency of y upon x can be thought of as a "functional" relationship

$$y = (g\,x)$$

with g denoting it. Of course, the y need not be *uniquely* determined by the choice of x – in general there will be (if $\forall x\, \exists y\, \varphi$ is true in some model M) several (possibly even infinitely many) individuals y such that $\varphi(x, y)$ is true in M. Our use of g corresponds to our making a choice of a *particular* y, when there is more than one y that fits the requirement.

A Skolem transform C' of a prenex ordinary sentence C is often misleadingly said to be in *Skolem normal form*. The implicit suggestion in this terminology is that $C \Leftrightarrow C'$, but it must be realized that, in general, we do *not* have this equivalence. While we *do* have the logical implication $C' \Rightarrow C$ of C by its Skolem transform C', the converse $C \Rightarrow C'$ does not in general hold, even if we consider C and C' as sentences of the larger calculus of which they are both members. For while, e.g.

$$\forall x\, \varphi(x(g\,x)) \Rightarrow \forall x\, \exists y\, \varphi(x, y) \tag{23}$$

the converse

$$\forall x\, \exists y\, \varphi(x, y) \Rightarrow \forall x\, \varphi(x(g\,x)) \tag{24}$$

can easily be refuted by displaying a model in which the meaning of φ and the meaning of g have no particular connection. Assertion (23) is really (intuitively)

for *all* g, $[(\forall x\, \varphi(x(g\,x)) \Rightarrow \forall x\, \exists y\, \varphi(x, y))]$

which is to say

$[$for *some* g, $\forall x\, \varphi(x(g\,x))] \Rightarrow \forall x\, \exists y\, \varphi(x, y)$

whereas assertion (24) is

$\forall x\, \exists y\, \varphi(x, y) \Rightarrow [$for *all* g, $\forall x\, \varphi(x(g\,x))]$

Thus (24) is too strong to be a true assertion. Those who have felt uncomfortable with the above remarks are invited to reflect on the *second order* predicate calculus sentences

$$\exists g \, \forall x \, \varphi(x(g\,x))$$
$$\forall x \, \exists y \, \varphi(x, y)$$

the first of which expresses the intuitive content of the Skolem transform of the second one. When the notion of logical consequence is suitably extended to *second* order calculi (in which we may quantify not only "individual" variables but also function symbols and relation symbols, regarded as "variables") then these two sentences, one of them *first* order and the other *second* order, *are* logically equivalent!

What is really going on, when we pass from the sequent (13) whose left-hand side is the set of sentences $\{C_1, \ldots, C_r\}$, to that whose left-hand side is the set $\{C'_1, \ldots, C'_r\}$ of their Skolem transforms, is this. It is the *sequent-as-a-whole*

$$C_1, \ldots, C_r \Rightarrow \tag{25}$$

that is being transformed to the *sequent-as-a-whole*

$$C'_1, \ldots, C'_r \Rightarrow \tag{26}$$

rather than the transformation being merely a sentence-to-sentence one. As we saw in the discussion, in passing from (25) to (26) we must take into account, at each single step of elimination of an existential quantifier and introduction of the corresponding Skolem function symbol, *the entire set of sentences*, and not just the sentence in which the existential quantifier happens to occur. The function symbol introduced at each step must be *new to the entire sequent*, not just to the sentence into which it is being introduced.

So: in the Skolem normal form we have rather a "higher level" notion of normal form – namely, one for sequents – than the notions of prenex normal form, conjunctive normal form, and so on, which are for sentences in isolation.

The two sequents (25) and (26) are either both true, or both false; and so we may safely analyse (26) in order to draw conclusions about the truth or falsehood of (25).

The transformation of a sequent $C_1 \ldots C_r \Rightarrow$ to Skolem normal form (when $C_1, \ldots, C_r$ are all in prenex normal form) involves the successive elimination of existential quantifiers from the prefixes of $C_1, \ldots, C_r$, to produce the sequent $C'_1, \ldots, C'_r \Rightarrow$. The idea of this transformation, however, is not restricted to sequents with empty succedents. In general, given a sequent

$$A_1, \ldots, A_m \Rightarrow B_1, \ldots, B_n$$

whose sentences are all in prenex normal form, we can transform it to a sequent

$$A'_1, \ldots, A'_m \Rightarrow B'_1, \ldots, B'_n$$

by successively eliminating all *existential* quantifiers from the prefixes of the A's, and successively eliminating all *universal* quantifiers from the prefixes of the B's, by steps identical to the step that takes (15) to (16) except for the interchange of $\forall$ and $\exists$ in their descriptions. Namely, we replace a sentence

$$\exists x_1 \ldots \exists x_k \; \forall y \; N(x_1, \ldots, x_k, y)$$

in the *succedent* of the sequent, by the sentence

$$\exists x_1 \ldots \exists x_k \; N(x_1, \ldots, x_k, (g \, x_1 \ldots x_k))$$

in which g is a k-ary function symbol *new to the entire sequent*.

After this Skolem transformation has seen to it that all existential quantifiers have been eliminated from the *antecedent* sentences and all universal quantifiers have been eliminated from the *succedent* sentences, the resulting sequent (the Skolem transform of the given sequent) is in Skolem normal form, in the sense of the following definition:

> an ordinary sequent is in *Skolem normal form* iff its sentences are all in prenex normal form and those in the antecedent contain no existential quantifiers while those in the succedent contain no universal quantifiers

So, for example, the sequent

$$Ha, \forall x(Hx \to Mx) \Rightarrow \exists x \, Mx$$

is in Skolem normal form, as is:

$$\forall x \, \forall y \, \forall z \, \forall u \, \forall v \, \forall w((Pxyu \wedge Pyzu \wedge Pxvw) \to Puzw),$$
$$\forall r \, \forall s \, P(g \, r \, s)rs,$$
$$\forall a \, \forall b \, Pa(h \, a \, b)b$$
$$\Rightarrow$$
$$\exists t \, P(k \, t)t(k \, t)$$

Our entire discussion so far may now be summed up by the proposition

> every ordinary prenex sequent is true if, and only if, its Skolem transform is true

Intuitively, the given sequent is "equivalent" to its Skolem transform; but we must not confuse this informal (metalanguage!) notion with the one we have been using for formal sentences of the predicate calculus.

In view of this proposition we can confine our attention, in developing procedures for establishing the truth of sequents, to sequents that are in Skolem normal form. We can in fact go one step further still, in the direction of devising a suitable normal form for sequents.

We can certainly assume, given a sequent $A_1, ..., A_m \Rightarrow B_1, ..., B_n$ in Skolem normal form, that we have both of the following:

(a)   the matrix of each of $A_1, ..., A_m$ is in *conjunctive* normal form;

(b)   the matrix of each of $B_1, ..., B_n$ is in *disjunctive* normal form.

For we can, if necessary, replace any matrix not already in the stated form, by a logically equivalent matrix that is. For example, the sequent

$$\forall x\, \forall y (\wedge(\vee Pxy)\,(\vee Qx\, Sx)) \Rightarrow \exists z(\vee(\wedge Qz\, \neg Sz)\,(\wedge Rzz)) \qquad (27)$$

is not only in Skolem normal form but also satisfies these extra constraints.

But now we can *distribute the prefixes* of each sentence onto the conjuncts and disjuncts that comprise their matrices. Doing this to (27) gives:

$$(\wedge \forall x\, \forall y(\vee Pxy)\,\forall x\, \forall y(\vee Qx\, Sx)) \Rightarrow (\vee \exists z(\wedge Qz\, \neg Sz)\,\exists z(\wedge Rzz)) \qquad (28)$$

for the new sentences are logical equivalents of the old. We may then *dissolve* the conjunctions in the antecedent, and the disjunctions in the succedent, into their several conjuncts and disjuncts; getting, e.g. from (28), the sequent

$$\forall x\, \forall y(\vee Pxy),\, \forall x\, \forall y(\vee Qx\, Sx) \Rightarrow \exists z(\wedge Qz\, \neg Sz),\, \exists z(\wedge Rzz) \qquad (29)$$

on the grounds that, in general, we have

$$(\wedge K_1 \ldots K_p),\mathscr{A} \Rightarrow \mathscr{B},(\vee L_1 \ldots L_q)$$

if, and only if, we have

$$K_1, ..., K_p,\mathscr{A} \Rightarrow \mathscr{B}, L_1, ..., L_q$$

Finally we may delete any "vacuous" quantifiers from prefixes; thus from (29) we can get

$$\forall x\, \forall y(\vee Pxy),\, \forall x(\vee Qx\, Sx) \Rightarrow \exists z(\wedge Qz\, \neg Sz),\, \exists z(\wedge Rzz) \qquad (30)$$

In general, these steps produce a sequent in Skolem normal form, all of whose antecedent sentences are *universal clauses*, and all of whose succedent sentences are *existential clauses*.

A universal clause is an ordinary sentence in prenex form whose quantifiers are universal, and whose matrix is a *disjunction* of *literals*, i.e., predications and negations of predications

An existential clause is an ordinary sentence in prenex form, whose quantifiers are existential and whose matrix is a *conjunction* of literals.

We say that such a sequent is in *clausal form*, and the total transformation, starting from an ordinary prenex sequent and first getting its Skolem transform, then refining this to a clausal form sequent as described above, is called the *clausal transformation* of the original prenex sequent; the final sequent so produced is the *clausal transform* of the starting sequent. Thus we have:

every ordinary prenex sequent is true if, and only if, its clausal transform is true

The clausal form is, as we shall see, a very convenient and effective normal form for ordinary sequents.

In the rest of this book we shall investigate some special techniques for the task of establishing the truth of clausal sequents, which are especially suited to the *mechanization* of this task on a computer.

9.   Herbrand Models and Maps

Because of their special form, clausal sequents are amenable to an exceedingly simple method of semantic analysis, which makes it possible to establish their truth by a special technique called *resolution*.

We may always suppose that the calculus *pure* (L) whose clausal sequents we are studying has a non-empty set of ordinary closed terms, by adding, if necessary, a zero-ary function symbol to L. In what follows, we assume this is done. (If a lexicon lacks zero-ary function symbols, then no *ordinary* closed terms can be written that contain only symbols from that lexicon.)

The non-empty set of ordinary closed terms in the calculus *pure* (L) is called its *Herbrand universe*. We may note that it is a proper subset of the logical universe of *pure* (L). Just as, in studying the semantics of sequents in general, we found that *logical models* – those whose universe of individuals is the logical universe and in which all terms denote themselves – sufficed for a complete survey of all the different kinds of semantic possibilities that needed to be accounted for, so we shall find that in studying the semantics of *clausal* sequents, it is enough to consider only *Herbrand models*. An Herbrand model of *pure* (L) is one whose universe of individuals is the Herbrand universe of *pure* (L), and in which each *ordinary* closed term (i.e. each member of the Herbrand universe!) denotes itself.

For example, the calculus whose lexicon is

$$\{H, M, a, b, c\} \quad (H, M \text{ in } P_1; a, b, c \text{ in } C_0) \tag{1}$$

has the Herbrand universe $\{a, b, c\}$; whereas the calculus whose lexicon is

$$\{H, M, a, b, c, g, h\} \ (H, M \text{ in } P_1; a, b, c \text{ in } C_0; g \text{ in } C_1, h \text{ in } C_2) \tag{2}$$

has an infinite Herbrand universe

$$\{a, b, c, (g\ a), (g\ b), (g\ c), (h\ a\ a), (h\ a\ b), \ldots\} \tag{3}$$

which contains all the possible results of using a, b, c, g, h to form a term, e.g.

$$(h(g(g\ a))(h\ a(h\ a(g(h\ a\ a)))))$$

Herbrand universes of *pure* (*L*) have the same property as its logical universes have, whereby if $t_1, \ldots, t_k$ are members of the universe and *c* is a *k*-ary function symbol in *L*, then the term $(c\, t_1 \ldots t_k)$ is also a member. It is this property that permits us to stipulate, in logical models and Herbrand models alike, that every member of the universe denotes itself; for we are thus tacitly taking each *k*-ary function symbol *c* to denote the *k*-ary function, defined at all *k*-tuples $t_1, \ldots, t_k$ of elements of the universe, which yields the *term* $(c\, t_1 \ldots t_k)$ when applied to such a *k*-tuple.

Clausal sequents involve only *ordinary* sentences. So in analysing their semantics we shall be able to ignore the behaviour of models for formulas containing the ∗-symbol.

The behaviour of an Herbrand model for ordinary sentences, and thus in particular for the universal and existential clauses that we find in clausal sequents, is completely fixed by its behaviour for ordinary *predications*. For example, in the calculus with (1) as its lexicon, we need only know the truthvalues denoted in an Herbrand model by the predications

$$\{Ha, Hb, Hc, Ma, Mb, Mc\} \tag{4}$$

in order to work out the truthvalue denoted in the model by *any* ordinary sentence in the calculus, e.g., the sentence

$$\forall x(Mx \rightarrow \exists y(Hy \wedge \neg Mx))$$

We call the set (4) the *Herbrand base* of the calculus with the lexicon (1). In general the Herbrand base of a calculus *pure* (*L*) is the set of all ordinary closed predications that are in *pure* (*L*), and it may of course be an infinite set, as indeed it is when *L* is the lexicon (2). The base then contains such sentences as

$$H(h(g(g\, a))(h\, a(h\, b(g(h\, b\, c)))))$$

and infinitely many others.

Note that an Herbrand model is not in general uniquely determined by the truthvalues it assigns to the members of the Herbrand base; for these assignments leave the freedom to assign denotations to ∗-terms, which is fettered only by the requirements of tables 5.1 and 5.2. However, we do not need to know anything about such aspects of Herbrand models when we are using them to study clausal sequents. From this point of view, the truthvalues assigned by the Herbrand model to the predications in the Herbrand base completely determine all of the model's properties that we are concerned about. So we pay particular attention to these assignments of truthvalues, and call the set of such assignments (i.e. equations $v(X) = w$, X an ordinary predication, w a truthvalue) the *Herbrand map* of the Herbrand model.

For example, there are $64 = 2^6$ different Herbrand maps for the calculus whose lexicon is (1). The calculus whose lexicon is (2) has infinitely many Herbrand maps – indeed an uncountable infinity of them. [For, if $X_1, X_2, \ldots$ is an enumeration of the (countably) infinite Herbrand base of this calculus, then each of its Herbrand maps is a sequence

$$v(X_1) = w_1, v(X_2) = w_2, \ldots$$

of equations. If we were given an *enumeration* of these sequences, say, by the two-way infinite array

$$v_1(X_1) = w_{11}, v_1(X_2) = w_{12}, \ldots, v_1(X_j) = w_{1j}, \ldots$$
$$v_2(X_1) = w_{21}, v_2(X_2) = w_{22}, \ldots, v_2(X_j) = w_{2j}, \ldots$$
$$\cdots$$
$$v_i(X_1) = w_{i1}, v_i(X_2) = w_{i2}, \ldots, v_i(X_j) = w_{ij}, \ldots$$
$$\cdots$$

we could immediately write down an Herbrand map not in the array, namely

$$v(X_1) = \overline{w}_{11}, v(X_2) = \overline{w}_{22}, \ldots, v(X_i) = \overline{w}_{ii}, \ldots$$

in which each sentence X_i is assigned the *opposite* truthvalue, $\overline{w}_{ii}$, to the truthvalue w_{ii} that it receives in the ith map of the array. This use of Cantor's "diagonal argument" shows that any such array must omit at least one map, and hence that no array can contain them all, i.e., that the set of all Herbrand maps is *un*countably infinite.]

Now the reason why Herbrand models are our main tool for studying the semantics of clausal sequents is similar to the reason why logical models are the main tool for studying sequents in general:

> a clausal sequent $\mathcal{A} \Rightarrow \mathcal{B}$ of *pure* (L) is true if, and only if,
> there is no Herbrand model of *pure* (L) that refutes $\mathcal{A} \Rightarrow \mathcal{B}$, i.e.,
> satisfies $\mathcal{A}$ and falsifies $\mathcal{B}$

Thus we can establish the truth of a *clausal* sequent by showing that *no Herbrand model refutes it*, just as we can establish the truth of *any* sequent by showing that *no logical model refutes it*.

But the question whether a given Herbrand model M refutes a given clausal sequent is completely determined by the Herbrand map of M. Indeed this is true of any sequent in Skolem normal form. Let us review why, and how, this is so.

Consider any closed sentence in prenex form:

$$Qx_1 \ldots Q_k x_k \; \varphi(x_1, \ldots, x_k) \tag{5}$$

in which the prefix $Q_1 x_1 \ldots Q_k x_k$ consists either entirely of universal quantifiers or entirely of existential quantifiers, and in which the matrix $\varphi(x_1, \ldots, x_k)$ is some Boolean combination of ordinary predications in which only the variables $x_1, \ldots, x_k$ are free. Each sentence (5) has associated with it its set of *ground instances*

$$\{\varphi(t_1, \ldots, t_k) \mid t_1, \ldots, t_k \text{ in the Herbrand universe}\} \tag{6}$$

i.e., the set of all sentences $\varphi(t_1, \ldots, t_k)$ obtained from the matrix $\varphi(x_1 \ldots x_k)$ by replacing each of its free variables x_j by some term t_j from the Herbrand universe.

Now, if (5) is universal (i.e. if all the quantifiers $Q_1 x_1 \ldots Q_k x_k$ are universal) then (5) is *true* in an Herbrand model M if and only if *every* sentence in (6) is true in M; while if (5) is existential (i.e., if all the quantifiers $Q_1 x_1 \ldots Q_k x_k$ are existential) then (5) is *false* in M if, and only if, *every* sentence in (6) is false in M.

However, the ground instances in (6) are simply Boolean combinations of members of the Herbrand base, and the Herbrand map of M tells us, for each member of the Herbrand base, what its truthvalue is. So each ground instance has its truthvalue completely determined by the Herbrand map of M, and hence so does (5).

In view of this relationship between sentences of the form (5) and their sets of ground instances (6), let us consider the following complete survey of the semantic possibilities of a sequent $\mathscr{A} \Rightarrow \mathscr{B}$ in Skolem normal form. We let $X_1, X_2, \ldots$, as before, be an enumeration of the Herbrand base of the calculus of which the sentences of $\mathscr{A} \Rightarrow \mathscr{B}$ are being considered to be members. We then associate the various Herbrand maps

$$v(X_1) = w_1, v(X_2) = w_2, \ldots \tag{7}$$

with the branches of a binary tree whose nodes are the sequences $(w_1, w_2, \ldots, w_n)$ of truth values:

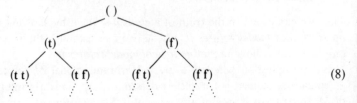

$$\tag{8}$$

so that (in the branch notation of chapter 4) the *branch*

$$(w_1, w_2, \dots \quad) \qquad (9)$$

is associated with the *map* (7).

We now construct from this tree an *Herbrand map tree*, which analyses the semantics of $\mathcal{A} \Rightarrow \mathcal{B}$ as follows. We traverse each branch of (8), constantly patrolling the possibility that, as we arrive at each node N, some ground instance of a sentence A in $\mathcal{A}$ has had all its predications assigned truthvalues and has thereby been determined as a *false* ground instance of A; or else that some ground instance of a sentence B in $\mathcal{B}$ has, by similar means, been determined as a *true* ground instance of B; in both cases, we will have found that in all maps corresponding to branches passing through that node, A will be false (or B will be true). So we *drop* all the nodes of (8) that are proper descendants of the node N, and we label N with the sentence A (or the sentence B).

The resulting Herbrand map tree T is a complete survey of the semantics of $\mathcal{A} \Rightarrow \mathcal{B}$ in this sense, that any Herbrand map of an Herbrand model M that fails to refute $\mathcal{A} \Rightarrow \mathcal{B}$ will correspond to a branch of T that terminates in a node labelled by either an A in $\mathcal{A}$ that M falsifies, or a B in $\mathcal{B}$ that M satisfies. On the other hand, an Herbrand map of an Herbrand model that *refutes* $\mathcal{A} \Rightarrow \mathcal{B}$ will correspond to a branch of T that does *not* so terminate. If the Herbrand base is infinite, such a branch of T will be an infinite branch; if the Herbrand base is finite, it will be a branch of T whose tip is not labelled by an A in $\mathcal{A}$ or a B in $\mathcal{B}$.

For example, let the calculus be that whose lexicon is (1) and whose Herbrand base is therefore (4). Then the binary tree (8) is in this case a finite tree of six levels corresponding to the enumeration, say,

$$Ha, Ma, Hb, Mb, Hc, Mc \qquad (10)$$

of the base (4). If we then draw up the Herbrand map tree T for the sequent

$$Ha, \forall x(Hx \to Mx) \Rightarrow Ma \qquad (11)$$

we get:

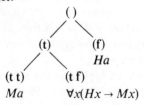

and we therefore conclude that no Herbrand model refutes (11) and that (11) is true. On the other hand if we construct the Herbrand map tree for the sequent

$$\neg Hb, Mb, Ha, \neg Ma \Rightarrow \exists x(Mx \wedge Hx) \tag{12}$$

we get the tree shown in figure 9.1, in which the branches with the unlabelled tips correspond to maps that refute (11). So we conclude (11) is false.

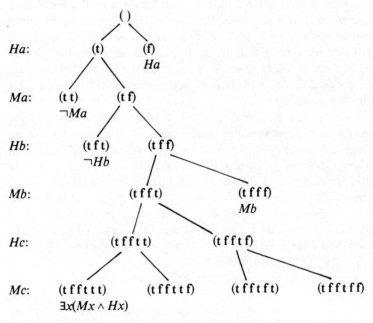

Figure 9.1

Only when the Herbrand base is finite, of course, will the survey produce a *finite* Herbrand map tree for a *false* sequent. But it will produce a finite Herbrand map tree for a *true* sequent (by König's Lemma!) whether or not the Herbrand base is finite, and indeed whether or not the sequent $\mathscr{A} \Rightarrow \mathscr{B}$ is finite.

[Herbrand map trees illustrate, once again, the compactness phenomenon: if an *infinite* sequent $\mathscr{A} \Rightarrow \mathscr{B}$ is true, any finite Herbrand map tree for it will yield a *finite* sequent $\mathscr{A}' \Rightarrow \mathscr{B}'$ that is true, and for which $\mathscr{A}' \subseteq \mathscr{A}$, $\mathscr{B}' \subseteq \mathscr{B}$; we just let $\mathscr{A}'$ and $\mathscr{B}'$ be the sentences from $\mathscr{A}$ and $\mathscr{B}$ that label the tips of the given map tree.]

Now the method of Herbrand map trees applies to *any* sequent in the Skolem normal form; but we are particularly interested in it when the sequent is a *clausal* sequent. The reason for this is that a certain pattern of inference for clausal sequents – called *resolution* – emerges directly and naturally from a closer analysis of Herbrand map trees for clausal sequents. The resolution principle is an inference principle that, in its full generality, requires rather more effort to apply than is usually associated with single inference steps. By packing more of the combinatorial linkages of a proof into the insides of their inference steps, rather than having them externally explicit as relationships between many more, but simpler, steps, a resolution proof of a sequent is a very much simplified total construction. However, the nature of each individual step in the proof is untraditionally complex – and is more suited to being taken, and certified as correct, by a computer than by a human. These remarks will become clear after we have examined the resolution principle in detail and have come to understand what it is and how it works. Our undertaking to do so marks a transition in this book, from a preoccupation with "human-oriented" inference principles to a concern with what can only be described as "machine-oriented" inference principles.

10. Quad Notation for Clausal Sequents

We will be saved from much needless mental effort and writing in our discussions of the resolution principle for clausal sequents, by using a economical notation that represents the essential features of a clausal sequent and dispenses with the inessential ones. This notation is called the *quad* notation, because of the use it makes of the special symbol $\Box$ ("quad") in representing clauses.

In the quad notation, a clausal sequent $\mathscr{A} \Rightarrow \mathscr{B}$, consisting essentially of *two* sets, a set $\mathscr{A}$ of *universal clauses* and set $\mathscr{B}$ of *existential clauses*, is written as a *single* set $\mathscr{S}$ of *clauses*, with no distinction, or indication, as to whether each clause is universal or existential. For example, the clausal sequent

$$\forall x\, \forall y(\vee \neg Pxy\, Qx\, \neg Qy),\ \forall x(\vee Pxx) \Rightarrow \exists x\, \exists y(\wedge \neg Pxy\, Qx\, \neg Qy) \qquad (1)$$

becomes, in quad notation, the set:

$$\{Pxy\, Qy\, \Box\, Qx,\ \Box Pxx,\ Qx\, \Box\, Pxy\, Qy\} \qquad (2)$$

of three *clauses*. The convention is that a *universal clause*

$$\forall x_1 \ldots \forall x_k (\vee \neg N_1 \ldots \neg N_r,\, P_1 \ldots P_s)$$

is represented as

$$\{N_1 \ldots N_r\}\, \Box\, \{P_1 \ldots P_s\}$$

and an *existential clause*

$$\exists x_1 \ldots \exists x_k(\wedge \neg N_1\, \neg N_r\, P_1 \ldots P_s)$$

as

$$\{P_1 \ldots P_s\}\, \Box\, \{N_1 \ldots N_r\}$$

with the curly brackets omitted unless confusion would result. All quantifiers are dropped. Thus each clause, in the quad notation for $\mathscr{A} \Rightarrow \mathscr{B}$, loses its identity as a universal clause in $\mathscr{A}$ or an existential clause in $\mathscr{B}$; the set $\mathscr{S}$ of "neutral" clauses that takes the place of $\mathscr{A} \Rightarrow \mathscr{B}$ is a kind of diagram showing merely what the essential structure of each *matrix* is in the universal and existential clauses of $\mathscr{A} \Rightarrow \mathscr{B}$: what predications it contains, and which are negated and which are not.

The quad notation (2) for the sequent (1) would be obtained also if we transcribed the sequent, say:

$$\Rightarrow \exists x(\wedge \neg Pxx), \exists x\, \exists y(\wedge\, Pxy\, Qy\, \neg Qx), \exists x\, \exists y(\wedge\, \neg Qy\, \neg Pxy\, Qx) \qquad (3)$$

as is easily verified:

$\exists x(\wedge \neg Pxx)$ becomes $\square Pxx$

$\exists x\, \exists y(\wedge\, Pxy\, Qy\, \neg Qx)$ becomes $Pxy\, Qy\, \square\, Qx$

$\exists x\, \exists y(\wedge\, \neg Qy\, \neg Pxy\, Qx)$ becomes $Qx\, \square\, Pxy\, Qy$

Thus the quad notation for clausal sequents provides a certain kind of *normal form* for clausal sequents. All clausal sequents having the same quad notation are, in a suitable sense, equivalent to each other: each is refuted by exactly the same models as the others are.

This means that we can convert a "quad sequent" back to ordinary notation in any of the ways we like that inverts a possible transcription *into* quad notation. We could, for example, convert (2) back into (1), or into (3), or indeed into any sequent $\mathscr{A} \Rightarrow \mathscr{B}$ that results from taking each clause

$$X_1 \ldots X_m \,\square\, Y_1 \ldots Y_n$$

in quad notation and writing it *either* as a universal clause

$$\forall x_1 \ldots x_k\, (\vee \neg X_1 \ldots \neg X_m\, Y_1 \ldots Y_n)$$

to be placed in the antecedent $\mathscr{A}$, *or* as an existential clause

$$\exists x_1 \ldots \exists x_k(\wedge X_1 \ldots X_m \neg Y_1 \ldots \neg Y_n)$$

to be placed in the succedent $\mathscr{B}$. In each case we quantify every variable.

That all sequents $\mathscr{A} \Rightarrow \mathscr{B}$ obtainable in this way from a given quad sequent are equivalent, is immediately clear from the fact that we have, in general, for all models M:

M refutes $\mathscr{A} \Rightarrow \mathscr{B}, X$ if, and only if, M refutes $\neg X, \mathscr{A} \Rightarrow \mathscr{B}$

and

M refutes $\mathscr{A} \Rightarrow \mathscr{B}, \neg X$ if, and only if, M refutes $X, \mathscr{A} \Rightarrow \mathscr{B}$

together with

$$\neg\, \forall x_1 \ldots \forall x_k(\vee \neg X_1 \ldots \neg X_m\, Y_1 \ldots Y_n) \Leftrightarrow$$
$$\exists x_1 \ldots \exists x_k(\wedge X_1 \ldots X_m \neg Y_1 \ldots \neg Y_n)$$

and

$$\neg\, \exists x_1 \ldots \exists x_k(\wedge X_1 \ldots X_m \neg Y_1 \ldots \neg Y_n) \Leftrightarrow$$
$$\forall x_1 \ldots \forall x_k(\vee \neg X_1 \ldots \neg X_m\, Y_1 \ldots Y_n)$$

So we shall work henceforth with "quad sequents"

$$\mathcal{S} = \{\mathcal{L}_1 \square \mathcal{R}_1, \dots, \mathcal{L}_p \square \mathcal{R}_p\}$$

which are sets of "quad clauses" $\mathcal{L} \square \mathcal{R}$ in which $\mathcal{L}$ and $\mathcal{R}$ are sets of predications containing, in general, variables. Always we shall be ready to invoke the fact that such a quad sequent $\mathcal{S}$ is simply a notation representing any one of the family of mutually equivalent clausal sequents that translate into $\mathcal{S}$ by the conventions we have described.

To fix ideas, it often helps to choose some particular clausal sequent to "see" when confronted with a quad sequent. The one that most people use for this purpose is that corresponding to giving each clause in the quad sequent the *universal* reading. Thus when confronted with (2) one would "see" the clausal sequent

$$\forall x\, \forall y (\vee \,\neg Pxy\; \neg Qy\; Qx),\; \forall x (\wedge\, Pxx),\; \forall x\, \forall y (\vee\, \neg Qx\, Pxy\; Qy) \Rightarrow \qquad (4)$$

which says in effect that the set of its clauses is unsatisfiable.

Either, or both, of the sets $\mathcal{L}, \mathcal{R}$ in a quad clause $\mathcal{L} \square \mathcal{R}$ may be empty. When both are empty, the quad clause becomes just $\square$, the quad symbol standing alone representing the empty clause. Considered as a universal clause it is the empty disjunction in the antecedent; but considered as an existential clause it is the empty conjunction in the succedent. In either case, the sequent must be true; in the first case its antecedent is unsatisfiable; in the second, its succedent is unfalsifiable.

We conclude that

if $\square$ is in $\mathcal{S}$ then $\mathcal{S}$ is true

for all quad sequents $\mathcal{S}$.

Now, consider the example used in the last chapter to illustrate the notion of an Herbrand map tree:

$$Ha,\, \forall x (Hx \rightarrow Mx) \Rightarrow Ma.$$

In clausal form, this is

$$Ha,\, \forall x (\vee\, \neg Hx\, Mx) \Rightarrow Ma$$

and so, in quad form, it is

$$\{\square Ha,\, Hx \square Mx,\, Ma \square\} \qquad (5)$$

The ground instances of a quad clause $\mathcal{L} \square \mathcal{R}$ are all the quad clauses $\mathcal{L}' \square \mathcal{R}'$ obtainable from $\mathcal{L} \square \mathcal{R}$ by replacing its variables with terms from the Herbrand universe. So, in this example, (with the Herbrand universe $\{a, b, c\}$) the ground instances of $Hx \square Mx$ are: $Ha \square Ma$, $Hb \square Mb$, $Hc \square Mc$. If we use the enumeration

$$Ha, Ma, Hb, Mb, Hc, Mc$$

of the Herbrand base, the Herbrand map tree of (5) is:

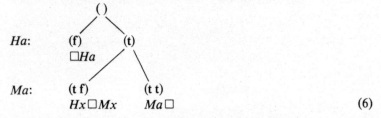

$$(6)$$

In this tree, we observe a very simple example of the following general pattern:

L:

$$(7)$$

in which some node (...) of the tree is not itself labelled by a clause, but has immediate successors (... f), (... t) both of which are labelled by clauses.

Intuitively, what this pattern reveals is that the Herbrand map "decisions" down to and including the node (...) have not yet been "adverse" for any clause in the sequent, but that the very *next* decision, whichever way it is made, is adverse for some clause in the sequent. If we make the predication L denote f, then $A \square B$ is adversely affected; if on the other hand we make L denote t, then $C \square D$ is adversely affected. By "adversely affected" we mean, of course, that some ground instance of $A \square B$, or of $C \square D$, finds itself with a left set and a right set whose members all denote truthvalues decided upon already, but none in the left set denotes f, and none in the right set denotes t. If we are "seeing" the quad clauses with the "universal" reading, these ground instances are thus *disjunctions*, which the decisions down to (... f) and to (... t) respectively have caused to denote f.

Note that, in (6), the pattern (7) shows up with $Hx \square Mx$ as the $A \square B$ and $Ma \square$ as the $C \square D$, and with the predication Ma as the L. By deciding that Ma shall denote f, we falsify the disjunction $Ha \square Ma$ (alias $(\vee \neg Ha\, Ma)$, which is a ground instance of $Hx \square Mx$; but by deciding that Ma shall denote t, we falsify the disjunction $Ma \square$ (alias $(\vee \neg Ma)$), which is (trivially) a ground instance of itself.

The two ground instances, then, in (6), which are the reasons for the labels $Hx \square Mx$ and $Ma \square$, are

$$Ha \square Ma, Ma \square$$

and the predication L, which just receives its truthvalue at those tips, is Ma. This illustrates another facet of the general pattern (7), which we exhibit as:

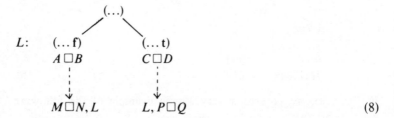

$$L: \quad (\ldots f) \qquad (\ldots t)$$
$$A \square B \qquad C \square D$$
$$M \square N, L \qquad L, P \square Q \tag{8}$$

showing, below each of the clauses $A \square B$ and $C \square D$, their ground instances that are the causes of the labellings. The predication L must occur in each, as shown. Here, we are writing the right-hand side of $M \square N, L$ as a set in which L occurs and whose remaining members, if any, comprise N. Similarly the left-hand side of $L, P \square Q$ is a set in which L occurs and in which the remaining members, if any, comprise the set P.

In (8) we say the node $(\ldots f)$ *fails* the clause $A \square B$, and that the node $(\ldots t)$ *fails* the clause $C \square D$; and we classify them as *failure nodes* of the Herbrand map tree. The node $(\ldots)$ is called an *inference node* of the Herbrand map tree. Inference nodes in general are those that are not failure nodes but whose immediate successors are both failure nodes. Note that in the tree (6), the node (f) is a failure node, and fails $\square Ha$; but ( ) is not an inference node since only one, not both, of its immediate successors is a failure node. However, (t) *is* an inference node, since *both* (t f) *and* (t t) are failure nodes.

Every Herbrand map tree whose branches all end in failure nodes (and which is therefore finite) is, as we have seen, direct evidence that the sequent it analyses is true. We say such a tree *fails*, thinking of this as meaning, intuitively, that it fails to find an Herbrand map that refutes the sequent being analysed. So: if an Herbrand map tree T for a quad sequent $\mathcal{S}$ fails, then

$\mathcal{S}$ is true;

but also, as we shall now see,

if $\square$ is not in $\mathcal{S}$ then T contains an inference node.

The proviso is needed: for if □ is in $\mathscr{S}$, the node ( ) would be a failure node, since it would fail □! The tree T would then be simply:

( )
□

and so of course it would not contain any inference node.

However, if □ is *not* in $\mathscr{S}$, but its Herbrand map tree fails, there *has* to be an inference node in T for much the same reason as the reason why König's Lemma is true. For *assume* T contains no inference node; then since ( ) is not one, at least one of (f), (t) is *not a failure node*. But, in general, if a node (...) in T is not a failure node, then *at least one of its immediate successors* (... f), (... t) is not a failure node; for otherwise (...) would be an *inference* node, and T has not got any. So just as in the proof of König's Lemma we get a branch of T consisting entirely of immortal nodes, so here we get a branch of T *consisting entirely of nodes that are not failure nodes*. However, since T *does* fail, such a branch does not occur in it. Hence our assumption that T contains no inference node was false, and we conclude that, as stated, T contains at least one of them.

What this shows is that when $\mathscr{S}$ is a true sequent and T is any Herbrand map tree of $\mathscr{S}$, there will always be at least one inference node in T, i.e., T will always exhibit the pattern (8), with $A\,\square\,B$ and $C\square D$ both in $\mathscr{S}$.

The reader may be wondering why we have chosen the term "inference node" to describe a node like (...) in (8). It is because, as we shall see, such a node represents the fact that *an inference can be made* (using the resolution principle) in which the sequent $\mathscr{S}$ is the premiss. The conclusion of that inference is a sequent $\mathscr{S}$, R obtained from $\mathscr{S}$ by adding to it clause R, which "resolves" (in the sense to be explained in the sequel) the clauses $A\,\square\,B$ and $C\square D$. The resulting sequent $\mathscr{S}$, R, and the sequent $\mathscr{S}$ itself are related by:

$\mathscr{S}$ is true if, and only if, $\mathscr{S}$, R is true

It is thus a correct inference to *add* to a sequent $\mathscr{S}$ a clause R that "resolves" two clauses in $\mathscr{S}$; but it is also a correct inference to *drop* a clause R from a sequent, provided it "resolves" two clauses in the sequent that remains.

In the example (6) the clause that "resolves" $Hx\square Mx$ and $Ma\square$ is the clause: $Ha\square$. Thus we are saying that the sequent

$\{\square\,Ha,\ Hx\square\,Mx,\ Ma\,\square\}$ (5)

is true if, and only if, the sequent

$$\{\Box Ha, Hx\,\Box Mx, Ma\,\Box, Ha\,\Box\} \tag{9}$$

is true.

Now let us compare the Herbrand map tree (6) of the sequent (5) with that for (9), using the same enumeration of the Herbrand base. We put them side by side, with (6) on the left:

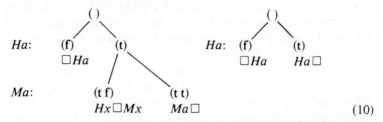

(10)

The map tree for the sequent (9) is smaller than that for the sequent (5), because the clause $Ha\,\Box$ causes a failure to occur at the node (t). This is typical of the relationship between an Herbrand map tree for a true sequent $\mathscr{S}$ and one for $\mathscr{S}, R$, where R "resolves" two clauses in $\mathscr{S}$: *if $\Box$ is not in $\mathscr{S}$, then the map tree for $\mathscr{S}, R$ is smaller than that for $\mathscr{S}$.* (In making this claim, we are assuming that both map trees are drawn up using the same enumeration of the Herbrand base.) We *also* are assuming that the clauses chosen to label failure nodes are selected by the same criterion (if more than one clause is failed by the node), but the claim holds independently of this assumption.

So: we are saying that each inference node in an Herbrand map tree for a true sequent $\mathscr{S}$ determines a clause R, which resolves two clauses in $\mathscr{S}$ *and which is not itself a member of $\mathscr{S}$.* Had R been in $\mathscr{S}$, the inference node would in fact have been a failure node, for it would have failed R.

The whole argument can be repeated for $\mathscr{S}, R$. In (10) the right-hand tree has an inference node; it is the root node ( ). The two clauses causing the respective failures are $\Box Ha$ and $Ha\,\Box$ and hence these two can be resolved; and the clause that resolves them is $\Box$. If we add $\Box$ to the sequent (9) we get the sequent

$$\{\Box Ha, Hx\,\Box Mx, Ma\,\Box, Ha\,\Box, \Box\} \tag{11}$$

whose map tree is:

( )
□

The overall process has thus moved us from (5) to (9) to (11) in two steps of "resolution" and has ended with a sequent containing □.

which is thus immediately recognisable as true. By reversing the sequence of inferences we can thus go from (11) to (9) to (5), "taking back" the certainty of the truth of (11) to (9) and thence to (5).

Now in this discussion, which was an informal first look at the general nature of the resolution principle and its relationship to the idea of Herbrand map trees for true sequents, we have simply declared, without explanation, that certain clauses "resolve" certain pairs of other clauses. We said that

$Ha \square$ resolves $Hx \square Mx$ and $Ma \square$
$\square$ resolves $\quad \square Ha$ and $Ha \square$

but we did not explain why. The explanation is partly given in the diagram (8), which shows that, in general, if we consider the two clauses $A \square B$ and $C \square D$ at the failure nodes of an inference node (...), there will be two ground instances

$$M \square N, L \text{ and } L, P \square Q \tag{12}$$

of $A \square B$ and $C \square D$ respectively, which contain the predication L which receives its truthvalue at these two failure nodes. If we ask what this tells us about $A \square B$ and $C \square D$, the answer is that it shows us that *there must be predications in B and C, of which L is a ground instance*. Indeed, we can redraw the diagram (8) to bring this out:

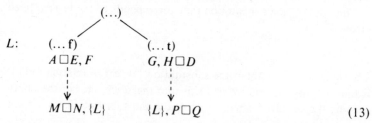

$$M \square N, \{L\} \qquad \{L\}, P \square Q \tag{13}$$

We are now exhibiting $A \square B$ with its right-hand side B decomposed into two disjoint sets E and F, and $C \square D$ with its left-hand side decomposed into two disjoint sets G and H, with the intention of showing that the sets F and G are those that contain the predications that "become" the predication L when we pass to the ground instances $M \square N, L$ of $A \square B$ and $L, P \square Q$ of $C \square D$.

At the same time, the sets A, E become the sets M, N; and the sets H, D become the sets P, Q. The broken-line arrow signifies the operation of "instantiating" $A \square B$, $C \square D$, namely, replacing the *variables* in each of them by *terms* from the Herbrand universe. In the case of (13), which occurs in (6) we have:

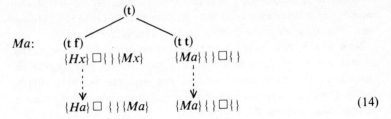

$$Ma: \quad (t\ f) \qquad\qquad (t\ t)$$

(14)

and so the broken-lined arrow signifies the operation of putting the term *a* for the variable *x*.

Such an operation is called a *substitution*. In general, a substitution consists of the act of simultaneously replacing each of a given list

$$(x_1, \ldots, x_k)$$

of variables by the corresponding term in a given list

$$(t_1, \ldots, t_k)$$

of terms. We denote this operation by writing the set

$$\{\langle x_1, t_k \rangle, \ldots, \langle x_k, t_k \rangle\}$$

of ordered pairs. It is understood that the variables $x_1, \ldots, x_k$ are all distinct.

Thus in (14) the substitution that corresponds to the broken-lined arrow is

$$\{\langle x, a \rangle\}$$

The thing to notice about the substitution $\{\langle x, a \rangle\}$ in relation to (14) is that it turns the sets $\{Mx\}$, $\{Ma\}$ into the *same* set; i.e., they both become the set $\{Ma\}$ when we carry out the substitution $\{\langle x, a \rangle\}$ on their members.

This fact about $\{\langle x, a \rangle\}$ and (14) is a simple special case of the following general one: we have a substitution θ and two sets F, G of predications, and the set $F \cup G$ becomes, under the substitution θ, a *singleton* set $\{L\}$; we write this:

$$(F \cup G)\theta = \{L\} \tag{15}$$

In (14),

       θ is $\{\langle x, a \rangle\}$
       F is $\{Mx\}$
       G is $\{Ma\}$
       L is Ma

Here is another, less simple example:

$$\theta = \{\langle x, (h(g\ a))\rangle, \langle y, (g\ a)\rangle, \langle z, (g(h(g\ a)))\rangle, \langle u, (h(g\ a))\rangle,$$
$$\langle v, (g(h(g\ a)))\rangle, \langle s, (g(h(g\ a)))\rangle, \langle w, a\rangle\}$$
$$F = \{(A\ x(g\ x)), (A(h\ y)z)\}$$
$$G = \{(A\ u\ v), (A(h(g\ w))s)\}$$
$$L = (A(h(g\ a))(g(h(g\ a)))) \tag{16}$$

which illustrates that, in general, F and G need not themselves be singletons. The main point is that the substitution θ, the sets F and G, and the predication L should satisfy the condition (15).

When (15) holds, we say that θ *unifies* the set $(F \cup G)$. Intuitively, a substitution unifies a set of predications if it "shrinks it down to a singleton" by making each predication in the set look like each other one in the set.

In the example (16) θ makes $(A\ x(g\ x))$ become $(A(h(g\ a))(g(h(g\ a))))$ and also makes $(A(h\ y)z)$ become $(A(h(g\ a))(g(h(g\ a))))$; hence θ unifies F; it also unifies G; and it unifies $(F \cup G)$.

Now, if we re-examine the diagram (13) and let θ be the substitution corresponding to the broken-lined arrows, we see that the essential feature of the two failure clauses

$$A \,\square\, E, F \quad G, H \,\square\, D \tag{17}$$

is that θ unifies $(F \cup G)$ and that the singleton to which θ shrinks $(F \cup G)$ is the one whose member is the very L which receives its truthvalue at these failure nodes.

It is from this feature of the situation that the resolution principle emerges. *Two clauses can be resolved if, and only if, they can be written as in (17) in such a way that there is a substitution θ which unifies the set $(F \cup G)$.* In writing the clauses in the pattern (17), the sets E, F must be disjoint, as must the sets G, H.

The clause R which resolves $A \,\square\, E, F$ and $G, H \,\square\, D$ is then;

$$R = (A \cup H)\sigma \,\square\, (E \cup D)\sigma \tag{18}$$

where σ is the substitution that unifies $(F \cup G)$ *in the most general way that this can be done.*

There is an R which resolves $A \,\square\, B, C \,\square\, D$ for each way that $A \,\square\, B, C \,\square\, D$ can be written in the pattern (17) so that $(F \cup G)$ can be unified; and this R is given by (18), where σ is the most general substitution that unifies $(F \cup G)$. For example, let $(F \cup G)$ be

$$\{(P\ x), (P(g\ y))\}$$

then all of the following unify it

$$\theta_1 = \{\langle x, (g(h\,a))\rangle, \langle y, (h\,a)\rangle\}$$
$$\theta_2 = \{\langle x, (g(ka(h\,a)))\rangle, \langle y, (ka(h\,a))\rangle\}$$
$$\sigma = \{\langle x, (g\,y)\rangle, \langle y, y\rangle\}$$

but only σ does so in the most general way that it can be done.

Note that

$$\{(P\,x), (P(g\,y))\}\theta_1 = \{(P(g(h\,a)))\}$$

while

$$\{(P\,x), (P(g\,y))\}\sigma = \{(P(g\,y))\}$$

so that

$$\{(P\,x), (P(g\,y))\}\theta_1 = \{(P\,x), (P(g\,y))\}\sigma\theta_1 \qquad (19)$$

where on the right-hand side we mean: first do σ, then do θ_1. The substitution σ will satisfy (19) no matter what substitution θ_1 is chosen, so long as θ_1 unifies the set $\{(P\,x), (P(g\,y))\}$. This is the technical content of the assertion that σ is the most general substitution that unifies $\{(P\,x), (P(g\,y))\}$: that $S\theta = S\sigma\theta$ for *all* sets S of predications or of terms, and *all* substitutions θ that unify $\{(P\,x), (P(g\,y))\}$. Now consider the equation (18) again, in relation to the diagram (13). We can now see that if we form the clause R as in (18), and if θ is the substitution that produces $M \square N$, $\{L\}$ and $\{L\}$, $P \square Q$ from $A\,\square\,E$, F and G, $H\square D$ respectively, then:

$$R\theta = (M \cup P)\,\square\,(N \cup Q) \qquad (20)$$

Since:

$$R = (A \cup H)\sigma\,\square\,(E \cup D)\sigma \quad \text{by (18)}$$

we have

$$\begin{aligned}
R\theta &= (A \cup H)\sigma\theta\,\square\,(E \cup D)\sigma\theta \\
&= (A \cup H)\theta\,\square\,(E \cup D)\theta \quad \text{appealing to } \theta = \sigma\theta \\
&= (A\theta \cup H\theta)\,\square\,(E\theta \cup D\theta) \\
&= (M \cup P)\,\square\,(N \cup Q) \quad \text{by definition of } \theta
\end{aligned}$$

But reflection on the contents of the sets M, N, P and Q shows that, in the diagram (13), the ground instance $(M \cup P)\,\square\,(N \cup Q)$ of R would be falsified at the node (...), if not already falsified at a higher node. This shows why it is that, if we add the clause R to the sequent $\mathcal{S}$, we get a smaller Herbrand map tree than we got for $\mathcal{S}$ itself: the ground instance $R\theta$ is failed by the inference node, or by some node even earlier than the inference node, which produced the clause R.

However, R need not have been unearthed by this process at all. There is no need to draw up an Herbrand map tree for the sequent $\mathscr{S}$ in order to discover which of its clauses, if any, will resolve. We need only examine the clauses of $\mathscr{S}$ in pairs, looking for the ways in which we can make the pattern:

$$A \,\square\, E, F \quad G, H \,\square\, D$$

occur in such a way that $(F \cup G)$ is unifiable; we then find the most general unifier σ of $(F \cup G)$ and form the clause:

$$R = (A \cup H)\sigma \,\square\, (E \cup D)\sigma$$

Since there are only finitely many ways in which this can be done, there are only finitely many clauses R that are immediately eligible to be added to $\mathscr{S}$ as "resolvent" clauses.

It remains to explain how we can determine whether $(F \cup G)$ is unifiable and how we can find, if so, its most general unifier σ. This is really the whole nub of the resolution principle, and requires a thorough study of the whole "unification" phenomenon. We shall devote the next chapter to this study.

11. Unification

In the previous chapter we were informally introduced to the main ideas behind the resolution principle, as we observed its emergence from a closer analysis of Herbrand map trees of true clausal sequents. Now we must set up these ideas carefully and fully in a form suitable for their intended use as practical tools. We begin with the subject of *substitutions* and the *unification* phenomenon.

From a proper mathematical point of view, a substitution is a certain kind of function, or operation, which is *applied* to the symbolic objects of our calculi – the symbols and the formulas built from them – to produce other symbolic objects of the same kind, as *results*.

For our purposes we take, as the domains of application of substitution operations, the sets whose elements are the Boolean operators, the constructor and predicate symbols of some lexicon, and all formulas constructible from these – i.e., all formulas of the pure calculus with that lexicon – that contain no *bound* occurrences of variables, hence no occurrences of $\forall$, $\exists$, or $*$.

We shall call the constructor and predicate symbols, and the Boolean operator symbols, *constants*. Our sets thus contain two kinds of *expressions*: the *symbols*, which are either constants or variables; and the *applicative expressions*:

$$(\Omega \, e_1 \dots e_n)$$

which are formed by making a list whose first component is a constant and whose remaining components are expressions in the set. The constant Ω in such an applicative expression may be a Boolean operator, a constructor symbol, or a predicate symbol; we do not, in the present context, need to distinguish between the different kinds of constant.

Let E be such a set of expressions. Then a substitution is a *function* $\theta: E \to E$, defined for each expression in E and yielding a result that is an expression in E, which satisfies the conditions:

(1) $s\theta = s$, for all *constants* s in E

(2) $(e_0\, e_1 \ldots e_n)\theta = (e_0\theta\, e_1\theta \ldots e_n\theta)$ for all
   applicative expressions $(e_0\, e_1 \ldots e_n)$ in E

(3) $x\theta$ is a *term* in E, for all *variables* in E

The first condition says that substitution operations do not change constants; thus $\neg\theta = \neg$, $\vee\theta = \vee$, $R\theta = \theta$, and so on (where R is some constant; in general we shall use capital letters for constructor and predicate symbols, and small letters for variables). We write the substitution symbol on the right of its argument.

The second condition says that substitution operations change applicative expressions in a certain characteristic way, namely, by changing their components *independently* of each other, and producing the applicative expression whose components are those expressions which are thereby produced.

The third condition says that variables always become *terms* under substitution operations; this in particular allows a variable x to stay unchanged

$$x\theta = x$$

or to become a different variable

$$x\theta = y$$

or to become an applicative expression whose operator is a constructor symbol and whose operand is a list of terms

$$x\theta = (\Omega\, t_1 \ldots t_n)$$

We use small Greek letters to denote substitutions, and we reserve the letter ε to denote the *identity substitution*, which leaves all expressions unchanged:

$$A\varepsilon = A, \text{ for all expressions } A \text{ in } E \tag{4}$$

Conditions (1), (2) and (3) govern our entire theory of substitutions. An immediate consequence of them is the fact that every substitution θ is completely determined in its effect on all expressions in E *by its effect on the variables in E*. We need only know what expression $x\theta$ is, for each variable x in E, to work out, using (1) and (2) repeatedly, the expression $A\theta$ for an arbitrary expression A in E.

For if A is a constant, (1) tells us that $A\theta$ is A, while if A is an applicative expression, say $(A_0 \ldots A_n)$, then (2) tells us that $A\theta$ is the applicative expression $(A_0\theta \ldots A_n\theta)$, so that to work out what $A\theta$ is we need only work out what $A_0\theta, \ldots, A_n\theta$ are, by the same techniques, and then assemble these expressions to form $A\theta$.

In practice, one finds $A\theta$, given θ at the variables only, by copying out or rewriting A, and whenever one encounters a variable x in A one writes into the copy, instead of x, whatever the expression $x\theta$ is. Thus, if A is

$$\neg(F\,x(G\,y\,x)) \to (F(H\,x\,y))$$

and we know that

$$x\theta = (H\,B)$$
$$y\theta = (G(H\,C))$$

then we can easily write out $A\theta$ in one pass:

$$\neg(F(H\,B)(G(G(H\,C))(H\,B))) \to (F(H(H\,B)(G(H\,C))))$$

This fact about substitutions allows us to use a simple, useful convention for describing them. We give a list of the variables that are *changed* by θ into terms different from themselves, with the term *into* which each variable is changed by θ. That is, we give the pairs $\langle x, x\theta \rangle$ such that $x \neq x\theta$. The convention is that, if $x \neq x\theta$, then we *must* give the pair, but if $x = x\theta$ (so that the pair is $\langle x, x \rangle$) we *need not* (although there is nothing wrong about doing so). So, if we write, e.g.

$$\theta = \{\langle x, (H\,B) \rangle, \langle y, (G(H\,C)) \rangle\}$$

we are saying, according to this convention, that if A is any variable other than x or y, then $A\theta = A$.

This notation is hardly of any use if θ changes each of *infinitely* many variables into some term other than itself. But we do not encounter the need to describe such substitutions very often, and when we do, we have to fall back on some other method of description to say what the substitution does.

Now it is also handy to be able to consider the resulting *set* of expressions when we apply a substitution θ to each expression in some given set S of expressions. We write $S\theta$ for the resulting set, with the understanding that $S\theta$ may well have fewer members than S does. For example, if S is the set

$$\{x, y, z, (H(G\,u))\} \tag{5}$$

and θ is the substitution

$$\{\langle x, (H(G\,B)) \rangle, \langle y, (H(G\,B)) \rangle, \langle z, (H(G\,B)) \rangle, \langle u, B \rangle\} \tag{6}$$

then $S\theta$ is the singleton set

   $\{(H(G\ B))\}$

since θ maps each expression in S into the *same* expression $(H(G\ B))$.
Indeed, this is an example of the *unification* of a set by a substitution.

   In general, if S is any set of expressions and θ is any substitution
we say that θ *unifies* S if, and only if, the set $S\theta$ is a singleton set.
The substitution θ is said then to be a *unifier* of S, and S is said to
be a *unifiable* set. A unifiable set may have many – indeed infinitely
many – distinct unifiers. For example, the set (5) just examined has
not only the unifier (6) but also

$$\sigma = \{\langle x, (H(G\ u))\rangle, \langle y, (H(G\ u))\rangle, \langle z, (H(G\ u))\rangle\} \tag{7}$$

which transforms (5) to the set

   $\{(H(G\ u))\}$

and

$$\lambda = \{\langle x, (H(G(H\ B)))\rangle, \langle y, (H(G(H\ B)))\rangle, \langle z, (H(G(H\ B)))\rangle,$$
$$\langle u, (H\ B))\rangle\} \tag{8}$$

which transforms (5) to the singleton set

   $\{(H(G(H\ B)))\}$

It is easy to see that if we take an arbitrary term A and perform the
substitution

$$\mu = \{\langle u, A \rangle\} \tag{9}$$

on the set $\{(H(G\ u)\}$, we get a set, namely $\{(H(G\ A))\}$, which could be
produced directly from (5) by the substitution

$$\rho = \{\langle x, (H(G\ A))\rangle, \langle y, (H(G\ A))\rangle, \langle z, (H(G\ A))\rangle, \langle u, A \rangle\} \tag{10}$$

That is, the effect of ρ upon (5) is the same as that of *first* doing σ
to (5) and *then* doing μ.

   Since substitutions are operations acting on a set and yielding
results in the same set, we may usefully consider their *composition*.
In general, if θ and λ are two substitutions, their *composition* $\theta\lambda$ is
the substitution defined by

$$A(\theta\lambda) = (A\theta)\lambda \text{ for all expressions } A \tag{11}$$

In other words: to find the expression yielded by $\theta\lambda$, one first finds
that yielded by θ and then performs λ on it. For example, the substitution ρ described by (10) is the composition $\sigma\mu$ of those described
by (7) and (9).

   It is very simple to write out the *description* of a composition $\theta\lambda$

if we have the descriptions of θ and of λ. Suppose the description of θ is

$$\{\langle x_1, A_1 \rangle, \ldots, \langle x_k, A_k \rangle\}$$

and that of λ is:

$$\{\langle y_1, B_1 \rangle, \ldots, \langle y_m, B_m \rangle\}$$

Then the description of $\theta\lambda$ is

$$\{\langle x_1, (x_1\theta)\lambda \rangle, \ldots, \langle x_k, (x_k\theta)\lambda \rangle, \langle y_1, (y_1\theta)\lambda \rangle, \ldots, \langle y_m, (y_m\theta)\lambda \rangle\} \quad (12)$$

that is, the effect of $\theta\lambda$ is totally determined by its effect on the variables changed by θ and those changed by λ; and the way these variables are changed by $\theta\lambda$ is that each of them is first changed to something by θ, which thing is then changed by λ.

For example, the description (7) of σ and the description (9) of μ yield, according to (12), the description of $\sigma\mu$

$$\{\langle x, (H(G\,A))\rangle, \langle y, (H(G\,A))\rangle, \langle z, (H(G\,A))\rangle, \langle u, A \rangle\} \quad (13)$$

which, by direct comparison with (10), is the description of ρ. So we have

$$\sigma\mu = \rho$$

It is possible that in (12) some of the variables x_i and y_j may be the same; but in that case so will the pairs $\langle x_i, (x_i \theta)\lambda \rangle$ and $\langle y_j, (y_j \theta)\lambda \rangle$ be the same; so the effect is simply that (12) contains fewer than $k + m$ distinct pairs. It is also possible that in (12), some of the pairs are trivial, i.e., that $x_i = (x_i \theta)\lambda$ or $y_j = (y_j \theta)\lambda$. In that case, they may be retained or dropped, whatever is most convenient.

It should be noted that we have

$$\varepsilon\theta = \theta\varepsilon = \theta \text{ for all substitutions } \theta \quad (14)$$

and

$$(\theta\lambda)\mu = \theta(\lambda\mu) \text{ for all substitutions } \theta, \lambda, \mu \quad (15)$$

Thus the substitutions form an algebraic system (known as a *monoid*) in which the binary operation combining the elements (i.e. the substitutions) is the *composition* of two substitutions to yield a further substitution. This composition is *associative* (property (15)), and the identity substitution ε is the *identity element* of the monoid (property (14)).

In general, the composition of substitutions is not *commutative*: we do not, in general, have $\theta\lambda = \lambda\theta$. For example, if θ is $\{\langle x, (G\,x)\rangle\}$ and λ is $\{\langle x, (H\,x)\rangle\}$ we have

$$\theta\lambda = \{\langle x, (G(H\,x))\rangle\}$$
$$\lambda\theta = \{\langle x, (H(G\,x))\rangle\}$$

However, *some* pairs of substitutions "commute", that is, the equation $\theta\lambda = \lambda\theta$ *is* true for some θ and λ. For example, (14) shows that the identity substitution commutes with any substitution. Furthermore, the various "powers" θ^n of a given substitution θ commute with each other. Here, we are defining the powers θ^n by

$$\theta^0 = \varepsilon$$
$$\theta^{n+1} = (\theta^n)\theta \quad \text{for all } n \geqslant 0$$

so that we have the familiar rule of "adding exponents" in multiplying powers:

$$(\theta^m)(\theta^n) = (\theta^{m+n}) \quad \text{for all } m, n \geqslant 0$$

and the usual identification of θ^1 with θ. It is then obvious that

$$(\theta^m)(\theta^n) = (\theta^n)(\theta^m) = \theta^{n+m}$$

so that θ^n commutes with θ^m for all m and n.

Nor, in general, are substitutions "invertible". We say that θ is invertible if, and only if, there is a substitution λ such that $\theta\lambda = \varepsilon$. Thus doing θ, and then doing λ, brings us back to the same expression we started with. The substitution λ is unique, if it exists, and is called the *inverse* of θ; it is denoted by θ^{-1}, in an extension of the exponent notation. The exponents of invertible substitutions can then be negative as well as positive integers: θ^{-n} means $(\theta^{-1})\ldots(\theta^{-1})$ (n times), and the "adding exponents" rule generalizes to arbitrary (positive, negative, or zero) integers for such substitutions.

Intuitively, an invertible substitution is a one-for-one replacement of some set of variables by *other variables*; i.e., each variable that is replaced is replaced by a distinct other variable; however, the new variable must be one of the replaced set. In other words, the substitution must merely "permute" the set of variables. For example, the substitution $\{\langle x, y\rangle, \langle y, x\rangle\}$ permutes the set $\{x, y\}$, and so it is invertible. Its inverse, in fact, is itself. The invertible substitution

$$\theta = \{\langle x, y\rangle, \langle y, z\rangle, \langle z, x\rangle\}$$

has the inverse

$$\theta^{-1} = \{\langle x, z\rangle, \langle y, x\rangle, \langle z, y\rangle\}$$

and so on; but, e.g., $\{\langle x, y\rangle\}$ is not invertible.

The "algebra of substitutions" is thus a system of ideas of a character entirely similar to those involved in many other contexts in which there is some set and we are interested in a family of transformations on the set that contains the identity transformation and is "closed under composition", i.e., the composition of any two transformations in the family is again a transformation in the family.

Now let us consider the unification of sets of expressions by substitutions, in more detail. If S is a set of expressions, its *unifiers* (i.e. the substitutions θ such that $S\theta$ is a singleton set) form a family that is uniquely determined by S and which has some useful properties with which we will now try to become familiar. Let us write $[S]$ to denote the set of all unifiers of S. It is possible that $[S]$ is the empty set: i.e., S may not be unifiable. However, if S is unifiable then $[S]$ is a non-empty set with some interesting properties.

For example, if θ is in $[S]$, and λ is *any* substitution, not necessarily in $[S]$, then $\theta\lambda$ is in $[S]$. Once unified, so to speak, S *stays* unified! (If $S\theta$ is a singleton set, so, obviously, is $S\theta\lambda$.)

Much less obvious, and indeed rather subtle, is the fact that $[S]$ contains at least one substitution σ that has the property that $\sigma\theta = \theta$, for all θ in $[S]$. That is, σ acts as a "left identity element" for the set $[S]$, just as ε does for the set of *all* substitutions.

Such a substitution σ is called a *most general unifier* of S (abbreviated to *m.g.u.*). The reason for this name is that, if θ is *any* unifier of S, we can "decompose" θ into a product $\sigma\theta$, which shows that its effect on S is *first* that of σ, *followed by* further modifications of the singleton set $S\sigma$ (or rather, of the only expression in it). Thus every particular way of shrinking S to a singleton in this sense must *include* the way that the m.g.u. σ does it.

Now, to see that if $[S]$ is non-empty, it contains at least one such m.g.u. we shall *construct* one, by performing a process called the *unification algorithm* on S. This algorithm, which is the heart of the resolution principle, is of considerable interest in its own right. It operates upon any set S of expressions and has two different ways to terminate (and it always *does* terminate): *either* it will terminate with an indication that the set S is *not* unifiable; *or* it will terminate with both an indication that the set S *is* unifiable, and a most general unifier of S.

As we shall see, it will suffice to give the unification algorithm for the case when S has *two* expressions in it; the cases when S has more than two expressions in it will be easy to handle once we work out the case of two expressions.

Suppose, then, that S contains two expressions, A and B. We shall construct a finite sequence of pairs (S_j, σ_j), for $j = 0, 1, \ldots$, in which S_j is a set of expressions and σ_j is a substitution. The initial pair (S_0, σ_0) is simply (S, ε), i.e., the given set S and the identity substitution ε.

Each successive pair (S_{j+1}, σ_{j+1}) in the sequence will be related to its predecessor (S_j, σ_j) by the simple equations

$$\left. \begin{aligned} S_{j+1} &= S_j \mu_j \\ \sigma_{j+1} &= \sigma_j \mu_j \end{aligned} \right\} \tag{16}$$

where μ_j is a substitution involving only one variable v_j

$$\mu_j = \{\langle v_j, t_j \rangle\} \tag{17}$$

which will be replaced by a term t_j *that does not contain* v_j. The variable v_j will be selected from those occurring in the (expressions in the) set S_j; and so we shall have that v_j is "eliminated" in passing from S_j to S_{j+1}.

However, the term t_j will also be selected from among those occurring in the (expressions in the) set S_j; so the substitution μ_j, in replacing v_j by t_j throughout these expressions, must *diminish by exactly one* the number of distinct variables that occur in them. That is, the number of distinct variables in the expressions in S_{j+1} is *one fewer* than the number for S_j. This means that the sequence (S_0, σ_0), (S_1, σ_1), ..., must terminate in no more than n steps, where n is the number of distinct variables occurring in A and B, i.e., in the expressions in S_0, alias S.

It remains to explain how the variable v_j and the term t_j are determined at the jth step. It is easy to see that we have

$$S_j = S \sigma_j \tag{18}$$

for all $j \geqslant 0$. For when $j = 0$, σ_j is ε and S_j is S; while if $j \geqslant 0$ and (18) holds for a given value of j, it will hold for value $j + 1$ since (16) gives $S_{j+1} = S_j \mu_j$, and $\sigma_{j+1} = \sigma_j \mu_j$; so we then have $S_j \mu_j = S \sigma_j \mu_j = S \sigma_{j+1}$. Thus $S_j = \{A \sigma_j, B \sigma_j\}$. Now, if $A \sigma_j$ and $B \sigma_j$ are the same expression (that is, if S_j is a singleton set) we *terminate* the algorithm, indicating that S is unifiable and supplying σ_j as the most general unifier of S.

However, if $A \sigma_j$ and $B \sigma_j$ are *not* the same expression, we must analyse them to find how they differ. To aid our doing so and our thinking about the whole process, let us define the *difference* $(diff\, X\, Y)$ between any two expressions X and Y to be the set of unordered pairs determined as follows:

if X and Y are the same expression then
$(diff\ X\ Y) = \{\ \}$, the empty set
if X and Y are not the same expression, but are lists $(X_0 \ldots X_n)$,
$(Y_0 \ldots Y_n)$ of the same length n, then
$(diff\ X\ Y) = (diff\ X_0\ Y_0) \cup \ldots \cup (diff\ X_n\ Y_n)$
if X and Y are not the same expression and are not lists of
the same length, then
$$(diff\ X\ Y) = \{\{X, Y\}\} \tag{19}$$

For example, if X is $(F(H\ x)(G\ x(K\ y)))$ and Y is $(F(K\ x)u)$ then
$(diff\ X\ Y)$ is $\{\{H, K\}\ \{(G\ x(K\ y)), u\}\}$. We compute this, using the
definition (19), in successive steps:

$(diff(F(H\ x)(G\ x(K\ y)))\ (F(K\ x)\ u))$
$= (diff\ F\ F) \cup (diff(H\ x)(K\ x)) \cup (diff(G\ x(K\ y))u)$
$= \{\ \} \cup (diff\ H\ K) \cup (diff\ x\ x) \cup \{\{(G\ x(K\ y)), u\}\}$
$= \{\{H, K\}\} \cup \{\ \} \cup \{\{(G\ x(K\ y)), u\}\}$
$= \{\{H, K\}, \{(G\ x(K\ y)), u\}\}$.

Now, we say that $(diff\ X\ Y)$ is *negotiable* if it is non-empty and every
pair $\{U, V\}$ in $(diff\ X\ Y)$ has the property:

at least one of U, V is a variable,
and
neither of U, V occurs in the other   (20)

For example, the pair $\{H, K\}$ does not satisfy (20), although the pair
$\{(G\ x(K\ y)), u\}$ does; hence the difference between $(F(H\ x)(G\ x(K\ y)))$
and $(F(K\ x)u)$, which we calculated above to be the set $\{\{H, K\},$
$\{(G\ x(K\ y)), u\}\}$, is not negotiable.

To take another example, the difference between $(F\ x)$ and $(F(G\ x))$,
which is the set $\{\{x, (Gx)\}\}$, is not negotiable either, since the pair
$\{x, (G\ x)\}$ fails to satisfy (20), because x occurs in $(G\ x)$.

However, the difference $\{\{x, (G\ y)\}, \{y, z\}\}$ between $(F\ x\ y)$ and
$(F(G\ y)z)$ *is* negotiable, since both of the pairs $\{x, (G\ y)\}$ and $\{y, z\}$
satisfy (20).

Well, let us now return to the unification algorithm. We were
discussing the action to be taken in case the expressions $A\sigma_j$ and $B\sigma_j$
are not the same expression. What we do is examine the difference
$(diff\ A\sigma_j\ B\sigma_j)$ between $A\sigma_j$ and $B\sigma_j$ to see if it is negotiable or not. If
it is *not* negotiable, we *terminate* the algorithm with an indication
that S, viz., $\{A, B\}$, is *not* a unifiable set.

However, if $(diff\ A\sigma_j\ B\sigma_j)$ *is* negotiable, we can immediately set up
the substitution μ_j as in (17), by choosing any pair $\{U, V\}$ from

(*diff Aσ_j Bσ_j*) and letting v_j be that one of U, V which is a variable and t_j be the *other* one of U, V. (If *both* of U, V are variables, as may happen, then it is immaterial which of U, V is chosen to be v_j; but then t_j must be the *other* one.)

Note the freedom of choice for the pair $\langle v_j, t_j \rangle$ which is the content of μ_j. We shall show, in a moment, that the unification algorithm's properties do not depend on the way the choice is made.

The substitutions $\mu_j = \{\langle v_j, t_j \rangle\}$ eligible to be chosen for the negotiable difference (*diff X Y*) are called *reductions* of (*diff X Y*). Thus, the reductions of the difference $\{\{x, (G\,y)\}, \{y, z\}\}$ between ($F\,x\,y$) and ($F(G\,y)z$) are three in number:

$$\{\langle x, (G\,y)\rangle\}, \{\langle y, z\rangle\}, \{\langle z, y\rangle\}$$

The unification algorithm can now be very succinctly described if we pull together all these pieces and make use of a few standard notions from the methodology of *programming*, or *algorithm specification*. We shall express the work of the algorithm as the successive building up of the final output σ, from its initial value of ε, to its final value. Each successive value will replace its old value; and we shall use the symbol σ throughout for the sequence $\sigma_0, \sigma_1, \ldots$ of substitutions that "converge" on our final answer σ. The algorithm then has three steps:

> *Unification Algorithm*, for two expressions A, B as input
> (1)   Put $\sigma = \varepsilon$
> (2)   **while**   (*diff Aσ Bσ*) is negotiable
> (2.1) **do**   replace σ by $\sigma\mu$,
>   **where** μ is any reduction of (*diff Aσ Bσ*)
> (3)   **if**   (*diff Aσ Bσ*) is empty
>   **then**   indicate that $\{A, B\}$ is unifiable, and output σ
>   **else**   indicate that $\{A, B\}$ is not unifiable

Its *input* is the set $\{A, B\}$. The *initialization* step 1 simply starts off the substitution σ to be the identity substitution ε. Step 2 is the *iteration* step. This is the step that is repeated for as long as the "**while** condition" remains true, namely, for as long as (*diff Aσ Bσ*) is negotiable. Note, however, that each time we find that (*diff Aσ Bσ*) *is* negotiable, we immediately modify σ in the "**do** operation"; so that in asking again whether (*diff Aσ Bσ*) is negotiable, we have changed the question, so that the answer may be "no" even though it was "yes" the last time. We know that every time the **do** operation is performed, a variable is eliminated, so eventually either (*diff Aσ Bσ*) will be empty (and thus not negotiable) or else $A\sigma$, $B\sigma$ will no longer contain any variables (hence (*diff A σ B σ*) will not be negotiable) or else (*diff A σ B σ*) will have turned out not to be negotiable anyhow. One way or the other, step 2 will eventually come to an end. Step 3 then simply classifies the termination into the appropriate one of the two possible kinds, and the process is concluded.

As we pointed out, the Unification Algorithm always terminates, since at each iteration within step 2, another variable is eliminated from the expressions $A\sigma$, $B\sigma$. What needs to be shown is that *when* it terminates, its indication as to the unifiability of the input pair $\{A, B\}$ is correct, and, in the case that the indication is positive, that the substitution σ is then a most general unifier of $\{A, B\}$. We formulate these facts in the

> ### Unification Theorem
> Let A and B be expressions. Then $\{A, B\}$ is unifiable if, and only if, the Unification Algorithm so indicates upon termination. Moreover, the substitution σ then available as output is a most general unifier of $\{A, B\}$.

It is immediately clear that if the Unification Algorithm indicates that $\{A, B\}$ is unifiable, then it *is* unifiable, for σ unifies it. The algorithm gives this indication *only* if (*diff A σ B σ*) is empty. So we need show only that *if* $\{A, B\}$ is unifiable *then* the Unification Algorithm will eventually so indicate, and that when it does, σ will be a most general unifier of $\{A, B\}$.

In showing this, we shall appeal to a basic proposition relating the notions of difference and unification, whose intuitive content is that *the difference between unifiable expressions is removable*. The proposition is the

> ### Negotiability Lemma
> If X and Y are distinct expressions and θ unifies $\{X, Y\}$ then (*diff X Y*) is negotiable, and θ unifies each pair in (*diff X Y*).

Let us assure ourselves of the truth of the Negotiability Lemma. We can do so if we reason by "induction", showing that it is true no matter what number d is taken as an upper bound on the depths of X and Y:

Suppose that d is taken to be 0. Then the expressions X and Y must both be symbols. If θ unifies $\{X, Y\}$, this can only be because at least one, and perhaps even also the other, of X, Y, is a variable. It also means that neither of X, Y, occurs inside the other. Since in this case (*diff X Y*) is $\{\{X, Y\}\}$, it is obviously negotiable, and obviously θ unifies every pair in (*diff X Y*).

Now, as "hypothesis of the induction", let us *assume* that *the*

Negotiability Lemma holds when both of X, Y have depths less than, or equal to, some number $d \geqslant 0$. And then let us *prove*, on the basis of this assumption, that the Negotiability Lemma must also hold when both of X, Y have depths less than, or equal to, $d + 1$. If we can do this, we shall have shown that the Negotiability Lemma is true no matter what number d is taken as an upper bound on the depths of X and Y – that is, that it is true for *all* expressions X and Y.

So: assuming the hypothesis of induction as stated above, let us consider a pair $\{X, Y\}$ of distinct expressions whose depths are less than, or equal to, the number $d + 1$, and for which we know that θ unifies $\{X, Y\}$. Unless the depth of at least one of X, Y actually *is* $d + 1$, there is nothing to prove (for the hypothesis of the induction already covers such a pair). So we shall assume that at least one of X, Y has depth $d + 1$. Since $d + 1$ is greater than 0, this means that *at least one of X, Y is a list*.

Now, as θ unifies $\{X, Y\}$, there are only two possibilities:
(a) not both of X, Y are lists, and the one that is not a list is a *variable* that does not occur inside the one that is a list;
(b) both of X, Y are lists, and these lists are of the *same* length, say, $(X_0 \ldots X_n)$ and $(Y_0 \ldots Y_n)$.
(i.e. we can rule out the possibility that one of the pair is a *constant*, or that X and Y are lists of *different* lengths, or that one is a variable that occurs *inside* the one that is a list; all these would clearly prevent $\{X, Y\}$ from being unified by θ).

In case (a), $(\textit{diff } X \; Y)$ is $\{\{X, Y\}\}$ and is negotiable since $\{X, Y\}$ contains a variable and neither of X, Y occurs inside the other; and θ unifies every pair in $(\textit{diff } X \; Y)$.

In case (b), $(\textit{diff } X \; Y)$ is

$$(\textit{diff } X_0 \; Y_0) \cup \ldots \cup (\textit{diff } X_n \; Y_n)$$

But since $\{X, Y\} = \{(X_0 \ldots X_n), (Y_0 \ldots Y_n)\}$ is unified by θ, we have

$$X\theta = Y\theta$$

that is:

$$(X_0 \ldots X_n)\theta = (Y_0 \ldots Y_n)\theta$$

that is:

$$(X_0\theta \ldots X_n\theta) = (Y_0\theta \ldots Y_n\theta)$$

In other words, we have that each of the pairs $\{X_0, Y_0\}, \ldots, \{X_n, Y_n\}$ is unified by θ. The hypothesis of the induction applies to all of these pairs; for the depths of each of $X_0, \ldots, X_n, Y_0, \ldots, Y_n$ cannot exceed d.

So we conclude that each of the differences $(diff\ X_j\ Y_j)$, $0 \leqslant j \leqslant n$, for which X_j and Y_j are distinct expressions, is negotiable. It then follows immediately that

$$(diff\ X\ Y) = (diff\ X_0\ Y_0) \cup \ldots \cup (diff\ X_n\ Y_n)$$

is, if it is non-empty, negotiable, and that each pair in $(diff\ X\ Y)$ is unified by θ. But $(diff\ X\ Y)$ is non-empty, since (the expressions in) at least one pair $\{X_j\ Y_j\}$ *are* distinct. Our reasoning is thus completed, and the Negotiability Lemma is now proved.

Let us then see why the Unification Theorem is true. We are going to show that, *if A and B are expressions for which* $\{A, B\}$ *is unifiable*, then the following proposition remains true *throughout the computation* that the Unification Algorithm performs if given A and B as input:

$$\text{for all unifiers } \theta \text{ of } \{A, B\}, \theta = \sigma\theta \qquad (21)$$

It follows immediately from (21) that

$$\text{for all unifiers } \theta \text{ of } \{A, B\}, \theta \text{ unifies } \{A\sigma, B\sigma\} \qquad (22)$$

for $A\theta = B\theta$, hence by (21) $A\sigma\theta = B\sigma\theta$, that is, $(A\ \sigma)\theta = (B\ \sigma)\theta$. Thus if (21) remains true throughout the computation, so does (22). Well: (21) is certainly true immediately after step 1 has been performed, for at that point σ is ε and (21) is thus trivially true.

We shall show that, in general, if (21) is true *before* step 2.1 is performed, i.e. the step

> **do**   replace σ by $\sigma\mu$
> **where** μ is any reduction of $(diff\ A\sigma\ B\sigma)$

then it is true immediately *after* this step. This is so because, no matter how μ is selected, it will have the form

$$\mu = \{\langle U, V \rangle\}$$

where $\{U, V\}$ is in $(diff\ A\sigma\ B\sigma)$, and by the negotiability of $(diff\ A\sigma\ B\sigma)$, the variable U will not occur inside the expression V. Hence it will follow that:

$$\mu\theta = \theta, \text{ for all unifiers } \theta \text{ of } \{A, B\} \qquad (23)$$

since $\mu\theta$ and θ will agree at all variables. They agree at U since:

$$
\begin{aligned}
U(\mu\theta) &= (U\mu)\ \theta \\
&= V\theta \qquad \text{since } \mu \text{ is } \{\langle U, V \rangle\} \\
&= U\theta \qquad \text{since } \theta \text{ unifies } \{U, V\}, \text{ by (22) and the} \\
&\qquad\qquad \text{Negotiability Lemma}
\end{aligned}
$$

They agree at each variable W other than U, since

$$W(\mu\theta) = (W\mu)\,\theta$$
$$= W\theta$$

Well, in view of (23) and the truth of (21) we have

$$\theta = \sigma\theta$$
$$= \sigma(\mu\theta)$$
$$= (\sigma\mu)\,\theta$$

for all unifiers θ of $\{A, B\}$. Thus when σ is replaced by $\sigma\mu$ (21) will still be true.

So (21) is preserved at each performance of step 2.1; and this step is repeated as long as $(\mathit{diff}\,A\sigma\,B\sigma)$ is negotiable. The only way that $(\mathit{diff}\,A\sigma\,B\sigma)$ can fail to be negotiable is for it to be empty, by (22) and the Negotiability Lemma. Hence, when we finally leave step 2, (21) will be true and $(\mathit{diff}\,A\sigma\,B\sigma)$ will be empty. Therefore, the Unification Algorithm in performing step 3 will indicate that $\{A, B\}$ is unifiable; and since (21) is still true it will be the case that σ is a most general unifier of $\{A, B\}$. This completes the proof of the Unification Theorem.

The Unification Algorithm solves a class of problems that can be arbitrarily complicated. It can be programmed for a computer almost directly from its three-step definition; but in practice one would pay attention to the question of its economical use of time and space and would program an equivalent, but slightly more complex, algorithm, which we shall describe later in the book.

Let us work an example to get the feel of a computation carried out by the Unification Algorithm. We shall take the input expressions to be:

$$A: (P\,x(F(G\,y))(F\,x))$$

and

$$B: (P(H\,y\,z)(F\,z)(F(H\,u\,v))).$$

Our first act is to perform step 1. The substitution σ is now ε. (Let us say σ_0 is ε, to distinguish the initial state of σ.) We are now at step 2. We compute the difference of $A\sigma$ and $B\sigma$, that is, of A and B. It is the set

$$\{\{x, (H\,y\,z)\},\ \{z, (G\,y)\},\ \{x, (H\,u\,v)\}\}$$

and we find that it is negotiable. Let us choose one of its pairs and use it to form the substitution μ. (There is complete freedom here; of course a computer program would have to have in it a particular way of "making up its mind".) Say our choice is $\{z, (G\ y)\}$. Then μ is the substitution

$$\{\langle z, (G\ y)\rangle\}$$

and we replace σ by $\sigma\mu$. Since σ was ε, it is now

$$\{\langle z, (G\ y)\rangle\}$$

(Let us say σ_1 is $\{\langle z, (G\ y)\rangle\}$; we shall keep track of the successive states of σ in this way throughout.) We now have

$$A\sigma = A\sigma_1 = (P\ x(F(G\ y))(F\ x))$$
$$B\sigma = B\sigma_1 = (P(H\ y(G\ y))(F(G\ y))(F(H\ u\ v)))$$

The difference of $A\sigma_1$ and $B\sigma_1$ is therefore

$$\{\{x, (H\ y(G\ y))\}, \{x, (H\ u\ v)\}\}$$

which is again negotiable. We again must choose a pair to use as μ; say, the pair $\{x, (H\ u\ v)\}$. So μ is

$$\{\langle x, (H\ u\ v)\rangle\}$$

Since $\sigma (= \sigma_1)$ is $\{\langle z, (G\ y)\rangle\}$ we must compute

$$\sigma\mu = \{\langle z, (G\ y)\rangle\}\ \{\langle x, (H\ u\ v)\rangle\}$$
$$= \{\langle z, (G\ y)\rangle, \langle x, (H\ u\ v)\rangle\}$$

So $\sigma (= \sigma_2)$ is now $\{\langle z, (G\ y)\rangle, \langle x, (H\ u\ v)\rangle\}$, and

$$A\sigma = A\sigma_2 = (P(H\ u\ v)(F(G\ y))(F(H\ u\ v)))$$
$$B\sigma = B\sigma_2 = (P(H\ y(G\ y))(F(G\ y))(F(H\ u\ v))).$$

The difference set is now:

$$\{\{u\ y\}, \{v(G\ y)\}\}$$

If we choose μ to be, say $\{\langle y, u\rangle\}$, then

$$\sigma\mu = \{\langle z, (G\ y)\rangle, \langle x, (H\ u\ v)\rangle\}\ \{\langle y, u\rangle\}$$
$$= \{\langle z, (G\ u)\rangle, \langle x, (H\ u\ v)\rangle, \langle y, u\rangle\}$$

and so the new value of $\sigma (= \sigma_3)$ is:

$$\{\langle z, (G\ u)\rangle, \langle x, (H\ u\ v)\rangle, \langle y, u\rangle\}$$

and

$$A\sigma = A\sigma_3 = (P(H\ u\ v)(F(G\ u))(F(H\ u\ v)))$$
$$B\sigma = B\sigma_3 = (P(H\ u(G\ u))(F(G\ u))(F(H\ u\ v)))$$

The difference set is now:

$$\{\{v, (G\ u)\}\}$$

so our μ is

$$\{\langle v, (G\ u)\rangle\}$$

and σ becomes:

$$\sigma_4 = \sigma_3\mu = \{\langle z, (G\ u)\rangle, \langle x, (H\ u(G\ u))\rangle, \langle y, u\rangle, \langle v, (G\ u)\rangle\}$$

and we have

$$A\sigma = A\sigma_4 = (P(H\ u(G\ u))(F(G\ u))(F(H\ u(G\ u))))$$
$$B\sigma = B\sigma_4 = (P(H\ u(G\ u))(F(G\ u))(F(H\ u(G\ u))))$$

so that the difference is now $\{\ \}$. Thus the computation goes to step 3 and indicates that A and B are unifiable with most general unifier

$$\sigma = \{\langle z, (G\ u)\rangle, \langle x, (H\ u(G\ u))\rangle, \langle y, u\rangle, \langle v, (G\ u)\rangle\}.$$

This computation may be summarised in table 11.1, which shows how the successive states of σ bring about, successively, pairs $\{A\sigma, B\sigma\}$ whose difference is "smaller" each time until it vanishes.

Table 11.1.

State	σ	$(diff\ A\sigma, B\sigma)$
0	$\{\ \}$	$\{\{x, (H\ y\ z)\}, \{z, (G\ y)\}, \{x, (H\ u\ v)\}\}$
1	$\{\langle z, (G\ y)\rangle\}$	$\{\{x, (H\ y(G\ y))\}, \{x, (H\ u\ v)\}\}$
2	$\{\langle z, (G\ y)\rangle, \langle x, (H\ u\ v)\rangle\}$	$\{\{u, y\}, \{v, (G\ y)\}\}$
3	$\{\langle z, (G\ u)\rangle, \langle x, (H\ u\ v)\rangle, \langle y, u\rangle\}$	$\{\{v, (G\ u)\}\}$
4	$\{\langle z, (G\ u)\rangle, \langle x, (H\ u(G\ u))\rangle, \langle y, u\rangle, \langle v, (G\ u)\rangle\}$	$\{\ \}$

The reader is encouraged to try a few examples on his own. The main tools needed are the computation of differences and the computation of compositions of substitutions, to get $(diff\ A\sigma\ B\sigma)$ and $\sigma\mu$ at each iteration.

Now we have given the Unification Algorithm for the case that the set to be analysed has no more than *two* members: $\{A, B\}$. This was in order to minimize the complexity of the discussion. Suppose, in fact, that we wish to analyse a non-empty set S of expressions to see if it is unifiable and if so to compute a most general unifier of S; where S has any finite number of members.

Consider the following more general Unification Algorithm, which accepts as input any non-empty finite set S of expressions:

Unification Algorithm, for a set S of two or more expressions
as input
(1)   Put $\sigma = \varepsilon$
(2)   **while** $(diff\,A\sigma\,B\sigma)$ is negotiable, or empty,
                    for all A, B in S, and negotiable for some A, B in S
        do   replace σ by $\sigma\mu$
        where μ is any reduction of $(diff\,A\sigma\,B\sigma)$
                    for some distinct A, B in S;
(3)   **if** $(diff\,A\sigma\,B\sigma)$ is empty
                    for all distinct A, B in S
        then   indicate that S is unifiable, and output σ
        else   indicate that S is not unifiable.

Comparison with the previous version shows that, when S is $\{A, B\}$
the two versions coincide. The more general version requires the
computation, at each iteration, of $n(n - 1)$ differences, if S has $n \geqslant 2$
members.

The Unification Theorem needs to be reformulated as follows:

Unification Theorem
Let S be any finite set of expressions. Then S is unifiable if
and only if the Unification Algorithm so indicates upon
termination. Morever, the substitution σ then available as
output is a most general unifier of S

This reduces to the previous version, when $S = \{A, B\}$. Of course,
if S is a singleton set, the S is unifiable with most general unifier ε.

The proof of the more general Unification Theorem is essentially the
same as that of the restricted version. We show that the proposition

$$\theta = \sigma\theta, \text{ for all unifiers } \theta \text{ of } S \tag{24}$$

remains true throughout the computation, noting that if θ unifies S
then θ unifies $\{A, B\}$, for all distinct A, B in S. Evidently, upon
termination, σ will unify S if $(diff\,A\sigma\,B\sigma)$ is empty for all A, B in S,
and the truth of (24) guarantees that σ is a most general unifier of S.

The computational *efficiency* of the general Unification Algorithm
is not high: it calls for very much more work than in fact is necessary
for the task. However, the equivalent but more efficient algorithms
are less easily understood and proved correct.

In the following chapter we define the resolution principle and
establish its basic properties. In the chapter after that, we give a
complete computer program for proving true clausal sequents by
means of the resolution principle.

12. Resolution

The resolution principle is a pattern of inference that applies to finite clausal sequents. For any such sequent S, certain clauses R are defined to be the *resolvents* of S, as explained below. *There are only finitely many of these resolvents of S*. The resolution principle is simply: *to infer the sequent S, R from the sequent S*.

None of the resolvents of S is in S already; so the sequent S, R is an expansion of the set S. However, a resolvent R of S is always a logical consequence of two clauses in S, so that we have:

for any resolvent R of a finite clausal sequent S,
S is true if and only if S, R is true $\qquad$ (1)

That is to say, the resolution principle is a "sound" inference principle for finite clausal sequents which works in both directions: we can reason *forwards*, by a series of resolution steps:

$$S_0, S_1, \ldots, S_n \qquad (2)$$

in which S_{j+1} ($0 \leqslant j < n$) is S_j, R_{j+1} for some resolvent R_{j+1} of the finite clausal sequent S_j, and know that S_n must be true if S_0 is; but by (1) we can also reason *backwards*, and will then also know that S_0 *must be true if S_n is*. It may happen that S_n is of such a form that its truth is immediately evident; in which case (2) will serve as a piece of reasoning, or *proof*, that S_0 is true.

For example, a sequent containing the empty clause $\square$ is obviously true (for this represents either the empty disjunction in the antecedent, or the empty conjunction in the succedent). So if S_n in (2) is such a "terminal" sequent, (2) will serve as a proof of its first member (indeed, of any of its members!) by virtue of (1).

A finite series of sequents like (2), whose final sequent S_n is a *terminal* sequent (one that contains $\square$) is called a *resolution proof* of its first sequent, S_0. The resolution principle enjoys the following *completeness property*:

every true finite clausal sequent has a resolution proof $\qquad$ (3)

The resolvents of a given finite clausal sequent S are the finitely many clauses in a set (*resolve S*) that is computed by an algorithm to be described below. The algorithm *resolve* is also, in effect, the definition of the notion of a resolvent: the resolvents of *S* are the clauses computed, for *S* as input, by the algorithm *resolve*.

The fact that the resolvents of *S* are computable from *S*, and are finite in number, means that the task of finding resolution proofs for true clausal sequents can be mechanized. Indeed the proof-finding procedure can be envisioned intuitively as a *path-finding* procedure in "resolution space".

The "points" in this "space" are the various finite clausal sequents – or, more precisely, they are the *sets* of finite clausal sequents that differ from each other only by changes of bound variables in one or more of their constituent clauses. We shall be treating such "variant" clausal sequents as essentially the same sequent, e.g., we "see" the sequent

$$Pxy\ Qy\,\square,\ \square Pab,\ \square Qz \tag{4}$$

as though it were:

$$Puv\ Qv\,\square,\ \square Puv,\ \square Qu \tag{5}$$

or:

$$Pab\ Qb\,\square,\ \square Pab,\ \square Qz \tag{6}$$

since they all three are variants of each other, in the sense that their constituent clauses are. We shall therefore often speak as if two clauses were identical when in fact they are merely mutual variants in this sense.

A sequence like (2) is a *path* in this space, if we regard two points in the space as *adjacent* when one is S and the other is S, R, for some resolvent R of S. The set of all points adjacent to S is then a finite set – the space is "locally finite". We may even elaborate the metaphor a little more and introduce an "up" and "down" direction in the space: we go *down* from S to its neighbour S, R, and *up* from S, R to S.

So, since (*resolve S*) is finite, we can go down from S to only finitely many adjacent points S, R; on the other hand S itself can be a lower neighbour S', R' of some point S' in only finitely many ways. Thus the entire collection of points, adjacent to S both above and below, is finite.

The resolution space being locally finite, the search for a downward path (2) starting at a given point S_0 and ending in a terminal sequent can be conducted in a "finitary fan-out" or "breadth-first" manner and be guaranteed of success, by (3), *if S_0 is true*. Such a search consists of constructing a series of finite sets of points:

$$T_0, T_1, \ldots,$$

in which T_0 is simply $\{S_0\}$, while T_{j+1} is the set of all points S, R such that S is in T_j and R is a resolvent of S. If S_0 is a true finite clausal sequent then (3) assures us that eventually, say, T_n will contain a terminal point S_n, whereupon we can extract points S_j from each T_j so as to trace a path (2) from S_0 to S_n, which will be a resolution proof of S_0.

This overall account of the resolution principle and its use in a mechanized proof-finding system for finite clausal sequents is intended to give some preliminary idea of what is going on before we become involved in details. As we shall see, there are, in practice, several different notions of resolvent that can be formulated, all of which descend from a simple common notion that we shall define first. All of the above ideas apply to each notion of resolvent: all are complete, i.e., proposition (3) holds in each case; and all are locally finite and computable, i.e., the proof-finding searches can all be conducted in the same way and be guaranteed of success by the completeness property.

Let us then examine the simplest and most general notion of resolvent. Let S be a finite clausal sequent. A *resolution of* S is a list $(M, N, A, E, F, G, H, D, R)$ of things satisfying the following conditions:

(1) M and N are variants of clauses in S, and have no variables in common

(2) M has the form $A \square E, F$ where E and F are disjoint sets of predications, and F is non-empty

(3) N has the form $G, H \square D$, where G and H are disjoint sets of predications, and G is non-empty

(4) the set $(F \cup G)$ is unifiable, with most general unifier σ

(5) R is the clause $(A \cup H)\sigma \square (E \cup D)\sigma$

(6) R is not subsumed by any clause in S

(7) R is not a tautology

In stating condition 6 we have used a notion hitherto not mentioned, which is of considerable importance in the resolution of clausal sequents. We say a clause $A \square B$ *subsumes* another clause $C \square D$ if there is a substitution θ such that $(A \square B)\theta$ is a *subclause* of $C \square D$, i.e., if $A\theta \subseteq C$ and $B\theta \subseteq D$. For example, variants subsume each other; so condition 6 says that R must not be a variant of a clause in S.

But the subsumption relationship is more general than the variant relationship. For example, the clause $\square PAAE$ is subsumed by the clause $\square PxxE$, since:

$$(\square\, PxxE)\ \{\langle x, A \rangle\} = \square PAAE$$

Thus, a clause subsumes its *instances*. However, the subsumption relationship is more general than the instantiation relationship; for example, $\square Qxy$ subsumes $Pxy \,\square\, Q(F\,x)(F\,x)$ since

$$(\square Qxy)\ \{\langle x, (F\,x) \rangle, \langle y, (F\,x) \rangle\} = \square Q(F\,x)(F\,x).$$

We can always compute whether one clause subsumes another, using the Unification Algorithm, and we shall show how to do this in the following chapter when we come to discuss computational details.

Condition 7 means that R does not contain the same predication in both its left and right hand side. Such clauses are always satisfied by every model.

The clause R is *the resolvent of S yielded by* the resolution $(M, N, A, E, F, G, H, D, R)$. The clause in S of which M is a variant is the *left clause* of the resolution; that of which N is a variant is its *right clause*. The set of predications in the left clause that corresponds to the set F in the right-hand side of M is called the *left field* of the resolution; the set of predications in the right clause that corresponds to the set G in the left-hand side of N is the *right field* of the resolution.

We regard resolutions of S that have the same left clauses, the same right clauses, the same left fields and the same right fields as essentially the same resolutions, and say that they are *equivalent* resolutions. It is easy to see that the resolvents yielded by equivalent resolutions are variants of each other. The only freedom we have in making a resolution of S with a given left clause, left field, right clause, and right field (i.e. with a given *analysis*, for short) is in the choice of variants M and N to use for the computation. Once M and N are chosen, the components A, E, F, G, H and D are determined since F and G are. The Unification Algorithm then determines whether or not the set $(F \cup G)$ is unifiable, and delivers the most general unifier σ if it is. This then determines R, and it is a matter of routine computation (using the methods explained in the following chapter) to see if R is subsumed by a clause in S.

To *resolve* S, we simply construct a resolution of S for each distinct analysis for which resolutions exist. We do this by taking all possible choices of left and right clause, and for each such choice then taking each possible choice of a (non-empty) left field and (non-empty) right field; for each such *possible* analysis of a resolution of S

we then determine whether it actually is one, by selecting variants M, N of the left clause and right clause and carrying through the construction, using the Unification Algorithm to see if condition 4 is met. If it is, and conditions 6 and 7 are also met, we have a resolution of S, and the resolvent R of this resolution of S is added to the set of clauses that will be the set (*resolve S*) after all possible analyses have been dealt with in this way.

Let us see how this works on a simple example, that of the sequent (4):

$$Pxy\, Qy\, \square, \square Pab, \square Qz$$

We note that there is only one clause that can be chosen as *right* clause, namely $Pxy\, Qy\, \square$, since the other clauses have empty left-hand sides and so would offer no chance to choose a right field. Each of the other two clauses can act as left clauses. Since the left and right fields must comprise a unifiable set, the predicate symbols must all be the same, and this precludes success for the selections

$$\{Qz\} \quad \{Pxy\}$$

or

$$\{Pab\} \quad \{Qy\}$$

as left and right fields. So there are only two analyses which might succeed:

$$\square\underline{Pab} \quad \underline{Pxy}\, Qy\, \square$$

and

$$\square\underline{Qz} \quad Pxy\, \underline{Qy}\, \square$$

where we have indicated the left and right fields by underlining their members. Since both left and right clauses are already in "separated variables" form, we can take them directly as the M and N. In the first case, then, we are to send $\{Pab, Pxy\}$ to the Unification Algorithm. It (as may be easily verified) finds this set unifiable, with most general unifier (say)

$$\sigma = \{\langle a, x\rangle, \langle b, y\rangle\}$$

so that R is the clause

$$Qy\square$$

In the second case, we unify $\{Qz, Qy\}$ and find a most general unifier (say)

$$\sigma = \{\langle y, z\rangle\}$$

so that R is the clause

$Pxz\,\square$

Thus (*resolve* (4)) is the set

$$\{Qy\,\square,\ Pxz\,\square\} \tag{7}$$

Of course, we might, in computing (*resolve* (4)), have chosen our variants M, N differently; in which case we would have obtained a set of resolvents that were *variants* of those in (7).

We see then that there are two different sequents that may be inferred from (4), in view of (7). They are:

$$Pxy\ Qy\ \square,\ \square Pab,\ \square Qz,\ Qy\,\square \tag{8}$$

and

$$Pxy\ Qy\ \square,\ \square Pab,\ \square Qz,\ Pxz\,\square \tag{9}$$

If we compute (*resolve* (8)), we find that it is

$$\{Pxz\,\square,\ \square\} \tag{10}$$

(up to within choice of variables) and that, similarly, (*resolve* (9)) is

$$\{Qy\,\square,\ \square\} \tag{11}$$

The possible analysis $\square\underline{Pab},\ \underline{Pxy}\ Qy\ \square$ for a resolution of (8) fails, because its R is a variant of $Qy\,\square$ that is already in (8). Similarly the possible analysis $\square\underline{Qz},\ Pxy\ \underline{Qy}\ \square$ for a resolution of (9) fails, since its R is a variant of the clause $Pxz\,\square$ that is already in (9).

The presence of $\square$ in (10) and in (11) shows that we can infer a terminal sequent from (8) and also from (9). In fact we can infer

$$Pxy\ Qy\ \square,\ \square Pab,\ \square Qz,\ Qy\,\square,\ \square \tag{12}$$

from (8), and

$$Pxy\ Qy\ \square,\ \square Pab,\ \square Qz,\ Pxz\,\square,\ \square \tag{13}$$

from (9).

In terms of "paths" in the "resolution space" these inferences look like figure 12.1, where we indicate terminality by a double under-

Figure 12.1

lining. There are thus two proofs of (4), each of length two. Of course, since (*resolve* (8)) and (*resolve* (9)) (viz., (10) and (11) above) contain *other* clauses besides □, we could also infer

$$Pxy \: Qy \: \Box, \: \Box Pab, \: \Box Qz, \: Qy \: \Box, \: Pxz \: \Box \qquad (14)$$

from (8) and also from (9). That is, we could add $Pxz \Box$ to (8) to get (14), or we could add $Qy\Box$ to (9) to get (14). So the space looks like figure 12.2.

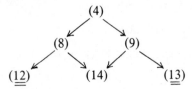

Figure 12.2

If we resolve (14) we find that (*resolve* (14)) is {□}, so that we can infer from (14) the sequent

$$Pxy \: Qy \: \Box, \: \Box Pab, \: \Box Qz, \: Qy \: \Box, \: Pxz \: \Box, \: \Box \qquad (15)$$

and can complete the picture of the resolution space (figure 12.3)

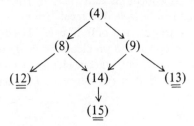

Figure 12.3

which exists below the sequent (4). This sequent is thus a true sequent, with four resolution proofs. The two longer proofs each contain an unnecessary step – and this is signalled by the fact that there are two different resolutions of (14), both of which yield □ as resolvent. One resolution of (14) that yields □ has left clause □*Pab* and right clause $Pxz \Box$. The other has left clause □*Qz* and right clause $Qy\Box$.

Figure 12.3 is, intuitively, a "map" of the resolution space, showing all of the different paths from the point (4) in the downward direction. It shows us how complex the search will be, if we begin at (4) and "fan out" downwards, looking for a terminal sequent.

Let us now return to the general procedure *resolve*. Although our little example did not illustrate it, there can be resolutions of a sequent S whose left and right clauses are the *same* clause in S. A clause can "resolve with itself". For instance, suppose S contains the clause $Pxy\ Qx \ \square \ Pyz\ Mz$. Then we could take it as both left and right clause of a resolution of S, with the left and right fields shown as underlined:

$$Pxy\ Qx \ \square \ \underline{Pyz}\ Mz;\ \underline{Pxy}\ Qx \ \square \ Pyz\ Mz$$

M and N would then be variants of this clause, with no variables in common; e.g., (showing F and G by underlining):

$$Pxy\ Qx \ \square \ \underline{Pyz}\ Mz;\ \underline{Pab}\ Qa \ \square \ Pbc\ Mc$$

The resolvent R would then be: (assuming $\sigma = \{\langle y, a \rangle, \langle z, b \rangle\}$)

$$Pxa\ Qx\ Qa \ \square \ Pbc\ Mb\ Mc$$

Now let us consider the general properties of resolution. It will help the understanding if we think of clausal sequents in their "universal disjunctive clause" form, so that the sequent (4), for example, is thought of as the sequent

$$\forall x \forall y (\neg Pxy \lor \neg Qy),\ \forall a \forall b (\lor\ Pab),\ \forall z (\lor\ Qz) \Rightarrow \qquad (16)$$

Suppose that we have such a sequent S, and that its Herbrand Universe is H and its Herbrand Base is B. We recall, from the discussion in chapter 9, that S is true if, and only if, every Herbrand map (i.e. assignment of truthvalues to the predications in B) of S falsifies at least one clause in S; and that a given Herbrand map V falsifies a clause C in S if, and only if, it falsifies some *instance* of C over H.

[For instance, let the Herbrand Universe of (16) be

$$\{A\}$$

its base, therefore, is

$$\{PAA, QA\}$$

Then the map

$$v(PAA) = \text{t},\ v(QA) = \text{t}$$

falsifies the clause $\forall x \forall y (\neg Pxy \lor \neg Qy)$ because it falsifies the instance

$$(\neg PAA \lor \neg QA)$$

but it does not falsify either of the clauses $\forall a \forall b (\lor\ Pab)$ or $\forall z (\lor\ Qz)$, whose instances over $\{A\}$ are $(\lor\ PAA)$ and $(\lor\ QA)$.]

Suppose S is true, and let R be a resolvent of S. If V is any Herbrand map of S, it must falsify at least one clause in S, and hence at least one clause in S, R, so that S, R is also true.

Suppose, in order to reason in the opposite direction and thus verify proposition (1), that S, R is true. Then if V is any Herbrand map of S, R, V falsifies at least one clause in S, R. Suppose it falsifies R. Let us remember that we have

$$R = (A \cup H)\sigma \, \square \, (E \cup D)\sigma$$
$$M = A \, \square \, E \cup F$$
$$N = G \cup H \square D$$

where $M, N, A, E, F, G, H, D, R$ is the resolution of S that yields R, and σ is a most general unifier of $(F \cup G)$. Then let θ be a substitution for the variables in R of terms from the Herbrand Base B such that V falsifies $R\theta$. Then we have

$$R\theta = (A \cup H)\sigma\theta \, \square \, (E \cup D)\sigma\theta$$
$$= (A\sigma\theta \cup H\sigma\theta) \, \square \, (E\sigma\theta \cup D\sigma\theta)$$

so that V assigns **t** to every predication in $(A\sigma\theta \cup H\sigma\theta)$ and **f** to every predication in $(E\sigma\theta \cup D\sigma\theta)$.

But $(F \cup G)\sigma\theta$ is a singleton (since $(F \cup G)\sigma$ is) say, $\{L\}$; and so V assigns **t** to every (i.e. *the*) member of $F\sigma\theta$ and of $G\sigma\theta$, or else V assigns **f** to every member of $F\sigma\theta$ and of $G\sigma\theta$. This means, therefore that *either*

> V assigns **t** to every member of $A\sigma\theta$ and **f** to every member of $(E\sigma\theta \cup F\sigma\theta)$, and hence falsifies $M\sigma\theta$

or

> V assigns **t** to every member of $(G\sigma\theta \cup H\sigma\theta)$ and **f** to every member of $D\sigma\theta$, and hence falsifies $N\sigma\theta$

and so in either event we have that V falsifies a clause in S (namely the left clause, or the right clause, of the resolution that yields R from S). Thus if S, R is true, every Herbrand map V of S, R falsifies at least one clause in S, and so S is true.

This verifies proposition (1), that resolution inferences are sound. Now let us verify proposition (3), that resolution is *complete*. Let S be a true clausal sequent, and, let U be its Herbrand Universe and B its Herbrand Base. We know that any Herbrand map tree T for S will be finite, and thus (by the discussion in chapter 9) contain at least one inference node with the analysis shown in figure 12.4, where $M = A \, \square \, E, F$ and $N = G, H \square D$ are variants, having no variables in common, of clauses in S, and θ is a substitution of terms in the Herbrand Universe U for the variables in M and N. The predication

L is the member of the singleton set $(F \cup G)\theta$, and the predications in $A\theta$, $E\theta$, $H\theta$ and $D\theta$ are all covered by the assignments in the branch leading to the inference node (...). Since $(F \cup G)$ is unifiable (by θ), we have that the $M, N, A, E, F, G, H,$ of figure 12.4 constitute a resolution of S if we add to them the clause

$$R = (A \cup H)\sigma \,\square\, (E \cup D)\sigma$$

where σ is a most general unifier of $(F \cup G)$.

$$\text{(...)}$$

L: $(...f)$ $(...t)$
$M\theta$: $A\theta\square E\theta, F\theta$ $G\theta, H\theta\square D\theta$ $: N\theta$

Figure 12.4

Since θ is a unifier of $(F \cup G)$ we have (by the Unification Theorem) that $\theta = \sigma\theta$; so that every subclause of a certain instance of R, viz., of

$$R\theta = (A \cup H)\sigma\theta \,\square\, (E \cup D)\sigma\theta$$
$$= (A \cup H)\theta \,\square\, (E \cup D)\theta$$
$$= (A\theta \cup H\theta) \,\square\, (E\theta \cup D\theta)$$

is falsified at (...) or even higher up the tree. It follows that R is not a tautology, nor is it subsumed by any clause in S (for *that* clause would have caused a failure at (...) or even higher up the tree). So R, or some variant of it, *is* a resolvent of S, and we can infer S, R from S.

However, the very same Herbrand map tree T for S can now be turned into one for S, R by simply pruning off the nodes below the one that we can now label with $R\theta$ as a failure node.

The entire argument can now be repeated, with a resolvent of the expanded sequent being produced in the same way. This leads to a sequence

$$S,$$
$$S, R_1$$
$$...$$
$$S, R_1, ..., R_n$$

of consecutive expansions of S by adding a resolvent R_{j+1} not already present in $S, R_1, ..., R_j$; until, after finitely many steps, say n of them, we have $R_n = \square$. This proves proposition (3).

The entire process of "shrinking the tree" T, which is the finite

Herbrand map tree of the true sequent S, is entirely automatic, the only room for choice at each step being that surrounding the choice of an inference node at which to generate the next resolvent. If there is more than one inference node to choose from, the choice may be taken arbitrarily; however, some choices may be more fortunate than others in the amount of shrinkage they cause in the tree. Indeed, this choice corresponds, to some extent, to the multiplicity of paths from the point S to some terminal point, in the resolution space.

Clauses containing no variables – "ground" clauses – consist, essentially, of two finite sets of predications from the Herbrand Base: $A_1 \ldots A_m \square B_1 \ldots B_n$, with the intuitive reading (in the "universal disjunction" convention)

$$(\neg A_1 \vee \ldots \vee \neg A_m \vee B_1 \vee \ldots \vee B_n)$$

Sequents whose clauses are all ground clauses ("ground" sequents), such as

$$(P(F\,A)B)(Q\,A) \,\square\, (Q\,B),$$
$$(Q\,B)\square,$$
$$\square(P(F\,A)B) \tag{17}$$

are very much simpler to resolve than sequents whose clauses contain variables. Resolutions always involve the left clause and right clause directly – there being no variants to consider – and the left field and right field are simply two singletons, one in each clause, containing the same predication. Thus:

$$\begin{array}{ccc} \square(\underline{P(F\,A)B}) & & (\underline{P(F\,A)B})(Q\,A)\,\square\,(Q\,B) \\ & \searrow \qquad \swarrow & \\ & (Q\,A)\,\square\,(Q\,B) & \end{array}$$

is a resolution of the sequent (17), and so is

$$\begin{array}{ccc} (P(F\,A)B)(Q\,A)\,\square\,(\underline{Q\,B}) & & (\underline{Q\,B})\square \\ & \searrow \qquad \swarrow & \\ & (P(F\,A)B)(Q\,A)\square & \end{array}$$

It is useful to separate the case of "ground resolution" – i.e., the inferences and proofs by resolution in which the sequents are ground sequents – for two reasons. First: it is very much easier to think about, there being none of the intricacies of the unification process to take into account. Second: one can study more refined forms of resolution, and prove them complete, by analysing resolutions at the ground level and then transferring one's conclusions to the general level. This technique of argument is used to develop a type of resolution, called *hyper-resolution*, whose search-space is very much sparser, and therefore more conducive to computerized proof-finding, than the basic resolution space that we have just been examining.

The basic observation that connects the two levels of resolution is the following. Suppose that we have a ground resolution:

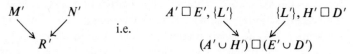

in which M' and N' are instances, by a substitution θ, of two clauses M and N that have no variables in common:

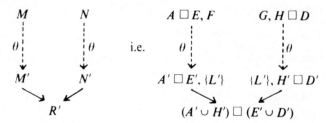

Then we know that there is a resolution $M, N, A, E, F, G, H, D, R$ in which $(F \cup G)\sigma\theta$ (where σ is the most general unifier of $(F \cup G)$) is the singleton $\{L'\}$ whose member is the very predication with respect to which M' and N' resolve to yield R', and that $M\sigma\theta = M'$ and $N\sigma\theta = N'$. This all follows easily from the fact that θ unifies $(F \cup G)$ to produce $\{L'\}$, whence $\theta = \sigma\theta$.

But this means that we can complete the diagram by introducing R, and getting R' from R by θ:

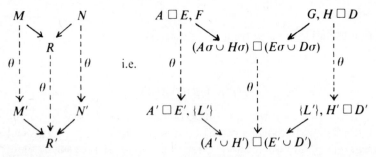

Suppose, then, that S is a finite clausal sequent and that S' is a finite clausal *ground* sequent, each of whose clauses is an instance, by some substitution of terms from the Herbrand Universe of S for its variables, of a clause in S. Suppose, further, that S', R' is a sequent inferred from S' by ground resolution, by adding the resolvent R' of S' to S'.

Then, by the basic observation explained above, we know that this ground inference corresponds to an inference from S to S, R in which the left and right clauses yielding R are those whose instances are the left and right clauses yielding R', and that R' is an instance of R.

In general we say that a ground level deduction from a sequent S'

$$S', R'_1, ..., R'_n \tag{18}$$

is an *instance* of a deduction from a sequent S

$$S, R_1, ..., R_n \tag{19}$$

if every clause in S' is an instance of a clause in S, and if each resolvent R'_j is an instance of R_j, and if the left and right clauses yielding R'_j are instances respectively of the left and right clauses yielding R_j, $1 \leqslant j \leqslant n$. The basic observation then allows us to say ("Lifting Lemma"):

> every deduction by resolution from a sequent S' which is a
> set of ground instances of clauses in a sequent S, *is an instance*
> *of a deduction from S*

Now there are certain properties of resolution deductions – called *instantiation invariants* – which are preserved in passing from a deduction (18) to one of which it is an instance, (19), and conversely. That is, such a property P either belongs to *both* (18) and (19) or to *neither*. Examples of instantiation invariants of resolution deductions are:

(a) being a deduction of a terminal sequent;
(b) being a deduction in which every resolution has
    a left clause with empty left-hand side;
(c) being a deduction in which every resolution has
    a right clause with empty right-hand side.

These are quite clearly instantiation invariants: if R'_n is $\square$, for example, then since it is an instance of R_n, R_n must be $\square$, as instantiation cannot create $\square$ from a non-empty clause.

Similarly, if the left clause M' in the resolution yielding R'_j has an empty left-hand side, then the left clause M in the resolution yielding R_j must *also* have an empty left-hand side, because M' is an instance of M, and instantiation cannot create an empty left-hand side from a non-empty left-hand side.

Let us call a ground sequent S', every clause in which is an instance of some clause in the sequent S, *a ground instance of S*. Now suppose we could prove a proposition of the following form:

for any true finite clausal sequent S, there is a resolution
deduction *from some finite ground instance of S* that has
the instantiation invariant P (20)

Then, by the preceding discussion we could immediately infer the
proposition:

for any true finite clausal sequent S there is a resolution
deduction *from S* that has the instantiation invariant P (21)

We would merely need to take the deduction provided by (20) and
"lift" it, by the Lifting Lemma, to obtain the one required by (21).

In fact we can prove some interesting and useful propositions of
the form (20). For example, we can prove (20) when P is the instantiation invariant *being a deduction of a terminal sequent*. Then (21)
becomes the proposition (3), asserting the completeness of resolution!

To prove (20) in this case, we need two results:

every true finite clausal sequent
has a true finite ground instance   (22)

and

every true finite clausal *ground*
sequent has a resolution proof   (23)

Proposition (23) is a very easy one to establish, using the Herbrand
map tree argument; one need only enumerate those members of the
Herbrand Base, say $L_1, ..., L_n$, which actually occur in a true finite
clausal ground sequent S', and construct the map tree down to at
most the n levels corresponding to this enumeration. Since S' is true,
every branch will end in a node labelled by some clause in S', and
there will be at least one inference node. The required resolution
proof of S' then is automatically generated.

Proposition (22) also follows from the Herbrand map tree argument. If S is a true finite clausal sequent its Herbrand map tree is
finite, and so the (finitely many) tips of it are labelled by clauses that
are ground instances of clauses in S. The set S' of these ground
instances is thus a true, finite ground instance of S.

Indeed (22) and (23) together are no more than a restatement of
the Herbrand map tree argument, broken down into two parts, which
(20) and (21) allow us to put back together again.

But we can prove (20) for more interesting cases of instantiation
invariants, such as the following one, which we label "P_1" for convenience:

P_1:   being a deduction of a terminal sequent in which every resolution

   has a *left clause whose left-hand side is empty*

   has a *right field* that contains *the leftmost predication on the left-hand side of the right clause*

In stating this property we are supposing (as is in practice the case) that the predications in a clause are written in linear order from left to right, and that *instantiation preserves this ordering* in the following sense. If $(A_1, ..., A_n)$ is a sequence of distinct predications then the sequence $(A_1, ..., A_n)\theta$, which is its instance under the substitution θ, is obtained by taking the sequence $(A_1\theta, ..., A_n\theta)$ and then *removing any duplicates from it, preserving only the leftmost copies*. Thus the sequence ($Px\ Qxy\ Py\ Qyz\ Pu$) becomes, under the substitution

$$\{\langle x, A \rangle, \langle y, A \rangle, \langle z, B \rangle, \langle u, A \rangle\}$$

the sequence

   ($PA\ QAA\ QAB$)

that is, we first take the sequence

   ($\underline{PA}\ QAA\ \underline{PA}\ QAB\ \underline{PA}$)

and then remove all but the leftmost of the underlined components. With this convention, the property P_1 is an instantiation invariant. This is readily apparent if we suppose that the right field G in the general "lifting diagram" for resolution:

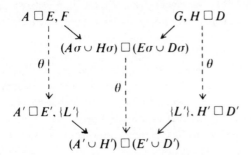

is marked (as in our illustrative examples) by underlining its members and the clause $\{L'\}, H'\Box D'$ is obtained from $G, H\Box D$ as explained above, treating the clauses as sequences of their predications and the sign $\Box$. Then L' will be the leftmost predication in $\{L'\}, H'\Box D'$ if, and only if, G contains the leftmost predication in $G, H\Box D$.

If the resolutions in the above diagram are to be "P_1-resolutions", then, we must have that:

> A is empty (hence A' also is)
> G contains the leftmost predication in $G, H \square D$ (hence $\{L'\}$ also does).

A resolution proof having property P_1 will be referred to as a *P_1-resolution proof.*

Thus with P_1 as P, proposition (21) is:

> every true finite clausal sequent has a P_1-resolution proof   (24)

and it is clear that in order to establish (24) it is enough to establish (in view of (22)) that

> every true finite clausal *ground* sequent has a P_1-resolution
> proof   (25)

Now, to prove (25), we actually need only show that the following holds:

> if S' is a true finite clausal ground sequent that does not
> contain $\square$, then there is a resolvent R' of S' for which the
> left clause has an empty left-hand side, and the right field
> is the singleton set containing the leftmost predication on
> the left-hand side of the right clause   (26)

Proposition (25) is an easy consequence of (26). For S' can involve only finitely many predications, say, $L_1, ..., L_m$, out of which all its clauses are built. The resolvent R' must be built entirely from $L_1, ..., L_m$. Thus, if we repeatedly apply (26) to obtain a deduction

$$S', R_1', R_2', ...$$

in which R_{j+1}' is the R', and $S', R_1', ..., R_j'$ is the S', of (26), each successive R_{j+1}' has to be a clause not already in the sequent S', $R_1', ..., R_j'$. There being only finitely many clauses that can be built from $L_1, ..., L_m$, we conclude that eventually one of these resolvents, say R_n', will be $\square$, precluding further application of (26) but providing the required P_1-resolution proof

$$S', R_1', ..., R_n'$$

of S'. So let us prove (26).

If S' is a true finite clausal ground sequent involving only the predications $L_1, ..., L_m$, then every assignment of truth values

$$\{v(L_1) = w_1, \ldots, v(L_m) = w_m\} \tag{27}$$

to $L_1, \ldots, L_m$ will falsify some clause in S'. (We are assuming, as usual, the universal disjunctive reading of each clause.) Let A be the set of clauses in S' that have empty left-hand sides. There are certainly assignments (27) that satisfy each clause in A; for example

$$\{v(L_1) = \mathbf{t}, \ldots, v(L_m) = \mathbf{t}\} \tag{28}$$

does so. Since $\square$ is not in S, every clause in A has a *non-empty right-hand side*. Furthermore, A has at least one member, for otherwise the assignment

$$\{v(L_1) = \mathbf{f}, \ldots, v(L_m) = \mathbf{f}\} \tag{29}$$

would satisfy every clause in S'. Let us then consider an assignment (27) that

satisfies every clause in A, and
assigns the fewest $\mathbf{t}$'s of any such assignment

That is, an assignment using fewer $\mathbf{t}$'s than (27) must falsify at least one clause in A. We may note that (27) must use at least one $\mathbf{t}$, otherwise it is (29) and will necessarily falsify at least one clause in A.

Well, (27) must falsify *some* clause in S'; and such a clause will of course have a non-empty left-hand side. Let us choose one of these, and let us choose it so that it has the smallest left-hand side of any such clause: thus it is a clause

$$H\square K \tag{30}$$

in which H is a non-empty subset of $\{L_1, \ldots, L_m\}$, and if any clause in S' has a *smaller* non-empty left-hand side than H, then (27) *satisfies* that clause.

Now, suppose L' is the leftmost predication in the left-hand side H, in (30). Since the assignment (27) falsifies $H\square K$, it must contain the equation $v(L') = \mathbf{t}$. We claim that there must exist a clause in A, say, the clause

$$\square G \tag{31}$$

in whose right-hand side L' occurs; in which, moreover, every member of the set $G - \{L'\}$ is assigned $\mathbf{f}$ by (27).

If no such clause existed, we could change the equation $v(L') = \mathbf{t}$ in (27) to $v(L') = \mathbf{f}$, thereby getting an assignment with *fewer* $\mathbf{t}$'s than (27) uses, which nevertheless satisfies every clause in A!

But now consider the clauses $\Box G$ and $H \Box K$. We know that G contains L' and that H contains L'. Hence the clause

$$R' = (H - \{L'\}) \Box (G - \{L'\}) \cup K \tag{32}$$

is a resolvent of S', with left clause $\Box G$ and right clause $H \Box K$, as required by (26), provided that R' is not a tautology and is not subsumed by any clause in S'.

R' *cannot* be a tautology, or subsumed by a clause in S', for the following reasons:

> If R' is $\Box$, then R' is not subsumed by a clause in S' because that clause would have to be $\Box$ and we are given that $\Box$ is not in S' in the hypothesis of (26); and $\Box$ is not a tautology.
> If R' has an empty left-hand side, then R' is not a tautology; and since (27) *satisfies* every clause in S' that has an empty left-hand side, this also means that no such clause could subsume R', for R' would then *also* be satisfied by (27).
> If R' does not have an empty left-hand side, then R' is not a tautology because (27) falsifies R'; and since R' has a *smaller* left-hand side than does $H \Box K$, this also means that any clause in S' that subsumed R' would be falsified by (27) and have a smaller left-hand side than does $H \Box K$, which is impossible.

The proposition (26) has thus been proved.

So we have arrived at a rather stronger version of resolution – "P_1-resolution" – which we have just shown to be complete. The proposition asserting its completeness, (24), corresponds to the proposition (3), which asserts the completeness of the more general, weaker, resolution.

If we contemplate the P_1-resolution space, we see that it consists of the *points* in resolution space (namely, the various finite clausal sequents) but has far fewer *paths* than resolution space. Two points are adjacent in P_1-resolution space if one is S and the other is S, R, where R is a P_1-resolvent of S; thus, points that *are* adjacent in resolution space may *not* be adjacent in P_1-resolution space.

Note that, in particular, we need no longer be concerned to "resolve clauses against themselves". In computing the set $(P_1$-*resolve S*$)$ of all P_1-resolvents of a given finite clausal sequent S, we confine our choices of left and right clauses to those pairs in which the left clause has an empty left-hand side and the right clause does not. Otherwise, the computation is exactly like that of (*resolve S*). Indeed, we obviously have

$(P_1\text{-}resolve\ S) \subseteq (resolve\ S)$

for all finite clausal sequents S.

We can now carry the argument one step further still. This will lead us to a version of resolution known as *hyper-resolution*, whose search-space has even fewer paths than that of P_1-resolution. Let us consider any P_1-resolution proof of a finite clausal sequent S, and let us display it in tree form, showing the left and right clauses of each resolution as the immediate parents

of each resolvent R. Such a tree will have $\square$ at its root, clauses in S at its tips, and will have left clauses M with empty left-hand sides. For example, such a proof might have the structure shown in figure 12.5, so that the clauses $M_1, M_2, M_5, M_7, N_1, N_3, N_6, N_7$ would all be in S and the remaining clauses, $M_3, M_4, M_6, N_2, N_4, N_5, \square$ would be inferred by P_1-resolution.

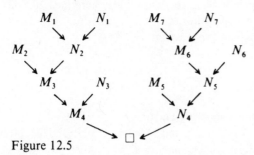

Figure 12.5

It is easy to see that any such P_1-resolution proof can be decomposed into subdeductions of the following general structure:

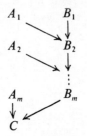

Figure 12.6

in which $A_1, \ldots, A_m$ and C are clauses with empty left-hand sides and
$B_1, \ldots, B_m$ are clauses with non-empty left-hand sides. One simply
enters the proof at each tip which has a non-empty left-hand side,
and traces down the branch until a clause is reached that has an
empty left-hand side. The proof in figure 12.5, for example, breaks
down in this way into the deductions:

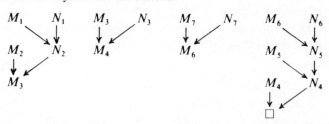

We call deductions by P_1-resolution, which have the form of
figure 12.6, *hyper-resolutions*. The clause C is the *hyper-resolvent*
yielded by the hyper-resolution, and the clause B_1 is its *right-hand
clause* while the (one or more) clauses $A_1, \ldots, A_m$ are its *left-hand
clauses*.

The general idea here is to "bury" the "intermediate" clauses
$B_2, \ldots, B_m$, ignoring them, in order to see the entire transaction displayed in figure 12.6 as a *single step*:

$$A_1 \ldots A_m \, B_1$$
$$\searrow \downarrow \swarrow$$
$$C$$

with the right-hand clause B_1 and the left-hand clauses $A_1, \ldots, A_m$
considered as the $m + 1$ "immediate ancestors" of the hyper-resolvent
C. (One can hardly say "parents" of C any longer.) In this way a
P_1-resolution proof of S can be restructured as a *hyper-resolution
proof* of S, with some economies obtained by omission of the "intermediate" clauses in each hyper-resolution. For example, the P_1-
resolution proof of figure 12.5 can be redrawn now as the hyper-
resolution proof:

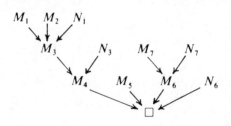

So: if we say that a clause R with empty left-hand side is a *hyper-resolvent* of a finite clausal sequent S when there is a hyper-resolution whose left-hand clauses and right-hand clause are in S and which yields R, we can contemplate inferences of sequents S, R from S in which R is a hyper-resolvent of S, and we know that these will always suffice to prove a true finite clausal sequent S:

> every true finite clausal sequent has a hyper-resolution
> proof (33)

Proposition (33), the completeness theorem for hyper-resolution, is, as the preceding discussion shows, essentially the same proposition as (24), the completeness theorem for P_1-resolution.

The search-space for hyper-resolution, however, contains fewer paths than that for P_1-resolution. Points in hyper-resolution space are adjacent only if one of them is S and the other is S, R, where R is a *hyper-resolvent* of S. The computation of all hyper-resolvents of S is done by the algorithm *hyper-resolve*, which produces its output set (*hyper-resolve S*) of clauses directly from its input set S.

It is noteworthy that since, in a hyper-resolution proof of S:

$$S, R_1, \ldots, R_n, \square$$

the successive hyper-resolvents $R_1, \ldots, R_n, \square$ are all clauses with empty left-hand sides, the successive inference steps must all reach back *into* S for their right-hand clauses.

We conclude this chapter with some examples of hyper-resolution proofs.

Example 1. Prove the sequent:

S_1: $\square(P\,x\,y), (P\,y(F\,x\,y))(P(F\,x\,y)(F\,x\,y))\square(Q\,x\,y),$
$\quad\quad (P\,y(F\,x\,y))(P(F\,x\,y)(F\,x\,y))(Q\,x(F\,x\,y))(Q(F\,x\,y)(F\,x\,y))\square$

The only hyper-resolvent of this sequent is the clause $\square(Q\,x\,y)$. A hyper-resolution that yields it is:

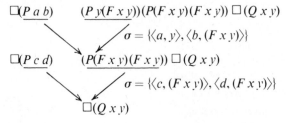

So we infer the sequent:

$S_1, \Box(Q\ x\ y)$

The only hyper-resolvent of which is $\Box$. A hyper-resolution that yields it is:

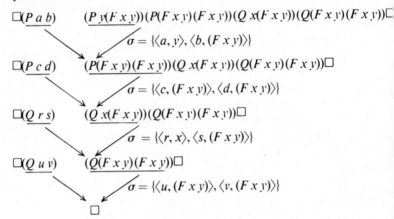

and so we infer the terminal sequent: $S_1, \Box(Q\ x\ y), \Box$. The entire hyper-resolution search space for this sequent looks like:

$$S_1$$
$$\downarrow$$
$$S_1, \Box(Q\ x\ y)$$
$$\downarrow$$
$$S_1, \Box(Q\ x\ y), \Box$$

Example 2. Prove the sequent:

S_2: $(P\ x\ y\ u)(P\ y\ z\ v)(P\ x\ v\ w)\ \Box(P\ u\ z\ w),$
       $(P\ x\ y\ u)(P\ y\ z\ v)(P\ u\ z\ w)\ \Box(P\ x\ v\ w),$
          $\Box(P(G\ r\ s)r\ s),$
          $\Box(P\ a(H\ a\ b)b),$
       $(P(K\ t)t(K\ t))\Box$

The set (*hyper-resolve* S_2) is:

$\{\Box(P\ y(H\ x\ x)y),$
$\Box(P\ x(H\ y(H(G\ y\ x)z))z),$
$\Box(P\ x(H(H(G\ y\ z)x)y)z),$
$\Box(P\ x(H(H\ y\ x)(H\ y\ z))z),$
$\Box(P(G(G\ x\ y)(G\ x\ z))yz),$
$\Box(P(G(G(H\ x\ y)z)x)zy),$
$\Box(P(G\ x(G(H\ x\ y)z))yz),$
$\Box(P(G\ x\ x)yy)\}$

If we infer the sequent

S'_2: $S_2, \square(P\,y(H\,x\,x)y)$

we then find that $\square$ is in the set $\{hyper\text{-}resolve\ S'_2\}$, so that from S'_2 we may infer the terminal sequent:

S''_2: $S_1, \square(P\,y(H\,x\,x)y), \square$.

The computations here are very laborious if done by hand. They were actually done by a computer, using methods we shall discuss in the next chapter.

Example 2 is a problem derived from an exercise given by Birkhoff and MacLane in their book *A Survey of Modern Algebra*. We are given that a set G is closed under a binary operation $\circ$, which is *associative*:

(A) $\forall x\ \forall y\ \forall z(x \circ y) \circ z = x \circ (y \circ z)$

and that "left solutions" g and "right solutions" h exist for all equations

$$g \circ r = s, a \circ h = b$$

where r, s, a, b are any elements of G:

(B) $\forall r\ \forall s\ \exists g\ g \circ r = s$
(C) $\forall a\ \forall b\ \exists h\ a \circ h = b$

We are then asked to prove, from the postulates (A), (B) and (C), the theorem (D) that there exists an element t of G that is a "right-identity" element:

(D) $\exists t\ \forall k\ k \circ t = k$.

Now if we represent the three-place relation $x \circ y = u$ by applying the 3-ary predicate symbol P to x, y, and u as arguments so as to form the predication $(P\,x\,y\,u)$, we can express the associativity of $\circ$, proposition (A), by the sentence

(A′) $\forall x\ \forall y\ \forall z\ \forall u\ \forall v\ \forall w(((P\,x\,y\,u) \wedge (P\,y\,z\,v)) \rightarrow ((P\,u\,z\,w) \leftrightarrow$
          $(P\,x\,v\,w)))$

which is the result of naming the anonymous "intermediate" entities in the equation of (A) as indicated below:

$$\underbrace{\underbrace{(x \circ y)}_{u} \circ z}_{w} \quad = \quad \underbrace{x \circ \underbrace{(y \circ z)}_{v}}_{w}$$

and construing (A) to say: "*if* $x \circ y$ *is* u *and* $y \circ z$ *is* v, *then* $u \circ z$ will be w *if, and only if,* $x \circ v$ *is also* w". The sentence (A′) is in fact logically equivalent to the conjunction of the two sentences:

(A$_1$) $\forall x \forall y \forall z \forall u \forall v \forall w(((P\,x\,y\,u) \wedge (P\,y\,z\,v) \wedge (P\,x\,v\,w)) \rightarrow (P\,u\,z\,w))$
(A$_2$) $\forall x \forall y \forall z \forall u \forall v \forall w(((P\,x\,y\,u) \wedge (P\,y\,z\,v) \wedge (P\,u\,z\,w)) \rightarrow (P\,x\,v\,w))$

and (B), (C), (D) go over respectively to:

(B$_1$) $\forall r \forall s \exists g(P\,g\,r\,s)$
(C$_1$) $\forall a \forall b \exists h(P\,a\,h\,b)$
(D$_1$) $\exists t \forall k(P\,k\,t\,k)$

If we consider the sequent

$$(A_1), (A_2), (B_1), (C_1) \Rightarrow (D_1)$$

we see that its truth corresponds to the fact that (D) is a logical consequence of (A), (B) and (C). Eliminating existential quantifiers in the antecedent and universal quantifiers in the succedent of this sequent produces its Skolem transform:

$\forall x \forall y \forall z \forall u \forall v \forall w(((P\,x\,y\,u) \wedge (P\,y\,z\,v) \wedge (P\,x\,v\,w)) \rightarrow (P\,u\,z\,w)),$
$\forall x \forall y \forall z \forall u \forall v \forall w(((P\,x\,y\,u) \wedge (P\,y\,z\,v) \wedge (P\,u\,z\,w)) \rightarrow (P\,x\,v\,w)),$
$\forall r \forall s(P(G\,r\,s)r\,s),$
$\forall a \forall b(P\,a(H\,a\,b)b)$
$\Rightarrow$
$\exists t(P(K\,t)t(K\,t))$

from which we can immediately write, in quad-notation, its clausal transform:

S_2: $(P\,x\,y\,u)(P\,y\,z\,v)(P\,x\,v\,w)\,\square\,(P\,u\,z\,w),$
    $(P\,x\,y\,u)(P\,y\,z\,v)(P\,u\,z\,w)\,\square\,(P\,x\,v\,w),$
    $\square(P(G\,r\,s)r\,s),$
    $\square(P\,a(H\,a\,b)b),$
    $(P(K\,t)t(K\,t))\square$

which we then prove by hyper-resolution, in two steps, as explained.

Example 3. Prove the sequent:

S_3: $(P\,x\,y\,u)(P\,y\,z\,v)(P\,x\,v\,w)\,\square\,(P\,u\,z\,w),$
    $(P\,x\,y\,u)(P\,y\,z\,v)(P\,u\,z\,w)\,\square\,(P\,x\,v\,w),$
    $\square(P\,E\,x\,x),$
    $\square(P\,x\,E\,x),$
    $\square(P\,x\,x\,E),$
    $\square(P\,A\,B\,C),$

$(P B A C)\Box$

This example again arises from a problem set by Birkhoff and MacLane in *A Survey of Modern Algebra* (p. 130, exercise *11; they attach an asterisk to exercises considered to be of greater than average difficulty). The algebraic problem is to show that if we have, in a *monoid* (an associative system containing an element E, which is both a left- and right-identity) the property that x^2 (i.e., $x \circ x$) is always identical to E, then the monoid is *commutative*, i.e.

(T) $\forall a\ \forall b\ a \circ b = b \circ a$

Using the same three-place relation representation as in example 2, we may express the desired theorem as

(T′) $\forall a\ \forall b\ \forall c((P\,a\,b\,c) \rightarrow (P\,b\,a\,c))$

construing (T) as saying, in effect: "*if $a \circ b$ is c, then so is $b \circ a$*". Thus we must prove the sequent

$(A_1), (A_2), \forall x(P\,E\,x\,x), \forall x(P\,x\,E\,x), \forall x(P\,x\,x\,E)$
$\Rightarrow$
$\forall a\ \forall b\ \forall c((P\,a\,b\,c) \rightarrow (P\,b\,a\,c))$

where (A_1) and (A_2) are as in example 2.

The Skolem transform of this sequent is:

$(A_1), (A_2), \forall x(P\,E\,x\,x), \forall x(P\,x\,E\,x), \forall x(P\,x\,x\,E)$
$\Rightarrow ((P\,A\,B\,C) \rightarrow (P\,B\,A\,C)).$

In transforming this sequent to clausal form, the sentence in the succedent becomes the pair of sentences:

$(\wedge \neg(P\,A\,B\,C)), (\wedge(P\,B\,A\,C))$

so that the clausal sequent we obtain is, in quad-notation, S_3.

Now a hyper-resolution proof of S_3 (obtained by the program PROVE given in the next chapter) is the four-step proof:

S_3

$S_3, \Box(P\,C\,B\,A)$

$S_3, \Box(P\,C\,B\,A), \Box(P\,C\,A\,B)$

$S_3, \Box(P\,C\,B\,A), \Box(P\,C\,A\,B), \Box(P\,B\,A\,C)$

$S_3, \Box(P\,C\,B\,A), \Box(P\,C\,A\,B), \Box(P\,B\,A\,C), \Box$

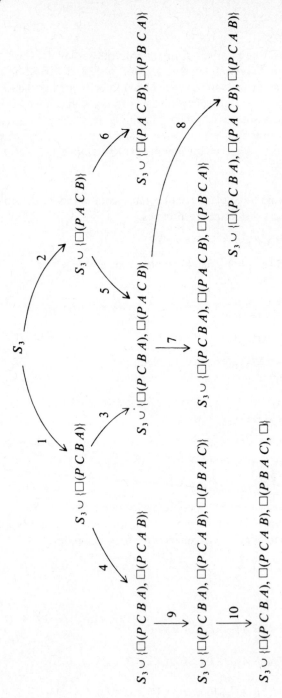

Figure 12.7

which corresponds intuitively to the algebraic argument:

> We are given that $A \circ B = C$, but that $B \circ A \neq C$.
> So, multiplying the equation $A \circ B = C$ by B on both sides
> $$\text{we have } A \circ B \circ B = C \circ B;$$
> But since $B \circ B$ is E, this means $A \circ E = C \circ B$;
> And since $A \circ E$ is A, this in turn means $A = C \circ B$.

(this takes us as far as the *first* hyper-resolvent, $\square(P\ C\ B\ A)$).

> So, multiplying this last equation by C on both sides:
> $$C \circ A = C \circ C \circ B;$$
> But, since $C \circ C$ is E, this means $C \circ A = E \circ B$;
> And, since $E \circ B$ is B, this in turn means $C \circ A = B$

(which takes us as far as the *second* hyper-resolvent, $\square(P\ C\ A\ B)$).

> Now, multiplying both sides of *this* equation by A:
> $$C \circ A \circ A = B \circ A;$$
> But, since $A \circ A$ is E, this means that $C \circ E = B \circ A$;
> And, since $C \circ E$ is C, this further means that $C = B \circ A$;

(which takes us as far as the *third* hyper-resolvent $\square(P\ B\ A\ C)$;

> But this *contradicts* what we were given, that $B \circ A \neq C$.

(which takes us to the *fourth* hyper-resolvent, $\square$).
The "clever" algebraic argument is, so to speak, invented by the internal processes taking place within the *hyper-resolve* computations.

The actual search conducted by the program **PROVE** for this example is pictured in figure 12.7. The numbers on the arrows give the order in which the corresponding steps were taken by the path-finding algorithm invoked by **PROVE** on being supplied with S_3 as its input. The diagram therefore illustrates a typical "trace" of a path-finding search in hyper-resolution space, showing not only the path eventually found between the input sequent and some terminal sequent, but also the extent of the total search that was required.

13. Resolution on the Computer

The actual programming of the processes we have been talking about is not an entirely trivial matter, and in this chapter we shall give some concrete examples of computer programs that embody some of the algorithms developed in earlier chapters. The reader who happens to have access to a computer with facilities for running LISP programs will be able to use the programs given in this chapter to do examples and to form the basis, if he is ambitious, of a more elaborate and finely-engineered system.

The programs to be described comprise the author's own set of experimental tools, devised over a period of years as a practical working system for research and teaching purposes. They have no high pretensions to elegance or maximal efficiency. They get the job done, and are fairly simple to understand, but no doubt contain enough infelicities to cause the professional programmer amusement, if not pain. Programming is a great art and has attracted some of the best minds of our time to its practice and study. The present writer is privileged to know some of these virtuosi, and is duly diffident about his own attempts to play their music.

The LISP programming system was developed in the late 1950's by John McCarthy (1960, 1962) and his colleagues at the Massachusetts Institute of Technology. Its purpose was to serve the computing needs of a growing community of research workers who were interested primarily in "non-numerical" computation, that is, the manipulation and construction of symbolic complexes such as scientific formulas; phrases, sentences and texts of natural language; diagrams and pictures; musical scores; and mathematical proofs.

In its twenty years of existence LISP has served these needs extremely well. It is the main – if not indeed the only – programming system of the "artificial intelligence" community, and is available at the computing centres of most universities and colleges. Several primers and manuals exist, (McCarthy *et al.* 1962, Weissman 1970), and a recent textbook (Winston 1977) on artificial intelligence devotes half of its space to explaining LISP. The design of the LISP system is, in itself, a contribution to the task of trying to understand the human mind as a kind of symbolic computer, and thinking as a kind of computing.

We cannot hope, in this chapter, to do more than give a bare outline of the main ideas of LISP for those who have not yet made its acquaintance. The reader who wishes to learn more can easily do so by consulting the references given above.

The objects manipulated by LISP computations are neutral, general-purpose symbolic complexes officially called *S-expressions* (for "symbolic expressions"). We shall also call them "LISP objects" or "objects".

There are two kinds of LISP objects: *atoms* and *pairs*. (The latter are officially called "dotted pairs" because of the way they are customarily denoted on paper.) If α and β are any LISP objects, so is the *pair* $(\alpha \cdot \beta)$, whose first component (or *head*) is α, and whose second component (or *tail*) is β.

The atoms are *strings of characters*, such as:

ABC, X, IS-VARIABLE, HYPER-RESOLVE, P1

taken from an alphabet of the 26 letters, the ten digits 0, 1, 2, 3, 4, 5, 6, 7, 8, 9, and various other characters found on a teletypewriter keyboard. Some of these atoms are interpreted in the usual way as *numbers* (the purist would perhaps insist on saying, *numerals*). Certain other atoms are given special status in LISP, and are called *reserved words*. The programmer is supposed to know which ones these are, and what they mean. We shall be meeting several of them very shortly.

The atoms that are not reserved words or numbers are the programmer's raw materials; he can do with them whatever he wishes. His *data* will be constructed out of them and his *programs* will be constructed out of them; but for our present purposes we shall not dwell on the latter fact. Such atoms are called *identifiers*.

Two basic reserved words are:

T and NIL

which are LISP's truthvalues, truth and falsehood, respectively. NIL also has another, enormously important role; it represents *the empty list*. Lists are the main data-structuring notion in LISP.

Lists are represented by (we shall just say, *are*) certain of the S-expressions. The set of lists is defined recursively by:

NIL is a *list* (the empty list)
if β is a *list*, and α is *any* S-expression,
then the pair $(\alpha \cdot \beta)$ is a *list*.

So, for example, the following are lists:

> NIL
> (X · NIL)
> (X · (Y · (Z · NIL)))
> ((X · NIL) · (X · (Y · (Z · NIL))))

The non-empty list $(\alpha \cdot \beta)$, that is, *must* have a list as its tail, but need not have a list as its head.

While the dotted-pair notation is always meaningful and usable in LISP computing, there is a more convenient notation for lists, which is the one mostly used. This is the "usual" notation, in which we write, e.g.

> (X Y Z)   for (X · (Y · (Z · NIL)))

and

> ((X) X Y Z) for ((X · NIL) · (X · (Y · (Z · NIL))))

"listing" the "components" of the list one after the other, with spaces (one or more, when typing) between them, surrounded by a single pair of parentheses. In this notation the head of a non-empty list is always the first item on it, while its tail is *the list of its remaining items*. Thus the head of (X Y Z) is X and the tail is (Y Z); the head of (X) is X, and the tail is ( ) or NIL, and so on.

In the LISP notation one uses in actual programming, the reserved words CAR and CDR (pronounced "kidder" by some and "kudder" by others) take the place of head and tail. (The reason is an almost-forgotten mnemonic code associated with an obsolete computer's instruction set, in terms of which the first LISP system was implemented.)

One of the main uses of identifiers by the programmer in LISP is as "variables". He can give them a *value* by executing an *assignment command*. The command, e.g.,

> (SETQ X 4)

is an assignment command whose effect is to make the identifier X have the value 4, or denote 4. The reserved word SETQ is LISP's "assignment operator". The list (SETQ $\alpha \beta$) is interpreted as the command to make the identifier α have as its value, or denote, *the value of the S-expression β*. Numbers, and the two truthvalues, have *themselves* as value, but in general an S-expression has to be *evaluated* in order to find out what its value is.

Every "properly written" S-expression has a value. The LISP machine is designed to obtain that value, given the expression, and to print it out, or display it, at the programmer's console (or to *use* it to obtain the value of still another, surrounding expression). Even the expression (SETQ $\alpha\,\beta$) has a value; it is that of β. Thus when the machine types out its "ready" symbol

*

we can type a LISP expression immediately to its right, e.g. as in

*(SETQ A (PLUS 2 2))

and the result will be that the machine prints out the expression's value

4

and again prints its "ready" symbol

*

This is a simple *transaction*, between "ready" symbols: we type in an expression, the machine evaluates it, displays its value, and fires another * to show it is ready for another transaction.

In general, an expression not only has a value, but also *causes a "side-effect"*, or change of some sort, inside or outside the machine, when it is executed. ("Executed" is a more general term than "evaluated"; it includes *both* the getting of the value *and* the causing of the side-effect.) Thus (SETQ A (PLUS 2 2)), when executed as above, has the *value* 4 and the *side-effect* of causing the variable "A" to have the value (or to denote) 4. The transaction:

*(SETQ Y (PLUS A (TIMES 3 A)))
16
*

assigns to "Y" the value, i.e., 16, of the expression

(PLUS A (TIMES 3 A))

(which would be written as, e.g.

A + (3 × A)

in a more "arithmetically-minded" system than LISP) and prints it out. The transaction

*(PLUS A (TIMES 3 A))
16
*

has a "null" side-effect; the value is found and printed out, but no changes have been left behind inside the machine. The programmer has to learn what values will be determined and what side-effects caused (if only, as above, the *null* side-effect), by the various expressions he can submit to the machine for execution. As the example shows, the value of an expression will depend on the internal state, or *environment*, of "bindings" that currently prevail between variables and the objects that happen to have been most recently made their values.

Not just a number, but *any S-expression at all*, can be a value of a variable. The transaction

⁎(SETQ Z (QUOTE (HELLO! I'M NOT A NUMBER!)))
(HELLO! I'M NOT A NUMBER!)
⁎

illustrates how a variable can be made to denote an arbitrary list, or indeed an arbitrary S-expression, as its value. The expression

(QUOTE α)

in general has as its value the very expression α that is its second component. Look at the difference between the first two and last two transactions that follow:

⁎A
4
⁎Y
16
⁎(QUOTE A)
A
⁎(QUOTE Y)
Y
⁎

One can *ask* the LISP machine to evaluate an expression by explicitly invoking its *evaluation function* EVAL:

⁎(EVAL (QUOTE (PLUS 3 2)))
5
⁎

which works in general by executing (EVAL α) just as all other "function applications" are executed: *first* the function expression and the argument expression or expressions are evaluated, and *then* the value of the function expression is applied to the value(s) of the argument expression(s). So, in general, the LISP programmer finds himself writing function application expressions, of the form

$$(\varphi \, \alpha_1 \ldots \alpha_n),$$ (1)

all the time; expecting them to be evaluated in the systematic way explained, which amounts to the general equation:

the value of $(\varphi \, \alpha_1 \ldots \alpha_n)$ = result of applying (the value of φ) to (the value of α_1) and ... and (the value of α_n)

Certain expressions of the form (1) are exceptions to this general pattern of evaluation, and must be learned separately. The case (SETQ $\alpha \, \beta$) is one of them, and (QUOTE α) is another. A third case is the *conditional expression*:

(COND $\alpha_1 \ldots \alpha_n$)

and a fourth case is the *program expression*:

(PROG $\alpha_1 \ldots \alpha_n$)

(COND and PROG and QUOTE are, of course, *reserved words*).

The argument expressions in a conditional expression are lists whose heads are "Boolean expressions", i.e. expressions that denote a truthvalue. The value of a conditional expression is determined by whichever of its components is the *earliest* in the sequence of lists $\alpha_1 \ldots \alpha_n$ to have a head whose value is other than NIL, e.g., T. *That* component, say, α_i, is singled out and *its* successive component expressions are executed, one after the other from left to right (causing side-effects, if any, as called for by the expressions executed); the value of the *last* expression in α_i is then delivered as the value of the entire expression (COND $\alpha_1 \ldots \alpha_n$). If none of the α_i has a head whose value is other than NIL, the value of (COND $\alpha_1 \ldots \alpha_n$) is some arbitrary object (NIL, in the author's local LISP machine), or is even left undefined.

Thus the value of (COND (NIL 8) (NIL (SETQ A 39) 7) (T (SETQ B 6) 42)) is 42; and in obtaining it there will have been caused a side-effect, namely, the assignment of the value 6 to the variable "B". Note that the command (SETQ A 39) is *not* executed! (Of course in general the heads of the lists that are components of conditional expressions can be arbitrarily complex expressions, not just bare truthvalues as in the above example.)

Certain *predicates* (functions yielding truthvalues) are built into the LISP machine and are associated with reserved words, which denote them. Thus NULL yields T at the empty list NIL, and yields NIL at all other S-expressions:

```
*(NULL 4)
NIL
*(NULL (QUOTE (A B C)))
NIL
* (NULL (CDR (QUOTE (A))))
T
*
```

The predicate ATOM yields T at every atom and NIL at every dotted-pair. The predicate NUMBERP yields T at numbers and NIL at all other S-expressions.

Certain predicates take more than one argument. A very basic one is EQ. The expression (EQ α β) has the value T if α and β are one and the same atom, and has the value NIL if α and β are distinct atoms. Its value when one or both of α and β are *not* atoms is left undefined.

The predicate GREATERP is defined for pairs of numbers; and (GREATERP n m) has the value T or NIL according as the number denoted by the expression n is greater than, or not greater than, that denoted by the expression m.

The programmer can define (by means we shall explain shortly) his own functions and predicates; indeed this is what he is doing when he is "programming in LISP".

The other exception mentioned above, the "program" (PROG $\alpha_1 \dots \alpha_n$), is a much-used LISP expression. In more detail, its form is

$$(\text{PROG } (\zeta_1 \dots \zeta_m) \, \varepsilon_1 \dots \varepsilon_n)$$

where the list $(\zeta_1 \dots \zeta_m)$ (which may be empty, i.e., we can write (PROG NIL $\varepsilon_1 \dots \varepsilon_n$) displays a collection of distinct identifiers that are called the "*local variables*" of the program. The other components, $\varepsilon_1, \dots, \varepsilon_n$, are the *steps* of the program, and are executed one after the other. They are, with one exception, executed as the LISP expressions that they are; their values, if any, are "thrown away", i.e., ignored, the point being *to obtain their side-effects*. The one exception is when an ε_i is a bare identifier. It is then called a *label* or *tag*, and serves to mark the place where it occurs. One can think of it as an expression with no value and no side-effect: it just sits there. Its purpose is to serve as the "destination" of "jump" commands that can occur in programs (but *only* in programs) in LISP. A jump has the form (GO α), where α is a label in the program. Thus if we type in and execute certain programs, we can get repetitive behaviour *ad infinitum*:

*(PROG (N) (SETQ N 1) A (PRINT N) (SETQ N (ADD1 N)) (GO A))

1
2
3
4
...

for the execution of the jump expression (GO A) causes the machine to go back to the point A and continue from there. Thus the above example shows a simple "loop" by which repetition can be obtained of the same commands several, or even arbitrarily many, times.

One normally programs in "tests" to determine when such loops should be left behind; for example:

(PROG (N) (SETQ N 1) A (PRINT N)
(SETQ N (ADD1 N)) (COND ((GREATERP N 3)
                        (PRINT (QUOTE FINISHED))
                        (RETURN (QUOTE (END OF PROGRAM)))))
(GO A))

INISHED
END OF PROGRAM)

(Here, we have shown the permissible "free lay-out" of LISP expressions: one starts a new line whenever one pleases and leaves spaces *ad libitum* for purposes of readability: the bracketing structure of the expression tells the machine, and the reader, what the expression is.) Note the conditional expression guarding against infinite repetition of the loop, and the use of (RETURN α) to *exit* from the program expression *with the value of α as the value of the program expression*. If the Boolean expression (GREATERP N 3) has the value NIL (as it will for the times when N has the values 1, 2, 3) then the conditional expression yields NIL and control flows to the next expression in the program, (GO A). But when (GREATERP N 3) has the value T (as it does when N has the value 4), the law of the conditional expression decrees that the expressions in the list it heads be executed one after the other.

The local variables $\xi_1, \ldots, \xi_m$, which are "declared" in the list which is the first "step" in the program

$$(\text{PROG} \, (\xi_1 \ldots \xi_m) \, \varepsilon_1 \ldots \varepsilon_n)$$

are not affected by (they do not even exist for) transactions taking place outside that of executing the program. We can use these identifiers as variables outside the program, but they are then *different* variables. The idea is the same as that of bound variables in formulas of predicate calculi. Local variables are bound variables of the program; their scope is the program; we could change them to other identifiers without changing the "meaning" of the program (it would be a *variant* of the first program). Witness the transaction:

```
*(SETQ N 5)
5
*(PROG (N) (SETQ N 3) (PRINT N) (RETURN (QUOTE DONE
3
DONE
*N
5
*
```

The value denoted by N, i.e. 5, is unaffected by the events taking place within the execution of the program that has N as its local variable. From within that program, we have no way to get at the external, or "global" N; we cannot change its value by assignment (that would change only the *local* N) nor use its value, say to print it (we can only use the *local* N).

We have now met a large part of the LISP system! One important primitive idea we have yet to meet, however, is the function CONS. The value of the expression (CONS $\alpha \, \beta$), for any S-expressions that are the respective values of α and of β, is the *dotted pair* of those values.

```
*(CONS 3 4)
(3 . 4)
*(CONS (QUOTE X) (QUOTE (Y Z)))
(X Y Z)
*(CONS 3 NIL)
(3)
*
```

CONS is the fundamental operation with which the LISP programmer *builds up* the S-expressions he wants; CAR and CDR are the fundamental operations he uses to *take them apart*.

Whereas, however, CAR and CDR have no side-effect, CONS does (that is, the side-effect of CAR and of CDR is null; that of CONS is not). Whenever (CONS α β) is executed, a new storage cell is allocated, inside the machine, to be the place where the dotted pair which is the value of (CONS α β) will exist. (Actually, the cell physically contains, not that dotted pair itself, which may be a huge object that would not fit into the cell; but rather a pair of "pointers", or cell-addresses, indicating where the S-expressions are that are the values of α and β. Thus, putting together two never-so-large S-expressions to make the dotted pair thereof, is always a simple, single, LISP step.)

The LISP programmer need not, unless he is working at a fairly advanced level, concern himself with this side-effect of CONS. The full story is elegant and powerful: a cell pre-empted by a CONS execution can later be retrieved by the LISP machine for re-use, when it detects that the dotted pair "contained in", or represented by, that cell *is no longer being referred to or used in any way in the computation*. This recycling of the storage cells is done entirely automatically and the programmer need not even know about it: it is part of the "autonomic nervous system" of LISP. In the slightly self-mocking jargon of the LISP designers, this automatic recycling of storage cells is known as "garbage collection".

The fundamental equations of CAR, CDR and CONS are:

$$(CAR\ (CONS\ \alpha\ \beta)) = \alpha$$
$$(CDR\ (CONS\ \alpha\ \beta)) = \beta$$
$$(CONS\ (CAR\ \gamma)\ (CDR\ \gamma)) = \gamma$$

The first two are true for *all* objects α and β. The third is true for all *pairs* γ. These equations should be read as assertions about α, β, and γ rather than as assertions about the storage cells in which they may be stored in the LISP machine.

As stated earlier, the programmer can define his own functions and have them incorporated into the LISP machine's repertory along with its own "built-in" functions. He does this by executing the command (or "definition")

$$(DE\ \varphi\ (\xi_1 \ldots \xi_m)\ \beta)$$

where φ is an identifier he has chosen to denote the function, and the list $(\xi_1 \ldots \xi_m)$ is a list of distinct variables that will denote, throughout the "body" β of the definition, the m arguments of the function. The expression β is any meaningful LISP expression.

After this definition has been executed, the identifier φ will *denote* (have as its value) the function intended by the programmer. He can "call" it by writing function application expressions with its name φ as the head and m expressions as argument expressions

$$(\varphi\, \alpha_1 \ldots \alpha_m)$$

The LISP machine will then evaluate this expression in the intended way: it will deliver, as its value, *the value of the "body" β when $\xi_1, \ldots, \xi_m$ are assigned the values of $\alpha_1, \ldots \alpha_m$.* An example shows how this works:

```
*(DE THRICE (N) (PLUS N N N))
THRICE
*(THRICE 2)
6
*(THRICE 4)
12
*(THRICE (THRICE (THRICE 5)))
135
```

The function denoted by φ is, in fact, represented by a certain S-expression that "describes" it for the LISP machine's purposes. Advanced LISP programmers know what S-expression this is, and how the LISP machine uses it as a description of a function when it is called upon to apply that function to given objects. For our present purposes we do not need to know about all this, and we shall simply take for granted that the definitions really do work, when we execute them, as described.

Note that the expression $(DE\, \varphi\, (\xi_1 \ldots \xi_m)\, \beta)$ has a value, namely, the identifier φ (as witness its being printed out when the definition is executed; see the THRICE example above). However, *we execute it for its side-effect*, which is *to assign to φ, as its value, the function described in the definition.*

Let us take another example. This time, we define a function "recursively", by referring, within the body β, to the very function we are defining: a very common and powerful technique in programming. Suppose we are given two *lists*, e.g. (3 4 8) and (9 2). We want to *append* them to form a single list, e.g. (3 4 8 9 2). The definitional transaction:

```
*(DE APPEND (A B)
      (COND ((NULL A) B)
            (T (CONS (CAR A)
                     (APPEND (CDR A) B)))))
APPEND
*
```

will assign to the identifier APPEND a function that has the property we want:

*(APPEND (QUOTE (3 4 8)) (QUOTE (9 2)))
(3 4 8 9 2)

*

Note that the body of the definition encapsulates the reasoning

> if A is the *empty* list, then the answer we want is simply B itself; but if A is, say, $(A_1 \cdot A_2)$, then what we want is the list $(A_1 \cdot C)$, where C is the result of appending A_2 and B

So the problem of appending (3 4 8) and (9 2) is solved by "CONSing" 3 with the result of appending (4 8) and (9 2), and so on.

The body β of a definition can contain references to other functions already defined by the programmer (or, for that matter, to functions not yet defined, provided that they will have been defined by the time the programmer executes a function application that will cause the LISP machine to evaluate β!). Every definition that is executed extends the repertory of functions the LISP machine "understands". Thus by executing definitions the LISP programmer is in a rather straightforward sense *extending* the LISP machine to a larger LISP machine, specially tailored to his own computing purposes.

This facility gives the LISP programmer tremendous power. The whole world is at his feet. He can make the LISP machine into a device ready and able to carry out *any symbolic task he understands well enough to define.*

That is what we shall be doing for the remainder of this chapter. We shall go over some definitions of functions (40 of them) which constitute an extension of the LISP machine to one that can be used to prove clausal sequents exactly as described in the previous chapter. In the course of thinking through each function we shall meet a few further features (and associated reserved words) of the LISP system itself. By the time we are done, at chapter's end, the reader will have understood, and quite literally will be ready to use (assuming availability of a LISP machine) a surprisingly formidable "automatic clausal sequent prover", which can be adapted to proving true sequents in general by further programming (to convert them to the clausal form).

The author's label (in the LISP "filing system", which is stored in the "library" that is part of the LISP machine) for these 40 functions is: RESLAB. When one wishes to extend the machine by adding these functions to its repertory, one simply carries out the following transaction:

```
*(DSKIN RESLAB)
RESLAB
***
*
```

The LISP system command DSKIN needs only to be given the label RESLAB to cause the side-effect of retrieving the collection of 40 definitions, so-labelled, which is stored on the magnetic-disc device in the computing centre under the author's name and account number. In a few seconds the label RESLAB is typed back at the requestor, followed by *** and the standard ready-character *. This means that all 40 definitions have been executed, and we are ready to invoke them in any way we please, by composing and typing in appropriate LISP expressions. It is just as though we had typed in and executed, one at a time, each of the 40 definitions – but very much less laborious!

The "top-level" function in RESLAB is: PROVE. If the identifier S denotes a clausal sequent S, then the transaction

```
*(PROVE S)
...
*
```

is one in which that sequent is proved (assuming it is true, and that there is enough time and storage space to carry out the task). The value of the expression (PROVE S) is a terminal sequent:

$$S, R_1, ..., \square$$

suitably represented (in a way to be explained shortly) by an S-expression, and this terminal sequent is a proof of S by hyper-resolution according to the ideas set forth in the previous chapter.

Let us begin our study of RESLAB by reviewing the author's representation of sequents, clauses, predications, and so on, as LISP objects.

In all programming, one has to decide on how to represent, inside the machine (and in transmitting to and from the machine one's "input" and "output") the various entities on which one's programs will do their work. These decisions are of very considerable import-ance in the overall design: poorly-chosen representations can make for obscure, inefficient programs; well-chosen ones can both *aid the mind*, by providing clear, simple structures subject to intelligible rules of combination and analysis-into-parts, and also *enhance the efficiency* of the computer's operations by affording quick, direct decompositions into sub-structures and assembly of constructs from their constituents. In RESLAB, all the functions are designed with the following plan of representation in mind.

Constants and variables are simply, *identifiers*. Whether a given identifier, say X, is a constant or a variable is a matter for inquiry — it depends on the user's taste, preference for mnemonic vibrations, etc., as to what identifiers he uses for his constants and variables. There is in RESLAB a function IS-VARIABLE, which we shall meet several times in use: the transaction

```
*(IS-VARIABLE (QUOTE X))
T
*
```

would occur if X were a variable, while

```
*(IS-VARIABLE (QUOTE X))
NIL
*
```

would show that X was a constant. There is a function in RESLAB that the user invokes to "make a variable" from an identifier: Thus the transaction

```
*(MAKE-VARIABLE (QUOTE X))
T
*
```

has the side-effect of changing certain information about X inside the machine so that X will be a variable. (The value T is just a formality: it's the side-effect we are after.)

Here are the definitions of IS-VARIABLE and MAKE-VARIABLE:

```
(DE IS-VARIABLE (#A)
  (GET #A (QUOTE IS-A-VARIABLE)))
(DE MAKE-VARIABLE (#A)
  (PUTPROP #A T (QUOTE IS-A-VARIABLE)))
```

To understand them, we must know about a hitherto-unmentioned feature of the LISP machine, which is one of its most attractive, useful and thought-provoking facilities: the *property-list* of an identifier.

Every identifier in use inside the LISP machine at a given time has a property-list. You can actually take a look at it if you wish:

⋆(CDR (QUOTE X))
(IS-A-VARIABLE T VALUE (X · 4) PRINT-NAME-165722)
⋆

because it is stored as the tail of a pair that occupies a cell associated with X, and which is consulted by the LISP machine whenever anything comes up, having to do with X, in the course of a computation. The property-list of an identifier is always changing, as a result of side-effects. We have shown above a typical snapshot in which the property-list has three *properties*: IS-A-VARIABLE, VALUE, and PRINT-NAME, each with an *entry*, i.e., T, (X · 4), and 165722. The latter two are of significance to the LISP machine (and to the cognoscenti; see the comment on EVAL, p.242) but the first *might well have been put there by a* MAKE-VARIABLE *command*. The LISP command

(PUTPROP α β γ)

causes the side-effect: the property-list of identifier α is modified so that it will have the entry β under the property γ. A property-list is just a list

$(\gamma_1 \beta_1 \dots \gamma_n \beta_n)$

of properties and corresponding entries. Some of the properties (such as VALUE and PRINT-NAME) are the concern of the LISP machine in its machinations: the entry under (i.e. immediately following) VALUE gives the value currently denoted by the identifier − by supplying the address of the storage cell where it may be found − and PRINT-NAME gives the coding details for printing out the characters comprising the identifier as far as the outside world is concerned.

The LISP command

(GET α γ)

has no side-effect; it simply "looks up" the property γ in the property-list of the identifier α and returns the entry under γ as value. Thus if the property-list of X is as above, the transaction

⋆(GET (QUOTE X) (QUOTE IS-A-VARIABLE))
T
⋆

could take place. If the property-list of α has no property γ on it, then the value of (GET α γ) is NIL:

```
*(GET (QUOTE X) (QUOTE NORWAY))
NIL
*
```

Now that we have seen how property-lists work, and what GET and PUTPROP do, the definitions of IS-VARIABLE and MAKE-VARIABLE become immediately clear.

It might also be noted, while we are on the subject of property-lists, that the side-effect of the assignment command (SETQ α β) is to change the property-list of the identifier α thus:

(PUTPROP (QUOTE α) (CONS (QUOTE α) β) (QUOTE VALUE))

However, LISP has *another* assignment operator, SET, which differs from SETQ in a subtle way. An example will show their difference:

```
*(SETQ X 5)
5
*X
5
*(SET (QUOTE X) 6)      changes the value of X to 6
6
*X
6
*(SETQ A (QUOTE X))    changes the value of A to "X"
X
*A
X
*(SET A 7)             changes the value of X to 7
7
*A                    not the value of A!
X
*X
7
```

In fact, SETQ is a sort of mnemonic for SET QUOTE in view of the sameness of meaning between, e.g.

(SET (QUOTE X) 4)

and

(SETQ X 4).

LISP also has a function (already mentioned in the introductory part of this chapter) EVAL, which gets the value of an expression.

When the expression is an identifier, the LISP machine must consult the identifier's property list for its value:

    *(EVAL (QUOTE X))
    4
    *

just as though we had executed (CDR (GET (QUOTE X) (QUOTE VALUE))) since (for esoteric, irrelevant reasons) the LISP machine puts the entry (CONS α β) rather than β as the entry under VALUE on α's property list, to represent that α's value is β. Thus when X's value is 4, the entry on its property list under VALUE is (X · 4).

After this digression on property-lists and the way they are changed by SET, SETQ, PUTPROP, and interrogated by GET and EVAL, let us return to the topic we were discussing: the representation of constants, variables, and other logical expressions as LISP objects.

We can make a whole lot of variables at once by the RESLAB command MAKE-VARIABLES, whose definition is:

    (DE MAKE-VARIABLES (#L)
       (COND ((NULL #L) T)
             ((MAKE-VARIABLE (CAR #L))
              (MAKE-VARIABLES (CDR #L)))))

and which uses the "one-identifier-at-a-time" MAKE-VARIABLE to process an entire *list* of identifiers. Note that this is another example of *recursive* programming. It is a typical piece of LISP writing: to do something to each thing on a list, by doing it to the head and invoking the entire process anew for the tail. Note that we are making use of the otherwise irrelevant fact that MAKE-VARIABLE *returns* T *as its value* as well as changing the property-list of the given identifier *as its side-effect*.

We can also *undo* this process of "making identifiers into variables". Note the two definitions:

(a)   (DE UNMAKE-VARIABLE (#A)
         (PUTPROP #A NIL (QUOTE IS-A-VARIABLE)))

which returns the value NIL, having modified the property-list; and

(b)   (DE UNMAKE-VARIABLES (#L)
         (COND ((NULL #L) T)
               ((NOT (UNMAKE-VARIABLE (CAR #L)))
                (UNMAKE-VARIABLES (CDR #L)))))

which makes use of the fact that UNMAKE-VARIABLE returns NIL.

Now, we represent *terms* and *predications* by lists. The constant (i.e. the constructor symbol or the predicate symbol) is the head of the list, while the terms which are the argument expressions form the tail. Thus the lists

(P X Y U)
(P (G R S) R S)
(P X (H Y (H (G Y X) Z)) Z)

are predications involving the 3-ary predicate symbol P, the 2-ary constructor symbols G and H, and the variables X, Y, Z, U, R and S. In order to have them so construed, we would have to have executed

(MAKE-VARIABLES (QUOTE (X Y Z U R S)))

so that the LISP machine would be able to discover our convention as to what symbols mean what. It would also have to be the case that all of the expressions

(IS-VARIABLE (QUOTE P))
(IS-VARIABLE (QUOTE G))
(IS-VARIABLE (QUOTE H))

denote NIL − we should not have made P, G, and H variables if we intend them to be treated as constants! So: identifiers are constants unless we *make* them variables.

A *clause* is represented by *a dotted pair of lists*, namely, the left-hand side L and the right-hand side R of a clause are represented by lists of the predications which are their members, and the clause $L \square R$ is then represented by $(\lambda \cdot \rho)$, i.e., by the value of (CONS $\lambda \rho$), where λ represents L and ρ represents R. So, for instance, the clauses in example 2 of the previous chapter are represented by the five pairs:

(((P %X %Y %U) (P %Y %Z %V) (P %X%V %W)) · ((P %U %Z %W)))
(((P %X %Y %U) (P %Y %Z %V) (P %U %Z %W)) · (P %X %V %W)))
(NIL · ((P (G %R %S) %R %S)))
(NIL · ((P %A (H %A %B) %B)))
(((P (K %T) %T (K %T))) · NIL)

after we have executed:

(MAKE-VARIABLES (QUOTE (%X %Y %Z %U %V %W %R %S %A %B %T)))

(It is because of the author's yearning for ease of perceiving formula-structure that the identifiers used for variables all begin with a special non-alphabetic character. They then spring to the eye as having a different status from the identifiers which are purely alphabetic. For similar reasons the LISP variables in the definitions of the RESLAB collection are made more discernible by being prefixed with #.)

A quirk of the LISP print-out convention results in a dotted pair *whose tail happens to be a list* being printed in the list notation instead of the dotted-pair notation: how can the poor printer know which notation one wants to see? So the five clauses shown above would actually come out, if we caused them to be printed, as:

(((P %X %Y %U) (P %Y %Z %V) (P %X %V %W)) (P %U %Z %W))
(((P %X %U) (P %Y %Z %V) (P %U %Z %W)) (P %X %V %W))
(NIL (P (G %R %S) %R %S))
(NIL (P %A (H %A %B) %B))
(((P (K %T) %T (K %T)))).

The reader will profit from the exercise of verifying that these S-expressions are the same ones, seen in the two different conventions.

A clausal sequent is then simply *a list of the clauses it contains*. Thus the sequent S_2 of example 2, chapter 12, is the list whose four components are the S-expressions shown above. We are, in the present version of RESLAB, under the constraint of ensuring that each clause is given as a variant, none of whose variables occur in other clauses of the sequent, when we submit a sequent as input. For convenience, example 2 can be entered into the machine by executing a simple function called EXAMPLE2, whose *value* is the sequent just described, and whose side-effect is to *make* the variables that are used. This function is defined by:

```
(DE EXAMPLE2 NIL
  (PROGN (MAKE-VARIABLES
            (QUOTE (%X %Y %Z %U %V %W %XX %YY %ZZ
                    %UU %VV %WW %R %S %A %B %TT)))
         (LIST (CONS (QUOTE ((P %X %Y %U) (P %Y %Z %V)
                             (P %X %V %W)))
                     (QUOTE ((P %U %Z %W))))
               (CONS (QUOTE ((P %XX %YY %UU) (P %YY %ZZ %
                             (P %UU %ZZ %WW)))
                     (QUOTE ((P %XX %VV %WW))))
               (CONS NIL (QUOTE ((P (G %R %S) %R %S))))
               (CONS NIL (QUOTE ((P %A (H %A %B) %B))))
               (CONS (QUOTE ((P (K %TT) %TT (K %TT)))) NIL))
  )
)
```

Here we have vertically aligned a couple of distantly-separated right parentheses below their mates, to aid the eye. This definition invokes two further L I S P features we have not yet mentioned. The *sequential composition* (PROGN $\epsilon_1 \ldots \epsilon_n$) is an expression that is executed by executing, from left to right, its *steps* $\epsilon_1 \ldots \epsilon_n$, thus causing any side-effects they may have, but ignoring their values, with one exception, that of ϵ_n. The value of the entire expression (PROGN $\epsilon_1 \ldots \epsilon_n$) is the value of ϵ_n. So, the value of (EXAMPLE2) is the value of its body, which is the value of the second of the two expressions in that sequential composition.

This involves the L I S P function LIST. As its name is intended to suggest, this function returns a list as its value (and has no side-effect of its own). The value of (LIST $\alpha_1 \ldots \alpha_n$) is the list whose components are the values of $\alpha_1, \ldots, \alpha_n$ respectively:

  ∗(LIST 3 (PLUS 3 4) (QUOTE EXCELSIOR!) (CONS 6 NIL))
  (3 7 EXCELSIOR! (6))
  ∗

and it is very handy to be able to create lists directly in this way instead of having to build them up using CONS, one item at a time.

L I S P provides a number of other useful functions for the programmer to use in working with lists. The ones we shall be using in RESLAB are: LENGTH, which gives the number of components of a list:

  ∗(LENGTH (QUOTE (3 4 7 6 2)))
  5
  ∗(LENGTH (QUOTE ((2 3))))
  1
  ∗(LENGTH NIL)
  ∅
  ∗

and MEMBER, which returns T if its first argument is one of the components of (the list that is) its second argument and NIL otherwise:

  ∗(MEMBER 3 (QUOTE (2 3 8 6)))
  T
  ∗(MEMBER 3 (QUOTE (2 4 8 6)))
  NIL
  ∗(MEMBER 3 NIL)
  NIL
  ∗

LISP also has the function APPEND built in, which we used earlier to illustrate how functions can be defined recursively.

It is very natural to use lists to represent *sets*. When considered as a set, a list may be ordered any old how and its components can be repeated more than once. It is still representing the same set; e.g. (3 4 3 8) and (4 3 8 8) both represent {3, 4, 8}. In RESLAB there are several functions devoted to this rôle of lists as set-representatives, since our representation of clauses and sequents is in fact using lists in that rôle.

Thus in RESLAB there is a function ENSEMBLE (the word SET, which would have been nicer for the purpose, is a reserved word, as we saw!) which takes a list and throws out any duplicates, to make it a bit more decent *as a set*:

```
(DE ENSEMBLE (#S)
  (COND ((NULL #S) NIL)
        ((MEMBER (CAR #S) (CDR #S))
         (ENSEMBLE (CDR #S)))
        (T (CONS (CAR #S) (ENSEMBLE (CDR #S))))
  )
)
```

We also have in RESLAB a function UNION, which returns the union of two "sets":

```
(DE UNION (#A #B)
  (ENSEMBLE (APPEND #A #B)))
```

and a function DELETE, which removes a given object from a given set, if indeed it is a member, and returns that set as value in any case:

```
(DE DELETE (#A #B)
  (COND ((NULL #B) NIL)
        ((EQUAL #A (CAR #B)) (DELETE #A (CDR #B)))
        (T (CONS (CAR #B) (DELETE #A (CDR #B))))
  )
)
```

The LISP function EQUAL tests two S-expressions to see if they are the same. One can consider EQUAL a generalization, to *all* S-expressions, of the function EQ (which is officially defined for *atoms* only). The following definition of EQUAL would give the same effect as the function that is in fact "built in":

```
(DE EQUAL (#A #B)
   (COND ((ATOM #A) (COND ((ATOM #B) (EQ #A #B))
                          (T NIL)))
         ((ATOM #B) NIL)
         (T (COND ((EQUAL (CAR #A) (CAR #B))
                   (EQUAL (CDR #A) (CDR #B)))
                  (T NIL)))
   )
)
```

One must simply know that S-expressions are equal *only* when *both are atoms*, and in that case are the *same* atom, or when *both are pairs*, and in that case have equal *heads* and equal *tails*.

We also have occasion in RESLAB to compute the set of all non-empty subsets of a given set (for the purpose of resolving two clauses in all possible ways, as we shall see). So we have a function POWER that does this. Its definition shows LISP at its best, allowing a messy data-processing task to be described recursively, with resulting intelligibility:

```
(DE POWER (#L)                    [#L is assumed to be non-empty]
   (COND ((NULL (CDR #L)) (LIST #L))    [if #L is a singleton
                                         set, the answer is {#L}]
         (T (PROG (#P #R)
            (SETQ #P (POWER (CDR #L)))
            (SETQ #R (APPEND (LIST (LIST (CAR #L)))
                             (DIST (CAR #L) #P)
                             #P))   [the built-in APPEND
                                     can take any number
            (RETURN #R)))           of arguments]
   )
)
```

[otherwise, #L is a list of two or more members, i.e., a pair $(\alpha \cdot \beta)$ with β a non-empty list; then, if (POWER β) is the list $(\beta_1 \ldots \beta_n)$, the answer is the list:

$$((\alpha) (\alpha \cdot \beta_1) \ldots (\alpha \cdot \beta_n), \beta_1 \ldots \beta_n)]$$

The auxiliary function DIST just takes its first argument α and forms a new list from its second argument β, which is a list, by tacking α onto each component of β:

```
(DE DIST (#A #L)
  (COND ((NULL #L) NIL)
        (T (CONS (APPEND (LIST #A) (CAR #L))
                 (DIST #A (CDR #L)))))
  )
)
```

Let us take time out to summarise the discussion so far. We have met the following ten of the forty functions from RESLAB:

IS-VARIABLE	ENSEMBLE
MAKE-VARIABLE	UNION
MAKE-VARIABLES	DELETE
UNMAKE-VARIABLE	POWER
UNMAKE-VARIABLES	DIST

and have considered their definitions. The function PROVE, which we have also met, has not yet been fully described. In the process of discussing the definitions of the ten functions above, we have encountered the property-list concept of LISP, and have learned about the meanings LISP attaches to the reserved words:

SET, GET, PUTPROP, PROGN,
LIST, EQUAL, MEMBER, LENGTH,
VALUE, PRINT-NAME

We have also been over the conventions for representing constants, variables, terms, predications, clauses, and sequents on which the design of the functions in RESLAB is based.

The ten RESLAB functions we have so far met are, one might put it, lower-level tools, or auxiliary devices, fashioned for the purpose of making the larger, loftier aspects of the design easier to grasp and to carry through. Here are four more: COMPONENT, VARIABLES, EMPTY-CLAUSE, and SPLIT, which can fairly be put into the same utilitarian category, and which can be understood now and recalled later when we come to use them in further definitions.

We need to be able to refer directly to the *j*th component of a given list, given *j*, and that list, as arguments. The function COMPONENT allows us to do this. Its definition is:

```
(DE COMPONENT (#A #J)
  (COND ((EQ #J 1) (CAR #A))
        (T (COMPONENT (CDR #A) (SUB1 #J)))))
```

The LISP function SUB1 returns the predecessor of its numerical (integer) argument, just as ADD1 returns the successor of its argument. Note that, in defining COMPONENT, we have not troubled to include tests against the given *j* exceeding the length of the given list – the discipline must therefore be observed (on pain of unwanted abortion of computations by the LISP machine on its being asked to do the meaningless) of invoking COMPONENT *only* with a non-empty list, and a positive integer no larger than the list's length, as arguments. The functions in RESLAB that call COMPONENT do observe this discipline.

We have occasion elsewhere in RESLAB to ask, of a given LISP object representing a logical one (a term, predication, clause, or sequent) what variables it contains. The function VARIABLES answers that question, as the following definition reveals:

```
(DE VARIABLES (#E)
  (COND ((NULL #E) NIL)
          ((ATOM #E) (COND ((IS-VARIABLE #E) (LIST #E))
                         (T NIL)))
          (T (UNION (VARIABLES (CAR #E))
                    (VARIABLES (CDR #E))))
  )
)
```

Our representation scheme has the empty clause □ represented by (NIL · NIL), or (in the other notation) by (NIL). To aid the eye, we make this object the one returned by the input-less function EMPTY-CLAUSE:

```
        (DE EMPTY-CLAUSE NIL (CONS NIL NIL)).
```

Thus whenever we wish to refer to □ in a LISP expression we need only write: (EMPTY-CLAUSE). This obviates the need to rummage in one's archives for the significance of the less-informative: (CONS NIL NIL).

Finally, the function SPLIT plays the humble part of separating, when invoked, the sequent that is its argument into two sets: a *left* set containing those clauses (if any) in the sequent that have an empty left-hand side, and a *right* set containing those clauses (if any) that do *not* have an empty left-hand side. Since we never invoke SPLIT to do this for a terminal sequent (one containing the clause □) we always know that the clauses in its *left* set have at least one predication in their right-hand sides. The behaviour of SPLIT is straightforward: it returns its two sets as the dotted pair of the lists representing them.

```
(DE SPLIT (#S)
  (PROG (#SPL)
        (RETURN
          (COND ((NULL #S) (CONS NIL NIL))                    [a]
                ((NULL (CAAR  #S))                            [b]
                 (SETQ #SPL (SPLIT (CDR #S)))
                 (CONS (CONS (CAR #S) (CAR #SPL))
                       (CDR #SPL)))
                (T                                            [c]
                 (SETQ #SPL (SPLIT (CDR #S)))
                 (CONS (CAR #SPL)
                       (CONS (CAR #S) (CDR #SPL))))))
          )
        )
  )
)
```

If the given sequent contains no clauses, this is discovered in line [a] and the dotted pair (NIL · NIL) is returned. If the first clause in the sequent has an empty left-hand side, it must be tacked on to the left set of the result of splitting the remaining clauses up into two sets. The left-hand side of the first clause in #S is (CAR (CAR #S)); the LISP system kindly permits one to abbreviate this by the expression (CAAR #S) used in the test in line [b]. At [c] we know that (CAAR #S) does *not* have an empty left-hand side, so we tack it onto the *right* set of the result of splitting the remaining clauses.

As an illustration of how SPLIT works, observe the transaction (recalling the definition of EXAMPLE2):

*(SPLIT (EXAMPLE2))
  (((NIL (P (G %R %S)) %R %S)) (NIL (P %A (H %A %B) %B)))
   (((P %X %Y %U) (P %Y %Z %V) (P %X %V %W)) (P %U %Z %W))
   (((P %XX %YY %UU) (P %YY %ZZ %VV) (P %UU %ZZ %WW))
    (P %XX %VV %WW))
   (((P (K %TT) %TT (K %TT)))))
*

The dotted pair has lost its dot since its tail is a list. The reader will acquire useful combat experience by verifying that the output displayed above is indeed a pair of lists, as required.

Many people find rebarbative, on first encounter, the thickets of brackets that LISP expressions display on being printed. The present author certainly did. He can only say, with d'Alembert: have faith!

press on! The discipline is rewarding, and one soon comes to value the bracketing convention for what it is: the *only* thing one has to remember in reading a LISP expression! The fact that LISP has *no other way* of indicating the structure of its objects is a tremendous blessing (in disguise, at least at first, one must admit) for there is thus *nothing to forget.* One can mitigate the difficulties of reading the bracketed expressions by various schemes of layout, indentation, and the like, and the LISP machine itself does print out S-expressions in various such ways, to assist the eye.

We are now in a position, having negotiated the foothills, to begin the ascent of the main peak of the RESLAB system, at whose summit is the function PROVE. If we were to follow this upward course, we would eventually arrive at PROVE, having mastered the successively higher-level functions on which it rests, without fully grasping what it was all about until the final revelation of "where it had all been leading". Such is the so-called "bottom-up" method of studying a hierarchically-structured system of functions in which the higher-placed ones invoke the lower-placed ones. As we shall see, the metaphor of up-down, and of hierarchic organization, is not always entirely apt. Some functions (as indeed we have already seen) invoke themselves, and so are "higher-up" than themselves: a somewhat strained posture and an exception to the generality that if function *A* calls function *B* then *A* is higher-up than *B*. In other cases, each of two functions may call the other ("mutual recursion") or a more elaborate inter-dependence may prevail (*A* calls *B*, who calls *C*, who calls *D*; who then calls *A*; and so forth). Nevertheless, it is customary, and useful, to pay careful attention, in thinking through the total meaning of a collection of inter-dependent functions, to the "up-down" orientation imposed by "who calls whom".

It is a widely-respected precept of the professional programmer to start, *not* at the bottom end of a hierarchy of functions, and work "bottom-up", but rather *to start at the top and work down.* For then one always knows *why* the subordinate functions are designed the way they are: "to serve the higher-ups". The "top-down" method is recommended not only for the exposition, but also for the composition, of one's functions. The art of programming itself, as well as the art of explaining the programs and understanding them, is thoroughly wedded to the principle of working from the top down.

And so we shall. The next function whose definition we shall study is that of PROVE! Contrary to what one might have expected, PROVE has a very brief definition for such a powerful function. Here it is:

(DE PROVE (#S) (SEARCH (LIST #S)))

Thus, in perhaps not unfamiliar fashion to those who study the hierarchical organizations in human enterprises, the top job consists of passing all the details on to an immediate subordinate, SEARCH, which expects to be given a *list* of (i.e., *set* of) sequents, and could (as its definition will show) cope just as well with a longer list.

The general idea of PROVE is to *initiate* a search in the hyper-resolution space that we studied in the previous chapter. The purpose of the search is to try to find a path, starting with the given sequent #S, which proceeds step-by-step via adjacent sequents until it reaches a terminal sequent. If and when such a path is discovered, it is returned as the value of (SEARCH (LIST #S)) and is promptly printed out by the LISP machine as the value of (PROVE #S), since it is, of course, a *proof* of #S by hyper-resolution. In fact what is printed out is the terminal sequent, not the whole path; this suffices to show the successive steps in the proof.

The search pattern used in RESLAB's SEARCH function is the rather prosaic one known as "breadth first": first all paths of length one, starting with the sequent *S*, are explored; then all paths of length two; and so on for steadily increasing path-lengths. It is much the simplest search plan, which is *guaranteed* to find a proof of the given sequent if the given sequent is true. It would be possible to contemplate more sophisticated search plans, but we shall not do so in this book. The breadth-first scheme is so called because the paths form a tree, e.g.

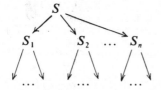

whose nodes are being visited in non-decreasing order of their distance from the origin of the search, i.e., breadth before depth.

So: to explain PROVE it will evidently suffice to explain SEARCH. Meanwhile, we know that (PROVE #S) returns, as its value, a hyper-resolution proof of the sequent #S. Indeed, the following transaction is exactly what one sees when using PROVE to do example 2, chapter 12:

```
*(PROVE (EXAMPLE2))
(5 1)
(6 8)
((((P Y X U) (P X V Z) (P Y Z W)) (P U V W))
(((P U X Y) (P X Z V) (P Y Z W) (P U V W))
(NIL (P (G X Y) X Y))
(NIL (P X (H X Y) Y))
(((P (K X) X (K X))))
(NIL (P Y (H X X) Y))
(NIL))
*
```

The two lines (5 1), (6 8) are simply helpful comments by SEARCH as it steps along paths. Each time it computes the hyper-resolvents of some sequent S it prints out the size of that sequent, and the number of other sequents currently awaiting their turn as ends-of-paths already traversed. So (5 1) says "I am just about to get the hyper-resolvents of a sequent of size 5, and there is just 1 sequent (namely, it!) in the queue at the moment". Then, when that has been done, and since apparently none of the resulting sequents, adjacent to the one just processed, is terminal, it says (6 8), that is: "I am just about to get the hyper-resolvents of a sequent of size 6, and there are just 8 sequents in the queue at the moment (namely, it and 7 more besides)". One of *these* hyper-resolvents is evidently □, and we are done. The final output is the sequent containing (standardized variants of) the clauses in the initial sequent, together with the successive hyper-resolvents

```
(NIL (P Y (H X X) Y))
(NIL)
```

of the proof.

How, then, does SEARCH work, that it should make things so easy and simple for PROVE? SEARCH farms out the hard parts to subordinates, and has only a small amount of "top-level" organizing to do. The subordinates are HYPER-RESOLVE, INFERENCES and STANDARDIZE. The first of these is the function discussed in the previous chapter: given a sequent S, it delivers as its output a list ($\equiv$ set) of all the clauses that are hyper-resolvents of S.

INFERENCES performs the simple job of transforming a sequent S and a list C of clauses into a list of the sequents obtainable by adding to S one of the clauses in C:

```
(DE INFERENCES (#S #C)
    (COND ((NULL #C) NIL)
          (T (CONS (APPEND #S (LIST (CAR #C)))
                   (INFERENCES #S (CDR #C))))
    )
)
```

STANDARDIZE takes a sequent and rewrites its clauses in a standard way, replacing each by a variant whose variables are easier on the eye than those (in general) that HYPER-RESOLVE picks. As we shall see, HYPER-RESOLVE and other functions down where all the real work is done must frequently introduce new variables in the course of their operations. They obtain these from an internal source of supply (GENSYM) which turns out, as we shall see, serviceable, but ugly, identifiers when called upon. So STANDARD-IZE merely gets rid of these in favour of nicer variables like X, Y, Z, U, V, and W.

Here is the definition, then, of SEARCH:

```
(DE SEARCH (#L)
    (PROG (HYPERS)
      A (COND ((NULL #L) (RETURN (QUOTE
                         (SEQUENT IS FALSE)))))       [a]
        (PRINT (LIST (LENGTH (CAR #L))
                     (LENGTH #L)))                    [b]
        (SETQ HYPERS (HYPER-RESOLVE (CAR #L)))        [c]
        (COND ((MEMBER (EMPTY-CLAUSE) HYPERS)         [d]
               (RETURN (STANDARDIZE (APPEND
                (CAR #L) (LIST (EMPTY-CLAUSE)))))))
        (SETQ #L (APPEND (CDR #L) (INFERENCES
                 (CAR #L) HYPERS)))                   [e]
        (GO A)
    )
)
```

This simple loop works by maintaining an orderly queue of se-quents, each sequent as it comes to the head of the queue giving rise to a set of inferred sequents that are then put on the back of the queue to await their turn. (This set might be empty; in which case the queue simply is shortened by losing its first member.) Once the sequent at the head of the queue has been processed it is discarded. If (line [a]) the queue becomes empty, the message is passed up (to PROVE, which prints it) that the original sequent is false — for it has been discovered that no hyper-resolution proof exists for it. At line [b], the little message is typed out saying what the state-of-affairs is at the current traversal of the loop. At line [c], the sequent at the head of the queue is sent off to HYPER-RESOLVE, who sends back the list of its hyper-resolvents; which is then called HYPERS for the sake of later reference. At [d] we ask: is □ one of those hyper-resolvents, by any chance? If so, we are done, and return the appropriate terminal sequent, nicely tidied-up by STANDARDIZE. If not, then we modify the queue by dropping its head and attaching at its rear the sequents inferrable from the dropped sequent.

One might note that there is the possibility that SEARCH will never empty the queue, nor ever turn up □ in line [d]. Once initiated, the search might never end! However, we know from the theory of hyper-resolution that this will *not* happen, if the sequent initiating the search is *true*.

There is also the possibility that the search may have to be aborted because of the limits on time, or storage space, or both, which locally prevail. The length of the queue may increase until it fills all the available storage. On the other hand, even though the queue never grows beyond a manageable length, it may be that the time taken to pursue the search to a given stage is all one can afford.

So: SEARCH can be seen to carry out a simple, repetitive scheme of management of a queue of sequents, whose members are the points on the frontier of an expanding region of the hyper-resolution space growing outward "in all directions" from the starting sequent. We can now say that we understand its behaviour, if we take on faith that HYPER-RESOLVE works as claimed. The relatively unimportant STANDARDIZE can be understood, if we similarly take, on faith, that *its* subordinate, STANDARD, works as claimed:

```
(DE STANDARDIZE (#S)
   (COND ((NULL #S) NIL)
         (T (CONS (STANDARD (CAR #S))
                  (STANDARDIZE (CDR #S))))
   )
)
```

since all STANDARDIZE does is apply STANDARD to each clause in the given sequent and return the sequent that results. STANDARD is the function that actually goes through the clause, chooses new variables properly, and delivers the clause that results.

So we have reduced the set of functions that are still to be explained to two: HYPER-RESOLVE and STANDARD. It will be best if we concentrate on the more important of the two, HYPER-RESOLVE, and postpone the details of how STANDARD accomplishes its relatively mundane chore until later.

As one might expect from the discussion of hyper-resolution in chapter 12, HYPER-RESOLVE relies completely on a function P1-RESOLVE, which, as its name suggests, takes two clauses (the first having an *empty left-hand side* and *non-empty right-hand side*, the second having a *non-empty left-hand side*) and delivers all their P1-resolvents.

Our explanation of HYPER-RESOLVE will, therefore, be given on the basis of an assumption that P1-RESOLVE does work as described. In addition to accepting P1-RESOLVE, we must also take on faith that a function called SUBSUMES works as claimed: namely it correctly returns T or NIL according as the clause that is its first argument does, or does not, subsume the clause that is its second argument. Both functions will, of course, be explained in the sequel.

We use SUBSUMES primarily to determine whether a given clause is subsumed by any clause in a given *list* ($\equiv$ sequent) of clauses. Accordingly we define the more convenient function LIST-SUBSUMES, which applies SUBSUMES to all the various pairs of clauses involved in such a determination:

```
(DE LIST-SUBSUMES (#S  #C)
   (COND ((NULL #S) NIL)
             ((SUBSUMES (CAR #S) #C) T)
             (T (LIST-SUBSUMES (CDR #S) #C))
   )
)
```

In HYPER-RESOLVE, we are interested to "filter" each collection of hyper-resolvents and other clauses by eliminating from it any clauses it contains that are subsumed by the lists of clauses we already have accumulated: for we are going to be adding *new* clauses to these lists, and we do not want to add them if they are subsumed by clauses *already* on those lists. This operation is nicely packaged all to itself in a function called FILTER, which, given two lists #L and #S of clauses will return the list of clauses in #L that are *not* subsumed by any clause in #S. Its definition uses LIST-SUBSUMES in a straightforward manner:

```
(DE FILTER (#L #S)
   (COND ((NULL #L) NIL)
             ((LIST-SUBSUMES #S (CAR #L))
```

```
                    (FILTER (CDR #L) #S))
                (T (CONS (CAR #L) (FILTER (CDR #L) #S)))
        )
    )
```

The only functions, then, whose explanations are being deferred until after we have explained HYPER-RESOLVE are:

P1-RESOLVE, SUBSUMES, STANDARD.

Let us then inspect the definition of HYPER-RESOLVE. The idea of its design is this. The input to HYPER-RESOLVE is a sequent #S. The output is to be a list of all clauses which are hyper-resolvents of #S, (and, hence, are not subsumed by any clause in #S). The way we compute these is to segregate the clauses in #S into two lists, LEFTS and RIGHTS. The clauses in LEFTS have empty left-hand sides and non-empty right-hand sides, and the clauses in RIGHTS have non-empty left-hand sides. We then *expand* RIGHTS by adding such further clauses to it as can be inferred by P1-resolution with left-clause in LEFTS and right-clause in RIGHTS. Each such P1-resolvent is added to RIGHTS if its left-hand side is *non-empty*, and to a list, HYPERS, if its left-hand side is *empty*. Every clause ever added to RIGHTS in this way is eventually used, as right clause, in an attempted P1-resolution with each clause in LEFTS as left-clause. By this means, all hyper-resolutions of the sequent #S are eventually considered, and HYPERS will contain all the resulting hyper-resolvents of #S. [The reader should, perhaps, refresh his recollection of the details of hyper-resolution by reading chapter 12's account of it again.] This work is managed by a simple "double loop" in which a pointer, I, is stepped through the numbers 1, 2, ..., NLEFTS (the number of clauses in LEFTS) for *each* value of another pointer, J. This second pointer starts at 1 and is stepped up (after each full cycle of I values) repeatedly until it eventually exceeds the length of RIGHTS; at which point the work is all done. For each pair of values of I and J, we invoke P1-RESOLVE with the Ith clause in LEFTS and the Jth clause in RIGHTS as its arguments.

While the number of clauses in LEFTS remains constant throughout this process, the number of clauses in RIGHTS will in general increase, and thus the pointer J is "chasing" the receding upper bound on the length of RIGHTS. Fears justifiably spring to the breast of the cautious programmer: what is to prevent J from never "catching up" with the ever-increasing number of clauses in RIGHTS? It *must* catch up, or else the work will never end! The answer is: only finitely many clauses can be added to RIGHTS; for the left-hand side of each clause that is added is *smaller* than the left-hand side of the right clause that is its parent. So J *will* catch up!

The form of the body of HYPER-RESOLVE is that of a 14-line PROG, the first 6 lines of which are executed just once, in order to initialize the working setup described above. The next 8 lines are the ones repeated as many times as called for in the loop.

The definition of HYPER-RESOLVE is the following:

```
(DE HYPER-RESOLVE (#S)
  (PROG (I J LEFTS RIGHTS NLEFTS HYPERS PR)
    (SETQ HYPERS NIL)
    (SETQ PR (SPLIT #S))                                        [a]
    (SETQ LEFTS (CAR PR))
    (SETQ RIGHTS (CDR PR))
    (SETQ NLEFTS (LENGTH LEFTS))
    (SETQ J 1)
  A (COND ((GREATERP J (LENGTH RIGHTS)) (RETURN HYPERS))) [
    (SETQ I 1)                                                  [c]
  B (COND ((GREATER I NLEFTS) (SETQ J (ADD1 J)) (GO A)))  [d]
    (SETQ PR (SPLIT (P1-RESOLVE                                 [e]
                (COMPONENT LEFTS I)
                (COMPONENT RIGHTS J))))
    (SETQ RIGHTS (APPEND RIGHTS (FILTER (CDR PR) RIGHTS)))  [f
    (SETQ HYPERS (APPEND HYPERS (FILTER             [g]
                          (FILTER (CAR PR) LEFTS)
                          HYPERS)))
    (SETQ I (ADD1 I))
    (GO B)))
```

Recall that SPLIT returns a dotted pair of lists of clauses, the head containing all the clauses with *empty* left-hand sides, and the tail containing all the clauses with *non-empty* left-hand sides, which are members of the list of clauses given to it as argument. Line [a] stores this pair, just to avoid repeated calls on SPLIT.

At line [b] we may detect that J has, at last, caught up with, and indeed has overtaken, the length of RIGHTS. In which case we are finished and return the list HYPERS as output. Otherwise we initiate, at [c], a fresh cycle of values for I. We expect to return to A repeatedly with a fresh value of J, as a consequence of the jump command in the step of the program marked [d].

At [e] we obtain, and duly segregate into candidates for RIGHTS and for HYPERS, the P1-resolvents whose left clause is (COM-

PONENT LEFTS I) and whose right clause is (COMPONENT RIGHTS J). These are then adjoined to RIGHTS and HYPERS respectively, after first, at [f], eliminating any RIGHTS-candidates subsumed by RIGHTS-incumbents, and, at [g], eliminating HYPERS-candidates already subsumed by clauses in LEFTS or in HYPERS.

Thus, if P1-RESOLVE and SUBSUMES work as claimed, we see that HYPER-RESOLVE does indeed do what is required. If we compare the following transaction with example 2 of chapter 12, we see an illustration of the fact that HYPER-RESOLVE is the LISP embodiment of the function *hyper-resolve* there being discussed:

```
*(HYPER-RESOLVE (EXAMPLE2))
 ((NIL (P GØ246 (H GØ247 GØ247) GØ246))
  (NIL (P GØ248 (H GØ249 (H (G GØ249 GØ248) GØ25Ø)) GØ25Ø))
  (NIL (P GØ251 (H (H (G GØ252 GØ253) GØ251) GØ252) GØ253))
  (NIL (P GØ254 (H (H GØ255 GØ254) (H GØ255 GØ256)) GØ256))
  (NIL (P (G (G GØ257 GØ258) (G GØ257 GØ259)) GØ258 GØ259))
  (NIL (P (G (G (H GØ26Ø GØ261) GØ262) GØ26Ø) GØ262 GØ261))
  (NIL (P (G GØ263 (G (H GØ263 GØ264) GØ265)) GØ264 GØ265))
  (NIL (P (G GØ266 GØ266) GØ267 GØ267))))
*
```

and we also see why there is a motive for interposing STANDARD-IZE between HYPER-RESOLVE and the public.

P1-RESOLVE follows the best tradition of passing on down the hierarchy all of the tricky bits to be handled by subordinates, and passing back up the relatively simple assemblies of their work which it constructs by itself. Its subordinates (that is, those we have not previously met) are Q-RESOLVE and PRUNE. Here is the definition of P1-RESOLVE:

```
(DE P1-RESOLVE (#C1 #C2)
   (Q-RESOLVE #C1 (PRUNE (POWER (CDR #C1)))     [a]
     #C2 (LIST (CAAR #C2))))                     [b]
```

Its inputs are two clauses, #C1 and #C2, which it assumes are "appropriate": it does not check whether #C1 has an *empty left-hand side* and a *non-empty right-hand side*, nor whether #C2 has a *non-empty left-hand side*. If they *fail* to be "appropriate" in this obvious sense, P1-RESOLVE will get into trouble: for example taking CAAR, at [b], of a #C2 with an empty left-hand side would cause an abortion of the entire computation. However, we never call P1-RESOLVE except after ensuring its arguments are "appropriate".

Recall that POWER yields a list of all non-empty subsets of its argument, as, e.g., the transaction

＊(POWER (LIST 1 2 3 4))
((1) (1 2) (1 2 3) (1 2 3 4) (1 2 4) (1 3) (1 3 4) (1 4)
 (2) (2 3) (2 3 4) (2 4) (3) (3 4) (4))

＊

illustrates. What does PRUNE do? Well, as its name suggests, it throws away some of the members of the list given to it as argument, or tries to. PRUNE treats each as a set of predications, and if it is not a *unifiable* set, PRUNE discards it. Thus, if L is a list of sets of predications, (PRUNE L) is a list containing just those sets in L that are unifiable. Indeed, here is PRUNE's definition:

(DE PRUNE (#L)
    (COND ((NULL #L) NIL)
          ((UNIFY (CAR #L) (TIME))
           (CONS (CAR #L) (PRUNE (CDR #L))))
          (T (PRUNE (CDR #L)))))

In order to do its job, PRUNE calls upon UNIFY, giving it, as first argument, the set (≡ list) of predications it currently wishes to test for unifiability. The second argument given to PRUNE comes as rather a surprise: it is the *time* at which the call of UNIFY is being made!

The LISP function TIME returns (without needing any input) the exact time, in thousandths of a second (milliseconds) since the inception of the LISP session, that the computer has actually spent working on one's requests. This length of time is not the same as that one has oneself spent sitting at the console since starting the session – for most of that time, the computer has been doing other things, or sitting idle, waiting to be asked to do other things; there being, in a "time-sharing" system, many people using the computer to execute their programs, all sitting at their various consoles thinking that they have the entire machine at their disposal. The computer fields requests as they come in, quickly does them, fires back the answer, takes another request, and so on. So (TIME) tells only how many milliseconds have been spent on *our* requests since we inaugurated the current session:

＊(TIME)
17216
＊(TIME)
17221

＊

(it takes 5 milliseconds, it would seem, just to tell us how many milli-seconds we have been charged with!).

The fact is that whenever we call UNIFY, we not only send a set to be unified but also a marker, or tag, which will help us recover the most general unifier (should we wish to do so) after the analysis is complete. The way this all works will become clear when we have explained UNIFY in detail; suffice it to say now that UNIFY returns T if its first argument is a unifiable set of terms or predications and NIL otherwise. From the point of view of its values, UNIFY is thus a predicate. However, its side-effect is all-important. If it returns T, then it will have left behind sufficient traces of its analysis (using the tag we gave to it as second argument) for us to recover the most general unifier of its first argument. However: *it will have not changed that first argument in any way.* Its side-effect consists of some "notes" on the way the substitution would be built, and these "notes" are all tagged by the given marker. If it returns NIL, these notes are still left behind: we cannot (as we would ideally like to) say that UNIFY has no side-effect if it returns NIL. But we can do almost as well: in all subsequent calls of UNIFY, the tag will be different from the one left behind on this activation, so that the new "notes" will simply be superposed over the previous ones, like a palimpsest with no explicit erasing.

The above is just an interim explanation of the general idea behind UNIFY. It will all be clear when we come to the official explanation of it. Given, then, that UNIFY returns T or NIL according as its first argument is unifiable or not (and ignoring, for now, its second argument) we see that PRUNE does indeed return just those items on its input list that are unifiable.

So: P1-RESOLVE is expecting that the list of P_1-resolvents of #C1 and #C2, which it must send out as its output, will be manu-factured by Q-RESOLVE when Q-RESOLVE is supplied with #C1 and #C2, together with:

(1)   a list of all the non-empty unifiable subsets of the right-hand side of #C1;

(2)   a list of the single predication which is the leftmost one in #C2's left-hand side.

as the other two arguments. This expectation is exactly right, since Q-RESOLVE stands ready to compute a resolvent of #C1 and #C2 for all the possible ways in which a left field can be chosen from the list (1) and the right field consists of the list (2):

```
(DE Q-RESOLVE (#A #A-LIST #B #B-LIST)
  (COND ((NULL #A-LIST) NIL)
        (T (PROG (#R)                                          [a
              (SETQ #R (P-RESOLVE #A (CAR #A-LIST)             [b
                                  #B #B-LIST
                                  (TIME)))
              (RETURN
                (COND ((NULL #R)                               [c
                       (Q-RESOLVE #A (CDR #A-LIST)
                                  #B #B-LIST))
                      (T (CONS #R                              [d
                          (Q-RESOLVE #A (CDR #A-LIST)
                                     #B #B-LIST)))
              )
            )
          )
        )
      )
    )
```

Note that Q-RESOLVE does its task by "recurring" down its argument #A-LIST. It invokes a junior colleague, P-RESOLVE, which expects to be given a left clause, a left field, a right clause, and a right field, and a tag (the latter for similar reasons to those alluded to, but not yet fully clarified, in the case of UNIFY). P-RESOLVE then returns NIL if a resolution does not exist with these ingredients, and the resolvent thereof, otherwise. At [a] we reserve the local variable #R to receive P-RESOLVE's output, which we then get, at [b]. We then return whichever of the lists is appropriate: at [c] we detect that #R was indeed NIL, so we send back whatever list comes of the recursive call on Q-RESOLVE with the truncated #A-LIST; at [d] we detect that we must tack onto the front of this list the resolvent #R.

With P-RESOLVE, we can say, with the late President Truman, that "the buck stops here". P-RESOLVE actually digs into its given arguments and determines if they constitute the essentials of a resolution. It returns NIL if they do not, but returns the resolvent of that resolution if they do. P-RESOLVE must deploy not only UNIFY, but also the function that goes off and recovers the most general unifier, namely SHOW. In addition, it calls upon a function TAUTOLOGY, to help it weed out any resolvents that are tautologies:

```
(DE TAUTOLOGY (#C)
   (COND ((NULL (CAR #C)) NIL)
         ((MEMBER (CAAR #C) (CDR #C)) T)
         (T (TAUTOLOGY (CONS (CDAR #C) (CDR #C)))))  [a]
   )
)
```

In line [a], (CDAR #C) is LISP's permitted abbreviation of (CDR (CAR #C)).

Finally, P-RESOLVE calls upon a function, NEW, which produces a fresh variant of any expression it is given as argument (it must also, like UNIFY and P-RESOLVE itself, be given a tag to use in its work). The purpose of P-RESOLVE's doing this is to deliver its resolvents as clauses whose (bound!) variables have never been used previously, in any other clause in the entire LISP session. Here, then, is the actual definition of P-RESOLVE:

```
DE P-RESOLVE (#LEFT-CLAUSE #LEFT-FIELD
              #RIGHT-CLAUSE #RIGHT-FIELD #TAG)
  (COND ((UNIFY (APPEND #LEFT-FIELD #RIGHT-FIELD) #TAG)   [a]
         (PROG (#K #LC #RC #R)
            (SETQ #K (SHOW (CAR #LEFT-FIELD) #TAG))        [b]
            (SETQ #LC (SHOW #LEFT-CLAUSE #TAG))            [b]
            (SETQ #RC (SHOW #RIGHT-CLAUSE #TAG))           [b]
            (SETQ #R (NEW (CONS (UNION (CAR #LC)           [c]
                                  (DELETE #K (CAR #RC)))
                           (UNION (DELETE #K (CDR #LC))
                                  (CDR #RC)))
                      (TIME)
                 )
            )
            (RETURN (COND ((TAUTOLOGY #R) NIL) (T #R)))
         )
         )
         (T NIL)
  )
)
```

The body of P-RESOLVE is a conditional expression, which says intuitively that P-RESOLVE returns NIL if there is no resolvent with the given left clause, left field, right clause and right field; and returns that resolvent otherwise.

At [a] the union of the left field with the right field is tested to see if it is a unifiable set. If it is not, we drop down to the bottom of the definition and send back NIL. If the test is successful, then (as we shall see) UNIFY will have left behind sufficient information, labelled with #TAG, that the subsequent calls of SHOW, using that very same #TAG, will be able to read all expressions as they would appear if the most general unifier had been applied to them which results from the unification algorithm's analysis.

Thus, in all three lines [b], the values of the expressions

$$(\text{SHOW } E \text{ \#TAG})$$

are the expressions $E\sigma$, where σ is the most general unifier resulting from the call on UNIFY in line [a]. This fact will be established once we have been over UNIFY, SHOW, and the other functions that comprise the unification machinery of the RESLAB system. Given that it is so, one can readily see that the expression that is the argument of NEW in line [c] is the resolvent, as defined in chapter 12, corresponding to the given inputs.

The functions that still require explanation are then:

UNIFY, SHOW, NEW, STANDARD, SUBSUMES

and whatever functions they in turn may invoke which have not already been explained. Let us begin with UNIFY. It has a very short definition, reducing its problems by passing on the hard part to a function called EQUATE, which is a specialist in "binary" unification:

```
(DE UNIFY (#L  #TAG)
    (COND ((NULL (CDR #L)) T)                          [a]
          ((EQUATE (CAR #L) (CADR #L) #TAG)            [b]
           (UNIFY (CDR #L) #TAG))                      [c]
          (T NIL)                                       [d]
    )
)
```

This UNIFY function is based on the following fact about unification. The set $\{A_1, A_2, ..., A_n\}$ of expressions is unifiable, with most general unifier $\sigma = \sigma_1\sigma_2$, if the set $\{A_1, A_2\}$ is unifiable with most general unifier σ_1, and the set $\{A_2\sigma_1, ..., A_n\sigma_1\}$ is unifiable with most general unifier σ_2. We shall not give the proof of this fact here; it is a sufficiently simple consequence of the basic definitions that it can be appropriately left as an exercise for the reader.

UNIFY says to itself: if #L is a singleton then of course I can unify it; send back T. Thus, line [a]. However, [b], if #L is, say,

$\{A_1, A_2, ..., A_n\}$ then if I can unify $\{A_1, A_2\}$ with most general unifier σ_1 and can unify $\{A_2\sigma_1, ..., A_n\sigma_1\}$ with most general unifier σ_2, then send back T; otherwise send back NIL.

The fact that the same #TAG is used in the calls of EQUATE and UNIFY is crucial. Let us now come to grips with this business of tags and most general unifiers.

What is going on here is that we are representing *substitutions* in a rather special, LISP-oriented way, which involves storing, on the property-list of a variable X, the information whether a given substitution θ *changes* it or not, i.e., whether $X\theta = X$ or $X\theta \neq X$. We do this by means of a property, IS-BOUND, on the property-list of the variable X; if we ask (IS-BOUND? (QUOTE X) θ) we shall be told T or NIL according as the substitution θ does or does not change X. We can, in fact, represent θ as the product:

$$\theta = \theta_1\theta_2 ... \theta_n$$

of several substitutions, and we can ask

(IS-BOUND? (QUOTE X) $\theta_1 ... \theta_n$)

and be told T if, in fact, it is recorded on X's property-list that X is changed by $\theta_1 ... \theta_m$, where $m \leqslant n$. Whatever substitution θ is named under IS-BOUND on X's property-list, the expression $X\theta$ is pointed at by the entry under VALUE on X's property-list, and so we can obtain it as (EVAL (QUOTE X)).

Here is a RESLAB function, SBST, which we have not met before but will meet frequently henceforth: it modifies the property-list of an identifier to record that, with respect to a given substitution #V, that identifier #A denotes a given expression #B:

```
(DE SBST (#A #B #V)
   (PROGN (SET #A #B)                          [a]
          (PUTPROP #A #V (QUOTE IS-BOUND))
          T
   )
)
```

SBST accepts whatever LISP object is given to it as the tag #V "naming" the substitution; it could be a number (as, e.g., when some higher-up uses (TIME) to invent a tag) or it could be a *list* representing – in reverse order – a product of substitutions. The operation at [a] simply enters, under the property VALUE, the expression that is the value of #B.

The function IS-BOUND? simply checks the property-list to see if the given substitution is the same as, or extends, the one recorded under IS-BOUND on the property-list of the given identifier:

```
(DE IS-BOUND? (#A #V)
    (EXTENDS #V (GET #A (QUOTE IS-BOUND))))
```

the actual investigation of #V and the recorded tag being carried through by the function EXTENDS:

```
(DE EXTENDS (#M #N)
  (COND ((ATOM #M)
            (COND ((ATOM #N) (EQ #M #N)) (T NIL)))      [a]
        ((ATOM #N) (MEMBER #N #M))                       [b]
        ((GREATERP (LENGTH #M) (LENGTH #N))              [c]
         (EXTENDS (CDR #M) #N))
        ((EQ (LENGTH #M) (LENGTH #N))                    [d]
         (EQUAL #M #N))
        (T NIL)                                          [e]
  )
)
```

which has to worry about several possible cases:

(i)   if both of #M and #N are atoms they must be the *same* atom (line [a]);

(ii)   if #M is a list and #N an atom, then #N must be *on* that list (line [b]);

(iii) if *both* #M and #N are lists, then if #M is longer than #N (line [c]) it must be that #N is in fact a final segment of #M, and if #M is the same length as #N they must be the *same* list (line [d]);

(iv) if both #M and #N are lists and #M is shorter than #N then #M does not extend #N.

This rather elaborate system is, it must be confessed, a piece of "tricky" programming whose motivation is the avoidance of as much unnecessary computation as possible. The real pay-off in this respect comes in the function SUBSUMES, which together with EQUATE forms the heart of RESLAB. SUBSUMES has to undertake an enormous exploration of all the various ways, given clauses A and B, that a substitution might exist satisfying $A\theta \subseteq B$. If it were not for the somewhat delicate arrangements we have set up for representing the effects of substitutions on expressions, SUBSUMES would be a formidably expensive computational luxury. As it is, it does its work in an acceptably expeditious manner.

Before we go into EQUATE and SUBSUMES, let us note how the

functions SHOW and NEW work, now that we have seen the scheme for representing substitutions.

We want (SHOW #E #V) to be the expression resulting from the application of the substitution #V to the expression #E. The following definition reveals how it is made to be so:

```
(DE SHOW (#E #V)
  (COND ((ATOM #E)
           (COND ((IS-BOUND? #E #V) (SHOW (EVAL #E) #V))    [a]
                 (T #E)))                                    [b]
        (T (CONS (SHOW (CAR #E) #V) (SHOW (CDR #E) #V)))))
)
```

All of the substitutions represented in RESLAB are created by the Unification Algorithm. We know, therefore, that they have the special form:

$$\theta = \{\langle x_1, t_1 \rangle\} \; \{\langle x_2, t_2 \rangle\} \; \ldots \; \{\langle x_n, t_n \rangle\} \tag{2}$$

of a product of "monic" substitutions $\{\langle x_j, t_j \rangle\}$ with the property that t_j does not contain any of the variables $x_1, \ldots, x_j$. (Recall that, at each step of the Unification Algorithm, we replace a variable by a term which does not contain it, and hence also does not contain any of the variables replaced in earlier steps.) The term t_j is that which is entered under VALUE on the property list of x_j, when x_j is tagged, under IS-BOUND, with the marker #V corresponding to θ: $t_j = $ (EVAL x_j). Now, in view of the fact that $x_1, \ldots, x_j$ do not occur in t_j, we have:

$$\theta = \{\langle x_1, t_1\theta \rangle\} \; \{\langle x_2, t_2\theta \rangle\} \; \ldots \; \{x_n, t_n\theta\} \tag{3}$$

so that, writing (SHOW E θ) for $E\theta$, we have:

(SHOW E θ) = if E is a *constant* or *a variable not in the list*
$$x_1, \ldots, x_n$$
then E
otherwise if E is x_j then (SHOW (EVAL E) θ)
otherwise if E is (CONS E_1 E_2)
then (CONS (SHOW E_1 θ) (SHOW E_2 θ))

and this is *exactly* what the body of the LISP function SHOW says.

A similar rationale explains the function OCCUR. We want to be able to tell whether a given variable x occurs in a given expression $E\theta$ – that is, we are given E, and θ of the form (2), and want to know if x occurs in $E\theta$ – at a crucial point in the Unification Algorithm. We *could* compute (SHOW E θ), as above, and then scan it symbol by symbol to see if x is one of its symbols. Instead, OCCUR uses the reasoning:

if E is a variable not in the list $x_1 \ldots x_n$ then x occurs in $E\theta$ iff x is identical with E;

if E is a variable in the list $x_1, \ldots x_n$, say, $E = x_j$, then x occurs in $E\theta$ iff x occurs in $t_j\theta$;

if E is a constant then x does not occur in $E\theta$;

if E is $(E_1 \cdot E_2)$ then x occurs in $E\theta$ iff either x occurs in $E_1\theta$ or x occurs in $E_2\theta$;

and so is defined accordingly:

```
(DE OCCUR (#X #E #THETA)
  (COND ((NULL #E) NIL)
        ((ATOM #E)
         (COND ((IS-BOUND? #E #THETA)
                (OCCUR #X (EVAL #E) #THETA))
               (T (EQ #X #E))))
        ((OCCUR #X (CAR #E) #THETA) T)
        (T (OCCUR #X (CDR #E) #THETA))
  )
)
```

This method uses no CONSes; it is a purely "read-only" operation, which scans $E\theta$ without actually creating it explicitly.

Now, NEW can be understood. Its purpose is to take an expression E and deliver a "fresh" variant of E, one, namely, which contains no variable that has ever been used previously (in the current LISP session). Its method is to *create* a substitution θ of the form (2), in which the variables x_j are all those occurring in E, and the terms t_j are *new* variables, obtained as needed from a useful LISP function known as GENSYM.

GENSYM is an input-less function that yields an *atom* each time it is called:

```
*(GENSYM)
G0001
*(GENSYM)
G0002
*(GENSYM)
G0003
*
```

and, as the above transaction illustrates, these atoms form a series of "improbable" identifiers, which the programmer is unlikely to have selected himself. We may now contemplate the definition of NEW:

```
(DE NEW (#E #V)
  (COND ((ATOM #E)
            (COND ((IS-BOUND? #E #V) (EVAL #E))              [a]
                   ((IS-VARIABLE #E)                         [b]
                    (PROG (#NEWVARIABLE)                     [c]
                      (SETQ #NEWVARIABLE (GENSYM))
                      (MAKE-VARIABLE #NEWVARIABLE)
                      (SBST #E #NEWVARIABLE #V)
                      (RETURN #NEWVARIABLE)))
                   (T #E)))                                  [d]
        (T (CONS (NEW (CAR #E) #V) (NEW (CDR #E) #V)))       [e]
  )
)
```

Note that NEW is given an expression and a "fresh" tag #V by the external caller; it is *itself* creating a substitution tagged by #V, for use in the *recursive* calls on NEW that, in line [e], it makes itself. Thus, at [a], NEW finds that a variable it has encountered is *one it has already replaced, itself*; so it reaches for the replacement. However, at [b] it finds that it is *one it has not already replaced*; hence at [c] it sets about getting a replacement for it, records the replacement, and returns the new variable. Subsequent encounters of the new variable will be picked up at [a]. At [d] NEW knows that #E must be a constant, and, at [e], a dotted pair.

The long-deferred explanation of STANDARD is now simple to give: its purpose is to make a "nice" variant of its clause-argument — one in which the variables are neat, short, and "look as though they really *are* variables". So, whatever the *n* variables in #E actually are, STANDARD replaces them with the first *n* variables in the standard list:

$$X, Y, Z, U, V, W, R, S, T, XX, YY, ZZ, UU, VV \qquad (4)$$

simply *assuming* that $n \leqslant 14$. This number is arbitrarily selected as being large enough for all foreseeable purposes (a clause with more than 14 variables would be a monster) and can be easily made larger if desired by changing the list (4) in the definition:

```
(DE STANDARD (#E)
  (PROG (#THETA)
    (SETQ #THETA (TIME))                                    [a]
    (SBST-LIST (VARIABLES #E)
               (QUOTE
                (X Y Z U V W R S T XX YY ZZ UU VV))
               #THETA)
    (RETURN (SHOW #E #THETA))
  )
)
```

At [a] we set up a tag for the substitution we are about to define. The function SBST-LIST merely iterates SBST down a list:

```
(DE SBST-LIST (#VARS #TERMS #TAG)
  (COND ((NULL #VARS) T)
        ((SBST (CAR #VARS) (CAR #TERMS) #TAG)
         (SBST-LIST (CDR #VARS) (CDR #TERMS) #TAG))
  )
)
```

using the fact that SBST, and SBST-LIST itself, both return T as value. We are now in a position to understand the central functions EQUATE and SUBSUMES.

EQUATE is the basic "binary unification algorithm" of the RESLAB system. It is called by external callers, who give to it a tag to use as the name of the most general unifier, which it is going to try to compute; but most of its calls are recursive ones that it makes upon itself, simply passing to itself the tag that names the substitution it is currently building up. It is, intuitively, engaged in a simultaneous scanning of the two expressions #A and #B that it is trying to unify, from left to right. When it discovers a difference between them, it ascertains whether this is negotiable or not, and if so it records the monic substitution that is a reduction of that difference. Most of the job of EQUATE is in the testing it must do to see which case it has been given. Its definition is shown opposite.

The reasoning underlying EQUATE's working is quite simple. If #V is thought of as representing the most general unifier σ, which EQUATE is trying to build up, then EQUATE is being given two expressions A and B, together with the σ it has so far constructed, and is being asked to modify σ, if necessary, in order to unify $\{A\sigma, B\sigma\}$.

If, at [a], it detects that *A is an atom*, then it must determine whether $A\sigma$ is A or is (EVAL A)σ, and in the latter case it must try

```
(DE EQUATE (#A #B #V)
   (COND ((ATOM #A)                                                 [a]
             (COND ((IS-BOUND? #A #V)                           ⎫
                       (EQUATE (EVAL #A) #B #V))               ⎬ [b]
                    ((ATOM #B)                                     [c]
                     (COND ((IS-BOUND? #B #V)                  ⎫
                              (EQUATE #A (EVAL #B) #V))) ⎬ [d]
                           ((EQ #A #B) T)                           [e]
                           ((IS-VARIABLE #A)                   ⎫
                            (SBST #A #B #V))                    ⎪
                           ((IS-VARIABLE #B)                  ⎬ [f]
                            (SBST #B #A #V))                    ⎪
                           (T NIL)))                            ⎭
                    ((IS-VARIABLE #A)                             [g]
                     (COND ((OCCUR #A #B #V) NIL)            ⎫
                           (T (SBST #A #B #V))))              ⎬ [h]
                    (T NIL)))                                     ⎭
          ((ATOM #B)                                              [i]
           (COND ((IS-BOUND? #B #V)
                    (EQUATE #A (EVAL #B) #V))
                 ((IS-VARIABLE #B)
                  (COND ((OCCUR #B #A #V) NIL)
                        (T (SBST #B #A #V))))
                 (T NIL)))
          ((EQUATE (CAR #A) (CAR #B) #V)                      ⎫
           (EQUATE (CDR #A) (CDR #B) #V))                    ⎬ [j]
          (T NIL)                                                  [k]
   )
)
```

to unify $\{(\text{EVAL } A)\sigma, B\sigma\}$; which it does at [b]. If the atom A really
is A (i.e., if $A\sigma = A$) then, at [c], attention turns to B; if B is *also* an
atom, then, at [d], EQUATE takes similar action to that in [b] in
case $B\sigma$ is not B but $(\text{EVAL } B)\sigma$. However, if the atom B really is B
(i.e., if $B\sigma = B$) then, if the atoms A and B are identical, we can
certainly unify them! Hence line [e]. If they are *distinct* atoms, we
can unify them only if at least one of them is a variable, and we can
do so by replacing it with the other; hence the five lines [f]. If B is
not an atom, but A *is*, we must ask, at [g] if A is in fact a variable; in
which case we can unify A and B only if A does not occur in B, and
that by replacing A with B; hence the three lines [h].

If A is *not* an atom then, at [i], a symmetric analysis is undertaken of the various possibilities with respect to B and its relationship with A, and the appropriate action is taken in each case, as in the preceding lines.

If *neither A nor B* is an atom then $\{A\sigma, B\sigma\}$ can be unified only if *both* $\{(CAR\ A)\sigma, (CAR\ B)\sigma\}$ *and* $\{(CDR\ A)\sigma, (CDR\ B)\sigma\}$ can be unified; and the most general unifier of $\{A\sigma, B\sigma\}$ will be that which results from first unifying one set, and then the second set in the light of the changes necessary to do the first. Hence line [j]. However (line [k]) if we cannot even unify the first set, then the job is hopeless.

Note that if a call on EQUATE using a tag τ should fail to unify the two expression arguments, there may be left behind, on the property-lists of some or all of the variables in those expressions, a collection of entries τ under IS-BOUND, and corresponding entries of sub-expressions (i.e., of pointers to them) under VALUE. These may be, and are, ignored. Subsequent calls on EQUATE, or indeed on any other function which uses the same mechanism for representing substitutions, will be with fresh tags, i.e., tags never used before; and only entries of *these*, not of old tags, will be "noticed".

We can represent substitutions in RESLAB in this way because of the very special constraints under which we are constructing substitutions. At any given moment in a computation there is *at most one* substitution that needs to be represented — namely that which is currently being constructed, or applied, by the process that is active at that moment. As we shall see, the process that takes place when SUBSUMES is being executed is one in which a substitution is being built up, torn back, then built up again in a different way, and so on, in a persistent attempt to create a substitution θ that will "embed" one clause A within another, B, and thereby reveal that A subsumes B. The combinatorial cost of SUBSUMES would be enormous unless we took every advantage of the fact that, at any moment, we need only know the current substitution. We can *extend* it by composing it with a further substitution; but then we are representing only the extended substitution; we can *undo* such an extension, restoring the original substitution; but then we are representing only that original substitution again. These *extendings* and *undoings* are managed by the function EMBED, which is SUBSUMES's main subordinate.

Our method of representing substitutions, then, really comes into its own with the function SUBSUMES. This function is probably the most difficult one in all of RESLAB to understand completely, but the one which "gets the most for the money" out of the total system design.

Recall that a clause A subsumes a clause B iff there is a substitution θ such that $A_L\theta \subseteq B_L$ and $A_R\theta \subseteq B_R$, where A is $A_L \square A_R$ and B is $B_L \square B_R$. We can state this more compactly if we represent A and B each as a single set, by *negating* each predication in A_L and B_L to form sets A'_L, B'_L of *negated predications*, and putting $A' = A'_L \cup A_R$, $B' = B'_L \cup B_R$. We call A' and B' the "antiquated" versions of A and B (since that was how we used to represent clauses in pre-RESLAB resolution programs). Then A subsumes B means: $A'\theta \subseteq B'$, for some θ. We have a function in RESLAB, called ANTIQUATE, which transforms a clause into this form:

```
(DE ANTIQUATE (#C)
    (UNION (NEGATIONS (CAR #C)) (CDR #C)))
```

calling upon the function NEGATIONS to negate all the predications in the left-hand side of #C. NEGATIONS just replaces each predication π in its list-argument by the list (NOT π):

```
(DE NEGATIONS (#L)
    (COND ((NULL #L) NIL)
          (T (CONS (LIST (QUOTE NOT) (CAR #L))
                   (NEGATIONS (CDR #L))))
    )
)
```

Now SUBSUMES merely *sets up* and *initiates* the real investigation of the two given clauses A and B. Its main subordinate, EMBED, is responsible for all the intricate work of the analysis.

SUBSUMES reasons as follows: if we "turn off" all the *variables* in B, so that they look like *constants*, then we shall have $B\theta = B$ for all substitutions θ, and so we can ask whether there is a θ such that $A'\theta \subseteq B'\theta$, instead of the unsymmetric question whether there is a θ such that $A'\theta \subseteq B'$. We can "turn on" B's variables after the investigation is over.

Accordingly, SUBSUMES is defined as follows:

```
(DE SUBSUMES (#A #B)
    (PROG (#RESULT #B-VARIABLES)
        (SETQ #B-VARIABLES (VARIABLES #B))           [a]
        (UNMAKE-VARIABLES #B-VARIABLES)              [b]
        (SETQ #RESULT                                [c]
            (EMBED (ANTIQUATE #A) (ANTIQUATE #B) 1
                                  (LIST (TIME))))
```

```
    (MAKE-VARIABLES #B-VARIABLES)                        [d]
    (RETURN  #RESULT)
  )
)
```

At [a], the variables in #B, if any, are saved so that they can be turned back on before sending back the result; and at [b] these variables are turned off. They then look like constants, to all concerned parties. At [c] the main call to EMBED is made, with the initial settings, 1 and a tag (LIST(TIME)), for EMBED's two control parameters; the significance of these will become clear only after we have understood EMBED. We can here, pending that understanding, only state the fact: $A'\theta \subseteq B'\theta$, for some θ, if and only if A' *embeds in* B'; by which is meant that there is a *subset* of B', say C', such that $A'\theta = C'\theta$, for some θ. We shall show, shortly, that the function EMBED correctly returns T or NIL according as it is true or false that A' embeds in B', and we call EMBED by (EMBED A' B' 1 λ) where λ is a "suitable" tag. We for the moment simply state that the tag used by SUBSUMES, in its call on EMBED, *is* "suitable". At [d] SUBSUMES turns the variables in #B back on before sending out its result.

It remains, then, to study EMBED. This is, in fact, the final function in RESLAB. Once we have been over EMBED, we will have completed our tour through RESLAB's forty functions.

EMBED is a "recursive back-tracking" procedure. It is a general device, which stands ready to determine, given two sets A, B of expressions, say:

$$A = \{A_1, ..., A_m\}, B = \{B_1, ..., B_n\}$$

whether there is a substitution θ and a list $j_1, ..., j_m$ of numbers in the set $\{1, ..., n\}$, such that all of the equations

$$A_1\theta = B_{j_1}\theta$$
$$...$$
$$A_m\theta = B_{j_m}\theta \tag{5}$$

are true.

Now, it is a trivial extension of the theory of unification to show that, if there is a solution θ to the equations (5), there is a most general one σ: i.e. σ satisfies

$$A_1\sigma = B_{j_1}\sigma$$
$$...$$
$$A_m\sigma = B_{j_m}\sigma \tag{6}$$

together with the further condition that

$$\theta = \sigma\theta \text{ for all solutions } \theta \text{ of (5).} \tag{7}$$

This is so because we can regard the m equations (5) or (6) as a single equation, i.e.

$$(A_1 \dots A_m)\theta = (B_{j_1} \dots B_{j_m})\theta$$

or

$$(A_1 \dots A_m)\sigma = (B_{j_1} \dots B_{j_m})\sigma$$

so that we are in effect still within the unification theory as already developed for the case of two expressions.

The most general unifier σ in (6) will be an m-fold composition:

$$\sigma = \sigma_1 \dots \sigma_m \tag{8}$$

of most general unifiers σ_i, $i = 1, \dots, m$, which satisfy

$$A_1\sigma_1 = B_{j_1}\sigma_1$$
$$\dots$$
$$A_i\sigma_1 \dots \sigma_i = B_{j_i}\sigma_1 \dots \sigma_i$$
$$\dots$$
$$A_m\sigma_1 \dots \quad \sigma_m = B_{j_m}\sigma_1 \dots \quad \sigma_m \tag{9}$$

and (with $\sigma_0 = \varepsilon$) for which σ_{i+1} is the most general unifier of

$$\{A_{i+1}\sigma_0 \dots \sigma_i, B_{j_{i+1}}\sigma_0 \dots \sigma_i\} \tag{10}$$

for $i = 0, \dots, m - 1$.

The numbers $j_1, \dots, j_m$ have to be "guessed". Each can, in general, be any number from 1 to n. The possibilities for these m numbers thus form the branches of a tree

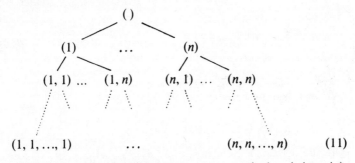

$$\tag{11}$$

of m levels, each node of which has n successors (unless it is a tip). There are thus n^m different branches.

We shall say that an i-tuple $(j_1, \dots, j_i)$ of numbers from the set $\{1, \dots, n\}$, together with an $(i + 1)$-tuple $(\sigma_0 \sigma_1 \dots \sigma_i)$ of substitutions, is a *partial solution of depth i* for the *embedding problem* (6) iff we have:

$$A_1\sigma_0\sigma_1 = B_{j_1}\sigma_0\sigma_1$$

$$\dots$$

$$A_i\sigma_0\sigma_1 \dots \sigma_i = B_{j_i}\sigma_0 \dots \sigma_i$$

and for each r, $r = 1, \dots i$, σ_r is a most general unifier of $\{A_r\sigma_0 \dots \sigma_{r-1},\ B_{j_r}\sigma_0 \dots \sigma_{r-1}\}$, (with $\sigma_0 = \varepsilon$). It is then clear that a partial solution of depth m is in fact a complete solution.

What EMBED does is to attempt to *extend*, in all possible ways, a given partial solution to a complete solution. If it finds such a way, it *succeeds*, and returns T. If it discovers that there is *no* way to extend the given partial solution to a complete solution, if *fails*, and returns NIL. Thus, the input of EMBED should be understood as *the description of a partial solution*.

The call

(EMBED A B j t)

has the following interpretation. The parameter A is the list $(A_{i+1}, \dots, A_m)$. The parameter B is the list $(B_1, \dots, B_n)$. The parameter t is a *list*

$$t = (j_i, \dots, j_1 t_0)$$

of numbers, and the parameter j is a number. The call is intuitively asking the question:

can the *partial* solution of length i
$$(j_1, \dots, j_i)$$
$$(\sigma_0, \sigma_1, \dots \sigma_i)$$
be extended to a *complete* solution in which j_{i+1} is greater
than or equal to j? (12)

in which the substitutions referred to *are represented by the tags*: $(t_0), (j_1\ t_0), \dots, (j_i, \dots, j_1\ t_0)$. That is, we have:

σ_0 is represented by the tag (t_0)
$\sigma_0\sigma_1$ is represented by the tag $(j_1 t_0)$
$\dots$
$\sigma_0\sigma_1 \dots \sigma_i$ is represented by the tag $(j_i \dots j_1 t_0)$ (13)

The number t_0 is the one sent in by SUBSUMES as the sole item on the tag list in the main call of EMBED. All the other numbers have been put in the tag by EMBED itself and delivered to EMBED in tag-parameters of recursive calls on itself.

Since EMBED can answer questions of the form (12) *it can ask itself such questions* and use the answers in arriving at its answers. Let us now look at the actual definition of EMBED to see how it calls itself in order to answer (12). The definition is:

```
(DE EMBED (#A #B #J #T)
   (COND ((NULL #A) T)                                    [a]
          ((GREATERP #J (LENGTH #B)) NIL)                 [b]
          ((EQUATE (CAR #A)                               [c]
                   (COMPONENT #B #J) (CONS #J #T))
          (COND ((EMBED (CDR #A) #B 1                     [d]
                        (CONS #J #T)) T)
                (T (EMBED #A #B (ADD1 #J) #T))))           [e]
          (T (EMBED #A #B (ADD1 #J) #T))                  [f]
   )
)
```

At [a] we find that the problem is solved, since the given partial solution is already a complete one. So EMBED answers: T. At [b] we find that there can be no completions of the given partial solution with $j_{i+1} \geqslant$ #J, since #J is already too large. So EMBED answers: NIL.

At [c] we ask whether $A_{i+1}\sigma$ ($A_{i+1} \equiv$ the head of #A) can be unified with $B_j\sigma$, where σ is the substitution given by the tag #T; if the answer is T, we want the substitution $\sigma\sigma_{i+1}$, where σ_{i+1} is the most general unifier of $A_{i+1}\sigma$ and $B_j\sigma$, to be represented by the tag (CONS #J #T). Suppose the answer *is* T: then we attempt, at [d], to complete *this* partial solution by asking EMBED question (12) again, this time with different data:

> can the partial solution of length $i + 1$
> $(j_1, ..., j_i, j_{i+1})$
> $(\sigma_0, \sigma_1, ..., \sigma_i, \sigma_{i+1})$
> be extended to a complete solution
> in which j_{i+2} is $\geqslant 1$?   (14)

If the answer to (14) is T then we are done; and EMBED indeed answers, in this case: T. If, however, the answer to (14) is NIL then EMBED must ask itself question (12) again at [e] exactly as it was first posed, except that the value of #J is one greater than before, and send back whatever answer it gets. The same recourse is taken at [f], in the event that the attempt to unify $A_{i+1}\sigma$ with $B_j\sigma$, at [c], meets with failure.

Throughout this questioning and answering of EMBED by and to itself, it is, one can imagine, moving about on the tree (11) attempting to push all the way down some branch without encountering any failures; but, when it does encounter a failure, "backtracking" up the branch it is on, to the last node it has passed at which there are still values of the parameter #J as yet untried; whereupon it tries the next such value, reverses its direction, and seeks to complete its downward quest anew.

Whenever the work backtracks in this way, the most-recently-added most-general-unifier is automatically "undone" *without any actual work to that end being performed*. This is a consequence of the tag system for representing products of substitutions. The present tag, then no longer relevant, will simply be *ignored* when next we come down the tree to the level from which we must now backtrack, for the then-prevailing tag will be different, in at least one component (but not the rightmost one, set by SUBSUMES from the clock).

The reader can now perhaps appreciate that SUBSUMES is indeed working very hard for its answers, at least vicariously through its back-tracking auxiliary, EMBED. All that SUBSUMES actually has to do is ask the right question of EMBED to begin with:

> can the partial solution of length 0
> ( )
> (σ_0)
> be extended to a complete solution
> in which j_1 is $\geqslant 1$?

which of course, as now can be seen, it does.

14. Historical Notes

Before Frege's 1879 publication of the *Begriffsschrift* opened up the modern period of logic, a number of noteworthy ideas, which have survived, had already been worked out, and Frege's formal system incorporated these along with much that was deep and original of his own.

The successful example of "mathematical" notations, which permitted and encouraged *symbolic* (i.e. also algebraic, as opposed to only numeric or arithmetical) *calculation* for solving scientific and practical problems, was from the sixteenth century onwards a strong influence on the thinkers in whose care logic gradually emerged from its ancient and medieval "pre-mathematical" form. The rapid development of mathematical knowledge and technique in the seventeenth and eighteenth centuries provided a source of intellectual power undreamed of in the former age. Modern science and technology, which has totally transformed the world as mankind sees it and interacts with it, is thoroughly permeated with the magical, miraculous idea of symbolic calculation. Think of it: by writing down formulas on some paper, and then "manipulating" them into further formulas, a human being can make discoveries about the universe, of the most unexpected and far-reaching kind. Isaac Newton's gift to posterity was not so much the *physical facts* he found out (the gravitational law, the principles of mechanics, the laws of optics, and so on) but the *mathematical formalism* he used in his investigations, the differential and integral calculus. This purely symbolic system of formula-writing and manipulating has in less than three centuries brought us from a higher-mammalian slumber to the threshold of an understanding of all reality, and of a mastery of all its forces.

Symbolic computation, or formula-manipulation, was what the philosopher Thomas Hobbes in 1655 declared *logic* really, at bottom, to be. In a large work, *De Corpore*, published in that year, he devoted to logic a first section entitled *Computatio Sive Logica* in which he advanced the view that reasoning might be reduced to and understood as a kind of calculation. He thought that it ought to be possible to work out the ways in which symbol-complexes are decomposed by

analytical rules into their simple constituents and these then re-
assembled into other symbol-complexes according to other rules of
combination or synthesis. Hobbes came late in life to mathematical
ideas. That delightful gossip John Aubrey tells how his friend Hobbes
at the age of forty first encountered geometry. Hobbes was visiting
a gentleman in whose library a copy of Euclid's *Elements* lay open at
the page where Pythagoras' Theorem is given:

> He read the proposition. "By God!" sayd he, "this is
> impossible!". So he reads the demonstration of it, which
> referred him back to such a proposition; which proposition
> he read. That referred him back to another which he also
> read. *Et sic deinceps*, that at the last he was demonstratively
> convinced of that trueth. This made him in love with geometry.

With *logic*, one gathers, rather than specifically with geometry. It
was the *method* that seduced Hobbes into devoting much of the
remaining fifty years of his life to reflection on the reasoning process
and its nature as a "kind of chemistry", in which things are taken
apart into simpler things and put together again into new things. "We
must not think", he wrote in *Computatio Sive Logica*, "that computation, that is ratiocination, has place only in numbers."

The philosopher and mathematician G.W.Leibniz was only eight
years old when Hobbes wrote down these ideas. Hobbes never
worked them out, but Leibniz – an intellectual giant who among
many achievements shares with Newton the credit for inventing the
differential and integral calculus – was ready to try to do so in 1666,
when he was still only nineteen. His *De Arte Combinatoria* of that
year acknowledges Hobbes' influence in the formation of Leibniz'
goal: to develop a universal logical notation and symbolic calculus in
which the sort of conceptual computing envisioned by Hobbes could
be carried out, as fluently and mechanically as numerical reckoning.

In 1679 – two centuries exactly before Frege was to reveal the
perfected system – Leibniz described the general idea behind his
proposed universal notation, which he called the *characteristica
universalis*. Every concept would be assigned a code number – its
characteristic number – which would be either *prime*, if the concept
was "primitive" and not further analysable into simpler ideas, or else
composite, if the concept was the "product", or conjunction, of two
or more ideas. The trick would be, to associate numerical multiplication of code numbers with the "logical multiplication" of the
concepts (i.e. their conjunction, or *and*-ing together) for which the
numbers stand. He illustrates this scheme:

> For example, the concept of *animal* enters into the formation

of the concept of *man*, and so the characteristic number of animal *a* (for example, 2) combines with some other number *r* (such as 3) to produce the number *ar*, or *h*, by multiplication (2 × 3), that is, the characteristic number of man. [The number *r* = 3 being the characteristic number of *rational*.]

So *man* gets the code number 6. Once all concepts have been numerically coded in this way (namely, numbers assigned so as to preserve the correspondence between numerical multiplication and logical conjunction) we can then operate a mechanizable calculus of question-answering or logical analysis – what Leibniz called a *calculus ratiocinator*, merely by doing numerical operations on code numbers. The proposition *all A are B* becomes (under the correspondence) the arithmetical assertion that *b exactly divides a*, where *a* and *b* are the characteristic numbers of the concepts *A* and *B*. *All men are rational?* ≡ *3 exactly divides 6? presto!*

The logical inference

all A are B, all B are C ⇒ *all A are C*

now becomes, under the correspondence, the arithmetical inference:

b exactly divides a, c exactly divides b ⇒ *c exactly divides a.*

The idea of finding structural analogues of *conceptual* and *propositional* combinations in the *numerical* combinations of arithmetic, and thus of obtaining a way of "reading" numerical processes as processes of logical reasoning and *vice versa*, is bold and original. It was already clear in Leibniz' day that at least some of the standard numerical operations could be mechanized; indeed he himself designed and built numerical calculating machines. The mapping of logical processes into numerical ones would therefore, Leibniz saw, amount to *showing how to mechanize logical processes too*.

However, Leibniz' scheme was limited severely by the restricted notion of logical form that he took as the basis of his analysis. He was committed to the traditional subject-predicate form of the Aristotelian syllogistic system, and this led him, apparently, to suppose that logical conjunction suffices as the sole mode of combination of two concepts, or propositions, which one needs in one's "logical chemistry" to explain all the concepts that there are or can be.

A correct view of logical form, whose complexities involve the notion of *application* of function to argument, the *abstraction* of *general* form from *particular* form by the use of bound variables or something equivalent, and the interaction of these with each other and with the simple combinational operations of the Boolean algebra, all this was to emerge only two hundred years later, in Frege's system.

In the interval between Leibniz' visions and Frege's first real step towards their achievement, the quest for a "mathematics of the laws of thought" was vigorously pursued, always, however, with the assumption that *logical* concepts and processes must somehow be modelled by *numerical* and *algebraic* ones, in other words by structural notions and patterns already present in the various number systems and their operations. Thus George Boole in 1854 published a sophisticated system of "logical algebra" which still finds its place, under the name *Boolean Algebra*, in modern logical theory. Boole's discovery was that the properties of the arithmetical operations of *plus*, *times* and "*complement*" provide very far-reaching abstract analogies with the logical operations of *and*, *or*, and *not*, especially if we think of the latter as operations on the logical "numbers" *truth* and *falsehood*. These may then be made the analogues of *one* and *zero*, and the correspondence between the two systems becomes exact if we then look at the arithmetic of "modulo 2" operations:

plus	0	1		times	0	1		"complement"	
0	0	1		0	0	0		0	1
1	1	0		1	0	1		1	0

in which we take the "complement" of n to be $(1 - n)$ for $n = 0, 1$. This then goes directly over to the logical system whose tables are

$\not\equiv$	f	t		$\wedge$	f	t		$\neg$	
f	f	t		f	f	f		f	t
t	t	f		t	f	t		t	f

where $\not\equiv$, "*exclusive or*", is to be distinguished from $\vee$, "*inclusive or*", whose table has a t, rather than an f, in the southeast corner.

This "algebra of logic" approach was also pursued by others, for example De Morgan, Jevons, and Schröder. It is fair to say that it was handicapped by the assumption alluded to: by being an explicit attempt to model logic in "mathematics proper". This was, at bottom, the same handicap that plagued Leibniz' relatively crude scheme: an inadequate understanding of the full complexity and subtlety of the logical structures that are to be modelled.

Logic could not become what it was destined to become without breaking out of this conceptual chrysalis. That is what it did in 1879.

Frege's system ushered in the modern epoch in the history of logic. At one stroke it:

> ... freed logic from an artificial connection with
> mathematics but at the same time prepared a deeper
> interrelation between these two sciences.
> (Jean van Heijenoort 1967, vi)

Frege deliberately avoided the temptation to seek numerical counterparts and analogies for every feature of the conceptual structures and processes which occur in logical thought. It was as though he was the first to appreciate, as Leibniz, Boole and the rest somehow did not, the wisdom of Hobbes' remark: "we must not think that computation has place only in numbers."

It is not because numbers are *numbers*, that we can "do mathematics" and "compute" with them. It is rather because they and their properties can be associated with the elements of an organized symbolic structure, defined by precise rules of formation and transformation. Numerical computation and algebraic manipulation of the traditional kind are simply *deductive reasoning* being carried out in the context of these rules within these symbolic systems. We manipulate *numerals* – symbols – not "numbers", whatever those might be.

Frege thoroughly understood this, and he found that he could design a complete symbolic calculus, using the highest standards of precision in his rules of formation and transformation, which was *not* in the least "numerical". It was a neutral, general-purpose, fully expressive symbolic notation for *representing logical form* and for manipulating these representations.

The name he used for his notation – *begriffsschrift* – means something like "concept-writing" or "ideography". It is for the expression of "pure thought"; no particular subject matter is associated with the notation. It is for the representation of logical form, in abstraction from the content, of whatever can be thought or said.

It is the system of the predicate calculus as we now have it. We do not, however, have it in Frege's own mode of written display of the formulas! He used a two-dimensional diagrammatic convention for displaying formulas, which has not survived the test of practical utility. The formula $A \rightarrow B$ is written

$$\begin{array}{l} {-}{\,}{\rule[0.5ex]{0.5em}{0.4pt}}\, B \\ {}{\rule[0.5ex]{0.5em}{0.4pt}}\, A \end{array}$$

and $C \rightarrow (A \rightarrow B)$ would be

while $(C \to A) \to B$ would be

To negate a formula, we hang a vertical stroke from its horizontal lead-in:

is $\neg A$; and $\neg(A \to B)$ is

So:

is the formula $\neg((B \to \neg A) \to \neg(\neg B \to A))$, or $A \not\equiv B$. To quantify a formula universally with respect to x one makes a little cup in its horizontal lead-in and puts "x" in it:

is $\forall x A$. The formulas A can be predications $A(x, y)$, etc. so we can represent, e.g. $\forall x(Ax \to \exists y Bxy)$ as:

The notation, viewed abstractly, is the one we use today (except for being confined to the logical symbols $\neg$, $\to$ and $\forall$, letting the rest be defined in terms of these). But the "syntactic sugar" opted for by Frege has not found its way into the mainstream, much, one might suppose, to the relief of those who must set up logical formulas in type. Frege was himself unrepentant, commenting: "the comfort of the typesetter is certainly not the *summum bonum*" (Van Heijenoort 1967, p.2).

The notation of the predicate calculus has been subject to numerous small variations in style as the system has been studied and extended during its century of existence. There has, in the author's opinion, been an unhealthy preoccupation with matters of *concrete* syntax, which has often tended to obscure, especially for the beginning student, what is of real importance in the syntactic analysis of formulas in the calculus. The point of view advocated in this book, that of *abstract* syntax, with maximal freedom allowed for the concrete written representations of it, seems both the most natural and the least confusing approach. The need to devise a representation of formulas as data objects inside computers almost forces this view upon one, in any case.

The history of the predicate calculus since 1879 is of a full, rich period of research in which the theory of the system has been pushed to its present highly developed state by a series of major mathematical discoveries. In these brief notes we can do no more than sketch in the main features of the story and refer the reader to the literature cited in the bibliography for further details.

A rigorous formulation of the semantical ideas – those of a *model* and of the relation of *denoting*, or *having as value*, between formulas and entities in the universe of a model – was not immediately arrived at. At first, these ideas were left informal and not entirely clear, during a somewhat stormy decade at the beginning of the present century when "logical paradoxes" bedevilled attempts to clarify and systematize the foundations of mathematics. These attempts took the form of laying down sets of axioms purporting to capture the essence of such notions as: *set, function, sequence, number*, and the like. It was at first thought (indeed Frege's own motivation for designing the *begriffsschrift* was to show) that all of mathematics could be derived, within a framework of formalized logical notation, from a few assumptions about "sets" and the "membership" relation of things to sets.

One such assumption, which seemed both true and innocent, was to the effect that to every "property" P there corresponds a *set*, namely, the set of all and only those things x such that x has P. Roughly:

$$\forall P \, \exists s \, \forall x \, (x \text{ is a member of } s \leftrightarrow x \text{ has } P) \tag{1}$$

It was Bertrand Russell (1902) who first noticed that this principle leads immediately to a contradiction, "Russell's Paradox", if for the property R we take that of "not being a member of oneself":

$$x \text{ has } R \Leftrightarrow x \text{ is not a member of } x \tag{2}$$

for, instantiating (1) with R we have

$$\exists s\ \forall x\ (x \text{ is a member of } s \leftrightarrow x \text{ has } R) \tag{3}$$

that is, applying (2):

$$\exists s\ \forall x\ (x \text{ is a member of } s \leftrightarrow x \text{ is not a member of } x) \tag{4}$$

But (4) obviously cannot be true, since the s asserted to exist would then be a set, call it B, which would have the property that:

$$\forall x\ (x \text{ is a member of } B \leftrightarrow x \text{ is not a member of } x) \tag{5}$$

Instantiating (5) with B then brings down the whole house of cards:

$$B \text{ is a member of } B \leftrightarrow B \text{ is not a member of } B \tag{6}$$

since (6) is a contradiction.

Something, clearly, was wrong somewhere; but at first no one was sure what. Could it be the logical principles themselves, despite all evidence to the contrary, that were *unsound*, i.e., that, after all, led from *true* assumptions to *false* conclusions? No: the problem lay rather in the fact that the apparently true assumption (1) is *not* true (a counter-example, after all, is the property R, in the above argument; and there are others). The notions of *set, membership, function, order*, and the like turned out to be slippery ones, whose formal characterization called for deep analysis and novel insights. This work is still in progress today; it is a branch of abstract mathematics known as "axiomatic set theory" whose purpose is to organize the concepts and propositions, constituting our knowledge about sets, into a coherent, consistent deductive system that permits us to prove as theorems everything that ought to be provable (i.e. everything that we think is *true* about sets) and nothing that ought not to be provable (i.e. nothing that we think is *false*).

This project has been pursued intensively throughout the modern period of logic, and has rather confused the purely logical story, with its fascinating, exceedingly difficult, but (from the neutral, abstract, *logical* viewpoint) *separate* concerns. To put it plainly: logic stands aloof from questions of truth and falsehood, being designed, as it is, to settle only "what follows from what". It is a *neutral* instrument; a tool for investigating such matters as what axioms to lay down in one's (e.g.) formal set theory *only in the sense that it will determine what follows from those axioms, not whether they are true*. If the set theorists do not like the consequences of their axioms, they must not blame logic; they must blame their axioms.

These developments in the early years of this century spurred on the attempts to clarify and strengthen both the *logical* theory associated with the predicate calculus as such, and the *non-logical* theory of the basic notions and truths that lie at the foundations of mathematics.

In order to keep logic itself free (or as free as possible) from the clouds of doubt and anxiety caused by the (misnamed) "logical" paradoxes, there developed a discipline of intellectual austerity that, it was thought, would make it all the more obvious that the logical calculi as such presupposed *no* dubious assumptions. David Hilbert led the way, under the banner of the "Hilbert Programme", to a position in which the logical formalism itself would be constructed and studied only from a "strictly finitist" point of view, in which the methods of proof used to establish properties of the formalism would themselves be open to no question as to their trustworthiness. With the security of the logical tools firmly established, Hilbert then hoped to move out into formalized mathematical theories (e.g. of arithmetic, set theory, and real analysis) and *prove* them to be consistent, i.e. to be incapable of having a contradiction as a theorem. Such *consistency proofs* would be "metamathematical" (that is, they would establish properties of particular calculi, considered as collections of formulas) rather than "mathematical" (that is, proofs concerned with propositions about the *subject matter*, such as numbers, sets, and the like, of the intended interpretations of the calculi). Of course one is *doing* mathematics even when one reasons about *formulas* rather than about what the formulas denote. But the subject-matter of *meta*-mathematics is in the relatively clear-cut transparent world of syntactic constructions and relationships, and the *method* of metamathematics can be (and, for Hilbert and his followers, *must* be) severely controlled so as to incur no commitment to assumptions that may not be true.

This discipline to some extent hampered the theoreticians who wished to strengthen and broaden the theory of the predicate calculus. In proposing what seemed to be the right formalization for the semantics of the system, Alfred Tarski (1936) found it necessary, if not indeed congenial, to make use of the full panoply of Cantor's (1895, 1897) general set theory and transfinite (cardinal and ordinal) number system to portray the totality of all *models* of a given pure calculus. Tarski's ideas are today accepted as the proper analysis of the intuitive notions of *truth*, *satisfiability*, *logical consequence*, and the like; but everyone realizes that the full characterization, precisely because it is the "right" one, reaches out beyond the simplicity, clarity and indubitability of Hilbert's "anschauliche" phenomena and imports, into the *semantical* part at least of the theory of the predicate calculus, all of the glory and power – and mystery! – of "Cantor's paradise".

Some of the great logical theorists – Herbrand (1930) and Gentzen (1936), to name the two most prominent – refused, on principle, to have truck with the Tarskian extravagances (as they saw them) and delicately picked their way to important discoveries by using finitist methodology and purely syntactic notions throughout. If *that* was semantics, their attitude seemed to be, then they wanted none of it.

So there came to be a distinction between two branches of logical theory: *proof* theory and *model* theory. The latter concerned itself with matters that could hardly be considered at all without at least tacit acknowledgement that there are such things as models, that their universes can be *any* non-empty set, and that one *is* interested in the *soundness* of the proof machinery in the (naive?) sense that it will not lead to *false* conclusions if applied to *true* premises. The reader is invited to reflect once again on what the content actually is of the judgment that a given sequent is true: it is that *no* model exists which satisfies its antecedent and falsifies its succedent. This apparently simple judgment thus is, in disguise, an enormous claim whose import ranges over *all* possible models in the full, Tarskian sense.

In *proof* theory, however, one eschews reference to truth, falsehood, satisfiability, and models. Instead one concentrates on the "intrinsic", combinatorial properties of formulas and sequents, considered as things-in-themselves, and on their derivability according to given formalized principles of inference or by given computational procedures. One cannot, in all strictness, from this viewpoint, *say* what is the really beautiful fact about the predicate calculus, its "completeness": *every true sequent is provable*. In the most austere form of proof theory one can say what "provable" means, but not what "true" means!

The fact itself, *completeness*, was discovered by Gödel (1930), and published in his doctoral dissertation at the University of Vienna. His proof also yields the Skolem-Löwenheim theorem, which had first emerged as a result of investigations in 1915 by Löwenheim (1915) and by Skolem (1920) and subsequently through the 'twenties. The *compactness* phenomenon was also established by Gödel (1930) in order to show that an infinite *unsatisfiable* set of formulas could, in a suitable sense, be *proved* so. Henkin (1949) proves the completeness result in a somewhat different way.

In 1931 Gödel proved an amazing theorem, which put paid to one of the aspirations of the Hilbert Programme, namely, the aim of formulating, and then proving both consistent and complete, the theory of the natural numbers ("arithmetic"). Gödel showed that any formalized theory of arithmetic must always be defective in one of two ways: either it would be *incomplete*, in the sense that some *true* formula (*true in the intended interpretation*, that is to say) would not be a *provable* formula, or else it would be *inconsistent* in the sense that *all* formulas, true and false alike, would be provable. Worse: he also showed that *if* the formalized theory is in fact consistent, *then* the proof of its consistency would of necessity have to transcend, in its methodology, the austere "finitist" techniques of argument captured in the formal inference-rules of the formalized theory itself. In a word: consistency of the theory can be proved in the metamathematics *only* (if at all) by appeal to principles "dubious" enough to have been left out of the theory itself! (Gentzen (1939) subsequently gave a consistency proof, whose methods, though not really dubious at all, nonetheless *were* "outside the theory".)

This work of Gödel is one of the greatest mathematical discoveries of all time. Its impact on foundational studies was so enormous that the ripples are still propagating. It was not, however, a "purely logical" result: it belongs in the domain of foundations of mathematics, just as does later work by Gödel on axiomatic set theory (1940).

As a "side-effect" or "spin-off" of Gödel's methods in the 1931 paper, a purely logical result was obtained by Alonzo Church (1936), which is directly pertinent to the subject-matter of the present book but which we judged to be too weighty a matter for inclusion in it. Church showed that, under certain plausible assumptions as to what the word *algorithm* means, there is not and cannot be an algorithm that, when given as input a finite sequent, will "decide" whether it is true or false: i.e., that will prove it, if it is true, and "disprove it" – or at least identify it as being false – if it is false. This result is of very great interest in view of the existence of algorithms that, given a *true* sequent as input, are *guaranteed* to prove it. The result means that if we submit to such a "proof-procedure" a sequent S and push the start button, the ensuing computation may (in principle) continue for ever *without our knowing whether it will eventually terminate or not*. The proof-procedures we have noted in this book *cannot*, by Church's theorem, be extended or strengthened so that they will always terminate and give the correct answer for *all* sequents.

In the 1930s Gerhard Gentzen (see the *Collected Papers*, Szabo 1969) pursued a series of profound investigations in both pure logic and foundations of mathematics. The notion of *sequent* is his, and he was the first to discover the fact that true sequents can always be given "cut-free" proofs. Herbrand (1930) had, however, unearthed essentially the same phenomenon (of the provability of any provable formula A by a proof that does not introduce any formulas that are not *subformulas*, in a suitable sense, of the formula A). Gentzen had to establish his result by the heroic course of demonstrating a method of *converting* an *arbitrary* proof (which may contain cuts) to a *cut-free* proof of the same sequent. This, because he was staying clear of direct, semantic argumentation. It is, indeed, far simpler and easier to prove directly the existence of a cut-free proof of any true sequent: but to do so one must appeal to the various relevant facts about models and satisfiability, and exploit such set-theoretical phenomena as that depicted in König's Lemma (König 1926).

Indeed, soon after the Second World War, a number of logicians (alas, not including Gentzen himself, who died in 1945 while a prisoner of war, nor Herbrand, who died in a mountaineering accident in 1931 at the age of twenty-three) went over the ground opened up by Gentzen with his sequent calculi and cut-elimination idea, and gave more direct expositions of the basic phenomenon. Evert Beth, and Jaakko Hintikka independently, hit upon the felicitous "semantic tableau" construction in which a cut-free proof of a given true sequent S can be obtained by carrying out a thorough, systematic attempt to build a counter-example for S and finding the attempt blocked at some stage, from being taken any further. This view of things showed that a proof is, in some sense, simply the record of "an unsuccessful attempt to describe a counterexample" (Hintikka 1969, p.4) and it seems to be an insight of considerable philosophical, i.e. epistemological, importance. A recent study of the semantic (he calls them "analytic") tableau approach, by Raymond Smullyan (1975), explores its nooks and crannies with elegant and unifying consequences for its exposition; and further exploration of the method was done by Kleene (1967).

The present author's debts to all of these sources will be apparent to those familiar with the literature. The system of the predicate calculus described in this book is an amalgam of the designs he has encountered in the work of the authors cited and, doubtless, in work whose influence abides but whose specific impact may have receded beyond recall.

One feature not yet mentioned in these historical notes is the use of "exemplifications" $*\forall xA$ and $*\exists xA$. These are the author's preferred notation for what are known as *Hilbert-terms*. David Hilbert

(1925, 1927) invented them in the early days of his Programme as a simplifying device in the formal system. He regarded them as auxiliary, proof-theoretical notations for use in obtaining proofs and shortening their presentation. He used (as do all others!) the notations:

εxA for $*\exists xA$

$\varepsilon x \neg A$ for $*\forall xA$

and so his idea is often referred to as "Hilbert's ε-operator". (The proposed change of notation in this book reflects the author's feeling that the usual ε-notation unduly favours one half of the thoroughgoing symmetry between $\exists$ and $\forall$, combined with his desire to get by with only *one*, not *two*, special symbols to represent a Hilbert-term.)

Hilbert showed (see Leisenring (1969) for an excellent account) that if an "ordinary" sequent is proved *with* Hilbert-terms occurring in the proof, it can be proved *without* them occurring in the proof: thus firmly establishing their status as purely auxiliary devices. It would seem that Hilbert-terms, auxiliary or not, do capture a certain intuitive manoeuvre, which is worth formalizing: to introduce a unique name for an entity whose *existence* has been established by some previous part of an argument, so as to continue with the argument and be able conveniently to refer to it if need arises.

A recent study by Leisenring (1969) makes out a strong case for admitting Hilbert-terms into the predicate calculus on a "full citizenship" basis, citing the above consideration of their naturalness, as well as the very extensive simplification of certain technical matters in the formal semantics, in support. There is, however, the matter of the intended meaning of Hilbert-terms. In this book we have given an account that leans as far as possible in the direction of saying *as little as we can* about the denotation of a Hilbert-term in a given model. It seems inherent in the intuitive understanding of what Hilbert-terms denote that it remain "indeterminate" in principle which of the one or more entities "eligible" to be denoted by a given Hilbert-term in a given model is actually denoted by it. The reader may, correctly, sense that here we impinge upon issues not entirely removed from contemporary debate, and which are therefore not as cut-and-dried as perhaps the expository flow of the explanations given earlier in the book may have suggested.

Starting in about 1957, when the large-scale automatic digital computer was becoming a fairly common resource in universities and other research centres, the thoughts of a number of logical theorists turned naturally enough to the idea of programming and running the predicate-calculus proof procedures – especially in view of the post-war revival of interest in the Herbrand-Gentzen cut-free proof techniques in the form of the semantic tableau concept.

By 1960, several such computer programs had been written and tried out (Gilmore 1960, Prawitz *et al.* 1960), with less than inspiring results. The problems of *actually computing* with a procedure whose original purpose had been only to supply an "existence proof" that such procedures really "were there" turned out to be disheartening. Yes: a proof *would* eventually be found by the computer – but only after running through combinations of instantiations that might be as many as (the exponents will be too tall if we write on the line!):

$$10^{10^{10^{10}}}$$

The "combinatorial explosions" caused by those early experimenters echoed through the corridors of computer centres and singed the eyebrows of the intrepid pioneers of "mechanical theorem-proving" several times, before sending them back to their drawing boards in search of more "machine-oriented" proof-procedures in whose design some explicit weight might be given to the *amount of computation* called for in any given case.

The present author began his own research in 1961, having studied carefully the publications of Prawitz (1960), Gilmore (1960), Davis and Putnam (1960), and having repeated their experiments to find that, indeed, the combinatorial explosions did seem to be inevitable and to block any attempts to prove other than trivially simple examples.

The idea that, instead of *trying* all instantiations over the Herbrand Universe, one might instead *predict* which ones would produce a "winning combination" by using what we have called the Unification Algorithm, turns out to have been sitting there all these years, unnoticed, in Herbrand's doctoral thesis (1930). Prawitz (1960), following out ideas of Kanger (1957), was, as far as the present author is aware, the first to describe this idea at length in print. His procedure was programmed and tried out, with one or two modifications, by the present author in 1962 and also by Martin Davis and his colleagues (1963).

Further reflection on the role played by unification, and especially on the interaction of unification with the analysis of the resulting sentences for being Boolean contradictions, led the author in 1963 to the resolution principle (1963, 1964, 1965a, 1965b). Since that time, resolution has been studied by many people, and there is a busy research literature in which much detailed work is reported on issues and questions arising from attempts to extend, refine, and improve the basic techniques and concepts of resolution as we have described them in this book. One would like to think that this may lead to the day when gentlemen in dispute about some issue as to "what follows from what" can pull out their pocket logical machines and say, as in Leibniz' favourite vision:

Calculemus.

Appendix: A Glimpse at Ordinal Numbers and Well-Ordered Sets

Let S be a set and let R be a collection of ordered pairs (x, y) of elements of S. The pair (S, R) is a *well-ordered set* (and S is *well-ordered* by R, and R is a *well-ordering* of S) if the following conditions hold:

A. For all x, y and z in S:
    (x, x) is in R
    if (x, y) and (y, x) are in R, then $x = y$
    if (x, y) and (y, z) are in R, then so is (x, z)
B. For all non-empty subsets X of S:
    there is an element a of X such that
    (a, x) is in R for all x in X

Condition A says that R is a *reflexive, antisymmetric* and *transitive* relation on S (and thus that R is a *partial ordering* of S).

Condition B says that in every non-empty subset of S there is a *first* (*earliest, smallest*) element with respect to the order R.

For example, the set N of natural numbers is well-ordered by the relation $\leqslant$ (less-than-or-equal-to); so $(N, \leqslant)$ is a well-ordered set. If we lay out N in an array or sequence according to the order $\leqslant$, we have

$$N = 0, 1, 2, \ldots$$

with 0 being the smallest element of N, 1 the smallest element of $N - \{0\}$, 2 the smallest element of $N - \{0, 1\}$, and so on.

A finite set containing k elements can be well-ordered in essentially only one way: the $k!$ distinct arrangements of its elements into a linear array all have the same order type, or "shape". In Cantor's system of ordinal numbers, the order type of a well-ordering is taken to be some particular ordinal number, and most appropriately so since, as we shall see, ordinal numbers themselves are well-ordered sets and their "shapes" run through all the "well-ordered shapes" that there are: so it is just a matter of selecting, as the representative of the "shape" of a given well-ordered set, the ordinal number whose own "shape" is that very one. A well-ordering of a finite set of k elements is said to have the number k as its order type.

An infinite set, however, can be well-ordered in a rich variety of different ways. For example, the well-ordered set $(N, \leqslant)$ is of type *omega*, the first of the infinite ordinal numbers. (Omega is denoted by the small Greek letter ω.) But consider the relation on N defined as follows (denoting it by P): (x, y) is in P if $y = 0$ or else if $x \neq 0$ and $x \leqslant y$. The reader can easily verify that P satisfies conditions A and B. If we consider the array into which P puts N we find that it looks like

$$N = 1, 2, 3, \ldots; 0$$

There is now a "last" element, namely 0, whereas the $\leqslant$-array of N has no last element. These two arrays have different shapes, and so $(N, \leqslant)$ and (N, P) have different order types: $(N, \leqslant)$ has type ω and (N, P) has type $\omega + 1$, the next ordinal number after ω in the sequence of ordinal numbers.

Again, consider the relation Q on N defined as follows: (x, y) is in Q if x is even and y is odd, or else if x and y both have the same parity and $x \leqslant y$. The array into which Q puts N then looks like

$$N = 0, 2, 4, \ldots; 1, 3, 5, \ldots$$

and (N, Q) is said to be of order type $\omega + \omega$, or $\omega \cdot 2$.

It is convenient to introduce the notation $R[\alpha]$ to denote the αth element in the well-ordered set (S, R). Thus $\leqslant [0] = 0$, $\leqslant [1] = 1$, and so on, while, for instance, $P[0] = 1$, $P[5] = 6$, and $Q[8] = 16$. In this notation we give the ordinal number α marking the position of the element in the array, starting out with 0 for the first position, 1 for the second position, and so on. The infinite ordinal numbers then serve to mark positions that are "transfinite", e.g. that of the element 0 in the P-array or of the element 5 in the Q-array. Indeed, we have $P[\omega] = 0$, and $Q[\omega] = 1$, $Q[\omega + 1] = 3$, $Q[\omega + 2] = 5$, etc.

What, then, are the ordinal numbers in general? The following sketch gives the main indeas of von Neumann's simple, elegant characterization (see his 1923 article in van Heijenoort 1967).

The number 0 is identified with *the empty set*. In general, the ordinal number α is identified with *the set of all ordinal numbers less than α*. Thus we have

$$1 = \{0\},$$
$$2 = \{0, 1\},$$
$$3 = \{0, 1, 2\}$$

and so on. Remembering that $0 = \{\ \}$, this means that the finite ordinal number n has exactly n elements.

The *set-inclusion relation* $\subseteq$ is the less-than-or-equal-to relation $\preceq$ that well-orders the ordinal numbers. Note that, e.g., $2 \subseteq 3, 0 \subseteq 1$.

Since ordinal numbers are sets, we can take the *union* of any set of ordinal numbers. For example, the union of $\{1, 2, 3\}$ is

$$
\begin{aligned}
\cup \{1, 2, 3\} &= 1 \cup 2 \cup 3 \\
&= \{0\} \cup \{0, 1\} \cup \{0, 1, 2\} \\
&= \{0, 1, 2\} \\
&= 3
\end{aligned}
$$

which illustrates the general fact that, *if A is a set of ordinal numbers that has a largest element m, then* $\cup A = m$.

But the union of A is *always* an ordinal number even though A has no largest member. For example, if A is the set of all *even* numbers

$$A = \{0, 2, 4, \ldots\}$$

its union is

$$
\begin{aligned}
\cup A &= 0 \cup 2 \cup 4 \cup \ldots \\
&= \{\,\} \cup \{0, 1\} \cup \{0, 1, 2, 3\} \cup \ldots \\
&= \{0, 2, 3, \ldots\} \\
&= \omega
\end{aligned}
$$

This illustrates the general fact that, *if A is a set of ordinal numbers that has no largest element, then* $\cup A$ *is the smallest ordinal number that is larger than every element of A.*

In the first case, $\cup A$ is called the *maximum* of A; in the second case, it is called the *limit* of A. Thus, ω is the limit of the set of even numbers (and indeed of every infinite set of finite ordinal numbers).

Note that every ordinal number α has an *immediate successor* $\alpha + 1$, which is the set containing α and all ordinal numbers less than α. So

$$\alpha + 1 = \alpha \cup \{\alpha\}$$

However, not all ordinal numbers are immediate successors of other ordinal numbers: 0 is not, for example, but is the only finite ordinal number that fails to be a *successor ordinal*. All other examples are infinite ordinal numbers. The first is ω; the next is $\omega + \omega$ (alias $\omega \cdot 2$), the limit of the set

$$\{\omega, \omega + 1, (\omega + 1) + 1, \ldots\}$$

Ordinal numbers that are limits of some set are called *limit ordinals*; it is these, and only these, which fail to be successor ordinals among the infinite ordinal numbers.

Consider the well-ordered set $(\omega + 1, \preceq)$: its characteristic array looks like

$$\omega + 1 = 0, 1, 2, \ldots; \omega$$

and has the same order type as the well-ordered set (N, P). The well-ordered set $(\omega \cdot 2, \preceq)$ has the characteristic array

$$\omega \cdot 2 = 0, 1, 2, \ldots; \omega, \omega + 1, \omega + 2, \ldots$$

and has the same order type as (N, Q). To have the same order types, two well-ordered sets (S, R) and (T, U) must be related by a one-to-one correspondence f from S onto T such that, for each x and y in S, (x, y) is in R if, and only if, $(f(x), f(y))$ is in U. This will mean that the element $f(R[\alpha])$ of T will be $U[\alpha]$, for every $\alpha \preceq \beta$, where β is the order type of (S, R) and of (T, U). The use of β as a set of "subscripts" for the "arrays" $R[\alpha]$ and $U[\alpha]$ is possible precisely because the well-ordered set $(\beta, \preceq)$ itself has order-type β.

The *sum* $\alpha + \beta$ of two ordinal numbers is defined to be the order type of a well-ordered set obtained from one of type α and one of type β by "juxtaposing" them in that order. More precisely, if (S, R) and (T, U) have types α and β respectively, where S and T are disjoint sets, then $\alpha + \beta$ is the type of $(S \cup T, V)$, where (x, y) is in V if x is in S and y is in T, or if x and y are both in S and (x, y) is in R, or if x and y are both in T and (x, y) is in U.

The *product* $\alpha \cdot \beta$ of two ordinal numbers is defined to be the order type of a well-ordered set obtained from one of type α and one of type β by "inserting" copies of the former in the positions of the latter. More precisely, if (S, R) and (T, U) have types α and β respectively, then $\alpha \cdot \beta$ is the type of the well-ordered set $(S \times T, V)$, where $S \times T$ is the set of all pairs (x, y) with x in S and y in T, and where $((x, y), (x', y'))$ is in V if (y, y') is in U or if $y = y'$ and (x, x') is in R. Thus the array of $(S \times T, V)$ looks like

$$(R[0], U[0]), (R[1], U[0]), \ldots, (R[0], U[1]), (R[1], U[1]), \ldots$$

with one "copy" of the array of (S, R) in the position 0 of (T, U), another in position 1, and so on.

The *power* α^β, with an ordinal number α as *base* and an ordinal number β as *exponent*, is then defined by induction on β, as follows. The power α^0 is the number 1. If β is a successor ordinal, say, $\gamma + 1$, then the power $\alpha^\beta = \alpha^{\gamma+1}$ is $\alpha^\gamma \cdot \alpha$. If β is a limit ordinal then α^β is the limit of the set of numbers α^γ, $\gamma \prec \beta$.

These arithmetical operations on the ordinal numbers have many (but not all) of the properties of their counterparts over the finite ordinal numbers, and when restricted to finite ordinals actually coincide with those operations. Thus, sums and products are associative, but not commutative. For example, $\omega \cdot 2 \neq 2 \cdot \omega$, and $\omega + 1 \neq 1 + \omega$.

The question naturally arises as to how we might represent ordinal numbers in a suitable notation using "numerals" of some kind, analogously to the way that we use "base ten" numerals to represent finite ordinal numbers.

While we cannot pursue the idea very far here, we may note that, just as each finite ordinal n can be represented uniquely as a sum of powers of 10:

$$n = 10^k \cdot a_k + 10^{k-1} \cdot a_{k-1} + \ldots + 10 \cdot a_1 + a_0 \qquad (1)$$

with the "digits" a_i satisfying $0 \leq a_i < 10$ and $a_k \neq 0$, so can each finite and infinite ordinal number $\alpha \leq \omega^\omega$ be represented uniquely as a similar sum of powers of ω:

$$\alpha = \omega^k \cdot a_k + \omega^{k-1} \cdot a_{k-1} + \ldots + \omega \cdot a_1 + a_0 \qquad (2)$$

with the "digits" a_i satisfying $0 \leq a_i < \omega$ and $a_k \neq 0$.

Just as, in the base ten notation for n, we use the sequence of decimal digits in (1)

$$a_k \, a_{k-1} \ldots a_0$$

as a numeral for n, so in precise analogy we can use the list of "base omega" digits in (2):

$$(a_k \, a_{k-1} \ldots a_0)$$

as a numeral for α.

Thus the base omega numeral for ω is (1 0). That for $\omega + 1$ is (1 1). That for $\omega \cdot 2$ is (2 0), and so on. The base omega numeral for n is simply (n), when n is finite.

Now, if we write the base omega numeral (0) for 0 as ( ), the *base omega numerals* are nothing other than the *indices* of chapter 3 (p.52). The relation $\prec$ among indices which was there defined is the same as the relation $\prec$ among the corresponding ordinal numbers. Just as we order *decimal* numerals in their ascending order first by their length and then by their "leftmost differences", so as to array them in numerical order, so we order the base omega numerals, in precisely the same way. The only difference in the two cases is that a digit of a base omega numeral can be any natural number, instead of being restricted to the ten possibilities of the familiar notational scheme.

The indices, then, are well-ordered by the relation $\preceq$, where $\prec$ is the relation defined on p.52, for this is just their numerical order when we read them as ordinal numerals.

Now, in the argument using indices on p.52 we needed to know that there are no infinite descending sequences of indices. This fact is an immediate consequence of their being well-ordered by $\preceq$. Indeed, for any well-ordered set (S, R) there can be no infinite descending sequence $x_0, x_1, \ldots$ of elements of S in the sense that, for $i \geqslant 0$, we have (x_{i+1}, x_i) is in R but $x_i \neq x_{i+1}$. Such a sequence would violate condition B, since the set $\{x_0, x_1, \ldots\}$ would have no first element with respect to R.

These ideas are merely the start of a journey into what Hilbert called "Cantor's paradise". If the reader's appetite has been whetted he or she will find Cantor's own expositions (Cantor 1895, 1897) an excellent source of further enjoyment.

References

BETH, Evert (1955) *Semantic entailment and formal derivability*, in Hintikka 1969, pp.9-41.

BIRKHOFF, Garrett, & MACLANE, Saunders (1953) *A survey of modern algebra* (revised ed.). New York: Macmillan.

BOOLE, George (1854) *An investigation of the laws of thought, on which are founded the mathematical theories of logic and probabilities*. London. Reprinted 1951 by Dover Publications Inc.

CANTOR, Georg (1895, 1897) *Contributions to the founding of the theory of transfinite numbers* (articles one and two). Translated and provided with an introduction and notes by Philip E. B. Jourdain, 1915. Reprinted by Dover Publications Inc.

—— (1899) *Letter to Dedekind*, in van Heijenoort 1967, pp.113-17.

CHURCH, Alonzo (1936) A note on the entscheidungsproblem. *J. Symbolic Logic 1*, 40-1. Correction, *ibid.*, 101-2. Also in Davis 1965.

DAVIS, Martin, ed. (1965) *The undecidable: basic papers on undecidable propositions, unsolvable problems and computable functions*. Hewlett, New York: Raven Press.

—— & PUTNAM, Hilary (1960) A computing procedure for quantification theory. *J. Assoc. Comput. Mach. 7*, 201-15.

FREGE, Gottlob (1879) *Begriffsschrift, a formula language, modelled upon that of arithmetic, for pure thought*, in van Heijenoort 1967, pp.1-82.

—— (1902) *Letter to Russell*, in van Heijenoort 1967, pp.126-8.

GENTZEN, Gerhard (1936) *Investigations in logical deduction*, in Szabo 1969, pp.132-213.

—— (1939) *The consistency of elementary number theory*, in Szabo 1969, pp.132-213.

GILMORE, Paul C. (1960) A proof method for quantification theory. *IBM J. Res. Dev. 4*, 28-35.

GÖDEL, Kurt (1930) *The completeness of the axioms of the functional calculus of logic*, in van Heijenoort 1967, pp.582-91.

—— (1931) *On formally undecidable propositions of Principia*

Mathematica and related systems I, in van Heijenoort 1967, pp.596-616.

—— (1940) *The consistency of the axiom of choice and of the generalized continuum-hypothesis with the axioms of set theory.* Princeton, New Jersey: University Press.

HENKIN, Leon (1949) The completeness of the first-order functional calculus. *J. Symbolic Logic 14*, 159-66. Reprinted in Hintikka 1969.

HERBRAND, Jacques (1930) *Researches in the theory of demonstration*, in van Heijenoort 1967, pp.525-81.

HILBERT, David (1925) *On the infinite*, in van Heijenoort 1967, pp.367-92.

—— (1927) *The foundations of mathematics*, in van Heijenoort 1967, pp.464-79.

HINTIKKA, Jaakko (1955) Form and content in quantification theory. *Acta Philosophica Fennica 8*, 11-55.

——, ed. (1969) *The philosophy of mathematics.* Oxford: University Press.

KANGER, Stig (1957) *Provability in logic.* Stockholm.

KLEENE, Stephen Cole (1952) *Introduction to metamathematics.* New York: Van Nostrand.

—— (1967) *Mathematical logic.* New York: Wiley.

KNEALE, William, & KNEALE, Martha (1962) *The development of logic.* Oxford: Clarendon Press.

KÖNIG, Dénes (1926) Sur les correspondences multivoques des ensembles. *Fundamenta Mathematicae 8*, 114-34.

LEISENRING, A. C. (1969) *Mathematical logic and Hilbert's ε-symbol.* London: MacDonald.

LÖWENHEIM, Leopold (1915) *On possibilities in the calculus of relatives*, in van Heijenoort 1967, pp.228-51.

McCARTHY, John (1960) Recursive functions of symbolic expressions and their computation by machine. *Commun. Assoc. Comput. Mach. 3*, 184-95.

—— et al. (1962) *The LISP 1.5 programmer's manual.* Cambridge, Mass: MIT Press.

NAGEL, Ernest, & NEWMAN, James R. (1958) *Gödel's proof.* New York: University Press.

PRAWITZ, Dag (1960) An improved proof procedure. *Theoria 26*, 102-39.

——, PRAWITZ, Hakan, & VOGERA, Neri (1960) A mechanical proof procedure and its realization in an electronic computer. *J. Assoc. Comput. Mach. 7*, 102-28.

302 *References*

QUINE, Willard van Orman (1950) *Methods of logic*. New York: Henry Holt & Co.

ROBINSON, John Alan (1963) A machine-oriented logic (abs.). *J. Symbolic Logic 28*, 302.

—— (1964) *On automatic deduction*. Rice University Studies.

—— (1965a) A machine-oriented logic based on the resolution principle. *J. Assoc. Comput. Mach. 12*, 23-41.

—— (1965b) Automatic deduction with hyper-resolution. *Int. J. Comput. Math. 1*, 227-34.

RUSSELL, Bertrand (1902) *Letter to Frege*, in van Heijenoort 1967, pp.124-5.

—— (1908) *Mathematical logic as based on the theory of types*, in van Heijenoort 1967, pp.150-82.

SMULLYAN, Raymond (1968) *First order logic*. Vol. 43 of *Ergebnisse der Mathematik und ihrer Grenzgebiete*. Berlin: Springer-Verlag.

SKOLEM, Thoralf (1920) *Logico-combinatorial investigations in the satisfiability or provability of mathematical propositions*, in van Heijenoort 1967, pp.252-63.

SZABO, M. E., ed. (1969) *The collected papers of Gerhard Gentzen*. Amsterdam: North-Holland.

TARSKI, Alfred (1956) *Logic, semantics, metamathematics: papers from 1923 to 1938*. Translated by J. H. Woodger. Oxford: Clarendon Press.

VAN HEIJENOORT, Jean, ed. (1967) *From Frege to Gödel: a source book in mathematical logic, 1879–1931*. Cambridge, Mass: Harvard University Press.

WEISSMAN, Clark (1970) *LISP 1.5 primer*. Encino, Calif: Dickenson Publishing Co.

WINSTON, Patrick Henry (1977) *Artificial intelligence*. Reading, Mass: Addison-Wesley.

Index